An Introduction to Applied Linguistics

An Introduction to Applied Linguistics

Contributors

Linxiu Yang et al.

AURIS
Reference

www.aurisreference.com

An Introduction to Applied Linguistics

Contributors: Linxiu Yang et al.

Published by Auris Reference Limited
www.aurisreference.com

United Kingdom

Copyright 2016

An Introduction to Applied Linguistics

ISBN: 978-1-78154-744-1

British Library Cataloguing in Publication Data
A CIP record for this book is available from the British Library

Printed in the United Kingdom

Contents

List of Abbreviations .... *vii*

List of Contributors...*ix*

Preface... ....*xi*

Chapter 1   **Evaluative Functions of Reporting Evidentials in English
Research Articles of Applied Linguistics** 1
Linxiu Yang

Chapter 2   **Towards a Character Language: A Probability in Language Use** 19
Jumanto

Chapter 3   **A Review Of Models In Experimental Studies of Implicit
Language Learning**... 45
Si Liu, Huangmei Liu

Chapter 4   **Some Polemical Issues in Applied Linguistics**..................................... 63
John Robert Schmitz

Chapter 5   **Language Politics and the Linguist** 81
Kanavillil Rajagopalan

Chapter 6   **Metaphor in Applied Linguistics: Four Cognitive Approaches** 91
Gerard Steen

Chapter 7   **Incorporating Linguistic Knowledge For Learning Distributed
Word Representations**... 115
Yan Wang, Zhiyuan Liu, Maosong Sun

Chapter 8   **Language Problems in Applied Linguistics: Limiting The Scope** 143
A. Effendi Kadarisman

Chapter 9   **A Comparative Study of Evidentiality in Ras in Applied
Linguistics Written by Ns and Chinese Writers** 165
Linxiu Yang

Chapter 10 **Cue Competition Between Animacy and Word Order: Acquisition
of Chinese Notional Passives By L2 Learners**.................................... 181
Jia Wang, Caihua Xu

Chapter 11   **The Archaeological Record Speaks: Bridging Anthropology and Linguistics** **201**

Sergio Balari, Antonio Benítez-Burraco, Marta Camps,
Víctor M. Longa, Guillermo Lorenzo, and Juan Uriagereka

Chapter 12   **Citation in Applied Linguistics: Analysis of Introduction Sections of Iranian Master's Theses** **243**

Alireza Jalilifar (Ahvaz) and Razieh Dabbi (Mahshahr, Iran)

Chapter 13   **Innovations in Structuring Article Introductions: The Case of Applied Linguistics** **259**

Ling Lin

Citations **281**

Index **283**

List of Abbreviations

ELT	English Language Teaching
AL	Applied linguistics
AGL	artificial grammar learning
CLT	communicative language teaching
DSM	Distributional semantic models
ESP	English for Specific Purposes
EN	English native speakers
FLT	foreign language teaching
GJT	Grammaticality judgment task
UPI	Indonesia University of Education
AILA	International Association of Applied Linguistics
IMRD	Introduction-Method-Results-Discussion
KRWR	Knowledge Regularized Word Representation
LL	Language Learning
LA	Linguistics Applied
MR	Margin Regularizer
NLM	neural language models
NNLM	neural-network language model
CBOW	continuous Bag-of-Words Model
RT	Reaction time
SRA	Science and Research Branch-Ahvaz
SLA	Second language acquisition
SL	Second-language
SCU	Shahid Chamran University of Ahvaz
SFL	Systemic Functional Linguistics
TQ	TESOL Quarterly
UG	Universal Grammar
UM	University of Malang
VSM	vector space models
WAN	Word Association Network

List of Contributors

Linxiu Yang
Foreign Languages School, Shanxi University, Taiyuan, China

Jumanto
Faculty of Cultural Studies (FIB), Dian Nuswantoro University, Semarang, Indonesia

Si Liu
School of Foreign Languages and Literatures, Lanzhou University, Lanzhou, China

Huangmei Liu
School of Foreign Languages and Literatures, Lanzhou University, Lanzhou, China

John Robert Schmitz
Universidade Estadual de Campinas,Brazil

Kanavillil Rajagopalan
Universidade Estadual de Campinas,Brazil

Gerard Steen
Department of English Language and Culture Vrije Universiteit; The Netherlands

Yan Wang
State Key Laboratory of Intelligent Technology and Systems, Tsinghua National Laboratory for Information Science and Technology, Department of Computer Science and Technology, Tsinghua University, Beijing, China

Zhiyuan Liu
State Key Laboratory of Intelligent Technology and Systems, Tsinghua National Laboratory for Information Science and Technology, Department of Computer Science and Technology, Tsinghua University, Beijing, China

Maosong Sun
State Key Laboratory of Intelligent Technology and Systems, Tsinghua National Laboratory for Information Science and Technology, Department of Computer Science and Technology, Tsinghua University, Beijing, China
Jiangsu Collaborative Innovation Center for Language Competence, Jiangsu, China

A. Effendi Kadarisman
Universitas Negeri Malang Jalan Semarang 5 Malang 65145, Indonesia

Linxiu Yang
Foreign Languages School, Shanxi University, Taiyuan, China

Jia Wang
Department of Linguistics and Translation, City University of Hong Kong, Hong Kong, China

Caihua Xu
College of Chinese Language and Culture, Beijing Normal University, Beijing, China

Sergio Balari
Departament de Filologia Catalana and Centre de Lingüística Teòrica, Universitat Autònoma de Barcelona, Edifici B, 08193 Barcelona, Spain

Antonio Benítez-Burraco
Departamento de Filología Española y sus Didácticas, Universidad de Huelva, Campus de El Carmen, 21071 Huelva, Spain

Marta Camps
Department of Anthropology, Center for the Advanced Study of Human Paleobiology, The George Washington University, Washington, DC 20052, USA

Víctor M. Longa
Departamento de Literatura Española, Teoría da Literatura e Lingüística Xeral, Universidade de Santiago de Compostela, Campus Norte, 15782 Santiago de Compostela, Spain

Guillermo Lorenzo
Departamento de Filología Española, Universidad de Oviedo, Campus El Milán, 33011 Oviedo, Spain

Juan Uriagereka
Department of Linguistics, University of Maryland, 1102 Marie Mount Hall, College Park, MD 20742, USA

Alireza Jalilifar (Ahvaz)
Shahid Chamran University of Ahvaz, Iran

Razieh Dabbi (Mahshahr, Iran)
Islamic Azad University in Mahshahr, Iran

Ling Lin
Hong Kong Polytechnic University (China)

Preface

Applied linguistics is an interdisciplinary field of linguistics that identifies, investigates, and offers solutions to language-related real-life problems. Some of the academic fields related to applied linguistics are education, psychology, computer science, communication research, anthropology, and sociology. The tradition of applied linguistics established itself in part as a response to the narrowing of focus in linguistics with the advent in the late 1950s of generative linguistics, and has always maintained a socially-accountable role, demonstrated by its central interest in language problems. The book, Applied Linguistics: An Introduction should be of utmost importance for students of applied linguistics and second language pedagogy as well as practicing teachers and researchers wishing to update their knowledge. First chapter shows that reporting evidentials not only function as indicating the information sources, but also have multiple evaluative functions. Second chapter explores about the main aspects of pragmatics are briefly introduced and then elaborated as building-blocks of character language. Third chapter reviews experimental research on implicit learning using linguistic stimuli, and proposes five key procedures of a framework for empirical studies of implicit learning. Fourth chapter expresses on some polemical issues in applied linguistics and fifth chapter focuses on language politics. Sixth chapter presents four different approaches to metaphor, based on the interdependence between language and thought as system and as use: metaphor in language as system; metaphor in thought as system; metaphor in language as use and metaphor in thought as use. Seventh chapter incorporates linguistic knowledge for learning distributed word representations. Eighth chapter critically discusses the paradigmatic shift in applied linguistics, resulting in a claim that countless real-world language problems fall within its scope, but in reality they weaken the discipline and make it lack a focus. Then it takes a closer look at the nature of these language problems, and picks out, for analysis, real examples of writing problems in ELT in Indonesian context. It further argues that, by focusing primarily on problems in ELT and SLA, applied linguistics reaffirms its well-defined position and underscores its significant contributions to both disciplines. Finally, it concludes the discussion by adding some notes on the question of autonomy in both applied linguistics and in ELT in Indonesia. Ninth chapter examines whether cultural factors influence the writer's choice concerning evidentiality and the interpersonal functions of evidentiality. First, it illustrates the necessity of the comparative study. Second, it presents the findings, including the similarities and the differences. Third, the pedagogical implications are pointed out. Tenth chapter support the universality of animacy cue proposed by Gass but also suggest that word order and pragmatic factors may affect L2 learners' cue strategies. The chapter also evidences the contribution of the input to the development of L2 cue strategies, which is in line with the predictions of the Competition Model. Eleventh chapter examines the origins of language, as treated within Evolutionary Anthropology, under the light offered by a biolinguistic approach. Twelfth chapter highlights on citation in applied linguistics. Appropriate reference to other sources is an important feature of academic writing. Last chapter explores the rhetorical structure of introductions that are followed by an independent Literature Review section.

Chapter 1

EVALUATIVE FUNCTIONS OF REPORTING EVIDENTIALS IN ENGLISH RESEARCH ARTICLES OF APPLIED LINGUISTICS

Linxiu Yang

Foreign Languages School, Shanxi University, Taiyuan, China

ABSTRACT

Reporting evidentials are frequently used in Research Articles. Based on the data analysis of 50 English research articles of applied linguistics, the study shows that reporting evidentials not only function as indicating the information sources, but also have multiple evaluative functions. The analyses have proved this by showing the evaluative functions of reporting evidential in choosing different information sources and different realization forms. At the same time the persuasive effects and discourse implications of these different choices are also discussed.

INTRODUCTION

As a hot research issue in recent years, evidentiality has been studied from various perspectives (e.g. Aikhenvald, 2003, 2004; Chafe, 1986; Palmer, 1990, 2001; Mushin, 2000, 2001; Halliday & Matthiessen, 2004; Hu, 1994, 1995; Fang, 2005; Tang, 2007; Yang, 2009, 2010). With different research focuses, goals and perspectives, these studies have provided us different understandings of evidentiality. Yet, up to now, few researchers have touched the evaluative functions of evidentiality, especially the functions of reporting evidential. As the frequently used evidential type in English research articles, it is necessary to study what reporting evidentials can do for the writer. Therefore, to fill this gap, this study intends to focus on the evaluative functions of reporting evidentials in English research articles, aiming to show how reporting evidential can help the writers to negotiate the relationship among the information, the writer and the reader.

Understanding of Evidentiality in the Current Study

As for what is evidentiality, there has been no consensus. There are narrow and broad understandings of it. For the working definition of evidentiality, the current study adopts the broad view of evidentiality. First, it treats evidentiality as a semantic notion rather than a grammatical one and admits all the potential realization forms rather than the grammaticalised ones. It adopts the "one-to-many" approach in Systemic Funtional Linguistics and admits the differences in different realizations for the same semantics. Second, the study agrees that evidentiality is interpersonal by nature and negotiating the interpersonal relationship is one of the most important functions of evidentiality, but at the same time it holds that the interpersonal functions of evidentiality are context-dependent. Only in certain concrete context, can the interpersonal functions of a certain evidential be decided. For instance, the reporting evidential it is said may perform different interpersonal functions in different contexts. It may denote the speaker's uncertainty of the source of saying, or it is a device for the speaker to conceal the information source and distance him or her from the information, or even escape from taking responsibility from the information. In this sense, context is much important in deciding the interpersonal functions of evidentials. Third, evidentiality is much related to genre convention. Many factors will affect the adoption of evidentiality, and genre is undoubtedly one of them. Each genre has its own linguistic manifestations. As far as evidentiality is concerned, in different genres, the forms and distributions of evidentials are different. For example, such subjective evidentials as I think, in my opinion are not preferred in academic genres. These understandings concerning evidentiality will decide the analytical orientation in the later part. This is also a starting point for the current research. It will examine in RAs what interpersonal functions reporting evidentials will perform and how they can help the writers to negotiate the relationship among the information, the writer and the reader.

Data and Methodology

English RAs of applied linguistics are chosen as the data. The corpus consists of 50 RAs in applied linguistics amounting to about 350,000 words. The journals selected for this study are: Journal of English for Academic Purposes (2004-2008), Journal of English for Specific Purposes (2004-2008), and Journal of Pragmatics (2004-2008). The data of RAs are confined to the same period because of the fact that genres are on the one hand quite stable in a certain period of time. On the other hand, they are also in a state of constant evolution, as Fairclough (1992) notes, "a genre implies not only a particular text type, but also particular processes of producing, distributing and consuming text...

Changes in social practice are both manifested on the plane of language in changes in the system of genre, and in part brought about by such changes". The genre of RAs also may change over time. Therefore, in order to examine the linguistic features of RAs, the study chooses RAs published during the same time for the validity of the research results. The data-coding of this research is done manually at the preliminary stage to identify and count all the potential lexical and discourse-based items that indicate different reporting evidential types. The material for data-coding includes the body of the articles, i.e. the complete text of the articles, excluding abstracts, notes, linguistic examples, tables, and figures. Then, Microsoft Office Excel is adopted to deal with the data and draw the figures accordingly. In addition, in order to take the context of evidentials into consideration to find the concordance patterns, a concordance software is also adopted. This quantitative approach is meant to identify the frequency of occurrences and to produce comparable data. The frequency of occurrence of each group of items is calculated in permillage.

Classification of Reporting Evidential and Its Lexicogrammatical Realizations in English RAs Based on the genre convention of English RAs, in the current research, reporting evidentials are classified into two types according to the information source: other-reporting and self-reporting evidentials. Self-reporting evidentials indicate that information comes from whatever related to the writer's own research, e.g. I, we, our, my, our analysis, our research, this article, and the participants involved in the experiments and so on, while other-reporting evidentials indicate that information is from the extra sources other than the writer's own research. Our data survey indicates that reporting evidentials are the most important and frequently adopted evidentials. They have various types of realizations. First, (author + date) form is a conventional way to realize reporting evidentials. For example: 1) Such evaluations can be said to be averrals which are expressed as though deriving from a source, in this case, implied consensus (Hunston, 2000). In Example (1), the evidential (Hunston, 2000) indicate the information comes from Hunston. At the same time it provides a way for the writer to give a summary or generalization of the cited information. This type of evidentials is typical in RAs. This type also includes (website) which indicates the information source is a certain website rather than an author. For example: 2) Negative judgments can also be made implicitly, with absence of items that carry negative values, but with tokens that evoke negative judgements from readers (http:// www.rammatics. com/appraisal/appraisalGuide/UnFrame   d/stage2-Attitude-judgment.htm). Example (2) reveals that the internet provides an alternative source of information. However, this type is not very frequently adopted in the data and only several cases are found. Second, reporting evidentials can be realized by verbal forms: verb + that structure, be verbed structure, it is verbed structure and as structure. The structure verb + that is a way in which the writer can show the specific information source, either human or nonhuman, specific or unspecific. This form presents the information source as the theme, which foregrounds the information source rather than the cited information. For example: 3) Tannen has demonstrated that controlling others involves them in a relationship (power entailing solidarity), the same way that claiming intimacy has an element of control (solidarity entailing power). 4) This body of literature suggests that L2 learners' relationship with their advisors dramatically impact their participation in academic literacy projects and, by extension, their attempts to gain admittance into target discourse communities. 5) Belcher's research suggests that a critical factor in high-level academic literacy activities is the quality and kind of relationship that L2 learners develop with their advisors. 6) Many researchers have argued that genre knowledge plays a pivotal role in advanced academic literacy. In the above examples, by foregrounding the information sources, the writers put more value on the information sources rather than the information itself, which shows the writers' respect for other researchers. The examples also show that the information may be human, as in (3) and (6), or inhuman, as in (4) and (5). It may be specific, as in (3) and (5), or unspecific, as in (4) and (6). The structures of be verbed and it is verbed allow the writer to omit the information source for whatever reasons. Consider the following two examples. 7) It is assumed that established genres such as case histories, experimental research reports and editorials constitute a natural part of readings in the medical sciences. 8) As can be seen in examples below, the DM te was found to function mainly as an information state marker and mostly marked shared and assumed knowledge between the speaker and the addressee. In Examples (7) and (8), instead of explicitly indicating the information sources, the writers choose to conceal them. In this case, the writers pay more attention to the reported information rather than where the information comes. The writers may not know the information source or they find no necessity to point it out. What they value is just the cited information, which is different from the case of the structure of verb+ that. Reporting evidentials can also be realized by as verb(ed) structure. Some examples of as structure are given below. 9) However, as Hyland (1998a) adds, expressions of certainty work towards the acceptance of by addressing readers as knowledgeable peers who are familiar with the ideas presented and able to follow the author's reasoning. 10) Moreover, as noted above, these labels are interactive: their use affects the reader's perception of the propositions and so enables the readers to perceive the organization and meaning that the writer intends. As verb(ed) structure is often chosen by the writer because of the flexibility of its occurrence. It can occur either at the beginning, in the middle or at the end of a clause. It is also a kind of textual meta-discourse which can smooth and guide the reader's understanding of the writer's argumentation, as in Example (10). This point will be elaborated in the following chapter. Third, non-verbal reporting evidentials include noun patterns or adjuncts. The typical nouns and adjuncts are such as fact, observation, agreement, finding, view, claim, evidence, argument, suggestion, according to X, in X's data, in X's view, in X's terms and so on. In this type of realization, the most frequently-used noun is fact which nearly constitutes 90% of the nouns as reporting evidentials, as shown in Example (11). 11) The use of nouns to construct stance in academic writing has so far attracted little attention, despite the fact that several researchers have identified a group of nouns which offer the possibility of incorporating interpersonal meanings in the text. The use of nouns as reporting evidentials have its own peculiar functions and characteristics. In some cases, the information source may be concealed. In addition, this form can also provide the writer with chances to evaluate the information source, e.g. One further interesting finding, the most striking finding for Harwood, Thomson's groundbreaking study. Furthermore, nouns allow the process to be a participant which can not be argued, negated and so on. Therefore, they have more persuasive power and they make it more possible for the reader to accept what the writer expresses. The adjunct according to is frequently adopted to indicate information source, which typically occurs at the beginning and gives prominence to information source. This type of realization is very objective because it just indicates information source without any of the writer's evaluation of information source and cited information. 12) According to Swales (1996), these are genres that "operate to support and validate the manufacture of knowledge directly as part of the publishing process itself or indirectly by underpinning the academic administrative processes of hiring, promotion and departmental review."

In Example (12), the writer chooses the adjunct "according to" to indicate the information source and shows no evaluations of the information source and the information itself. This type of reporting evidentials are identical to the objective nature of RAs. Table 1 will present a clear picture of the lexicogrammtical realizations of reporting evidential in English RAs of Applied Linguistics.

Evaluative Functions of Reporting Evidential

Based on the descriptive result of Section 3, in this section, we will look at the evaluative functions of reporting evidential in four aspects: the phraseological patterns of reporting evidential, the evaluative functions of information sources, the evaluative functions of reporting verbs and evaluative functions of nouns.

Phraseological Patterns of Reporting Evidentials

First consider the distribution pattern of reporting evidentials in RAs, as is shown in the Table 2. As seen from Table 2, to express reporting evidentiality, the writer prefers verbal forms, either in active forms or in passive forms. Verbal forms nearly constitute 61.4% of all the realization forms. The second frequently used forms are (author +

Table 1: Lexicogrammatical realizations of reporting evidentials

Evidential type	Realization type	Lexicogrammatical realizations	Typical examples
Reporting evidential types	Verbal realization	(Author + year) or (website + year)	(Hunston, 2000)
		Verb that structure, *be verbed* structure,	X argue, maintain, found, ... that
		It is ved structure	It is argued, it has been revealed
		As structure	As indicated by...
	Non-verbal realization	Noun that	Fact, observation, agreement, finding, view, claim,
		Adjunct	According to X, in X's data, in X's view

Table 2: Distribution of reporting evidentials

	Realization forms	Other-reporting	Self-reporting	Total & percentage	
Verbal	Author/date	647	0	647	30.7%
	Verb that structure	400	550	950	
	(It) is ved structure	53	50	103	61.4%
	As structure.	70	107	177	
Non-verbal	*Noun* that	117	3	120	
	Adjunct	37	10	47	7.9%

date) forms, constituting 30.7%. Therefore, verbal forms are prominent in reporting evidentials. The effect of this foregrounding feature will be discussed in Section 4.3. The results also show that (author + date) convention is a very specific form of reporting evidentials in RAs. It generally occurs at the end of a proposition with the only purpose of indicating the information source of that proposition. For example: (13) It sends the message to teachers that voice is critically important, and this message, if passed down to students, may result in learners who are more concerned with identity than ideas (Stapleton, 2002). In Example (13), to show that the proposition "It sends the message to teachers that voice is ..." comes from the other source other than the writer himself, he chooses (author + date) form. Compared with other forms, (author + date) forms are the objective ways to present the information sources in that the writer only reveals where the information is from without any subjective intrusion into the proposition. The writer will leave his "imprint" on choosing how to indicate the information sources. When he chooses (author

+ date) forms, he will be quite distanced from the proposition. It is the cited authors, but not the writer, who bear the full responsibility for the validity of the proposition. This kind of form is also identical to the objective nature of RAs in which not too much subjectivity is involved. Another important point peculiar to (author + date) form is that by indicating the exact date, sometimes with exact page number (e.g. Stapleton, 2002: p. 187), the reliability of the propositions is greatly improved. It can be certain enough that the reader tends to believe the information with specific sources. Therefore, this form contributes much to the persuasive and rhetorical purposes of the whole genre. First, it can improve the reliability of the information. Second, the improved reliability adds to the credibility of the writer. The writer will be made more detached from the information presented, therefore with less commitment and responsibility for the validity of the information. Third, the form is almost the most objective way for the writer to present the information from other sources, which consolidates the objectivity of RAs. As shown above, (author + date) forms are an objective way to function as reporting evidentials, but it is a different picture for verbal and noun forms as evidentials. The choice of reporting verbs and nouns will show the writer's subjective evaluation of the reported information and also the information sources. Sections 4.3 and 4.4 will elaborate the evaluative functions of reporting verbs and nouns as reporting evidentials.

Table 3: Information sources of reporting evidentials

Information sources		Other-reporting		Self-reporting		Total reporting	
Human	Specific	1037	88.6%	83	14.3%	1120	64%
	Unspecific	7	0.6%	13	2.3%	20	1.1%
Non-human		37	3.2%	363	62.7%	400	22.9%
Concealed		90	7.6%	120	20.7%	210	12%
Total		1171	100%	579	100%	1750	100%

Evaluative Functions of Information Source

In addition to the evaluative potential in different phraselogical patterns of reporting evidentials, the choice of information source is also evaluative in function and related to the overall persuasion of RAs. As can be seen in Table 3, specific human sources are most frequently chosen as information sources. Non-human and concealed sources are relatively low in frequencies. However, the different distributions between other-reporting and self-reporting should be devoted much attention to. In other-reporting, the writer tends to choose specific human sources which constitute 88.6% of the total number. This shows that in presenting others' work, the writer gives much prominence to the cited authors than the cited information. In so doing, there are at least two persuasive effects. First, by giving prominence to the cited authors, the writer will show his respect for the previous related researchers, which helps to build a professional persona. Second, this strategy adds much to the reliability of information and also the credibility of the writer. Nesler et al. (1993) points out that people tend to accept beliefs, knowledge, and opinions from what they see as authoritative, trustworthy, or credible sources, such as scholars, professionals, experts or reliable media. In addition, with reference to specific sources, the reliability of information will be improved. For example, Hu (1994) points out that a specific source will add to the reliability of information because the reader has specific persons and sources to refer to. The situation is different for self-reporting evidentials. The prominent information source adopted by the writer is nonhuman source (62.7%), including the findings, data, figures, analysis, tables and so on. This is different from other-reporting evidentials. However, they have the similar ultimate purposes. When presenting his own work, in order to let the facts speak for themselves, the writer tends to choose the research as the information sources, such as the research shows rather than we show. In so doing, the reliability of information is improved and at the same time contributes to the objectivity of RAs because not so many Is and wes are involved. When the writer chooses human sources as information sources, in addition to Is and wes, it is worth noting that the participants in the research are chosen as the information sources, e.g. the interviewees and the research participants. This also adds to the reliability of the information, for these people are direct experiencers and eyewitnesses of the information presented. The above discussion has shown that choosing different information sources is also meaningful and evaluative. It also presents the differences between other-reporting evidentials and self-reporting evidentials in this respect. In spite of the differences, they both serve the ultimate persuasive purpose of RAs.

Evaluative Functions of Verbs as Reporting Evidentials

Verbal forms are the most frequently adopted in RAs to function as reporting evidentials. By adopting verbal forms, the writer does not just show where the information is from. Instead, he presents his subjective evaluation. This section will focus on the evaluative functions of reporting verbs. In RAs, reporting verbs do not simply function to indicate the sources of the information reported, but they also reveal the writer's own position. The selection of an appropriate reporting verb allows the writer to intrude into the discourse to signal his assessment of the evidential status of the reported proposition and to demonstrate his commitment. For example, the verbs say and insist in He says/insists he is innocent differ in discourse implications in that insist explicitly conveys the speaker's insistence on the part of the information presented. Sometimes, reporting verbs are used with adverbials (e.g. As sb correctly asserts). This explicitly evaluative strategy allows the writer to open a discursive space within which the writer either exploits his opposition to the reported message or to build on it. However, this is not a common case in RAs. Most of the time, the writer chooses to intrude into the proposition implicitly. Hyland (1999: pp. 349-350) finds that reporting verbs in academic texts, such as X observe, X advocate, X establish, X ignore, X fail, and so on, can help the writer to differentiate his various degrees of commitment to the cited messages, which at the same time demonstrate implicitly the writer's personal stances towards the cited authors. Thompson (1991) agrees with Hyland on the evaluative functions of reporting verbs in academic discourse. As Thompson & Ye's (1991) ground-breaking study shows, the choice of reporting verbs is a key feature which enables the writer to position his work in relation to that of other members of the discipline. Their study offers a threefold analysis of the evaluative potential of reporting verbs (Thompson & Ye, 1991: pp. 372-373). First, reporting verbs show the cited author's stances towards the information. Second, reporting verbs can construct the writer's stance of acceptance, neutrality or rejection of the cited research. Third, they allow the writer's interpretation of the author's behaviors or discourse. Thompson and Ye (1991) also distinguish three categories of reporting verbs according to the activities they perform: "textual" verbs in which there is an obligatory element of verbal expression (e.g., state, write); "mental" verbs, which refer to mental processes (e.g. think, believe); and "research" verbs, which refer to the processes that are part of research activity (e.g. find, demonstrate). Later studies such as those by Thomas & Hawes (1994) and Hyland (2002) also admit the evaluative functions of reporting verbs. Hyland's category of reporting verbs, which are diverged from Thomson and Ye's rather complex system, is shown in Figure 1. The figure clearly shows Hyland's opinion toward the evaluative functions of reporting verbs. The above has shown that many researchers have paid much attention to the evaluative functions of reporting verbs. The use of a reporting verb to introduce the work of others is also a significant rhetorical choice (Hunston, 1993; Tadros, 1993; Thomas & Hawes, 1994; Thompson & Ye, 1991). The importance of these verbs lies in the fact that they allow the writer to convey clearly the kind of activity reported and to distinguish an attitude to that information, signaling whether the claims are to be accepted or not. This study totally agrees the evaluative function of reporting verbs. The following will discuss the evaluative functions of reporting verbs as evidentials. To categorize reporting verbs, the book adopts the classification of Francis et al. (1996) for V that clause pattern. According to his classification, three groups of reporting verbs are categorized in our corpus: ARGUE group,

THINK group, SHOW and FIND group. The explanations and verb samples are adapted from Francis et al. (1996: pp. 97-101), as shown in the following: A: ARGUE verbs are concerned with writing and other forms of communication, e.g., argue, suggest, point out, write, conclude, claim, add, maintain, propose, imply, mention. B: THINK verbs are concerned with thinking, including having a belief; knowing, understanding, hoping, fearing, e.g., think, assume, feel, hold, believe. C: SHOW and FIND verbs are concerned with indicating a fact or situation or with coming to know or think something, e.g., show, demonstrate, reveal, find, observe, discover, indicate. It is important to note that the categorization of verbs is dependent on the context where the verbs occur. That is, a verb can occur in more than one group, and the context needs to be examined in order to determine the appropriate category the verb belongs to. For example, the verb observe can appear in FIND group when it refers to the visual evidence with the meaning of "noticing" and also can be in ARGUE group when it refers to the language activity.

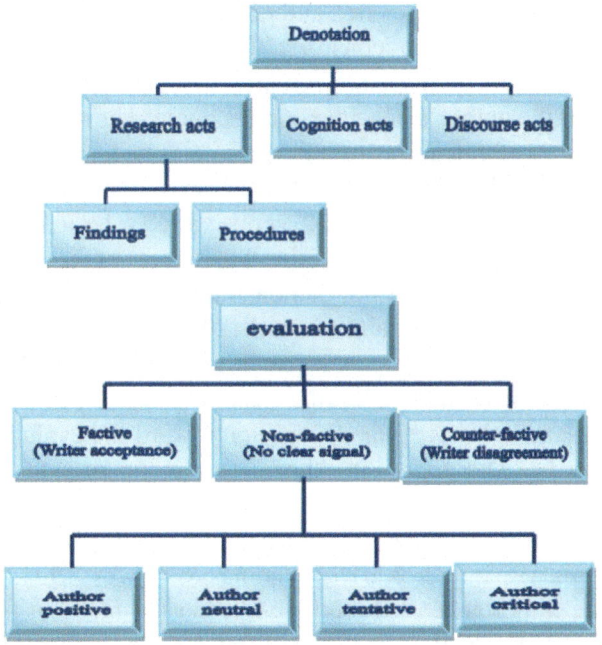

Figure 1: Categories of reporting verbs (after Hyland, 1999: p. 350).

This categorization may overlap or be similar to those of Thompson and Ye's and Hyland's. ARGUE verbs parallel the textual group and discourse group, THINK group, the mental and cognition group and SHOW and FIND group, the research group. In spite of the similarities and overlaps, the categorization adapted from Francis et al. (1996) is chosen by the current study for the following two reasons. First, this categorization reveals better the ways information is acquired, either through language activity (ARGUE verbs), through visual channel (FIND verbs), or through thinking (THINK verbs). Second, verbs of different categorizations may denote a line of different commitment and certainty. For example, FIND and SHOW group tend to bear high certainty than the other two groups in that FIND and SHOW verbs are always factive. They indicate different degrees of reliability of information. Based on the above categorization, a statistic picture of reporting verbs in NS corpus is presented in Table 4. Table 4 shows the distribution of verb groups in reporting evidential type. There are great differences in the distribution of verbal groups and also between other-reporting evidential type and self-reporting evidential type. It shows that THINK verbs are seldom adopted as reporting evidentials. Especially in selfreporting evidential type, no THINK groups occur, which can be explained by the fact that this book categorizes THINK group with self sources as brief evidentials. However, for the other two types of verbs, significant differences are presented. In other-reporting evidential type, ARGUE verbs predominate. In fact, 61.1% of the total appear with an ARGUE verb. The most frequently adopted ARGUE verbs are argue, point out, suggest, claim which constitute nearly half of the total number, as shown in the following examples. 14) Swales (1990) suggests that citation convention (numerical or author/date) may affect the choice between integral and non-integral and he argues that numerical conventions predispose the writer to use non-integral citation. 15) As Johns and Swales (2002: p. 13) point out, uncertainty over "what role there might be for a personal voice" is one area of difficulty that affects student writing at all levels, including the thesis. The situation is quite different for self-reporting evidentials. Unlike other-reporting evidentials, FIND and SHOW verbs predominate with the occurrence of 73.6% of the total. FIND and SHOW verbs are mainly concerned with the writer's own researches, such as the results, situations, findings and analyses. For example:

Table 4: Distribution of the verb groups in reporting evidentials

Verb groups	Other-reporting		Self-reporting	
	% of total	The most frequent verbs (total number of occurrence)	% of total	The most frequent verbs (total number of occurrence)
ARGUE group	61.1	Argue 70 Point out 43 Suggest 40 Claim 37	26.4	Suggest 70 Explain 33 Note 23 State 20
THINK group	3.8	Assume 10 Think 3 Hold 3	0	0
FIND and SHOW group	35.1	Show 43 Note 20 Reveal 17 Observe 13 Indicate 10	73.6	Show 117 Find 100 Reveal 63 Indicate 53 Demonstrate 13

16) Our study of conversation in noisy settings shows that there are also identifiable patterns in the ways that noise and impaired language perception during conversation affect grammatical and discourse structures, language processing, language use, and patterns of interaction in conversations. 17) Our data has demonstrated that the acoustic constraints have clear repercussions on grammatical constructions, including effects on utterance lengths, grammatical complexity, and questioning strategies. The two examples above show that the information sources of self-reporting evidentials are mainly about the writer's own study such as our data, our study and so on. In fact, our study has found very low percentage of personal pronouns such as I and we for information sources. This finding is also different from that of other-reporting evidentials, which can be explained by the fact that when referring to other sources, the writer tends to give prominence to the cited authors themselves, while when referring to self sources, he will put more value on the studies rather than the writer himself. This is a persuasive strategy. When presenting his own studies and researches, the writer lets his studies and researches speak for themselves, but not his own subjective demonstration. This strategy of "objectiveness" adds to the reliability of information. Thus, the reader will be more likely to accept the claims the writer makes. To sum up, the choice of reporting verbs in reporting evidential type positions the writer in relation to the reported authors and the reported information. With different reporting verbs, the writer shows his evaluation and stances towards the reported authors and the reported information.

Evaluative Functions of Nouns as Reporting Evidentials

The above has shown that (author + date) and reporting verbs are often adopted in reporting evidential type in RAs. In spite of this, significant numbers of nouns as reporting evidentials (e.g. fact, finding, evidence, suggestion, and observation) also occur in the data. These nouns often occur with that-clause (e.g. Swales' suggestion that review of literature does not only occur...). It is thought that the use of noun with that-clause as reporting evidentials is worthy of study for their distinct evaluative functions. This pattern enables the writer to give his evaluations of the propositions following that. Nouns as evidentials have their specific advantages. In fact, Biber et al. (1999) have stated that nouns are one of the primary devices used to express the writer's evaluation and stance in academic writing. Based on the close examination of this pattern used in the corpus, their evaluative functions will be shown in the following, which will indicate how theses nouns can help the writer express his own evaluations and construct a convincing argument. First, evaluative functions of nouns as evidentials are realized by choosing appropriate nouns.

The use of Noun thatclause pattern encapsulates the proposition in the clause, summarizing and representing it to the reader, which enables the writer to incorporate his own evaluations of the propositions through the choice of different types of nouns. Biber et al. (1999) find that the evaluative functions of nouns may either be attitudinal or epistemic. They show the writer's evaluation of and different degrees of commitment to the information. For example, the use of "suggestion" is very different from the nouns of "claim", "findings", or "fact". Thus, in order to understand the evaluative functions of nouns as reporting evidentials, it is necessary to examine the nouns that occur in this pattern. To categorize these nouns, the dissertation adopts the semantic criteria by Francis et al. The categories of nouns as evidentials are as follows: Fact and Findings Group: these nouns refer to the facts, or the findings in the research (e.g. fact, findings, observation). Idea group: these nouns refer to belief, ideas, wishes, and thought processes (e.g. suggestion, idea, assumption, view, belief). Argument Group: these nouns refer to something that is written or spoken (e.g. argument, claim, point, agreement). Table 3 shows the different frequencies of the occurrence of every category of nouns as evidentials in the corpus. Table 5 shows that there are significant differences among the categories of nouns as reporting evidentials. The writer particularly favors the noun category of Fact and Finding which nearly constitutes 73% of the total number of nouns as evidentials. This result shows that by using nouns indicating Fact and Finding, the writer puts more value on the factual status of the information presented. If something is presented as a fact or a finding, a reader is more likely to accept it. Therefore, this type of knowledge may occupy higher reliability than the other two types. In this sense, choosing an appropriate noun is critical for the reader's acceptance of the claims. Second, nouns as reporting evidentials provide the writer with a relatively objective way to evaluate. Different from other

Table 5: Categories of nouns as evidentials

Noun category	Raw data	Frequency per 1000 words
Fact and finding	87	0.277
Idea	23	0.075
Argument	10	0.032
Total	120	0.384

types of reporting evidentials, nouns as evidentials can facilitate the construction of a seemingly 'objective' evaluation of the proposition in the that clause since the writer can avoid indicating the source of the proposition just as verbs as evidentials do (excluding the passive forms of verbs). In fact, the data has shown that the majority of the nouns as evidentials do not occur with specific names or personal pronouns for the purpose of attribution. Actually only 6 cases of nouns are found to occur with the sources, which comprise 16.7% of all the cases. The absence of information sources enables the writer to obscure the origin of any evaluation that is carried out. Therefore, the information appears objective and is less open to dispute. Third, evaluation of nouns as reporting evidentials is multilayering. Nouns as reporting evidentials are sometimes without a head. For example, with no specific names or personal pronouns to indicate the information sources, they have the function of multi-layering evaluation. By multi-layering, it is explained by reference to the notions of attribution and averral (Sinclair, 1986; Tadros, 1993). According to Sinclair, a text is made up of propositions which may be put forward by the writer (averrals) or attributed by the writer to some other person or entity (attributions). In RAs, all assertions are taken to be averrals, unless the writer clearly shows the source of the assertions. In making an averral, the writer is responsible for the veracity of the proposition advanced. Consider the following examples. 18) Specifically, the use of parentheses by the Spanish writers ($p = 0.0016$) put forward the idea that Spanish opinion columns may exhibit a greater freedom to include what the English-speaking rhetorical principles consider "supplementary or digressive" material. 19) As far as the limitations observed by Samraj (2002) are concerned, the introduction of an optional step (step 2), "presenting positive justification", in Move 2 accounts for her first criticism, and Swales' (2004) suggestion that review of literature does not only occur throughout the introduction but can occur throughout the article as a whole accounts for her second criticism. In Example (18), no information source is indicated. Thus, it is the writer who is responsible for the truth of the statement and it is the writer who holds the idea of "Spanish opinion columns may exhibit a greater...". However, in (19), the information source is clearly indicated through "Swales'". It is Swales not the writer who takes the responsibility for the statement "review of literature does not only occur throughout...". However, it is only superficially so. As Sinclair (1986) points out, it is the writer who bears the ultimate responsibility for all the propositions in his texts. In this sense, all the attributions are also averrals. It is the writer who bears the responsibility for the whole statement "As far as the limitations observed..." and for the choice of the noun "suggestion". In this case, superficially, the information source "Swales" seems to be responsible for the statement. Actually the writer's own evaluation is also incorporated in it. For example, he chooses the noun "suggestion" rather than "claim" or "finding", which shows that even in attribution, the writer's evaluation is also revealed. Thus, the evaluation of nouns as reporting evidential is sometimes multi-laying. In such cases, writers show their evaluations which they assign to others or entities, but which simultaneously express their own positions. This multi-layering of evaluation provides a resource which writers can adopt to incorporate their own evaluations, while appearing to report that of others.

Fourth, nouns as evidentials make a verbal process an entity or phenomenon, such as "suggestion" rather than "suggest". It appears that what the writer presents is something that exists in the world and it is more likely for the reader to accept what has existed in the world than what others say. Fifth, in addition to the above evaluative functions and characteristics of nouns as reporting evidentials, it is also found that in some examples the nouns are modified by attributives such as "general finding, the most striking finding for Harwood, another important, though not surprising finding" and so on. Allowing different modifiers to modify nouns as evidentials may also be a great advantage for the writer to add explicit evaluations toward propositions. In sum, nouns as evidentials have great evaluative potential and provide the writer with an alternative to present the information with his own evaluations and stances.

CONCLUSION

This study has shown that in construing reporting evidential type, the writer has great power because he has various linguistic forms to choose for his presentation. How the writer chooses to present information is as important as the information he wants to present. Just as Berkenkotter & Huckin (1995) say, "you are what you cite". No matter what kind of forms he chooses, the writer leaves his imprint there and expresses his evaluation or stance. The analyses have proved this by showing the evaluative functions in choosing different information sources and different realization forms. At the same time it shows the persuasive effects and discourse implications of these different choices. This study intends to help to raise the writers' awareness in choosing reporting evidentials in RA writing. Theoretically, it is a beginning to study what evidentiality can do for the language users other than indicating the information source. It may lay a foundation for the future research and provide orientation for further study. There are more areas to be further studied. First, the functions of other evidential types can be further studied; Second, because of the genre convention, evidential use in other genres, even evidential use across genres is worthy of more research; Third, evidential use in different cultures may vary, which is believed to be an interesting topic in evidential study.

ACKNOWLEDGMENTS

This work was supported by Chinese Educational Bureau [grant number: 11YJC740128] and Program for the Outstanding Innovative Teams of Higher Learning Institutions of Shanxi (OIT).

REFERENCES

1. Aikhenvald, A. (2004). Evidentiality. Oxford: Oxford University. Aikhenvald, A., & Dixon, R. (2003). tudies in evidentiality. Amsterdam/ Philadelphia:John Benjamins Publishing Company.

2. Berkenkotter, C., & Huckin, T. (1995). Genre knowledge in disciplinary communication. Hillsdale, NJ: Lawrence Erlbaum.

3. Biber, D., et al. (1999). Longman grammar of spoken and written English. Edinburgh: Pearson Education Ltd.

4. Chafe, W. (1986). Evidentiality in English conversation and academic writing. In W. Chafe, & J. Nichols (Eds.), Evidentiality: The linguistic coding of epistemology (pp. 261-272). Norwood, NJ: Ablex.

5. Chafe, W., & Nichols, J. (1986). Evidentiality: The linguistic coding of epistemology. Norwood, NJ: Ablex.

6. Fairclough, N. (1992). Discourse and social change. Cambridge: Polity Press.

7. Fang, H. M. (2005). A Systemic-functional Approach to evidentiality. Unpublished Doctoral Dissertation, Shanghai: Fudan University.

8. Francis, G., Hunston, S., & Manning, E. (1996). Collins COBUILD grammer patterns 1: Verbs. London: Harper Collins.

9. Halliday, M. A. K., & Matthiessen, C. M. I. (2004). An Introduction to Functional Grammar. London: Arnold.

10. Hu, Z. L. (1994). Evidentiality in language. Foreign Languages Teaching and Research, 1, 9-15.Hu, Z. L. (1995). Evidentiality in Chinese and discourse analysis.Journal of Hubei University, 2, 13-23.

11. Hunston, S. (1993). Evaluation and ideology in scientific writing. In M. Ghadessy (Ed.), Register analysis: Theory and practice. London and New York: Pinter Publishers.

12. Hyland, K. (1999). Academic attribution: Citation and the construction of disciplinary knowledge. Applied Linguistics, 20, 341-367.doi:10.1093/ applin/20.3.341

13. Hyland, K. (2002). Activity and evaluation: Reporting practices in academic writing. In J. Flowerdew (Ed.), Academic discourse (pp. 115-130). London: Longman.

14. Mushin, I. (2000). Evidentiality and deixis in narrative retelling. Journal of Pragmatics, 32, 927-957.doi:10.1016/S0378-2166(99)00085-5

15. Mushin, I. (2001). Evidentiality and epistemological stance: Narrative retelling. Amsterstam/Philadelphia: John Benjamins Publishing Company.

16. Nesler, M. S., et al. (1993). The effect of credibility on perceived power. Journal of Applied Social Psychology, 17, 1407-1425. doi:10.1111/j.1559-1816.1993.tb01040.x

17. Palmer, F. (1990). Modality and the English modals. London: Longman. Palmer, F. (2001). Mood and modality. Cambridge: Cambridge University Press.

18. Sinclair, J. (1986). Fictional worlds. In M. Coulthard (Ed.), Talking about text (pp. 43-47). Birmingham: University of Birmingham ELR.

19. Tadros, A. (1993). The Pragmatics of text averral and attribution in academic texts. In M. Hoey (Ed.), Data, description, discourse (pp. 99-114). London: Harper Collins.

20. Tang, B. (2007). Systemic-functional approach to discourse features of evidentiality in English news reports of epidemic situation update.

21. Unpublished Doctoral Dissertation, Shanghai: Fudan University. Thomas, S., & Hawes, T. P. (1994). Reporting verbs in medical journal articles. Englsih for Specific Purposes, 2, 134-155.

22. Thompson, G., & Ye, Y. (1991). Evaluation in the reporting verbs used in academic papers. Applied Linguistcs, 4, 365-382.

23. Yang, L. X. (2009). Evidentiality in English research articles. Unpublished Doctoral Dissertation, Xiamen: Xiamen University.

24. Yang, L. X. (2010). Genre perspective on evidentiality. Proceedings of 36th ISF. Sydney: Macquarie University Press.

Chapter 2

TOWARDS A CHARACTER LANGUAGE: A PROBABILITY IN LANGUAGE USE

Jumanto

Faculty of Cultural Studies (FIB), Dian Nuswantoro University, Semarang, Indonesia

ABSTRACT

This opinion paper is about a probability in language use, about how a competent speaker should be aware of speaking for politeness or for camaraderie, and be capable of avoiding impoliteness. The main aspects of pragmatics are briefly introduced and then elaborated as building-blocks of character language. The proposed building blocks are: 1) elaboration of meaning and form strategies, 2) distant language and close language strategies, 3) politeness and camaraderie strategies, 4) object language and metalanguage strategies. A view on character language in Indonesian context is given, on how politeness, camaraderie, and impoliteness are elaborated; and then, six phases of character language building are proposed as a verbal social project: 1) interaction phase, 2) teaching-and-learning process phase, 3) evaluation phase, 4) re-evaluation phase, 5) verification phase, 6) selection phase. Upon the completion of a character language building, a competent speaker is presumably well-equipped for using language in a particular situation that may call.

INTRODUCTION

I am not very sure whether this idea works or not, despite my preference or earnest hope on the former to the latter. Rather than standing idle imagining what I have been thinking about for years upon completion of my PhD in Linguistics (Pragmatics) from University of Indonesia (Jumanto, 2006), (Jumanto, Phatic Communication among English Native Speakers, 2008), and after considering the article in an international journal (Jumanto, Phatic Communication: How English Native Speakers Create Ties of Union, 2014), this writing of article has recently come into being. I have been thinking about the development of linguistics so far, and a thought has tempted me whether this thesis can affect the linguistic world we live in or not, whether what I am heading for is indeed there in a speech society or not, and whether what I have in mind is true or not. However, as I once presented this topic in an international conference on English Language Teaching(ELT) in 2011[1], and, in the following year, in an international BIPA (Indonesian for Non-Native Speakers) Conference in 2012[2], both held in distinguished private universities in Indonesia, I found out that, not unexpectedly, because people kept talking about how character students should be in the language teaching and character building in the 2011 conference, and because people talked more about Indonesian language teaching (BIPA) in the 2012 conference—both missed the talk about language with character—this raw concept of thesis did not find its path.

I have myself observed that the development of linguistics has been quite a bitter quarrel between formal linguistics and functional linguistics. I see that it is of no problem, just like two siblings have different opinions for the betterment of their home. Something missing was together searched on by the two siblings. The search on meaning has its long history, side by side with that on form. The search on form, in my observation, has developed the so-called formal linguistics; and on the other hand, the search on meaning has contributed to the development of functional linguistics. Though the search on meaning has long been done since de Saussure (de Saussure, 1916) and Peirce (Peirce, 1940) in the early 1900, Bühler (Bühler, 1918), Malinowski (Malinowski, 1923), and Morris (Morris, 1946) and Jakobson (Jakobson, 1960), it has been interrupted by the search of form since Bloomfield (Boomfield, 1930), Fries (Fries, 1979), and Chomsky (Chomsky, 1950). The search on meaning was then revived by Austin with his speech acts theory (Austin, 1957), and then advocated by Searle (Searle, 1965), i.e. pragmatics, a branch of functional linguistics we can enjoy learning today. This cultural perspective on language use has been elaborated by functional linguists, e.g. Halliday (Halliday, Language as Social Semiotic, 1978), Lincoln and Guba (Lincoln & Guba, 1985), Holmes (Holmes, 1992), Thompson (Thompson, 1997), and Hinkel (Hinkel, 1999), to mention a few.

I have been long interested in the fact that our linguistic founding fathers have developed linguistics functionally, i.e. how they blended or combined linguistics and some other discipline into what we have heard or followed or advocated today, i.e. sociolinguistics, psycholinguistics, neurolinguistics, or some other branch with the—linguistics suffix. Here, the meaning carried out by a particular form or text is elaborated into or is made to function in a particular discipline. Thus, sociolinguistics has been a blend of sociology and linguistics, psycholinguistics of psychology and linguistics, neurolinguistics of neurology (medicine) and linguistics, and some other blend of a particular discipline and linguistics.

In this very sense, I have been aware of the fact that speakers are indeed bound to context, one property of which is when we are speaking to a close hearer or a notclose hearer. Types of hearer then come into effect due to this sense. Brown and Gilmanhave elaborated this thesis with their grand article The pronouns of power and solidarity (Brown & Gilman, 1968). I myself have made a little benefit of their findings when researching Phatic communication among English native speakers (Jumanto, 2006), on how it functions differently to different types of hearer and on what types of form the English native speakers elaborated to show politeness or friendship.

Politeness and friendship (or better: camaraderie) have become a central issue in what has tempted me for years, whether language use is to hearers with power factor or whether it is to hearers with solidarity factor. This far, we have come to the so-called distant language or close language (Jumanto, Teaching a Character BIPA (Indonesian for Non-Native Speakers), 2012). Distant language brings politeness, and close language brings camaraderie. This is, then, leading to what I am now proposing to the world as character language, the proposal of which is probably lacking advocation, but is hopefully getting a little attention.

In this article, we are talking about character language, or about politeness and camaraderie in language use, or about politeness or impoliteness in language use, i.e. about a probability in language use. Language use is, we believe together, a matter of probability, advocating the properties of language use, or communicative competence, first introduced by Hymes in the late 1960s (Hymes, On communicative competence, 1972); (Duranti, 1998). Meanwhile, the text analysis here employs Indonesian language corpus data, the researcher's opinion of which is based on three academic facts: 1) that the researcher is an Indonesian native speaker, 2) that the data collection as well as the direct observation is more authentic around the researcher's daily Indonesian-speaking atmosphere, and 3) that languages, commonly believed by formal as well as functional linguists, are most probably universal around the world.

CHARACTER LANGUAGE

A character language is a language with a character. The word character, in one sense, refers to nature, quality, of a thing (OLPD, 1987) or to ability, qualities, validity (CALD, 2008). A character language thus is able to function as a means of communication (ability), has qualities with which the language is different from the others (quality), and is effective in a correct formality (validity).

A character language should function as a means of communication, i.e. human communication, interpersonal and social. In an interpersonal communication, a character language should consider the speakers, the values and idiosyncrasies they believe in and hold, and their background knowledge as well. This is an interpersonal context. A character language should also involve the social values and norms, and other social aspects the speakers may elaborate in their verbal interactions. This is a social context. Thus, to be able to function as a means of communication, a character language should consider the interpersonal context and the social context of the speakers involved in verbal interactions. This is the first content: ability.

The second content of a character language is qualities. Qualities in this case may refer to everything special which distinguishes a particular language from the others. Thus, a language with a character is then a language distinguishable from the other languages. In this sense, a character language is unique despite some universal aspects of languages in the world. Here, we can say that a character language has an identity.

The third content of a character language is validity. Validity in this case may refer to effectiveness in a correct formality (CALD, 2008). Formality refers to high or strict attention to rules, forms, and convention we hold and believe in together in society. Informality then does the reverse. In this light, a character language should have formal forms and informal forms. Formal forms are high forms (or of high variety) and informal forms are low forms (or of low variety).

High and low varieties of language exist in some speech society, as they meet the demands of verbal interacttions of the members. Here, we are speaking of a diglossic situation. A diglossic situation in a speech society is a situation where people usually speak two varieties or variants of their language, i.e. high language and low language, or for more ease to say, formal language and informal language.

From the accounts above, we can finally sum up here that a character language is a language which can function as a means of communication in a diglossic situation, i.e. either in formal situations or in informal situations.

Is English a character language? Is Indonesian a character language? Is your language a character language? What is a character language to do with pragmatics? What is pragmatics to do with a character language? How do we build a character language through pragmatics? These are questions to deal with in this opinion paper.

PRAGMATIC VIEW ON CHARACTER LANGUAGE

To begin with, let us talk about some significant pragmatic aspects here, i.e. interaction of meanings, form in pragmatics, distant language and close language, politeness and camaraderie, and object language and metalanguage. The aspects are to be discussed in the accounts below.

Pragmatics and Interaction of Meanings

Pragmatic linguistics or linguistic pragmatics or, for short, pragmatics is not merely talking about locution, illocution, or perlocution. It inevitably is. A speech is an act with the three meanings, i.e. locutionary, illocutionary, and perlocutionary meanings. In pragmatics, this each meaning can be a force, an illocutionary or a pragmatic force. We are speaking and doing something at the same time, or to be more pragmatically specific: we do the act of saying something, implying something, and affecting someone at the same time. In the context that a speaker is talking to a cold wall or even a beautiful statue, or is speaking alone (soliloquy), we miss the perlocution. This is what Austin has elaborated in his grand theory of speech acts How to Do Things with Words (Austin, 1957). Austin's elaboration of speech acts theory is, in the writer's opinion, in line with Malinowski's argument that language is a mode of action (Malinowski, 1923).

Pragmatics is of human interactions every day (pragmeme = a human act (Mey, 2001)). Pragmatics is about interaction of meanings (Thomas, 1996); (Jumanto, Pragmatics: Linguistic World is Broad, 2011b). Though the search of meaning has long been done since de Saussure and Peirce in the early 1900, Bühler (Bühler, 1918), Malinowski (Malinowski, 1923), and Morris (Morris, 1946), it has been interrupted by the search of form since Bloomfield (Boomfield, 1930), Fries (Fries, 1979), and Chomsky (Chomsky, 1950). The search of meaning was then revived by Austin with his speech acts theory (Austin, 1957), and then advocated by Searle (Searle, 1965).

Pragmatics is the study of language use within context. Language use or spoken/written communication is a discourse (Richards, Platt, & Platt, Longman Dictionary of Language Teaching and Applied Linguistics, 1985); (Mey, 2001); (CoBuild CoBuild English Dictionary, 2003); (Jumanto, Discourse Analysis and Ideology Critics, 2011a). Utterances are the concrete forms of language use which we analyze as text (Carter, 1997). The analysis of pragmatics is then basically a discourse analysis on text within context (Cook, 1989); (Schiffrin, 1994); (Mey, 2001); (Jumanto, Pragmatics: Linguistic World is Broad, 2011b). Pragmatics is thus the study of meaning of language use in communication between the speaker and the hearer, within context, i.e. linguistic context and context of situation, in a particular speech society (Jumanto, Pragmatics: Linguistic World is Broad, 2011b).

Pragmatics regards communication as interaction of meanings, not interaction of forms. However, form or text is important as the vehicle of meaning. Without the form or text, language use or communication or discourse never happens, as there is nothing to be perceived or there is no text (Jumanto, Pragmatics: Linguistic World is Broad, 2011b).

The meaning (explicature or implicature) interacted in pragmatics is later developing or is open to probable elaboration by the speaker into the so-called ideology and then the myth. Here, the vehicles of meaning are not only an utterance or a speech act (or an idio text), but also an ideo text (a text bearing an ideology of a particular societal group or a political party) and a socio text (a text bearing an ideology of a particular society) (Jumanto, Language of Advertising: An Ideology Critic, 2010); (Jumanto, Discourse Analysis and Ideology Critics, 2011a).

How does pragmatics deal with form to find out meaning, as the form is the vehicle of meaning? To come to this answer, let us observe the account below.

Form in Pragmatics

Forms of utterance in pragmatics can be observed in three dichotomy types: 1) formal-informal, 2) direct-indirect, and 3) literal-non literal (Jumanto, Pragmatics and Character Language Building, 2011c). The word "formality" refers to high or strict attention to rules, forms, and convention (Hornby, 1987), and, therefore, informality does the reverse. Formal utterances have more complete, longer forms, and are in a good order. Informal utterances have incomplete, shorter forms, and are not in a good order, and sometimes cut-down, reversed-up, and changed in favor of the speaker.

Direct utterances are the utterances whose meanings can be soon interpreted directly from parts of the utterances, i.e. the meanings based on linguistic context (cohesive meanings). This meaning is called explicature in pragmatics. The opposite of this is called implicature. Implicatures are the meanings of indirect utterances, i.e. the meanings based on context of situation (coherent meanings). To come to an implicature of an indirect utterance, a hearer usually thinks a bit longer than he does to an explicature of a direct utterance.

Similar to direct and indirect utterances are literal and non-literal utterances. Literal utterances are the utterances in their usual and obvious sense. The opposite is non-literal or figurative utterances. Non-literal utterances use allegories and metaphors. Allegories are stories, paintings, or descriptions of ideas such as anger, patience, purity, and truth by symbols of persons with those characters. Metaphors are imaginative ways to describe something by referring to something else with the similar characteristics or qualities. A metaphoric language is thus the language with no usual or literal meaning but the language which describes something by images or symbols. Direct and literal utterances include banter, while indirect and non-literal utterances involve irony and hedges (Leech, 1983); (Jumanto, Pragmatics and Character Language Building, 2011c).

How do forms of utterance affect the meanings in pragmatics? Let us talk about distant language and close language in the next account.

Distant Language and Close Language

Distant language and close language here refer to and derive from the notion social distance. Social distance is the physical as well as psychological distance between the speaker and the hearer (Jumanto, Pragmatics: Linguistic World is Broad, 2011b). Social distance is not distant or close. It is a flexible concept of relative relationship between the speakers. Social distance is assumed to be zero when the speaker is talking to themselves[3].

From this context, pragmatics regards a diglossic situation of a speech society as having two variants of language, i.e. distant language and close language. Distant language refers to formal, indirect, and non-literal utterances, while close language refers to informal, direct, and literal utterances. As referring to formal, indirect, and non-literal utterances, distant language is usually carefully elaborated and uses safe and common topics. Meanwhile, as referring to informal, direct, and literal utterances, close language usually involves contractions, slangs, reverse-ups, changes, taboos, swearing, f-words, and uses any topics, personal and private (Axtell, 1995). The speaker tends to use distant language to the hearers with power factor (superiors); on the other hand, the speaker tends to use close language to the hearers with solidarity factor (close hearers)[4].

What are distant language and close language to do with politeness? Please watch our manners and read the following account carefully.

Politeness and Camaraderie

Considering the summary critique of politeness theories by Gino Eelen (Eelen, 2001), and apart from various theories of politeness (Leech, 1983; Brown & Levinson, 1987; Spencer-Oatey, 1992; Lakoff, 1990; Fraser & Nolen, 1981; Gu, 1990; Ide, 1989; Blum-Kulka, 1992; Arndt & Janney, 1985; Watts, 1989; Thomas, 1996; Coupland, 2000) Jumanto is trying to define what politeness is (Jumanto, Pragmatics: Linguistic World is Broad, 2011b). Jumanto proposed a theory of politeness among Javanese speakers, advocating the theory of Gunarwan (Gunarwan, Implicatures of Linguistic Codes Selection in some dialogues of Ludruk, 2001). Many of the politeness theories above are the results of violating Grice's Cooperative Principles (Grice, 1975), though some proposed a new atmosphere. However, few have proposed a working definition of politeness. Jumanto tried to offer a definition that politeness is everything good that has been uttered as well as acted by the speaker to the hearer within a particular context, to maintain their interpersonal face as well as their social face (Jumanto, Pragmatics: Linguistic World is Broad, 2011b).

The notion of face in politeness has come into high attention and importance since it was borrowed by Brown and Levinson (Brown & Levinson, 1987) from Goffman (Goffman, 1959, 1967). In Goffman's grand theory, everyone in interaction has two faces, positive face and negative face. Face refers to the will, intention, and other associations of ideas and values in the self of the speaker. In short, positive face refers to appreciation of the speaker's self and negative face refers to no depreciation of the speaker's self. The elaboration of face by Brown and Levinson has resulted in face management for two major politeness strategies, positive politeness strategies (which refer to positive face) and negative politeness strategies (which refer to negative face).

Under the light of this face management theory, Jumanto (Jumanto, Pragmatics and Character Language Building, 2011c) argues that the politeness theories in verbal interactions fall into or lead to two major poles, i.e. one is directed to distancing politeness and the other is directed to closeness politeness. Distancing politeness refers to Goffman's negative face (Goffman, 1959),Brown and Levinson's negative politeness strategies (Brown & Levinson, 1987), Renkema's respect politeness (Renkema, 1993), and Jumanto's politeness (Jumanto, Phatic Communication among English Native Speakers, 2008); (Jumanto, Pragmatics: Linguistic World is Broad, 2011b). Closeness politeness, on the other hand, refers to Goffman's positive face (Goffman, 1959), Brown and Levinson's positive politeness strategies (Brown & Levinson, 1987), Renkema's solidarity politeness (Renkema, 1993), and Jumanto's friendship or camaraderie (Jumanto, Phatic Communication among English Native Speakers, 2008); (Jumanto, Pragmatics: Linguistic World is Broad, 2011b). This tendency has been wellstrengthened and highlighted by the results of Jumanto's research on phatic communication among English native speakers (Jumanto, 2006).

From the accounts above, with high gratitude to the former theorists and researchers, we can see clearly that distancing politeness and closeness politeness are in line with distant language and close language the writer has just proposed above. Here, so far so good, we can sum up that distant language brings politeness, and close language brings friendship or camaraderie. Distant language and close language to show politeness and camaraderie finally meet the demand of language as a means of communication, i.e. a real-life everyday use of language in all situations or pragmatic use of language in a diglossic situation.

A BIG QUESTION is rising here: HOW DOES PRAGMATICS BUILD A CHARACTER LANGUAGE? Please wait a minute and be patient. We still have to deal with object language and metalanguage below.

Object Language and Metalanguage

The subtitle above of the two levels of language has long been advocated by de Saussurians and Peircians since early 1900. Indeed, as grand theorists of the states of the linguistic arts, their influences have persisted in linguistic areas to date. The first level of language function is called object language. This level is also noted as denotative level, which is the usual and obvious sense of language, based on some convention, which is objecttive. In this level, language is seen as an object (object language). The word RAT in this level, for example, refers to an animal, i.e. a four-footed mammal of the rodent family.

The second level of language is called metalanguage. This level is also noted as connotative level, which is the level of additional meaning to give an image or imagination based on some convention, which is subjective. This metalanguage level is metaphorical. A metaphor, as mentioned above, is an imaginative way to describe something by referring to something else with the similar characteristics or qualities. The word RAT in this level, for example, may be used to describe a person who breaks or deserts the duty. In this similar context, for another example, the word HEART as object language is the center of blood circulation in the human body, but the word HEART as metalanguage may refer to somebody the speaker is in love with.

Object language and metalanguage, the writer argues, exist in every living language in this world, the two levels of which serve human language as a means of communication, within interpersonal or social context.

Now we are coming to the discussions of character language below. However, before we are talking about the building of it, let us talk about the probability of it.

CHARACTER LANGUAGE: A PROBABILITY IN LANGUAGE USE

This heading is indeed intriguing. Why language use is a probability is now coming into our attention. As have been mentioned above, the talk on character language comprises politeness, camaraderie, and awareness of potential rude situations and awkward situations to happen in verbal interactions. In this light, we are about to observe how character language is elaborated in Indonesian context. Here, cases of politeness and impoliteness in Indonesian language are taken into account. A preliminary view on types of utterances in Indonesian language is given as leading points to politeness and camaraderie.

Character Language: Cases of Politeness and Impoliteness in Indonesian Language

The presentation of politeness and camaraderie in Indonesian language here means discussing politeness and camaraderie in the Indonesian languages. Politeness and camaraderie in Indonesian language is basically the language use in form of everyday verbal interactions, so that distant language and close language are there in real-life practices in the Indonesian diglossic speech situation. The pragmatic aspects discussed above are applied here, i.e. 1) elaboration of meaning and form, 2) distant language and close language, 3) politeness and camaraderie, 4) object language and metalanguage. The four pragmatic aspects are as the building blocks of politeness and camaraderie in Indonesian language, the discussion of which is carried out through two major accounts below.

Types of Utterances in Indonesian Language

The talk on types of utterances in Indonesian language consists of three sub-points, i.e. 1) formality-based utterances, 2) directness-based utterances, and 3) meaning-based utterances.

1) Formality-Based Utterances Formality-based utterances in the Indonesian language discussed here may fall into two categories, i.e. formal utterances and informal utterances. Formal utterances tend to have more complete, longer forms, and are in a good order. Whereas, informal utterances have incomplete, shorter forms, and are not in a good order, and sometimes cut-down, reversed-up, and changed in favor of the speaker. The two variants can be illustrated in Table 1.

   Examples in shorter utterances can also be found in daily use, as illustrated in Table 2.

2) Directness-Based Utterances

Table 1: Formality-based utterances

Formal utterances	Informal utterances
Saya mengucapkanterima kasih banyak. "I thank you very much"	Terima kasih; Makasih; Kamsia; Tks; Thanks; Thx. "Thank you", "Thanks", "Thx"

Table 2: More examples on formality-based utterances

Formal utterances	Informal utterances
memberikan "giving"; "give them"	berikan; beri; kasihkan; kasih "givin"; "giv'em"
Selamat pagi! "Good morning!"	Met pagi!; Pagi! "Morning!"
Semoga Anda segera sembuh "May you get better soon"	Cepet sembuh; Cepet baikan; Lekas sehat "Get better soon"; "Better soon"
membantu "helping"; "help them"	mbantu; bantu "helpin"; "help'em"
lelah sekali "extremely tired"	capek banget; ka-o; ngos-ngosan "exhausted"
berlebihan "superfluous"	lebay [?]
jarang dibelai "seldom cared for"	jablay [?]
tidak "No, I do not"	tak; tdk; nggak; gak "No", "I don't", "don't"
meskipun "although", "even though"	meski; mskpn "though"
tetapi "however", "nevertheless"	tapi; tp; but "but"
ayah "father"	yah; papa; daddy; bokap "daddy", "dad"
ibu "mother"	bu; mama; mammy; nyokap "mommy"; "mom"
Bapak Budi "Mister Budi"	Pak Budi; P Budi "Mr. Budi"
Ibu Rini "Mistress Rini"	Bu Rini; B Rini "Ms. Rini"
Saya "I would…"	Aku; Gue; Ai; Ike "I will…"
Anda "You would…"	Kamu; Lu; Situ; You "You will…"
Saudara "You would…"	Sdr "You will…"
dan sebagainya "et cetera"	dsb "etc."

Directness-based utterances in the Indonesian language may also fall into two categories, i.e. direct utterances and indirect utterances. Direct utterances are the utterances whose meanings can be soon interpreted directly from parts of the utterances, i.e. the meanings based on linguistic context (cohesive meanings). This meaning is called explicature in pragmatics. The opposite of this is called implicature. Implicatures are the meanings of indirect utterances, i.e. the meanings based on context of situation (coherent meanings). To come to an implicature of an indirect utterance, a hearer usually thinks a bit longer than he does to an explicature of a direct utterance. The two variants can be illustrated in Table 3.

Other examples of direct and indirect utterances can also be found in daily use, as illustrated in Table 4.

3)   Meaning-Based Utterances Meaning-based utterances in the Indonesian language may also fall into two categories, i.e. literal utterances and non-literal utterances. Literal utterances are the utterances in their usual and obvious sense. The opposite are non-literal or figurative utterances. Non-literal utterances use allegories and metaphors (CALD, 2008). Allegories are stories, paintings, or descriptions of ideas such as anger, patience, purity, and truth by symbols of persons with those characters. Metaphors are imaginative ways to describe something by referring to something else with the similar characteristics or qualities. A metaphoric language is thus the language with no usual or literal meaning but the language which describes something by images or symbols. Direct and literal utterances include banter, while indirect and non-literal utterances involve irony and hedges (Leech, 1983); (Jumanto J., Pragmatics and Character Language Building, 2011c). The two variants can be illustrated in Table 5.

Other examples of literal and non-literal utterances can also be found in daily use, as illustrated in **Table 6**.

Politeness and Camaraderie in Indonesian Language

Politeness is everything good that has been uttered as well as acted by the speaker to the hearer within a particular

Table 3: Directness-based utterances

Direct utterances	Indirect utterances
Saya tidak setuju dengan Anda. "I do not agree with you"	Menurut saya, sebaiknya begini··· "I think that it is better like this···"

Table 4: More examples on directness-based utterances

Direct utterances	Indirect utterances
Saya sedang sibuk dan tidak bias diganggu sekarang. "I am busy. You should not disturb me now"	Bagaimana jika besok saja? "What if we do this tomorrow?"
Tolong hidupkan AC-nya! "Please turn on the AC!"	Ruangannya kok panas, ya. "It is hot here, isn't it?"
Cinta mereka tidak serius. "Their love is not very serious"	Mereka sedang cinta monyet. "They are in puppy love"
Panggilkan Pak Kebun! "Call the gardener!"	Pak Kebun di mana, ya? "Where is the gardener?"
Saya tidak minum kopi. "I do not drink coffee"	Bisa minuman yang lain? "Do you have something else to drink?"
Lama. "Long time"	Tidak sebentar. "Not a short time"
Terlambat. "Late"	Tidak tepat waktu. "Not on time"
Bodoh. "Stupid"	Tidak begitu pintar. "Not very smart"
Maaf, saya harus pergi. "Excuse me, I have to go now"	Maaf, saya ada urusan lain. "Excuse me, I have something else to do"
Sudah tua. "Already old"	Tidak begitu muda. "Not very young"

Table 5: Meaning-based utterances

Literal utterances	Non-literal utterances
Koruptor merugikan negara. "Corruptors corrupt a country"	Tikus berdasi merugikan negara. "Rats in the government corrupt a country"

Table 6: More examples on meaning-based utterances

Literal utterances	Non-literal utterances
Pelari itu tidak kenal lelah. "That runner is never tired"	Pelari itu seperti kuda. "That runner is like a horse"
Selalu datang terlambat. "Always come late"	Pakai jam karet. "Have a rubber time"
Terlalu banyak berbicara. "Talk too much"	Tong kosong berbunyi nyaring. "A gasbag"
Kencing. "Urinate"	Buang air kecil. "Pass water"
Toilet/WC. "Toilet/bathroom"	Kamar kecil. "Restroom"
Mau ke kamar mandi. "Go to the bathroom"	Mau ke belakang. "Go wash one's hands"
Naik pesawat ke Singapura. "Take a plane to Singapore"	Terbang ke Singapura. "Fly to Singapore"
Menyelesaikan masalah kecil secaraberlebihan. "Settle a minor problem in a super fluousmanner"	Membunuh tikus dengan membakar gudang. "Burn the warehouse to kill a rat"
Pemuda itu besar, tegap, kuat, dan gagah. "That young man is big, strong, and steady"	Pemuda itu Superman. "That young man is Superman"
Marah dan melabrak apa saja. "Be mad and destroy everything"	Membabi buta. "Run amuck"

context, to maintain their interpersonal face as well as their social face (Jumanto, Pragmatics: Linguistic World is Broad, 2011b). Politeness in the Indonesian language is basically distant language and close language together in context, as proposed by Jumanto (Jumanto, Pragmatics and Character Language Building, 2011c). Distant language and close language refer to and derive from the notion social distance, i.e. the physical as well as psychological distance between the speaker and the hearer.

Pragmatics regards a diglossic situation in a speech society as having the two variants of language above. Distant language refers to formal, indirect, and non-literal utterances, while close language refers to informal, direct, and literal utterances. As referring to formal, indirect, and non-literal utterances, distant language is usually carefully elaborated and uses safe and common topics. Meanwhile, as referring to informal, direct, and literal utterances, close language usually involves contractions, slangs, reverse-ups, changes, taboos, swearing, fwords, and uses any topics, personal and private (Jumanto, Pragmatics and Character Language Building, 2011c). The speaker tends to use distant language to the hearers with power factor (superiors); on the other hand, the speaker tends to use close language to the hearers with solidarity factor (close hearers). Examples of superiors are our bosses, our supervisors, our parents, and others, those who can relatively be close or not close to us. Examples of subordinates are our employees, our younger siblings, our servants, and others, those who can relatively be close or not close to us[5].

From the accounts above, we can see clearly that distant language and close language are in line with distancing politeness and closeness politeness. Distant language brings politeness, and close language brings friendship or camaraderie (Jumanto, Teaching a Character BIPA (Indonesian for Non-Native Speakers), 2012). Distant language and close language to show politeness and camaraderie finally meet the demand of language as a means of communication, i.e. a real-life everyday use of language in all situations or pragmatic use of language in a diglossic situation. Back to politeness and camaraderie in the Indonesian language, we should be aware of the two variants of language above; and therefore, to find out the distant Indonesian language and the close Indonesian language, we should relate the types of forms of utterances in the Indonesian language with politeness and camaraderie. A probable data-based illustration is shown in Table 7. From the categories illustrated in Table 7 we can say that the distant Indonesian language (politeness) tends to have formal, indirect, and non-literal utterances, while the close Indonesian language (camaraderie) tends to have informal, direct, and literal utterances, the tendencies of which can be shown in Table 8. With reference to the distant Indonesian language and the close Indonesian language illustrated in

Table 8, we can transfer the previous data of utterances into three derivative tables. Here, for more ease to say and to learn, we refer the utterances in the three tables to the so-called distant utterances and close utterances. Distant utterances bring politeness, while close utterances bring camaraderie, as illustrated in Tables 9-11.

Impoliteness in Indonesian Language

Politeness in using the Indonesian language happens when we use the distant Indonesian language and the close Indonesian language eligibly, i.e. when we use the distant language and the close language to superiors and close hearers respectively (Jumanto, Teaching a Character BIPA (Indonesian for Non-Native Speakers), 2012). Here, as we speak of politeness and camaraderie in the Indonesian language, the Indonesian speakers adjust their utterances to a particular situation that may call. They can perform the so-called code-switching, whether to use the distant Indonesian language or to use the close Indonesian language. Impoliteness in using the Indonesian language happens when we do not learn the distant language and the close language. When we use the close language to superiors, probably due to our lack of knowledge about distant Indonesian language, we are being not polite or we are being rude, or impoliteness happens. On the other instance, when we use the distant language to close hearers, probably intentionally due to some interpersonal friction, we are also being not polite or impoliteness (or irony) happens. In this case, we are trying to be distant to close hearers. Awkwardness is in the air and there is usually less harmony between us.

Illustrations on rude situations and awkward situations in using Indonesian language are given below.

1)   Rude Situations (Impoliteness): Using the Close Indonesian Language to Superiors Examples of rude situations are as follows:

a) "Cepet baikan, ya Pak Bud!" (?)[6]

"Better soon, OK, Mr. Bud!" (?)

[It should be:]

"Semoga segera sembuh, Bapak Budi."

"May you get better soon, Mister Budi."

b) "Saya tidak setuju dengan Anda." (?)

"I do not agree with you." (?)

[It should be:]

"Menurut saya, sebaiknya begini···"

"I think that it is better like this···"

c) "Maaf, Pak. Saya mau ke WC dulu." (?)

"Excuse me, Sir. I want to go to the toilet first." (?)

[It should be:]

"Maaf, Bapak. Saya ijin ke kamar kecil dulu."

"Excuse me, Sir. May I go to the restroom, please?"

Rude situations may happen in the three utterances above, as the speakers are speaking to superiors by using a close language. Here, a) "Cepet baikan, ya Pak Bud!", b) "Saya tidak setuju dengan Anda.", and c) "Maaf, Pak. Saya mau ke WC dulu." are all of close language, i.e. informal, direct, and literal respectively.

2) Awkward Situations (Impoliteness): Using the Distant Indonesian Language to Close Hearers Examples of awkward situations are as follows:

a) "Saya mengucapkan terima kasih banyak atas bantuan Anda, ya Susanto!" (?)

"I thank you very much for your help, OK, Susanto!" (?)

[It should be:]

Table 7: More examples on meaning-based utterances

Types of utterances	Politeness (to superiors)	Camaraderie (to close hearers)
formality-based	formal utterances	informal utterances
directness-based	indirect utterances	direct utterances
meaning-based	non-literal utterances	literal utterances

[6]A query (?) is used here to show a rude or an awkward situation that may happen.

Table 8: Types of forms of utterances in Indonesian language in relation with distant language and close language

Types of language	Types of forms of utterances
Distant Indonesian language	formal utterances, indirect utterances, non-literal utterances
Close Indonesian language	informal utterances, direct utterances, literal utterances

Table 9: Formality-based utterances in Indonesian language in relation with politeness and camaraderie

Distant Indonesian language (politeness) with formal utterances	Close Indonesian language (camaraderie) with informal utterances
Saya mengucapkanterima kasihbanyak "I thank you very much"	Terima kasih; Makasih; Kamsia; Tks; Thanks; Thx "Thank you"; "Thanks"; "Thx"
memberikan "giving"; "give them"	berikan; beri; kasihkan; kasih "givin"; "giv'em"
Selamat pagi! "Good morning!"	Met pagi!; Pagi! "Morning!"
Semoga Anda segera sembuh "May you get better soon"	Cepet sembuh; Cepet baikan; Lekas sehat "Get better soon"; "Better soon"
membantu "helping"; "help them"	mbantu; bantu "helpin"; "help'em"
lelah sekali "extremely tired"	capek banget; ka-o; ngos-ngosan "exhausted"
berlebihan "superfluous"	lebay [?]
jarang dibelai "seldom cared for"	jablay [?]
tidak "No, I do not"	tak; tdk; nggak; gak "No"; "I don't"; "don't"
meskipun "although"; "even though"	meski; mskpn "though"
tetapi "however", "nevertheless"	tapi; tp; but "but"
ayah "father"	yah; papa; daddy; bokap "daddy", "dad"
ibu "mother"	bu; mama; mammy; nyokap "mommy"; "mom"
Bapak Budi "Mister Budi"	Pak Budi; P Budi "Mr. Budi"
Ibu Rini "Mistress Rini"	Bu Rini; B Rini "Ms. Rini"
Saya "I would…"	Aku; Gue; Ai; Ike "I will…"
Anda "You would…"	Kamu; Lu; Situ; You "You will…"
Saudara "You would…"	Sdr "You will…"
dan sebagainya "et cetera"	dsb "etc."

Table 10: Directness-based utterances in Indonesian language in relation with politeness and camaraderie

Close Indonesian language (camaraderie) with direct utterances	Distant Indonesian language (politeness) with indirect utterances
Saya tidak setuju dengan Anda. "I do not agree with you"	Menurut saya, sebaiknya begini··· "I think that it is better like this···"
Saya sedang sibuk dan tidak bias diganggu sekarang. "I am busy. You should not disturb me now"	Bagaimana jika besok saja? "What if we do this tomorrow?"
Tolong hidupkan AC-nya! "Please turn on the AC!"	Ruangannya kok panas, ya. "It is hot here, isn't it?"
Cinta mereka tidak serius. "Their love is not very serious"	Mereka sedang cinta monyet. "They are in puppy love"
Panggilkan Pak Kebun! "Call the gardener!"	Pak Kebun di mana, ya? "Where is the gardener?"
Saya tidak minum kopi. "I do not drink coffee"	Bisa minuman yang lain? "Do you have something else to drink?"
Lama. "Long time"	Tidak sebentar. "Not a short time"
Terlambat. "Late"	Tidak tepat waktu. "Not on time"
Bodoh. "Stupid"	Tidak begitu pintar. "Not very smart"
Maaf, saya harus pergi. "Excuse me, I have to go now"	Maaf, saya ada urusan lain. "Excuse me, I have something else to do"
Sudah tua. "Already old"	Tidak begitu muda. "Not very young"

"Makasih banget bantuanmu, ya Sus!"

"Thanks so much for your help, OK, Sus!"

b) "Ruangannya kok panas, ya." (?)

"It is hot here, isn't it." (?)

[It should be:]

"Tolong hidupkan AC-nya!"

"Please turn on the AC!"

c) "Wah, Anda pakai jam karet terus, nih!" (?)

"Well, you always have rubber time, don't you!" (?)

[It should be:]

"Ngapain kamu kok datang terlambat terus?"

"Why the hell d'you always come late?"

Awkward situations may happen in the three utterances above, as the speakers are speaking to close hearers by using a distant language. Here, a) "Saya mengucapkan terima kasih banyak atas bantuan Anda, ya Susanto!", b) "Ruangannya kok panas, ya.", and c) "Wah, Anda pakai jam karet terus, nih!" are all of distant language, i.e. formal, indirect, and non-literal respectively.

Cases of Confusion Due to Factors of Power and Solidarity: Code-Mixing for Camaraderie

In the case that confusion happens due to the factors of power and solidarity in the hearer, i.e. whether a superior is close or a close hearer has power, for example, the so-called code-mixing happens. However, as the terminology suggests, the code-mixing in language use belongs to informality, thus using a close language (camaraderie)[7]. Cases like these usually happen between close speakers, i.e. a superior to a close subordinate or a subordinate to a close superior. Examples on these cases are given below:

a) "Aku mengucapkan terima kasih banyak atas bantuanmu, ya Sus!"

 "I thank you very much for your help, OK, Sus!"

Table 11: Meaning-based utterances in Indonesian languagein relation with politeness and camaraderie

Close Indonesian language (camaraderie) with literal utterances	Distant Indonesian language (politeness) with non-literal utterances
Tikus membawa penyakit. "Rats carry disease"	Tikus berdasi merugikan negara. "Rats in the government corrupt a country"
Pelari itu tidak kenal lelah. "That runner is never tired"	Pelari itu seperti kuda. "That runner is like a horse"
Selalu datang terlambat. "Always come late"	Pakai jam karet. "Have a rubber time"
Terlalu banyak berbicara. "Talk too much"	Tong kosong berbunyi nyaring. "A gasbag"
Kencing. "Urinate"	Buang air kecil. "Pass water"
Toilet/WC. "Toilet/bathroom"	Kamar kecil. "Restroom"
Mau ke kamar mandi. "Go to the bathroom"	Mau ke belakang. "Go wash one's hands"
Naik pesawat ke Singapura. "Take a plane to Singapore"	Terbang ke Singapura. "Fly to Singapore"
Menyelesaikan masalah kecil secara berlebihan. "Settle a minor problem in a superfluous manner"	Membunuh tikus dengan membakar gudang. "Burn the warehouse to kill a rat"
Pemuda itu besar, tegap, kuat, dan gagah. "That young man is big, strong, and steady"	Pemuda itu Superman. "That young man is Superman"
Marah dan melabrak apa saja. "Be mad and destroy everything"	Membabi buta. "Run amuck"

[7]Analogy of this is just like wearing a T-shirt and a tie. Using a language is, indeed, like wearing clothes (Jumanto, Pragmatics Linguistic World is Broad, 2011b).

This is a probable situation between a superiorto a close subordinate, i.e. using a code-mixing of distant and close language. Here the expressions "Aku", "OK", "Sus", and "-mu" are informal, while the expression "mengucapkan terima kasih banyak atas bantuan-" is formal.

b) "Saya tidak setuju dengan rencana kamu, lho."

 "I do not agree on your plan, you know."

This is another probable situation between a subordinate to a close superior, i.e. using a code-mixing of distant and close language. Here the expressions "setuju", "kamu", and "lho" are informal, while the expressions "saya" and "tidak" are formal. The whole expression "Saya tidak setuju dengan rencana kamu, lho" itself is a direct utterance, thus used between close speakers.

    c) "Wah, kamu ini pakai jam karet terus, sih!"

    "Well, you always have rubber time, you see!"

The example (3) above is another probable situation between a superior to a close subordinate, i.e. using a code-mixing of distant and close language. Though the expressions "wah", "kamu", and "sih" are informal (thus, part of close language), the expression "jam karet" is non-literal, and thus, part of distant language.

From the three examples above, however, as the code-mixing happens only between close speakers, awkwardness does not usually happen and politeness between them is maintained. Camaraderie instills. Language use is a matter of probabilities.

Phases of Character Language: A Proposal to the Open Linguistic World

The building of a character language means applying the accounts on politeness, camaraderie, and impoliteness discussed above in verbal interactions so that distant language and close language are learned, internalized, personalized, and socialized or practiced in everyday life, and, therefore, rude situations as well as awkward situations can be avoided. Many parties are involved in this verbal social project: parents, teachers, communities, societies, and the authorities: the school managers, the local government, and the national government. Pragmatics is applied in this character language building in a context as if a native speaker is trying to acquire their language.

The pragmatic aspects to be applied are the four strategies, i.e. 1) elaboration of meaning and form strategies, 2) distant language and close language strategies, 3) politeness and camaraderie strategies, 4) object language and metalanguage strategies. The strategies function as building blocks of a character language building, the developing steps of which are the six phases of verbal social project as follows:

Interaction Phase

In this early phase, elaboration of meaning is more important than elaboration of form. Close language strategies should also be more emphasized in the daily experience than distant language strategies, and therefore, camaraderie strategies are more elaborated. As the learning speaker just starts building their character language, object language and metalanguage should be experienced in a 75:25 ratio of probabilities. The parties to help encouraging this phase are parents and close communities.

Teaching-and-Learning Process Phase

This phase is done at school, i.e. the teaching-and-learning phase. In this phase, elaborations of meaning and form strategies, distant language and close language strategies, politeness and camaraderie strategies, and object language and metalanguage strategies are equally experienced by the learning speaker of a character language. The speaker should experience an equal 50:50 ratio of probabilities encouraged by their character language teacher. The parties most responsible for helping encouraging this phase are teachers, and all the authorities, parents, close and distant communities, and societies.

Evaluation Phase

This phase is also done at school, i.e. the evaluation phase. The evaluation phase here is of formal and structured evaluation processes: progress, mid-term, and final-term evaluations. The elaborations of meaning and form strategies, distant language and close language strategies, politeness and camaraderie strategies, and object language and metalanguage strategies are equally evaluated by the teacher teaching a character language. The teacher should evaluate an equal 50:50 ratio of probabilities of character language material having learned by the learning speaker. Written reports are given upon the evaluation processes. The parties most responsible for helping encouraging this phase are teachers, and all the authorities.

Re-Evaluation Phase

This phase is also done at school, i.e. the re-evaluation phase. The re-evaluation phase here is an informal and unstructured evaluation atmosphere: in fun classrooms, in the school doorways, in sudden encounters between the teacher and the learning speaker, in the school yard, and in other school spaces at relaxed situations. The teacher should verify on the learning speaker's verbal performance on their character language in indirect and relaxed manners: whether the verbal performance is appropriate or not yet. When doing so, the teacher should minimize the threat to the learning speaker. Compliments and discussions are given upon the learning speaker's verbal performance. The parties most responsible for helping encouraging this phase are teachers, and all the authorities.

Verification Phase

This phase is done everywhere, i.e. the verification phase. This phase is to strengthen the re-evaluation phase at school. The verification phase should be done everywhere by the character language competent speakers upon the verbal performance of the learning speakers. Thus, every competent speaker is responsible for encouraging the learning speaker to complete their character language building. This phase is also done in an informal and unstructured atmosphere everywhere in the country. The verification should also be done in indirect and relaxed manners. Compliments and discussions should also be given upon the learning speaker's verbal performance. All the parties are most responsible for encouraging this phase.

Selection Phase

This is the final phase of the character language building project, i.e. the selection phase. This phase is for the speaker to apply the character language they have just completed learning, in a particular situation that may call. The speakers are now smart enough in using the language pragmatically, as they have equipped themselves with all the strategies required for character language use in a diglossic situation. The competent speaker may now select to use either distant language or close language, i.e. either formal utterances, indirect utterances, and nonliteral utterances in the formal situations, or informal utterances, direct utterances, and literal utterances in the informal situations. In this final phase, all parties as well as members of the speech society are responsible for encouraging one another in using and maintaining the character language.

CONCLUSION

The character language building proposed and discussed in this paper is a verbal social project. A social project here implies that the whole speech society is invited as well as involved in the project: parents, teachers, communities, societies, and the authorities: the school managers, the local government, and the national government.

This verbal social project is costly but is not impossible to carry out. The four pragmatic strategies elaborated as the building blocks of character language building are worth applying in the efforts to equip the state children of tomorrow with a character language for the future of a character nation.

A character language is inevitably important as part of character nation building. In this light, pragmatics serves to character nation building in the scope of verbal performances of a competent character speaker. A competent character speaker is a good speaker who in time will probably be a good character leader in a particular country.

As a character language equips the speakers with politeness and camaraderie and with awareness of avoiding impoliteness, both in rude situations and in awkward situations, the teaching and learning of it, and later the acquisition of it, will contribute to interpersonal, communal, social, and, in time, national harmony.

ACKNOWLEDGEMENTS

I would like to acknowledge all the distinguished people here for contributing their thoughts as well as precious opinions to the linguistic world I have academically lived in. The first group is nine English native speakers: (1) Samantha Custer (New England, US), John Custer (Pennsylvania, US), Bradford Sincock (Michigan, US), Patricia Mary O'Dwyer (South Ireland, GB), Patrick Bradley (Scotland, GB), Simon Colledge (London, UK, GB), Ian Briggs (Northern Territory, Australia), Anastasia de Guise (New South Wales, Australia), and Katrina Michelle Langford (Victoria, Australia). They have inspired me on how a linguist should perform in the linguistic world as well as on how I should learn more to observe people talking and to get real-life lessons for developing the pragmatic world.

I would also like to extend my gratitude to the second group of nine Indonesian professionals, Indonesian native speakers, without whom my linguistic world is not as enough as it is today: (1) Putri Mayangsari (freelance interpreter, Jakarta), Ria Herwandar (language consultant, Jakarta), Joseph Poerwono (company manager, Jakarta), Soetanto Hoetomo (school manager, Jakarta), Esther D. Tamtama (lecturer, Semarang), Herni Ambarwati (senior secretary, Semarang), Agus Sururi (hotel manager, Semarang), Didi Pribadi (restaurant manager, Semarang), and Siti Subiantari (liaison/guide, Jakarta).

Last but not least, I owe a lot to former linguists as well as researchers, whose works are both significant and helpful for making this article happen. May God the Almighty be with and bless you all.

REFERENCES

1.   Arndt, H., & Janney, R. (1985). Politeness Revisited: Cross-Modal Supportive Strategies. International Review of Applied Linguistics in Language Teaching, 23, 281-300.

2.   Austin, J. (1957). How to Do Things with Words. Oxford: Oxford University Press.

3.   Axtell, R. E. (1995). Do's and Taboos of Using English around the World.

New York: John Wiley & Sons, Inc.

4. Blum-Kulka, S. (1992). The Metapragmatics of Politeness in Israeli Society. In S. I. Richard Watts (Ed.), Politeness in Language: Studies in its History, Theory, and Practice. Berlin: Mouton de Gruyter.

5. Boomfield, L. (1930). Language. New York: Holt.

6. Brown, P., & Levinson, S. C. (1987). Politeness: Some Universals in Language Usage. New York: Cambridge University Press.

7. Brown, R., & Gilman, A. (1968). The Pronouns of Power and Solidarity. In J. A. Fishman (Ed.), Readings in the Sociology of Language (pp. 252-275). The Hague: Mouton & Co. N.V. Publishers. http://dx.doi.org/10.1515/9783110805376.252

8. Bühler, K. (1918). Theory of Language: The Representational Function of Language. Amsterdam: John Benjamins Publishing Co.

9. CALD (2008). Cambridge Advanced Learner's Dictionary. Cambridge: Cambridge University Press.

10. Carter, R. E. (1997). Working with Texts: A Core Book For language Analysis. London: Routledge. http://dx.doi.org/10.4324/9780203468470

11. Chomsky, N. (1950). Aspects of the Theory of Syntax. Cambridge: MIT Press.

12. CoBuild CoBuild English Dictionary (2003).

13. Cook, G. (1989). Discourse. Oxford: Oxford University Press.

14. Coupland, J. (2000). Small Talk. Harlow: Pearson Education Limited.

15. de Saussure, F. (1916). Pengantar linguistik Umum. Yogyakarta: Yogyakarta: Gadjah Mada University Press.

16. Duranti, A. (1998). Communicative Competence. In J. L. Mey (Ed.), Concise Encyclopedia of Pragmatics (pp. 147-148). Amsterdam: Elsevier.

17. Eelen, G. (2001). A Critique of Politeness Theories. Manchester: St. Jerome Publishing.

18. Fraser, B., & Nolen, W. (1981). The Association of Deference with Linguistic Form. International Journal of the Sociology of Language, 1981, 93-109.

19. Fries, C. C. (1979). Review of Grammatical Analysis. In K. L. Pike, & E. G. Pike (Eds.), Language (Vol. 55, pp. 907-911). London: Longman.

20. Goffman, E. (1959). The Presentation of Self in Everyday Life. New York: Anchor Books.

21. Goffman, E. (1967). Interaction Ritual: Essays on Face to Face Behavior. New York: Anchor Books.

22. Grice, H. P. (1975). Logic and Conversation. In P. Cole, & J. Morgan (Eds.), Syntax and Semantics, Speech Acts (Vol. 3, pp. 33-49). New York: Academic Press.

23. Gu, Y.G. (1990). Politeness Phenomena in Modern Chinese. Journal of Pragmatics, 14, 237-257. http://dx.doi.org/10.1016/0378-2166(90)90082-O

24. Gunarwan, A. (2001). Implicatures of Linguistic Codes Selection in Some Dialogues of Ludruk. PELLBA, 14, 23-35.

25. Gunarwan, A. (2005). Articles on Loose Papers in PhD Study Classes, University of Indonesia. Papers, Jakarta: University of Indonesia.

26. Hinkel, E. (1999). Culture in Second Language Teaching and Learning. Cambridge: Cambridge University Press.

27. Holmes, J. (1992). An Introduction to Sociolinguistics. London: Longman Group Ltd.

28. Hornby, A. (1987). Oxford Advanced Learner's Dictionary of Current English. Oxford: Oxford University Press.

29. Hymes, D. (1972). On Communicative Competence. In J. Pride, & J. Holmes (Eds.), Sociolinguistics (pp. 269-285). Harmondsworth: Penguin Books.

30. Hymes, D. (1974). Foundations in Sociolinguistics. Philadelphia, PA: University of Pennsylvania Press.

31. Ide, S. (1989). Formal Forms and Discernment: Two Neglected Aspects of Universals of Linguistic Politeness. Multilingua, 8, 223-248. http://dx.doi.org/10.1515/mult.1989.8.2-3.223

32. Jakobson, R. (1960). Concluding Statement: Linguistics and Poetics. In T. Sebeok (Ed.), Style in Language (pp. 350-377). Cambridge: MIT Press.

33. Jumanto, J. (2006). Komunikasi Fatis di Kalangan Penutur Jati Bahasa Inggris. Unpublished PhD Dissertation, Jakarta: Universitas Indonesia.

34. Jumanto, J. (2008). Phatic Communication among English Native Speakers. Semarang: WorldPro Publishing.

35. Jumanto, J. (2010). Language of Advertising: An Ideology Critic. In Languages and Science (BIP) (pp. 11-19). Semaranga: Akaba 17 Semarang.

36. Jumanto, J. (2011a). Discourse Analysis and Ideology Critics. In Lingua Komunika (pp. 44-51). Semarang: University of 17 August 1945.

37. Jumanto, J. (2011b). Pragmatics: Linguistic World Is Broad. Semarang: WorldPro Publishing.

38. Jumanto, J. (2011c). Pragmatics and Character Language Building. The 58th TEFLIN International Conference on Language Teaching and Character Building (pp. 329-340). Semarang: IKIP PGRI College.

39. Jumanto, J. (2012). Teaching a Character BIPA (Indonesian for Non-Native Speakers). The 2012 KIPBIPA VIII-ASILE International Conference (pp. 1-20). Salatiga: UKSW University.

40. Lakoff, R. T. (1990). Talking Power: The Politics of Language in Our Lives. Glasgow: HarperCollins.

41. Leech, G. (1983). Principles of Pragmatics. New York: Longman Group Limited.

42. Lincoln, Y., & Guba, E. (1985). Naturalistic Inquiry. Beverly Hills, CA: Sage.

43. Malinowski, B. (1923). The Problem of Meaning in Primitive Languages. In C. K. Ogden, & I. A. Richards (Eds.), The Meaning of Meaning (pp. 296-336). London: K. Paul, Trend, Trubner.

44. Mey, J. L. (2001). Pragmatics: An Introduction (2nd ed.). Oxford: Blackwell.

45. Morris, C. (1946). Signs, Language, and Behavior. New York: Prentice-Hall.

46. Ogden, C. K., & Richards, A. (1923). The Meaning of Meaning. London: K. Paul, Trend, Trubner.

47. OLPD (1987). Oxford Learner's Pocket Dictionary. Oxford: Oxford University Press.

48. Renkema, J. (1993). Discourse Studies: An Introductory Textbook. Amsterdam: John Benjamins Publishing Company.

49. Richards, J., Platt, J., & Platt, H. (1985). Longman Dictionary of Language Teaching and Applied Linguistics. Essex: Longman.

50. Schiffrin, D. (1994). Approaches to Discourse. Cambridge: Blackwell Publishers.

51. Searle, J. (1965). Speech Acts. Cambridge: Cambridge University Press.

52. Spencer-Oatey, H. (1992). Cross-Cultural Politeness: British and Chinese Conceptions of the Tutor-Student Relationship. Unpublished PhD Thesis, Lancaster: Lancaster University.

53. Thomas, J. (1996). Meaning in Interaction: An Introduction to Pragmatics. London: Longman.

54. Thompson, L. (1997). Children Talking: The Development of Pragmatic Competence. London: Multilingual Matters Publisher.

Chapter 3

A REVIEW OF MODELS IN EXPERIMENTAL STUDIES OF IMPLICIT LANGUAGE LEARNING

Si Liu, Huangmei Liu

School of Foreign Languages and Literatures, Lanzhou University, Lanzhou, China

ABSTRACT

The present review analyzes experimental research on implicit learning using linguistic stimuli, and proposes five key procedures of a framework for empirical studies of implicit learning. Our review begins with a brief overview of the current state of research on implicit learning, and then presents the procedures in detail: 1) choosing theoretical assumptions from psychology; 2) designing stimuli; 3) exposing subjects to information; 4) testing implicit learning; and 5) measuring subjects' state of awareness. This framework is intended to assist researchers in designing experiments on implicit learning both more comprehensively and with fewer flaws.

INTRODUCTION

Shanks (2005) uses nine examples of earlier research to give more explicit concept of implicit learning, and concludes that implicit learning can generally be characterized as learning that takes place both unintentionally and unconsciously. Interests in implicit learning have lasted about 50 years. Since Reber coined the term "implicit learning" for the first time in 1967, numerous experiments have been done in this field. Until now, it seems that the central issue of implicit learning studies has been proved that what researchers thought to have been learned implicitly really was acquired by implicit learning, and then to find the cognitive processes of implicit learning, rather than more fundamentally to prove whether implicit learning did in fact exist(Frensch & Rünger, 2003; Williams, 2009). Both psychologists and linguists are interested in the matter. Psychologists study it to learn more about human psychological mechanisms; linguists study it to learn more about human language developmental mechanisms. In this review, we would focus on clinical research with linguistic features.

Researchers like Williams (2004, 2005, 2009), endeavor to develop clinical methodologies and models that will make studies of implicit learning more reliable and persuasive. Clinical models are important gains from clinical studies. There are three general kinds of models: first, models based on offline methodology (Jiménez et al., 1996); second, models based on online methodology, mostly using RT, ERP or fMRI (Cleeremans & McClelland, 1991; Clegg et al., 1998; Leung & Williams, 2006; Williams, 2004, 2005); and third, models based on computational methodology, mostly constructed according to constructivist and emergentist views (Cleeremans & McClelland, 1991;Dienes, 1992; Estes, 1957; Hintzmann, 1986; Perruchet & Vinter, 1998). Following these three general models, there are detailed models developed by experimental practices. One of the most popular models using RT is the one developed by Williams in 2004, which examined implicit learning through a series of explicit training sessions that controlled subjects' attention, recording reaction time (RT) and drawing conclusions on which items had been learned implicitly (Chen et al., 2011; Leung & Williams, 2006; Williams, 2004, 2005).

Numerous models have been developed, but none of them is beyond dispute. On one hand, almost all contain some elements or procedures that make them less reliable; on the other hand, a more scientific criterion has not been found to guide researchers in planning their experimental procedures. In contrast, a surgeon follows a series of detailed and standardized preparation procedures before he or she enters the operating room. We, then, seek to give the best suggestions on developing and standardizing such necessary procedural steps for researchers in the clinical field of implicit learning.

METHOD OF OUR REVIEW

Literature Search Strategy

We tried to identify published studies through searches of Elsevier, Science-direct, Springer, Google Scholar and Google using keyword, title and abstract information. Each of these databases allows searches of articles before July of 2013. The following search terms were used: implicit learning, implicit knowledge, artificial grammar learning, sequence learning, unconscious learning and learning without attention. Manual searches were also important to consult for identifying other items from the references of other relevant reviews and book chapters.

Inclusion and Omission

Only English-language articles are included in the present review. To review critically and ensure manageability, our review focuses on clinical studies of implicit learning in relation to artificial grammar learning (AGL) and sequence learning (SL) but it is not exhaustive. Other paradigms, such as probability learning (Millward & Reber, 1968), melody learning (Rohmeier & Cross, 2010), visual search in complex stimulus environments (Chun & Jiang, 1999) and dynamic system control, have not been considered.

CONTROVERSIAL THEORETICAL ISSUES IN IMPLICIT LEARNING

Though this review focuses on the experimental models on implicit learning, this section will give a very brief summary about three theoretical issues that are quite controversial and need to be settled, because these theoretical issues seem to be the sources of the inconsistency of experimental results of implicit learning. The first issue is the definition of implicit learning. In the introduction section, we mentioned Shanks' conclusion about implicit learning as learning that takes place both unintentionally and unconsciously (Shanks, 2005). Definitions elsewhere (Cleeremans & McClelland, 1991; Clegg et al., 1998; Jiménez et al., 1996; Leung & Williams, 2006; Reber, 1967) also give descriptions like this. It is not difficult to find that the description itself is quite vague, because words like "unintentionally" and "unconsciously" are words without settled definition. Another difficulty in defining "implicit learning" is whether it should only include learning that occurs implicitly or all kinds of learning except ones occurring explicitly (Frensch & Rünger, 2003), since "implicit" does not absolutely equal to "unaware", and neither does "explicit" equal "aware". The inconsistency in defining implicit learning causes researchers to design experiments of implicit learning with different concepts of implicit learning in mind (Cleeremans & McClelland, 1991; Clegg et al., 1998; Jiménez et al., 1996; Leung & Williams, 2006), and consequentially makes the results of their experiments incomparable (Frensch & Rünger, 2003).

The second theoretical problem is that the processing mechanism of implicit learning and explicit learning is unsettled. There are disputes between the multiple-system hypothesis and single-system hypothesis (Frensch & Rünger, 2003). The former holds that implicit learning and explicit learning use different processing systems, whereas the latter holds that the two use the same processing system, and even some hypothesize that explicit learning should developed from implicit learning. This also makes the results of research incomparable with different concepts about processing mechanisms (please see Frensch & Rünger, 2003, for detail).

The third theoretical issue is also very troublesome: it is the uncertainty of attention mechanisms. In experiments, researchers need to make the acquisition of stimuli implicit or unaware by controlling subjects' attention. This problem will be given a more detailed discussion in Sections 4.1 and 4.3.

Though these theoretical issues do exist and do have passive consequences on the research of implicit learning, it is unlikely to be settled any time soon. However, to some extent, we might be able to complement this by adopting more controllable models in clinical studies.

A CRITICAL REVIEW ON EXPERIMENTAL MODELS IN CLINICAL STUDIES

After analytical work, we find that experimental models in clinical studies of implicit learning are usually involved in the following essential procedures: (1) choosing theoretical assumptions from psychology; (2) designing stimuli; (3) exposing subjects to information; (4) testing implicit learning; and (5) measuring subjects' state of awareness

Choosing Theoretical Assumptions from Psychology

Researchers have conceived of various presuppositions about implicit learning. The two most famous are the following: (1) the shadow theory (Searle, 1992), which holds that there is an unconscious mind and a conscious mind, and that the two are just the same, only with consciousness absent in the former; and (2) the not-reallyexisting theory (Shanks & St. John, 1994), which holds that results in experiments are about instances rather than rules, and thus learning about any kind of knowledge is explicit rather than implicit. Though there is still much to say about such presuppositions, we will not focus on them, instead, on psychological suppositions adopted in clinical experiments.

In designing experiments that test implicit learning, all or at least most researchers (Cleeremans & McClelland, 1991; Clegg et al., 1998) try to find their ground in the achievements of psychology, since implicit learning is thought to be an integral part of psychology. In the training section, researchers usually try to create conditions that promote implicit learning by controlling how subjects allocate attention, thus the most commonly cited supposition pertains to attention. "In psychology, the basic assumptions concerning attention have been that it is limited, that it is selective, that it is partially subjective to voluntary control, that attention controls access to consciousness, and that attention is essential for action control and for learning" (Schmidt, 2001: 11). These assumptions are basically used in the design of training, thus, we will review their roles in a later section on exposure.

Designing Stimuli

Usually, clinical research on implicit learning has essentially been focused on two stimulus paradigms: artificial grammar learning (AGL) and sequence learning (SL). The following sections will give more insight on the two paradigms with a critical view.

Artificial Grammar in Stimuli

Artificial grammar learning is arguably the most influential paradigm (Cleeremans & Dienes, 2008). In studies adopting artificial grammar, subjects are usually asked to memorize or look at a series of materials, and then to select from test materials the ones that conform to the materials they have seen before and to describe what rules they depend on to make the selection decisions. Reber (1967) was one of the first researchers to adopt AGL as experimental information in the study of implicit learning. He asked subjects to learn a series of letter strings within a limited time and then told them that these strings were all constructed according to a particular set of rules (an artificial grammar created by him). Later he conducted a test on the subjects with new strings and with such questions as which strings conformed to the rules earlier referred to. Subjects made decisions with better-than-chance accuracy; but results showed low correctness in description of the rules. Hence Reber concluded that the learning of the artificial rules was a phenomenon of implicit learning. Though Reber's conclusion was criticized heavily, since then, many researchers have taken to using artificial grammar to study implicit learning. Later versions of artificial grammar, however, have undergone many modifications (e.g. Reber, 1989; Berry & Dienes, 1993; Cleeremans et al., 1998; Pothos, 2007; Shanks, 2005; Wan et al., 2008).

What is arguably more worthy of note lies in the following experiments, which try to make the clinical stimuli closer to natural language. Williams (2004) used artificial nouns, artificial determiners and their artificial determiner-noun relationship as stimuli of implicit learning, but the determiners used had strong characteristics of gendered language determiners. Leung & Williams (2006) used artificial determiners, artificial syntax structure and the artificial determiner-agent/patient relationship as stimuli in Experiment 1. In Experiment 2, they used artificial nouns, artificial determiners and their artificial determiner-noun relationship as stimuli of implicit learning, having removed the features of gendered language determiner, using English nouns instead of artificial nouns, and using pictures to make up for the lack of context; Rebuschat & Williams (2009)adopted a semi-artificial grammar, which consists of English words and German syntax. Chen et al. (2011) conducted experiments in Chinese implicit learning, base on Williams' (2004) model, using extremely low-frequency Chinese characters as determiner, and Chinese nouns and an artificial determiner-noun relationship.

Although closer to natural language, these stimuli still have their own defects. The defect ofWilliams' (2004) stimuli is the gender features of the determiners; in Leung & Williams (2006), the stimulus defect results from its use of pictures, which might arouse other visual processing with the same effect as implicit learning. The stimuli in Rebuschat & Williams' (2009) experiments, from German syntax, may be too close to those of English. In Chen et al. (2011), the stimuli themselves seemed good, but Chen classified them in Chinese as "structure": in fact, the stimuli, though in the position of determiner, were more likely to be elements of adjectives belonging to a semantic field in Chinese that is completely ideographic. More modifications, therefore, are expected in future experiments. It is expected that one of the new directions will call for stimuli closer to natural language in a natural context with semantic and pragmatic features taken into consideration.

Sequence

In experiments in the paradigm of sequence learning, subjects are usually meant to learn the order of elements in a sequence during a training course that asks them to react as fast as possible to the elements that appear. If a subject has learned the sequential feature of the elements, he needs much less time to decide the features of the elements coming up (Clegg et al., 1998). Nissen and Bullemer (1987), the first adopted sequence learning in clinical study of implicit learning, demonstrated the effect of learning without awareness of the sequential rules. Cleeremans and McClelland (1991) used a sequence of stimuli whose locations were determined by a finite-state grammar. Fu et al. (2008, 2010) adopted two second-order conditional sequences of numbers in a target-location task, in which the location of each number was determined by the locations of the previous two numbers. Implicit sequence learning was also studied frequently in psychological studies of aging and other issues as a window through which to look inside human brain function (Rieckmann & Bäckman, 2009).

Artificial sequences are popular in today's implicit learning studies, but they are more or less too artificial to attract subjects, or unable to consider various meanings. This makes those experiments more likely to be in the situation of a mathematic or logic test. Even specialists in mathematics and logic believe that language is what we depend on to think. We believe that more linguistic features, particularly semantic and pragmatic features, should be added to the sequences in the future.

Models of Exposing Subjects to Information

Now we discuss two crucial methodology problems in the exposure phase. The first problem is the balance of exposure: researchers are expected to be able to ensure an environment that helps implicit learning happen while reducing the probability that implicit learning becomes explicit. That is to say, any break in the balance of exposure, too much or too little, would render the experiments questionable. The second problem is the control of attention allocation. As we discussed in Section 3.1, psychological presuppositions about attention are the theoretical foundation upon which researchers depend to design their training course. Attention and awareness are two inseparable sides of the same coin (Carr & Curran, 1994; James, 1890; Posner, 1994). Discussing the development of knowledge, Schmidt (2001) said, "perhaps the only role for attention is that, presumably, at least the crucial evidence that triggers changes in the unconscious system must be attended." That is to say, in clinical experiments, researchers need to control any kind of attention to implicit features, to reduce all likelihood of arousing attention to implicit features, or even to try to distract subjects' attention from implicit features. In terms of these two problems, we can see the strengths and the weaknesses of the most commonly adopted exposure paradigms.

Chiefly, there are four kinds of exposure paradigms: (1) implicit goal not mentioned + activities connected to implicit features; (2) explicit goal + explicit goal training + activities connected to implicit features + implicit goal not mentioned; (3) explicit goal + explicit goal training + implicit goal not mentioned; (4) only stimuli + implicit goal not mentioned.

Most sequence learning studies belong to the first type (Clegg et al., 1998; Cleeremans & McClelland, 1991; Nissen & Bullemer, 1987; Rieckmann & Bäckman, 2009): subjects are not told anything about the existence of rules, but only asked to react to questions as by pressing a fixed key when seeing an element or to memorize sequences in order. These kinds of inductive activities, however, are very likely to lead attention to orders and bring about the construction of hypotheses about sequence. For example, a person who had taken GRE test would easily tend to try to find rules in an exposure like of the one used by Fu et al. (2008). Likewise, clinical studies following the design of Reber (1967) which based on sequential rules might fall also this kind of trap.

Paradigms 2 and 3 have become popular since Williams (2004) adopted paradigm 3 in his experiment about implicit learning of a four-determiner-artificial grammar. Both Williams (2004)and Chen et al. (2011), which replicated models of Williams (2004), asked subjects to study four determiners' explicit features without mentioning anything about the implicit features of the stimuli. Between Williams (2004) and Chen et al. (2011), Leung & Williams (2006) replicatedWilliams (2004) by following Paradigm 2, adding activities about implicit features but still not mentioning the implicit goal. They used pictures to help subjects to build the implicit connection between the target words and the implicit features by asking them to decide whether the objects are in the pictures were near or far. This activity was connected strongly with the implicit feature in that experiments that targeted words also functioned as determining "near" and "far". In Paradigm 2, activities with connection to the implicit features might easily draw subjects' attention to implicit features, leading them to form hypotheses. Though the later debriefing still gave no obvious sign that hypotheses were formed, we are still not sure that the subjects knew about the existence of their subconscious hypotheses. We argue, however, that both Paradigms 2 and 3 seem more reasonable than Paradigm 1, because they set up an explicit goal to attract subjects' attention away from implicit features; and training about explicit features may leave subjects no room in attention recourse to be aware of implicit features. Would the paradigm work in the way the researchers expect? We doubt it, since to experimental subjects training is a passive way to obtain knowledge, and some of them, very weak in passive learning, might be inclined instead to explore knowledge by themselves. In this way, explicit training would fail as a distracter; a better way to attract subjects might be to let them allocate their attention to explicit features initially, by presenting more meaning-focused tasks in text form.

Paradigm 4 has been used more commonly in computational models (Elman, 1990; Perruchet & Vinter, 1998; Sun, 2002). Though computational models have proven the implicit learning ability of computer programs, we still wish to ask how one can determine whether a computational model provides a good explanation of human learning, a thing which is so complicated and multi-determined (Cleeremans & Dienes, 2008).

Models of Testing Implicit Learning

In this section, we discuss three main measures used in testing the effect of subjects' implicit learning: (1) classical tests, (2) SRT, and (3) measures in computational model.

Classical tests are the ones adopted very widely by researchers in clinical studies of implicit learning. Commonly, they test only students' accuracy of judgment on the use of implicit learning. For example, in clinical experiments with artificial grammars and sequences as stimuli, subjects' knowledge of the artificial rules or sequential rules was tested by their accuracy rate in picking out elements conforming to the rules from new strings shown to them as testing materials (e.g. Chen et al., 2011; Dienes & Altmann, 1997; Reber 1967; Wan et al., 2008; Williams, 2004). There are still a considerable number of experiments adopting the classical test model with modification. For example, Wan et al. (2008) added familiarity rating into tests; Kinder & Shanks (2003) added visual noise and string movements in their AGL experiment. These types of tests, however, would give subjects hints, or they might draw subjects' attention to implicit features, which would make test results less reliable.

Serial reaction time measurement results are considered more convincing than classical ones, since they allow retrieval cues observed when subjects take tests. Usually two facets of learning effects are recorded: accuracy rate and reaction time on test items (e.g. Cleeremans & McClelland, 1991;Clegg et al., 1998; Jiménez et al., 1996; Leung & Williams, 2006; Nissen & Bullemer, 1987). To prove that the results of reaction time reflects qualities of implicit learning, both controlled or grammatical items and violation or ungrammatical items are randomly distributed and tested in the test (Leung & Williams, 2006). If the reaction time of controlled items is significantly shorter than that of the violation items, the target implicit knowledge is thought to be learned. Whether it is learned implicitly depends on result measures of awareness, which we will discuss in the next section. Leung & Williams (2006) designed an artificial grammar expressing meaning as "near or far". The test section asked students to point out whether the phrases containing "near" or "far" elements of the artificial grammar conformed to the picture on the screen. If a phrase containing an element of "far" was shown under a picture whose target object was in the foreground, then it was a violation item, and the reaction time to it should have been longer than that of control items. The design in Leung & Williams (2006) was better, but it still left a future step to be more scientific and convincing: to add another dimension to distinguish explicit knowledge from implicit knowledge, rather than only learned from unlearned. How do we make this move? More experiments and researches need to be done. For example, researchers could conduct another experiment immediately after with a small group from the same subjects to find a time scale for an explicit reaction and an implicit reaction, and then do their analysis of implicit learning.

Another sub-model of RT was developed by adding familiarity as a variable to measure memory strength (e.g. Shanks & Perruchet, 2002; Shanks et al., 2003). Researchers following this model take the assumption that greater familiarity or priming effects would lead to faster reaction, thus, the test items that need less time are considered to be more familiar to subjects and are more likely to belong to the learned group. This assumption was proved by standard signal detection theory models for recognition judgments (Pike, 1973; Ratcliff & Murdock, 1976). However, if we do take measurement like this in a clinical study of implicit learning, we must admit firstly that it was graded rather than dichotomous between implicit and explicit (Cleeremans, 1997). Then the conclusions made by researchers under this model could be trapped in an embarrassing state.

Models of tests in computational studies usually focus on measuring the learnability of the computer programs. Most of the results are positive (e.g. Cleeremans & McClelland, 1991; Perruchet & Vinter, 1998; Sun, 2002), however, it is the design of a computational model which might put its result into doubt. Shanks (2005) argued that between two most dominant computational model of implicit learning, symbol processing models (O'Brien & Opie, 1999; Shanks, 1997) were more successful than distributed models (Dienes et al., 1999; Kinder & Shanks, 2001), since the former was able to give information to distinguish implicit representational state from explicit ones. Until now, however, experiments using distributed models have seemed more successful in learning, which might delay the development of symbol processing models.

Measuring Subjects' State of Awareness

This is usually the last phase of a clinical experiment on implicit learning, which unveils the subjects' awareness states. It is used to find whether the subjects learned the target implicit features implicitly or explicitly. The measurement models of awareness tests enjoy much more attention from researchers than models of the other phases discussed above, because of the join-in researchers in psychology in the literature. Models have been updated and renewed from time to time, and new models are published almost whenever new discoveries or related inventions come up.

Researchers (Rebuschat, 2008) essentially divide the awareness measurement models into three groups. Table 1 presents a clear classification of these models.

SUMMARY

We identify the five key procedures that are necessary to an implicit learning experiment. For each procedure, we had double-way analyses: finding flaws of a type of procedure's design and comparing different designs of different experiments. By doing this, we gave detailed comments of each procedure of the framework. Table 2 summarizes the main message of our comments.

CONCLUSION AND FUTURE DIRECTIONS

Merikle & Reingold (1991: 226) argue strongly that one measure is hardly enough to identify learning know

Table 1: Summary of awareness measurements models

Model	Sub-model	Researches	Techniques	Strength	Weakness
Verbal reports	Free reporting	Abrams & Reber, 1988; Dienes et al., 1991; Leung & Williams, 2006; Payne, 1994; Williams, 2004	Interview; open questions	Subjects can say what they want; sounds like with no information omitted.	Dissociation between acquired knowledge and its verbalizability; insensitive and incomplete measure of awareness;
	Closed questionnaire	Berry & Broadbent, 1984; Broadbent, 1977	Multiple choice	Focus on the state features of subjects wanted by the research	
Objective test	Offline objective test	Holender, 1986; Stadler, 1998	Forced-choice test, or free generation task	Providing retrieval cues; more sensitive to conscious knowledge.	Lack of exclusivity; underestimating the influence of unconscious knowledge
	Computational objective test	O'Brien & Opie, 1999; Shanks, 1997	Symbol-processing system to distinct implicit and explicit knowledge	Completely objective and self-controlled	Not widely used and still under the way of polishing
Subjective test		Chen et al., 2011; Dienes, 2008; Dienes & Berry, 1997; Dienes & Scott, 2005	Confidence ratings; source attributions; binary confidence technique; SDT measure of sensitivity;	Exclusivity; sensitivity; more easily to absorb scientific or new techniques	Difficulty in selection of the type of confidence scale; lack of a standardized procedure

Note: Thanks are given to Berry & Dienes (1993), Dienes (2008), Dienes & Scott (2005), Merikle et al. (2001), Reingold & Merikle (1990), and Shanks & St. John (1994), and special thanks go to Rebuschat (2008), from which we get important information for this table.

Note: Thanks are given to Berry & Dienes (1993), Dienes (2008), Dienes & Scott (2005), Merikle et al. (2001), Reingold & Merikle (1990), and Shanks & St. John (1994), and special thanks go toRebuschat (2008), from which we get important information for this table.

Table 2: Summary of clinical procedure related findings in implicit learning

Procedure	Models	Researches	Format	Comments & suggestions
Theoretical assumptions	Attention assumption	Chen et al., 2011; Leung & Williams, 2006; Williams, 2004; Williams, 2005	Not clear in most of researches.	Assumptions of each procedure had better be discussed.
Clinical stimuli	Artificial grammar	Starter: Reber, 1967; Variants: Berry & Dienes, 1993; Leung & Williams, 2006; Pothos, 2007; Reber, 1989; Shanks, 2005; Wan et al., 2008; Williams, 2004;	Computerized/pen & paper	More interesting to reduce subjects' nerve; more close to nature language in nature context with semantic and pragmatic features taken into consideration
	Sequence strings	Starter: Nissen and Bullemer, 1987; Variants: Cleeremans & McClelland, 1991; Clegg et al., 1998; Fu et al., 2008, 2010.	Computerized	
Exposure	Implicit goal not mentioned + activities with connection to implicit features	Clegg et al., 1998; Cleeremans & McClelland, 1991; Nissen & Bullemer, 1987; Rieckman & Backman, 2009	Computerized/pen & paper	Researchers need to ensure no attention to implicit feature, to reduce any kind of probability that might arouse attention to implicit features, or even to try to distract attention from implicit features; but all should be done with subjects in an initiative state.
	Explicit goal + explicit goal training + activities with connection to implicit features + implicit goal not mentioned	Leung & Williams, 2006	Computerized/pen & paper	
	Explicit goal + explicit goal training + implicit goal not mentioned	Williams (2004), and Chen et al. (2011)	Computerized/pen & paper	
	Only stimuli + implicit goal not mentioned	Elman, 1990; Perruchet & Vinter, 1998; Sun, 2002	Computerized/pen & paper	
Learning testing	Classical test	Chen et al., 2011; Dienes & Altmann, 1997; Reber, 1967; Wan et al., 2008; Williams, 2004	Computerized/pen & paper	Providing retrieval cues; avoiding being hints or drawing attention to implicit feature
	SRT	Cleeremans & McClelland, 1991; Clegg et al., 1998; Jiménez et al., 1996; Leung & Williams, 2006; Nissen & Bullemer, 1987	Computerized	Testing items should be more scientific avoid being hints or drawing attention to implicit feature; trying to distinct explicit knowledge form implicit one
	Computational model	Perruchet & Vinter, 1998; Sun, 2002	Computerized	Trying in symbol processing models
Awareness states	Verbal reports	Abrams & Reber, 1988; Berry & Broadbent, 1984; Broadbent, 1977; Dienes et al., 1991; Leung & Williams, 2006; Payne, 1994; Williams, 2004	Computerized/pen & paper/ recording	Reducing dissociation between acquired knowledge and its verbalizability; improving insensitivity to awareness
	Objective tests	Holender, 1986; O'Brien & Opie, 1999; Shanks, 1997; Stadler, 1998	Computerized/pen & paper	Increasing exclusivity; improving sensitivity to unconscious knowledge
	Subjective tests	Chen et al., 2011; Dienes, 2008; Dienes & Berry, 1997; Dienes & Scott, 2005	Computerized/pen & paper	Finding a proper and standardized confidence scale

ledge and awareness. This is true. It is exactly why we do need to maintain a whole framework to ensure that, although one step has a flaw, the steps before or after can make up for it. This is like what a food security department does when a pig becoming pieces of pork in meat stores: though the farm fails to find disease in one pig, the butchering factory may be still able to stop the pig from entering the market; if the butchering factory fails, the quarantine still has a chance. Of course, the framework of clinical experiments cannot be as standardized as that set up by official departments, because even today any tasks designed are not process-pure and completely exclusive, since a clear and comprehensive theory of awareness has not yet settled. However, at least a framework can be set up as guidance and advice for researchers to avoid design flaws or omissions. That is what we endeavor: to conduct a detailed comparison and search for a great amount of literature, though the comments and suggestions we bring forward still await empirical verification in which implicit learning can be studied exclusively and comprehensively.

Our recommendations to future studies on implicit learning are as follows: (1) developing a more valid control on attention allocation to ensure implicit learning to take place; (2) using materials or stimuli closer to natural language in natural context with semantic and pragmatic features taken into consideration to gain more understanding about human implicit learning in real situation; (3) adopting or developing new techniques to increase sensitivity to implicit learning and explicit learning; (4) allowing researchers in computational simulation fields still to have opportunities in symbol-processing models; (5) urging more efforts in online researches using ERP or fMRI technologies; (6) exploring implicit learning in second language acquisition.

In conclusion, by furthering a comprehensive understanding of procedural mechanisms that contribute to improvement in research designs, we may be able to gain a better understanding of implicit learning. In turn, new understanding gains may contribute to new suppositions that later help design more effective empirical studies. Thus, even though theoretical and empirical difficulties are far from resolution in the near future, there is an unprecedented opportunity for advancing our understanding of implicit learning.

REFERENCES

1. Abrams, M., & Reber, A. S. (1988). Implicit Learning: Robustness in the Face of Psychiatric Disorders. Journal of Psycholinguistic Research, 17, 425-439.

2. Berry, D. C., & Broadbent, D. (1984). On the Relationship between Task Performance and Associated Verbalisable Knowledge. Quarterly Journal of Experimental Psychology, 36, 209-231. http://dx.doi.org/10.1080/14640748408402156

3. Berry, D. C., & Dienes, Z. (1993). Implicit Learning: Theoretical and Empirical Issues. Hove, UK: Lawrence Erlbaum.

4. Broadbent, D. (1977). Levels, Hierarchies and the Locus of Control. Quarterly Journal of Experimental Psychology, 29, 181-201. http://dx.doi.org/10.1080/14640747708400596

5. Carr, T. H., & Curran, T. (1994). Cognitive Factors in Learning about Structured Sequences: Applications to Syntax. Studies in Second Language Acquisition, 16, 205-230.http://dx.doi.org/10.1017/S0272263100012882

6. Chen, G., Tang, Z., Yang, & Dienes (2011). Unconscious Structural Knowledge of Form-meaning Connections. Consciousness and Cognition, 20, 1751-1760.http://dx.doi.org/10.1016/j.concog.2011.03.003

7. Chun, M. M., & Jiang, Y. (1999). Top-Down Attentional Guidance Based on Implicit Learning of Visual Covariation. Psychological Science, 10,

360-365.http://dx.doi.org/10.1111/1467-9280.00168

8.   Cleeremans, A. (1997). Principles for Implicit Learning. In D. Berry (Ed.), How Implicit Is Implicit Learning? (pp. 196-234). Oxford: Oxford University Press.http://dx.doi.org/10.1093/acprof:oso/9780198523512.003.0008

9.   Cleeremans, A., Destrebecqz, A., & Boyer, M. (1998). Implicit Learning: News from the Front. Trends in Cognitive Sciences, 2, 406-416. http://dx.doi.org/10.1016/S1364-6613(98)01232-7

10. Cleeremans, A., & Dienes, Z. (2008). Computational Models of Implicit Learning. In R. Sun (Ed.), Cambridge Handbook of Computational Psychology (pp. 396-421). Cambridge: Cambridge University Press. http://dx.doi.org/10.1017/CBO9780511816772.018

11. Cleeremans, A., & McClelland, J. L. (1991). Learning the Structure of Event Sequences. Journal of Experimental Psychology: General, 120, 235-253.http://dx.doi.org/10.1037/0096-3445.120.3.235

12. Clegg, B. A., DiGirolamo, G. J., & Keele, S. W. (1998). Sequence Learning. Trends in Cognitive Sciences, 2, 275-281. http://dx.doi.org/10.1016/S1364-6613(98)01202-9

13. Dienes, Z. (1992). Connectionist and Memory-Array Models of Artificial Grammar Learning. Cognitive Science, 16, 41-79. http://dx.doi.org/10.1207/s15516709cog1601_2

14. Dienes, Z. (2008). Subjective Measures of Unconscious Knowledge. Progress in Brain Research, 168, 49-64. http://dx.doi.org/10.1016/S0079-6123(07)68005-4

15. Dienes, Z., & Altmann, G. (1997). Transfer of Implicit Knowledge across Domains? How Implicit and How Abstract? In D. Berry (Ed.), How Implicit Is Implicit Learning? (pp. 107-123). Oxford: Oxford University Press.http://dx.doi.org/10.1093/acprof:oso/9780198523512.003.0005

16. Dienes, Z., Altmann, G. T. M., & Gao, S. J. (1999). Mapping across Domains without Feedback: A Neural Network Model of Transfer of Implicit Knowledge. Cognitive Science, 23, 53-82. http://dx.doi.org/10.1207/s15516709cog2301_3

17. Dienes, Z., & Berry, D. C. (1997). Implicit Learning: Below the Subjective Threshold. Psychonomic Bulletin and Review, 4, 3-23. http://dx.doi.org/10.3758/BF03210769

18. Dienes, Z., Broadbent, D. E., & Berry, D. C. (1991). Implicit and Explicit Knowledge Bases in Artificial Grammar Learning. Journal of Experimental Psychology: Learning, Memory, & Cognition, 17, 875-

882. http://dx.doi.org/10.1037/0278-7393.17.5.875

19. Dienes, Z., & Scott, R. (2005). Measuring Unconscious Knowledge: Distinguishing Structural Knowledge and Judgment Knowledge. Psychological Research, 69, 338-351.http://dx.doi.org/10.1007/s00426-004-0208-3

20. Elman, J. L. (1990). Finding Structure in Time. Cognitive Science, 14, 179-211.http://dx.doi.org/10.1207/s15516709cog1402_1

21. Estes, W. K. (1957). Toward a Statistical Theory of Learning. Psychological Review, 57, 94-107. http://dx.doi.org/10.1037/h0058559

22. Frensch, P. A., & Rünger, D. (2003). Implicit Learning. Current Directions in Psychological Science, 12, 13-18. http://dx.doi.org/10.1111/1467-8721.01213

23. Fu, Q., Dienes, Z., & Fu, X. (2010). Can Unconscious Knowledge Allow Control in Sequence Learning? Consciousness & Cognition, 19, 462-475.http://dx.doi.org/10.1016/j.concog.2009.10.001

24. Fu, Q., Fu, X., & Dienes, Z. (2008). Implicit Sequence Learning and Conscious Awareness. Consciousness and Cognition, 17, 185-202.http://dx.doi.org/10.1016/j.concog.2007.01.007

25. Hintzmann, D. (1986). "Schema Abstraction" in a Multiple-Trace Memory Model. Psychological Review, 93, 411-428. http://dx.doi.org/10.1037/0033-295X.93.4.411

26. Holender, D. (1986). Semantic Activation without Conscious Identification in Dichotic Listening, Parafoveal Vision, and Visual Masking: A Survey and Appraisal. Behavioral and Brain Sciences, 9, 1-23. http://dx.doi.org/10.1017/S0140525X00021269

27. James, W. (1890). Principles of Psychology. New York: Holt.http://dx.doi.org/10.1037/11059-000

28. Jiménez, L., Méndez, C., & Cleeremans, A. (1996). Comparing Direct and Indirect Measures of Implicit Learning. Journal of Experimental Psychology: Learning, Memory, and Cognition, 22, 948-969. http://dx.doi.org/10.1037/0278-7393.22.4.948

29. Kinder, A., & Shanks, D. R. (2001). Amnesia and the Declarative/Nondeclarative Distinction: A Recurrent Network Model of Classification, Recognition, and Repetition Priming. Journal of Cognitive Neuroscience, 13, 648-669.http://dx.doi.org/10.1162/089892901750363217

30. Kinder, A., & Shanks, D. R. (2003). Neuropsychological Dissociations

between Priming and Recognition: A Single-System Connectionist Account. Psychological Review, 110, 728-744.http://dx.doi.org/10.1037/0033-295X.110.4.728

31. Leung, J., & Williams, J. (2006). Implicit Learning of Form-Meaning Connections. In R. Sun, & N. Miyake (Eds.), Proceedings of the Annual Meeting of the Cognitive Science Society (pp. 465-470). Mahwah, NJ: Lawrence Erlbaum Associates.

32. Merikle, P. M., & Reingold, E. M. (1991). Comparing Direct (Explicit) and Indirect (Implicit) Measures to Study Unconscious Memory. Journal of Experimental Psychology: Learning, Memory and Cognition, 17, 224-233. http://dx.doi.org/10.1037/0278-7393.17.2.224

33. Merikle, P. M., Smilek, D., & Eastwood, J. D. (2001). Perception without Awareness: Perspectives from Cognitive Psychology. Cognition, 79, 115-134.http://dx.doi.org/10.1016/S0010-0277(00)00126-8

34. Millward, R. B., & Reber, A. S. (1968). Event-Recall in Probability Learning. Journal of Verbal Learning and Verbal Behavior, 7, 980-989. http://dx.doi.org/10.1016/S0022-5371(68)80056-8

35. Nissen, M. J., & Bullemer, P. (1987). Attentional Requirement of Learning: Evidence from Performance Measures. Cognitive Psychology, 19, 1-32. http://dx.doi.org/10.1016/0010-0285(87)90002-8

36. O'Brien, G., & Opie, J. (1999). A Connectionist Theory of Phenomenal Experience. Behavioral and Brain Sciences, 22, 127-196.http://dx.doi.org/10.1017/S0140525X9900179X

37. Payne, J. W. (1994). Thinking Aloud: Insights into Information Processing. Psychological Science, 5, 241-248. http://dx.doi.org/10.1111/j.1467-9280.1994.tb00620.x

38. Perruchet, P., & Vinter, A. (1998). PARSER: A Model for Word Segmentation. Journal of Memory and Language, 39, 246-263. http://dx.doi.org/10.1006/jmla.1998.2576

39. Pike, R. (1973). Response Latency Models for Signal Detection. Psychological Review, 80, 53-68. http://dx.doi.org/10.1037/h0033871

40. Posner, M. I. (1994). Attention in Cognitive Neuroscience: An Overview. In M. Gazzaniga (Ed.), The Cognitive Neurosciences (pp. 615-624). Cambridge, MA: MIT Press.

41. Pothos, E. M. (2007). Theories of Artificial Grammar Learning. Psychological Bulletin, 133, 227-244. http://dx.doi.org/10.1037/0033-2909.133.2.227

42. Ratcliff, R., & Murdock, B. B. (1976). Retrieval Processes in Recognition Memory. Psychological Review, 83, 190-214. http://dx.doi.org/10.1037/0033-295X.83.3.190

43. Reber, A. S. (1967). Implicit Learning of artificial Grammars. Journal of Verbal Learning and Verbal Behavior, 6, 855-863. http://dx.doi.org/10.1016/S0022-5371(67)80149-X

44. Reber, A. S. (1989). Implicit Learning and Tacit Knowledge. Journal of Experimental Psychology: General, 118, 219-235. http://dx.doi.org/10.1037/0096-3445.118.3.219

45. Rebuschat, P. (2008). Implicit Learning of Natural Language Syntax. Unpublished Doctoral Dissertation, Cambridge: University of Cambridge.

46. Rebuschat, P. & Williams, J. (2009). Implicit Learning of Word Order. In N. A. Taatgen & H. van Rijn (Eds.), Proceedings of the 31st Annual Conference of the Cognitive Science Society. Austin, TX: Cognitive Science Society.

47. Rieckmann, A & Bäckman, L. (2009). Implicit Learning in Aging: Extant Patterns and New Directions. Neuropsychology Review, 19, 490-503. http://dx.doi.org/10.1007/s11065-009-9117-y

48. Reingold, E. M., & Merikle, P. M. (1990). On the Interrelatedness of Theory and Measurement in the Study of Unconscious Processes. Mind and Language, 5, 9-28.http://dx.doi.org/10.1111/j.1468-0017.1990.tb00150.x

49. Rohmeier, M., & Cross, I. (2010). Narmour's Principles Affect Implicit Learning of Melody. In Demorest et al. (Eds.), Proceedings of the 11th International Conference on Music Perception and Cognition (ICMPC 2010), Seattle, 23-27 August 2010.

50. Schmidt, R. (2001). Attention. In P. Robinson (Ed.), Cognition and Second Language Instruction (pp. 3-32). Cambridge: Cambridge University Press.http://dx.doi.org/10.1017/CBO9781139524780.003

51. Searle, J. R. (1992). The Rediscovery of the Mind. Cambridge, MA: MIT Press.

52. Shanks, D. R. (1997). Distributed Representations and Implicit Knowledge: A Brief Introduction. In K. Lamberts & D. Shanks (Eds.), Knowledge, Concepts and Categories (pp. 197-214). Hove: Psychology Press.

53. Shanks, D. R. (2005). Implicit Learning. In K. Lamberts & R. Goldstone (Eds.), Handbook of Cognition (pp. 202-220). London: Sage. http://dx.doi.org/10.4135/9781848608177.n8

54. Shanks, D. R., & Perruchet, P. (2002). Dissociation between Priming and Recognition in the Expression of Sequential Knowledge. Psychonomic Bulletin and Review, 9, 362-367.http://dx.doi.org/10.3758/BF03196294

55. Shanks, D. R., & St. John, M. F. (1994). Characteristics of Dissociable Human Learning Systems. Behavioral and Brain Sciences, 17, 367-447. http://dx.doi.org/10.1017/S0140525X00035032

56. Shanks, D. R., Wilkinson, L., & Channon, S. (2003). Relationship between Priming and Recognition in Deterministic and Probabilistic Sequence Learning. Journal of Experimental Psychology: Learning, Memory, and Cognition, 29, 248-261.http://dx.doi.org/10.1037/0278-7393.29.2.248

57. Stadler, M. A., & Roediger III, H. L. (1998). The Question of Awareness in Research on Implicit Learning. In M. A. Stadler & P. A. Frensch (Eds.), Handbook of Implicit Learning (pp. 105-132). Thousand Oaks, CA: Sage.

58. Sun, R. (2002). Duality of the Mind. Mahwah, NJ: Lawrence Erlbaum.

59. Wan, L. L., Dienes, Z., & Fu, X. L. (2008). Intentional Control Based on Familiarity in Artificial Grammar Learning. Consciousness & Cognition, 17, 1209-1218.http://dx.doi.org/10.1016/j.concog.2008.06.007

60. Williams, J. N. (2004). Implicit Learning of Form-Meaning Connections. In B. VanPatten, J. Williams, S. Rott, & M. Overstreet (Eds.), Form-Meaning Connections in Second Language Acquisition (pp. 203-218). Mahwah, NJ: Erlbaum.

61. Williams, J. N. (2005). Learning without Awareness. Studies in Second Language Acquisition, 27, 269-304. http://dx.doi.org/10.1017/ S0272263105050138

62. Williams, J. N. (2009). Implicit Learning. In W. C. Ritchie, & T. K. Bhatia (Eds.), New Handbook of Second Language Acquisition (pp. 319-353). Bingley: Emerald Group Publishing Ltd.

Chapter 4

SOME POLEMICAL ISSUES IN APPLIED LINGUISTICS

John Robert Schmitz

Universidade Estadual de Campinas,Brazil

ABSTRACT

In this paper, I look at three polemical issues in Applied Linguistics. I argue, first of all, that the desire for a stable definition of applied linguistics has by no means prevented research in the discipline. Secondly, I contend that the notion or "tradition" of "linguistics applied" (corpus linguistics or lexicography) is broader and more serious than "applicationism" (the use of linguistic formalisms, artificial practices, and terminology) in teaching material that are problematic and motivated by commercial interests. Thirdly, I argue that Educational Linguistics and Applied Linguistics have overlapping research objectives. In the course of the paper, I present some reservations about Educational Linguistics. KEYWORDS: Applied Linguistics, Linguistics Applied, Educational Linguistics, theory and practice.

INTRODUCTION

My objective here is to examine what I consider to be three controversial issues in the field of Applied Linguistics (henceforth, AL): (i) conflicting definitions of the discipline in the literature, (ii) the relationship between AL and Linguistics Applied, (iii) the existence of "educational linguistics" alongside of "applied linguistics". This paper is motivated by my own work in AL over the years and based on my thoughts, and in some cases, on some personal struggles, misgivings as well as a bit of stress with respect to the issues to be examined here. My intention is to encourage dialogue, debate and, no doubt, rebuttal with both colleagues and students of AL.

CONFLICTING DEFINITIONS OF THE DISCIPLINE

Some applied linguists, different from specialists in other areas such as psychology, chemistry and law, are unsure of what their discipline entails. Over the course of the years, one observes often conflicting definitions of what the field of AL is. Widdowson (2000a, p.3) a renowned applied linguist states that AL is "conceptually elusive" devoid of a "... stable definition". He argues that there exists a "... persistent and pervasive uncertainty about the nature of the enquiry." Similarly, Hasan and Perrett (1994, p. 222) complain that AL has not found its "center of gravity". James (1993, p. 17) also considers it as "under-defined" with "ragged boundaries" that are "much too wide". These definitions are surprising for a number of reasons. First, Widdowson's plea for stable definition would appear to conflict with the very nature of disciplines for they are situated in time and can change slowly, in some cases, and rapidly, in others. A desire for stable disciplines and neatly delineated boundaries between them suggests an essentialist view of AL, that is, the field is deemed categorically to consist of endeavor x, but not endeavor y. The wish for a fixed view of AL, I would argue, narrows the field and discourages multi-, inter- and cross-disciplinarity. Schulte and Biguenet(1992, p. 10) warn that members of disciplines "... tend to separate subject matters that by their nature are intricately connected." Such a policy would be a disaster for AL. In this regard, Foucault (1979, p. 218) views academic disciplines as "techniques for ordering of human affairs"; he observes that they tend to exercise surveillance on their membership. Secondly, it would seem to be contradictory to lament that the boundaries of AL are "ragged" and its scope "much too wide" and at the same time consider it to be interdisciplinary or cross-disciplinary where the widening of the boundaries would be the rule. Jacobs and Schumann (1992, p. 282) provide a definition that suggests a markedly different view of AL: At present, applied linguistics is perhaps more accurately characterized as the application of various research areas (for example, psychological, sociological, anthropological, neurocognitive) to basic issues in language acquisition, use, analysis, policy, assessment and several other domains. Students new to AL and perhaps for those students in the Brazilian context who are in the midst of writing up their theses or dissertations for advanced degrees might be perplexed about the uncertainty of what exactly AL entails based on the writings of a number of founding fathers of the field (WIDDOWSON, 2000a; HASAN; PERRET, 1994; JAMES, 1993). But quite surprisingly, a number of younger researchers still harbor doubts about the scope of AL. Edmondson (2005, p. 390) states that he does not "... see how a clear and workable definition of applied linguistics can be agreed on at this point in time". Lantolf (2006, p.

148) considers the fact that AL "… has expanded its interests beyond language teaching" has contributed to make it difficult "… to figure out what applied linguists is". Many of these same students in Brazil are, no doubt, quick to observe that a good number of their own instructors hold a different view of AL than some of their colleagues in Europe or the USA. Here is a definition by a Brazilian scholar in AL: Applied Linguistics, in its present form, is an emergent multidiscipline, or trans-discipline, developed on a multidisciplinary basis of inquiry into language in use, more specifically, into verbal communication within a given social and/or institutional context (SIGNORINI, 2004, p. 74).

Moita Lopes (2006, p. 19) points to a new perspective of AL that "… has contributed to the understanding of AL not as disciplinary knowledge, but as indisciplinary or anti-disciplinary and transgressive one (following PENNYCOOK1 (2001 and 2006))". I would conjecture that these views of AL are consensual in Brazil, for the most part, and most likely few practitioners in the field would want to return to the consideration of AL as being solely concerned with language teaching methodology. Absent also in Brazilian AL (as far as I can detect) is the view of the discipline held by Brown (1992, p. 144-145) who maintained that it "… must lean on models provided by theoretical disciplines" and is "… essentially exploratory and descriptive… ." In France, AL or "linguistique appliqué" was synonymous with methods of teaching foreign languages (didactique de enseignement des langues, Galisson, 1972).This is no longer the case for the editors of the Revue Française de Linguistique Appliquée (RFLA) inform that the periodical serves as " … a meeting point for interdisciplinary interaction and confrontation. The RFLA aims to reflect international research in the field of applied linguistics …" (http:// www. reflajournal.org/presentation.html). It would be important for students new to the field not to conclude (my emphasis) that views of AL held over 40 years ago were misguided. They served the discipline over the years at a certain point in time but now they have outlived their usefulness. A sense of where the discipline has been and where it is at the present time are essential for a feeling of the history of the discipline that would include knowledge about the contributions of the forerunners and founders of the area in addition to the new voices in LA. The "classics" in the field should be read in addition to the large number of books, important handbooks and seminal articles published in the last twenty years. The canonical texts should not be "revered" but respected. Even though there are practitioners who agonize over the fact that they cannot find a clear definition of what the field is, I would argue that applied linguists in Brazil and in other parts of the world are not letting the concern about an "adequate" definition deter them from actually getting on with their research in AL. There exist results in the form of reports, theses, books, articles and reviews in scholarly journals pointing to the fact that the researchers are actually contributing to the discipline in its many guises. The many international, national and regional conferences in AL also attest to the productivity of its practitioners. To my mind, there is something wrong about the quest for the definition (my emphasis). It would seem to me that we all know what AL entails (these views are, to be sure, often personal or defined institutionally) and how it can be distinguished from the discipline of linguistics. A paper dealing with second language acquisition would most likely be found in Language, Language Learning or Applied Linguistics. All practitioners in the field of language studies know what type of paper would be accepted by Linguistic Inquiry and what would not be appropriate. It is quite clear to most linguists or applied linguists what would be a good contribution for Language Problems and Planning or TESOL Quarterly. The Indian Journal of Applied Linguistics advises prospective contributors in the following terms: Articles from fields of sociolinguistics, first/ second language acquisition and pedagogy, bilingualism, language planning and others that can be usually covered under applied linguistics are invited. Articles of strictly theoretical linguistic persuasion are outside its scope (Statement of Purpose, Indian Journal of Applied Linguistics, http://www.acquire-content/com/titles/ indian-journal-of-applied-linguistics).

The widening of AL has contributed to making the discipline far more intellectually stimulating and challenging. Its cross-disciplinary stance, critical view and engagement with social issues have linked AL to the social sciences. In fact, for SEALEY and CARTER (2004), AL is a social science (my emphasis). With respect to the area of language teaching which was the initial interest of applied linguists, that very concern has also broadened to include reflective teaching, action-research, empowerment, teacher and student identities, chaos-complexity theory, language awareness among others, not limited to important topics such as classroom methodology or management. De Bot, Verspoor and Lowie (2005, p. 116) are quite pleased with the opening up of AL and not all worried about its being, in their words, "indeterminate in definition". In their words: The fact that AL as a field is not narrowly focused and constrained has allowed us to explore methods and theories that may have something to say about what language is and how it functions. In the next part of this paper, I want to look at the notion "linguistics applied" in relation to AL as well as the words "applied", "applying" and "application" that occur frequently in the case of the many other applied disciplines ranging from applied geology to applied sociology.

The Relationship between Applied Linguistics and Linguistics Applied

In the city of Stockholm in 1963, the Council for Cultural CoOperation of the Council of Europe discussed the idea of creating an International Association of Applied Linguistics (AILA). The first meeting of this Association was held in Nancy, France in 1964. Some two hundred linguists were invited to present their theories about language in order to ascertain if linguistic theory had any practical applications. In the report published by the Council in 1967, the distinguished linguist Eugeniu Coseriu (1921-2002)2 read a paper entitled "Lexical structure and the teaching of vocabulary" that was critiqued by the French linguist Antoine Culioli3 who quite bluntly declared that Coseriu´s paper had nothing to do with AL! Here are Culioli´s words: The domain of applied linguistics is, quite simply, the application of linguistics to other fields. There is, therefore, a theory and a practice of the application of linguistics to such and such a field, that is to say, in fact, of the articulation of two fields, the one being linguistic, the other being automation, or teaching, or neuropsychology, etc. (p. 62). Michael Halliday, to be sure, needs no introduction to students and teachers of AL. Not everybody knows that he was also present at the first AILA meeting and expressed the hope that the newly established association would attempt to "… include within its scope the application of linguistics to the teaching of the mother tongue." (p. 179).

One can easily say, in retrospect, that the belief that linguistics can be simply "applied" is naïve; but that was indeed the viewpoint in the mid 60s during the inaugural years of the young discipline. The very question "Does linguistic theory have any applications?" was indeed an appropriate question at that historic period or "situation". Such a question would not be posed at the present time. The report of the linguists ("Linguistic Theories and their Application") who met at the first AILA meeting in Nancy is indeed emblematic for the endeavors called AL as well as "the application of linguistics" were born and came to be known as "linguistics applied". In the mid 70s this notion quickly began to trouble practitioners of the discipline, yet, in spite of the criticisms (WIDDOWSON, 1980, 2000a) there were many instances of "Linguistics Applied" in the course of the years and, for good (or bad?), the notion is still present (as I will indicate shortly). There are two questions not always asked in discussions about AL and particularly "linguistics applied". The first one is: just what is "applied"? And the second is: precisely what it is applied to? What is being applied is not always made explicit. In the first place, it could be the grammatical findings of a specific linguistic theory or model; secondly, the complete linguistic model might be appropriated. And thirdly, the psychological underpinnings of a linguistic theory might be used as a framework to how language is acquired. This was attempted by some psycholinguists who used Chomsky´s ideas to explain how language was acquired by children. To answer both questions, I present below (FIG. 1) the following diagram:

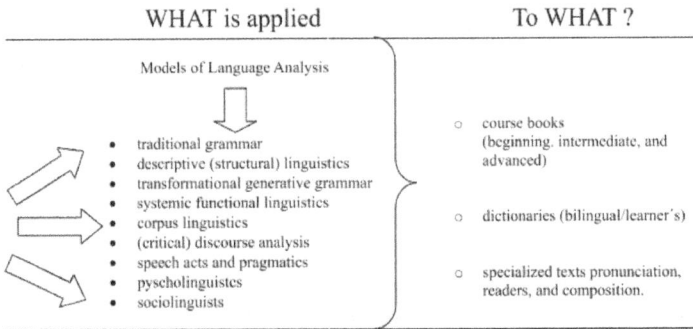

WHAT is applied	To WHAT ?
Models of Language Analysis	
• traditional grammar • descriptive (structural) linguistics • transformational generative grammar • systemic functional linguistics • corpus linguistics • (critical) discourse analysis • speech acts and pragmatics • pyscholinguistcs • sociolinguists	○ course books (beginning, intermediate, and advanced) ○ dictionaries (bilingual/learner´s) ○ specialized texts pronunciation, readers, and composition.

Let us look now at some of the published "applications". The first one is by Quirk, Greenbaum, Leech and Svartik (1972, p. vi) in their monumental grammar of English, A Grammar of Contemporary English point to the underpinnings of their text. Here are the beliefs of the authors in the early 70s:

Each of those [=theories] propounded from the time of Saussure and Jespersen onwards has its undoubted merits, and several (notably the transformational- generative approaches) have contributed very great stimulus to us as to other grammarians.

The work of Quirk et. al is an example of the first type of application, that is, the use of the grammatical findings of transformational theory (dominant at that time, particularly in the USA and other countries); the second type of application is the use of the whole underlying linguistic theory: examples are two textbooks (both designed for native speakers of English), the first entitled English Transformational Grammar and the Teacher of English by Owen Thomas (New York: Holt, Rinehart and Winston, Inc. 1965) and second English Series organized by Paul Roberts (New York: Harcourt, Brace World, Inc., 1964). Another example for English as a second/foreign language is William Rutherford´s Modern English (New York, Harcourt Brace Jovanovich, 1968, 2nd ed., 1975). Although Davies (1991, p. 52) quite rightly observes that linguistics applied was more influential in North America and in Continental Europe than in the United Kingdom, Cook, a renowned British applied linguist, in a recent article, (2007) describes his use (back in the 60s of the last century) of phrase structure rules introduced in Chomsky's Syntactic Structures (Janua Linguarum 4, The Hague: Mouton, 1957) in the highly popular textbook Realistic English authored by Abs, B., Cook, V. and Underwood, M. (Oxford, Oxford University Press, [1968], 1978), adopted in many universities and language institutes in Brazil in the 70s and later on. Celce-Murcia and Larsen-Freeman (1983, p. v) state in their preface to The Grammar Book: An ESL/EL Teacher's Course that linguistics has a great deal to offer teachers of English as a foreign or a second language "… in the way of insights into English grammar". In their text, they inform that they have resorted to transformational-generative grammar to deal with "basic sentence parsing" and the use of "syntactic operations such as the formation of negative sentences and questions". For understanding the function of prepositions and verb tenses, the authors state that they have "drawn insights from traditional grammar and case grammar. To inform learners about the role of the definite and indefinite articles, Celce-Murcia and Larsen-Freeman (1983, ibid) resort to a "discourse perspective". Indeed the authors "applications" are varied and eclectic. As far as I know, these applications of linguistics were never evaluated critically to ascertain if those students who used the different texts in their university courses actually learned something about language or not.

With respect to linguistics applied, it is indeed the case that some of the "applications" were simplistic and downright opportunistic (written for the purpose of earning royalties). Textbook exercises that required students to draw "trees", that is, phrase markers (in the technical vocabulary of linguistics) to illustrate the supposed "deep structure" of sentences were far from being pedagogically sound, to put it mildly. A few textbooks for the teaching of Portuguese in Brazilian schools presented linguistic formulas and trees, mere formalisms quite distant from real language input (which is what learners need). Teaching a language is one thing (far more complex than some people believe) and teaching linguistics is indeed quite another matter. Such applications or misapplications are in my view what Moita Lopes (2006, p.18) considers as "applicationalistic". I agree that some of these instances were indeed cases of "misapplied" AL. But I would not want to go so far as to condemn all "applications" and to discourage those who look to linguistics or to other disciplines as psychology, discourse analysis or education in the attempt to prepare teaching materials. A radical anti-application stance could impede well-intentioned attempts to create and innovate. I find it surprising that Hasan and Perrett (1994, p. 222) criticize AL for taking advantage of "… whatever might be the new bright idea of the decade." In the 60s the audio-lingual approach was in vogue and the use of structural exercises called "pattern drills" were used and, to be sure, in many cases, overused. Widdowson (2000b, p. 27) takes issue with Skehan4 (1998, p. 268) who argues that a transformational drill "… does not happen in the real world." Widdowson argues that "… activities such as a transformation drill can be converted by learners into something real and meaningful whereby they exploit the very foreignness of the language…" In this regard, Leffa (2008) takes Wong and Van Patten5 (2003) to task for their claim that the pattern drill has no use in the language classroom. Certainly many teachers exaggerated their use of structural exercises. I agree with Widdowson and Leffa. Anything can be real if the students find it useful. It is no surprise that students, depending on their needs, may find a tourist phrase book, a menu, a map or a railroad timetable to be relevant.

I must confess that in the midst of attempting to prepare teaching materials for different levels of English in schools and in the university, I often felt guilty about looking at the literature on speech acts, on metaphor or on conversation analysis for some insight or inspiration to prepare a handout for my classes. I would argue that "applications" cover a wide variety of endeavors ranging from using the terminology and/or formalisms in the language class (no doubt a misuse) to using data derived from the results of corpus analysis or data from functional linguistics or transformational linguistics. I would not consider corpus linguistics, lexicography or conversation analysis as examples of "applicationalism". To be sure, the three endeavors can be viewed as Linguistics Applied (L-A). One would think that lexicography is entirely dependent on the discipline of linguistics. The structure of dictionary entries may owe little to linguistics, but certainly corpus (my emphasis) linguistics has contributed language data for dictionaries, both bilingual and learner's dictionaries.6 Corpus linguistics might owe more to the computer science and the organization of the data by specialists in that area than to specific models of linguistics. Generative-transformational linguistics rejected corpus linguistics but systemic-functional linguistics has been used by some corpus linguists. It would seem that word "applied" or its cognates "applying" and "application" are in some cases are an embarrassment to AL. It is surprising that while applied linguists hail interdisciplinary and cross-disciplinarity, they, as far as I know, have had little or no contact with other "applied" disciplines such as applied sociology, applied psychology or applied philosophy. It is surprising that applied linguists based on their interdisciplinary or crossdisciplinary orientation have not looked at the "sister" applied disciplines. The discourse of the disciplines is similar to AL. Let us examine three "applied areas":

Applied Anthropology: "Applied anthropology is a complex of related, researchbased, instrumental methods which produce change or stability in specific cultural systems through provision of data, initiation of direct action and/or the formation of policy" (van WILLIGEN, J. Applied Anthropology: An Introduction. Boston, Mass., Bergin & Garvey Publishers, Inc., 1986). Applied Geography: "The application of geographical knowledge and skills to the solution or resolution of problems within society" (JOHNSON, R.; GREGORY, D.; SMITH, D. (Orgs.) The Dictionary of Human Geography.

London: Blackwell References, 1983). Applied Philosophy: "The International Journal of Applied Philosophy is committed to the view that philosophy can and should be brought to bear upon the practical issues of life." . Applied Anthropology deals with "research-based instrumental methods", applied geography focuses on the "resolution of problems within society" (similar to LA) and applied philosophy looks at what are considered "practical issues of life". What is interesting about applied philosophy is the issues examined; according to the journal, applied philosophers write about: "... affirmative action, alcohol abuse on college campuses, animal rights, business ethics, gambling, journalism ethics, just-war theory, liberalism, medical ethics, retribution, terrorism, and torture." I am sure that many of topics would be of interest to applied linguists given the cross-disciplinary and transgressive ("indisciplinary") stances in AL (MOITA LOPES, 2006). One might conjecture that the relationship between anthropology and applied anthropology, between geography and applied as well as between philosophy and applied is different (more integrated?) than that between linguistics and AL. I am not aware, based on my readings, if there exist two traditions in, say, philosophy, on one hand, and "philosophy applied", on the other, as in the case of "A-L" and "L-A". It would be interesting to prepare detailed comparisons or perhaps a taxonomy to confirm or not the assumption that the relation should be something that exists between physics and engineering or between medicine and biology. 7 It would indeed be instructive but it would take a bit of time to navigate on the internet or to interview specialists in applied fields to discover if there exist separate "applied" departments of philosophy, anthropology or geology.

Not all practitioners in AL were pleased with the notion "applied" but for different reasons. The first journal that bore the name "applied linguistics" for 45 years was Language Learning: A Journal of Applied Linguistics. Beginning with volume 43, number 1, the subtitle was changed to: A Journal of Language Studies (henceforth LL). I agree with Alistair Cumming, editor of this journal that the change is not "a radical difference". The first motivation for the change is to recognize the existence of "... the wide range of foundation theories and research methodologies now used to study language issues." The second motivation for the change in subtitle is to

[...] encourage the submission of more manuscripts from (a) diverse disciplines, including applications (my emphasis) of methods and theories from linguistics, psycholinguistics, cognitive science, ethnography, ethnomethodology, sociolinguistics, sociology, semiotics, educational inquiry, and cultural or historical studies to address (b) fundamental issues in language learning, such as bilingualism, language acquisition, second and foreign language education, literacy, culture, cognition, pragmatics and intergroup relations.

To be sure, the disciplines cited in (a) and the issues in (b) are all part and parcel of AL. Davies and Elder (2004, p. 4) consider that LL "… seems to have finally accepted the broader church that represents an Applied-Linguistics (A-L) as distinct from a Linguistics- Applied (L-A) approach to language problems." Widdowson (2000a) criticizes corpus linguistics, a more encompassing instance of linguistics applied than the appropriation of the results of the grammatical analysis of a particular linguistic theory. He argues that the theories of language and the models of language description that derive from "linguistics applied" are determined by the parent discipline of AL and therefore are "conformist". While he recognizes that corpus linguistics has contributed a great deal to the preparation of learner's dictionaries with computer-based examples, he contends that many of the examples would not be adequate in the language classroom for they would not be "real" or "authentic". For Widdowson, corpus linguistics applied to language teaching and learning is based on "third person data", that is what the computer reveals. This data is not real for the learner for he needs first person data ("when do I use the word?") as well as second person data ("when do you use the word?"). To be sure, Widdowson is rightly concerned with providing instances of real language for the learner. Would it be possible to incorporate in learning materials what is possible (what can/may occur) as well as what is contextually appropriate? In realistic terms, is it possible to include data from all three persons? Certainly all this would be daunting not only for learners but also for those who prepare teaching materials. Indeed Widdowson's reservations about corpus linguistics may have to be revised in the course of the coming years. After all, his remarks were published back in the year 2000, almost ten years ago.

In the penultimate sentence of Wissowson's paper (2000a, p. 24), he makes a very important statement that may have been overlooked by some readers. To quote him: "Linguistics applied of the kind of I have criticized in this paper thus poses a challenge to applied linguistics and in the respect is an important influence." I think it would be fair to ask where AL would be today if linguistics applied had not, over the years, challenged AL. Those colleagues who are fortunate to have access to the excellent Handbook of Applied Linguistics edited by Davies and Elder (2004) have undoubtedly observed that the book is divided into two main sections. The first part, labeled "Linguistics Applied"/ "L-A" consists of six sections with a total of 16 different chapters while the second part contains five sections also with 16 chapters. Certainly it is no simple task to place thirty-two different articles on varied topics into a coherent organizational framework that will please all the many applied linguists who work in its various dimensions. The editors are quite straightforward in declaring that the division into the two traditions, either

"L-A" or "A-L" is fraught with difficulties. They recognize the complexity. In their words:

What we have been compelled to realize is that the L-A/A-L distinction is sustainable only at the extremes. Thus the chapters on language attrition or language description may be regarded as largely L-A, while the concerns of second language learning or of computer assisted language learning are mainly to do with A-L. But in between the distinction is hard to make. It is probably easiest for topics in AL which deal with issues of language learning and language teaching because they have to do with the "real world", that locution we all refer to when we think of how language is used rather than how it is studied (p. 12).

What this boils down to is the fact that it is often difficult to make a distinction between AL and its use or application. I agree with Davies and Elder´s (ibid, p. 13) position with regard to "L-A" and "A-L":

Is there, then, still a distinction between L-A and A-L? Our answer is that there is but that it cannot easily be found in the topics of interest. Rather, it is found in the orientation of the researchers, and why they are investigating a problem and collecting their data. Do they regard themselves as linguists applying linguistics or as applied linguists doing applied linguistics? Are they investigating because they wish to validate a theory? If so, that is L-A. Or is it because they seek a practical answer to a language problem? That is A-L. We do, of course, recognize that in some, perhaps many, cases the researcher will have both interests at heart (p. 13).

In my own reading in the area of language studies, I have come to find it curious that there exists alongside AL another activity called "Educational Linguistics" (henceforth EL). Here is an additional instance in which the word "applied" seems to pose a problem and is duly "erased". Unfortunately I have not found in the specialized literature any discussion of the motivation for the existence of two activities outside of the two proponents of the endeavor. I will examine this in the next section.

Applied Linguistics / Educational Linguistics: Two Names for the Same Discipline or Competing Ones?

Spolsky's dislike for the word "applied" motivated him to prefer the term "educational linguistics" rather than "applied linguistics". In Spolsky's (1970, p. 145) view, the term "applied linguistics" encompasses too much and does not inform just what linguistics is applied to, and worse still "... it suggests a level of practicality that lacks the dignity of pure linguistics." There are a number of problems with this position. First of all, what is wrong with the possibility of encompassing "too much"? One just has to compare the early AILA meetings with the more recent ones. The number of papers presented in different fields is larger than it was at the first congress in 1964. To be fair to Spolsky, his remarks were written almost forty years ago and no doubt his views have changed. AL was indeed situated differently in the 70s. Who attributes "dignity" in the academy? Relative status in all endeavors is constructed and subjective. In university contexts, professors of accounting or management may indeed earn a lot more that professors of classical, modern foreign languages as well as linguists, discourse analysts, and applied linguists but none of them have problems with dignity. In his book Educational Linguistics Spolsky (1978, p. vii) remarks that his dissatisfaction with the term applied linguistics (his emphasis) is due to the "... suggestion linguistics is there just to be applied to any problem". In his words:

I prefer a less imperialistic approach, one that suggests that the various fields of linguistics have useful and relevant implications for many practical language related problems.

What is exactly imperialistic in the word "applied"? AL also covers a variety of sub-areas similar to educational linguistics. Spolsky's preference for the term "educational linguistics" can be attested many years after the publication of his Educational Linguistics (1978). In 1991, he published an article "Educational Linguistics" for the International Encyclopedia of Curriculum (LEVY, Arieh (Org.), 1991). While, on one hand, Spolsky cites in his bibliography seminal books and articles authored by "applied linguists", he chooses, on the other hand, not to use it for the title of his text. The motivation for his preference for educational linguistics is, no doubt, his belief that AL has been associated exclusively with pedagogical techniques for teaching foreign language as study skills, use of the overhead projector, preparation of visuals and basic classroom management, important activities indeed, but far removed from research in how learners acquire languages. It is also possible that the existence of some "terminal" graduate courses in AL that entail teacher inservice preparation for American high school teachers who have no intention of becoming researchers has contributed to a search for a new identity. Hence a new name to avoid old associations. I would, however, contend that his description of what educational linguists do and where they can be found could also define what applied linguists do and where they might work. Spolsky (1990, p. 585) observes: "...educational linguistics are found and trained in various parts of the university, most often where there is collaboration between scholars in education, linguistics, anthropology, and language departments."

Educational and applied linguists in many cases tend to overlap. In this regard, Crandall (1995, p. 425) quite rightly remarks: "This is an exciting time for applied linguists interested in education" (My emphasis). In addition to Spolsky, there is another important specialist in the field of language studies who views himself as an educational linguist. Van Lier (1997, p. 95) inserts EL within the "more specific sub-classification of applied linguistics, which in turn he considers "... as a more specific sub-classification of linguistics". He (1994, p. 201) contends that it is premature to consider educational linguistics as a discipline or field. In his view, to make EL a fullfledged discipline, "political action, lobbying, fund raising and arm twisting" will be necessary. The problem here is that if EL is not a field or a discipline, what is it exactly?

Van Lier's remarks reveal a certain tension in the field of language studies. Those who prefer the title "educational linguistics" are concerned with issues of classroom interaction and discourse. They tend to be unhappy with their colleagues who deal with second language acquisition (SLA) for they feel that the acquisitionists fail to deal with the consequences or relevance of acquisition studies for the classroom and teaching. Van Lier (1997, p.103) also points to problems with both "applied" and "linguistics". In the first place, he states that "applied" might imply that theory building is not a legitimate activity. This appears to be contradictory for Van Lier employs the modal might and goes on to state that the "practice-theory combination" is what AL is all about. There is nothing inherent in the word "applied" that suggests that "theory-building is not a legitimate activity" (p. 103). In this regard, Tomic (1987, p. 93), quite some time ago, argued that "... applied linguistics disciplines are themselves developing theory and thus have a theoretical and a descriptive aspect..." In the second place, with regard to the term "linguistics", van Lier points to the danger of it being associated with a dominant (hegemonic) model. I do not believe that AL was ever controlled by specific linguistic theory. Widdowson has to be given credit for his efforts to maintain AL independent of subservience to linguistics and its many currents. For van Lier, EL is a subfield of AL which is in turn a sub-field of Linguistics. This entails having a field within a field or a discipline within a discipline. I would view Linguistics as the parent discipline of AL but consider it to be a separate discipline (both academically and institutionally, in some cases) from Linguistics. With respect to different linguistic models and their relation to AL, Sridhar (1990, p.170) remarks that formal linguistics, specifically generativetranformational theory, excluded the notions of (i) function, (ii) performance, and (iii) context in language analysis. These three aspects of language are pertinent to the goals of AL. It is no wonder then that some applied linguists attached little or no value to linguistic models that excluded real people in real situations. The shift in linguistics from formal autonomous models to socially relevant linguistics, that is, "user-friendly linguistics" (in WEI's terms, 2007, p. 118) has indeed brought AL and Linguistics closer together for many researchers are involved in applied work within AL departments as well as in other departments such as education and communication.

Van Lier (1994, p. 202) states that researchers in Second Language Acquisition (SLA) have "... distanced themselves from practical educational matters" and as a result have contributed to leaving AL "seriously fractured". I would maintain that SLA researchers have the right to design their own research, but wouldn't it be possible for applied linguists to step in where the acquisitionists have left off and deal with "practical educational matters"? With respect to SLA, I interpret Gass (1993, p. 109) who writes that "... the language classroom needs to be seen as an integral part of the entire research agenda" to mean that she views SLA to be concerned with theory as well as with the practical aspects of acquisition in formal and informal contexts. Her remarks lead me to consider that not all SLA practitioners ignore the sociopolitical consequences of L2 acquisition and bilingual education in the countries where they work. Therefore, I do not view AL as being "fractured" by the disinterest on the part of L2 acquisitionists in the social or political consequences of their work. And there is nothing to impede applied linguists from looking at the political and social and practical implications of L2 acquisition as well as bilingual education. This stance would follow the ideas expressed by the authors in the text edited by Moita Lopes (2006). In addition, I find it strange that van Lier (1997, p. 103) suggests that the notion "...linguistics" might be too narrow in terms of the diverse knowledge-base and expertise that is required in the applied linguist's job." Once again, van Lier uses the modal might. "Narrow" or "un-friendly linguistics (de BOT, et. al., 2005) is not, for the most part, useful to most applied linguists. Formal linguistic models tend to look inward while sociallyrelevant ones look outside and offer a wide view of language practices (SRIDHAR, 1990). I do not deny van Lier's right to attempt to establish a field or a discipline or "church" (to use DAVIES; ELDER's, 2004, p. 4) term, hopefully without the necessity of "pushing and shoving", as he jokingly states. What troubles me is that his remarks (van LIER, 1997, p. 103) contradict his views about the word "applied" in AL when he concludes that:

I think that it is the applied linguist, who works with language in the real world, who is the most likely to have a realistic picture of what language is, and not the theoretical linguist who sifts through several layers of idealization.

What is indeed interesting in "educational linguistics" is certainly the term education. But what theories of education would be used? And what would be the role of linguistics with respect to theories of education? It would be remiss to think that AL has not interacted with education. Mcdonough (2002) devotes a number of chapters of his book to encouraging interaction with educational theories and classroom-based methods of research. The title of this section is in the form of a question: To repeat: are AL and EL the same discipline or competing ones? I would answer that they have the same focus but they are in competition. Competition between both endeavors is felicitous for it can contribute to academic excellence and to a deeper understanding of language and its role in society. One would hope also that both applied and educational linguists will continue to interact with one another. Dialogue between the two areas of interest can encourage collaboration and discourage duplication of effort.

In Conclusion

The frequent statements that AL is a "slippery object" (CAMERON, 2004, p. 121) attest to a desire for an orderly and essentialist view of the discipline. Definitions should be conceived as "working" ones, for disciplines change their scope over times. Research interests are situated in specific historic moments and different communities of practice in the world have varying conceptions of what their disciplines encompass. I would also contend that the case is similar with respect to other fields of knowledge such as education, linguistics and discourse analysis. I argue for a distinction between the notion "Linguistics Applied" ("L-A"), on one hand, and examples of "applicationism", on the other. The former, in Davies and Elder's view (2004, p. 11) "[...] looks inward, concerned not to solve language problems "in the real world" but to explicate and test theories about language itself." Examples of "L-A" are all-encompassing and academically serious such as Corpus Linguistics, Language Testing, and Lexicography. "Applicationism" I argue is carried out in classroom situations when teachers prepare teaching materials based on their readings in phonology, discourse analysis or pragmatics. In certain cases, "applicationism" has been infelicitous when, for example, elements of a linguistic theory are presented to learners rather than examples of real language in context. Those endeavors were not pedagogically sound and just developed to make a quick dollar. However, an extreme anti-applicationalist view can inhibit teachers from attempting to be original and creative, that is, from "trying things out". I shudder to think what the state of the art in AL, with respect to the teaching of grammar, would be without the work of Quirk et. al. (1972) and that presented by Celse-Murcia; Larsen-Freeman (1983).

While EL may indeed add new insights to our knowledge about the field of education and its relation to language studies, there is a possibility of duplication of research projects, unless there exists a dialogue between the two practices to avoid repetition. While AL has a "janus-like function" (DAVIES; ELDER, op. cit., p. 24) with its two traditions, one "L-A" and the other "AL", EL can only be that and not, I would imagine, *Linguistics educational", but maybe EL could mean linguistics (properly taught, of course!) to educators. Based on my references to the work of van Lier, I conclude that it is in fact another name for Applied Linguistics, as he duly recognizes. There is nothing sacred about names. We could call them both "applied language studies", "language studies" or "theoretical applied language studies" or Applied Linguistics. A rose is a rose but in Turkish it is gül, in Hungarian rózsa, in Japanese bara, in Maltese warda and in Mayan, nikte´. A rose smells just as sweet in all of the languages cited. What is in a name, really? In conclusion, I would say that we all have our preferences (and our prejudices). With respect to naming, I favor the term AL for it has accompanied me for over 50 years. I identify with it and relate to it.

REFERENCES

1. BROWN, G. Very much like a whale: shifting paradigms in applied linguistics. In. PUTZ, M. (Org.). Thirty years of linguistic evolution: studies in honor of René Dirven on the occasion of his sixtieth birthday. Philadelphia: John Benjamins, 1992.

2. CAMERON, L. Review of S. McDonough. Applied Linguistics in language education. System. v. 32, p. 121-122, 2004.

3. CELSE-MURCIA, M.; LARSEN-FREEMAN, D. The Grammar Book: An ESL/ EFL Teacher's Course. New York: Newbury House/ Harper & Row, Publishers, Inc., 1983.

4. COOK, V. Chomsky´s Syntactic Structures fifty years on. International Journal of Applied Linguistics. v. 17, n. 1, p. 120-131, 2007.

5. COUNCIL FOR CULTURAL CO-OPERATION OF THE COUNCIL OF EUROPE. Linguistic theories and their application. Strasbourg: International Association of Publishers of Applied Linguistics (AIDELA), 1967.

6. CRANDALL, J. Reinventing (America´s) schools: the role of the applied linguist. In: ALATIS, J. E.; Straehle, C. A.; Gallenberger, B.; Ronkin, M. (Org.).

7. Georgetown University Round Table on Languages and Linguistics 1995. Washington, D.C.: Georgetown University Press, 1996.

8. CUMMING, A. Editor´s Statement. Language Learning: A Journal of Research in Language Studies. v. 43, n. 1, p. 1-3, 1993.

9. DAVIES, A. British applied linguistics: the contribution of S. Pit Corder. In: PHILLIPSON, R.; KELLERMAN, E.; SELINKER, L.; SHARWOODSMITH, M.; SWANN , M. Foreign/Second Language

Pedagogy Research.Clevedon: Multilingual Matters, Ltd., 1991.

10. DAVIES, A.; ELDER, C. The Handbook of Applied Linguistics. (Org.). Malden, Mass.: Blackwell Publishers, 2004.

11. DE BOT, K.; VERSPOOR, M.; LOWIE, W. Dynamic systems theory and applied linguistics: the ultimate "so what"? International Journal of Applied Linguistics. v. 15, n. 1, p. 116-118, 2005.

12. EDMONDSON, Willis. Prejudice and practice in applied linguistics. Applied Linguistics. v. 15, n. 3, p. 389-398, 2005.

13. FOUCAULT, M. Discipline and punish: the birth of the prison. New York:Vintage Books, 1979.

14. GALISSON, R. Que deviant la linguitique appliqué? Qu'est-ce que la methdologie des langues? Études de Linguistique Appliquée. juillet-septembre, 1972.

15. GASS, S. Second language acquisition: past, present and future. Second Language Research. v. 9, n. 2, p 99-117, 1993.

16. HASAN, R.; PERRETT, G. Learning to function with the other tongue: a systematic functional perspective on second language teaching. In: T. ODLIN et. al. Perspectives on pedagogical grammars. Cambridge: Cambridge University Press, 1994.

17. JACOBS, B.; SCHUMANN, J. Language acquisition and the neurosciences: toward a more integrated perspective. Applied Linguistics. v. 13, n. 3, p. 282-303,1992.

18. JAMES, C. What is applied linguistics? International Journal of Applied Linguistics, v. 3, n. 1, p. 17-32, 1993.

19. LANTOLF, J. Review of Alan Davies and Catherine Elder (Org.). The handbook of applied linguistics. Applied Linguistics. v. 27, n. 1, p. 147-152, 2006.

20. LEFFA, V. Malhação na sala de aula: o uso do exercício no ensino de línguas. Revista Brasileira de Linguística Aplicada. v. 8, n. 1, p. 139-159.

21. MCDONOUGH, S. Applied linguistics in language education. London: Arnold, 2002.

22. MOITA LOPES, L. P. (Org.). Por uma Linguística Aplicada Indisciplinar. São Paulo: Parábola, 2006.

23. PHILLIPSON, R.; KELLERMAN, E.; SELINKER, L.; SHARWOODSMITH, M.; SWANN, M. Foreign/Second Language Pedagogy Research.Clevedon: Multilingual Matters, Ltd., 1991.

24. QUIRK, R.; GREENBAUM, S.; LEECH, G.; SVARTIK, J. The Grammar of Contemporary English. London: Longman, 1972.

25. SCHULTE, R.; BIGUENET, J. B. Theories of Translation: an anthology of essays from Dryden to Derrida. Chicago: The University of Chicago Press, 1992.

26. SEALEY, A; CARTER, B. Applied Linguistics as Social Science. London: Continuum, 2004.

27. SIGNORINI, I. Applied Linguistics: an Overview. In: STRAZNY, P. (Org.). Encyclopedia of Linguistics. New York: Routledge, 2004.

28. SPOLSKY, B. Linguistics and Language Pedagogy-Applications or Implications? In: ALLATIS, J. (Org.). Georgetown University Roundtable on Language and Linguistics. Washington, D.C.: Georgetown University Press, 1970.

29. SPOLSKY, B. Educational Linguistics: An Introduction. Rowley, Mass: Newbury House Publishers, Inc., 1978.

30. SPOLSKY, B. Educational Linguistics. In: LEVY, A. (Org.). The International Encyclopedia of Curriculum. Oxford: Pergamon Press. 1991.

31. SRIDHAR, S.N. What are Applied Linguistics? Studies in the Linguistic Sciences. v. 20, n. 2, p. 165-176, 1990.

32. TOMIC□, O. M. The integrity of applied linguistics. In: TOMIC,□ O. M.; SHUY, R.W. (Org.). The relation of theoretical and applied linguistics. New York: Plenum Press, 1987.

33. VAN LIER, L. Educational linguistics: field and project. In: ALATIS, J.E.(Org.). Georgetown University Round Table on Languages and Linguistics.

34. Washington, D.C.: Georgetown University Press, 1994. VAN LIER, L. Apply within, apply without. International Journal of Applied Linguistics. v. 7, n. 1, p. 95-105, 1997.

1. WEI, L. A user- friendly linguistics. International Journal of Applied Linguistics. v. 17, n.1, p. 117-119, 2007.

2. WIDDOWSON, H. Models and fictions. Applied Linguistics. v. 1, n. 2, p. 165- 170, 1980.

3. WIDDOWSON, H. On the Limitations of Applied Linguistics. Applied Linguistics. v. 12, n. 1, p. 3-23, 2000a.

4. WIDDOWSON, H. Object language and the language subject: on the mediating role of applied linguistics. Annual Review of Applied Linguistics. v. 20, p. 21-33, 2000b.

Chapter 5

LANGUAGE POLITICS AND THE LINGUIST

Kanavillil Rajagopalan

Universidade Estadual de Campinas,Brazil

ABSTRACT

This paper focuses on language politics as it is currently unfolding in Brazil. Thanks to a legislative bid by a member of the House of Representatives to curb the wide-spread use of English in the country, large segments of the country's population have suddenly become interested in language-related issues. Professional linguists were taken by surprise and have, by and large, been reduced to the status of mere spectators. In an attempt to address the issue, I argue that there is an urgent need to attend to the wider public and engage them in a fruitful dialogue.

INTRODUCTION

When it comes to talking about language, let alone theorising it, the linguist and the lay person are notoriously known to diverge drastically from each other. The former tends to dismiss the views of the latter as "pre-scientific" and at best deserving of some vague anthropological interest. In fact, as pointed out by a number of scholars and historians of ideas, modern linguistics itself was founded on an outright rejection of what it has since then systematically reviled as "folk linguistics" (HUTTON, 1996; AITCHINSON, 2001; JOHNSON, 2001). The lay person typically does not know (or, for that matter, does not even care to know) what the linguist really does for a living and, when pressed for a response, all too frequently comes up with such oft-repeated platitudes as that the linguist is a polyglot or someone interested mostly in dead or "outlandish" languages. "I am not half good a linguist as you are, Holy Father" – these were the opening words used by President Clinton as he welcomed Pope John Paul II on the Pontiff's last visit to the U.S. Whereas the President of the United

States may arguably be excused for not knowing what an academic speciality is really all about, one cannot

but lament the fact that many dictionaries confer the stamp of authority upon the common misconception just referred to. Thus the Webster's New Collegiate Dictionary (1976) registers two meanings for the word linguist, the first of which says "a person accomplished in languages esp: one who speaks several languages" (rather unhelpfully, the second says: "one who specializes in linguistics") (p. 669). MacMillan English Dictionary for Advanced Learners (2002) follows suit by rephrasing the two meanings as "someone who studies or speaks a lot of languages" and "someone who teaches or studies linguistics" (p. 832). Both dictionaries, though, do make up for the lack of clarity in the definitions by defining linguistics in separate entries that say "the study of human speech including the units, nature, structure, and modification of language" (p. 669) and "the study of language and how it works" (p. 832), respectively. Cambridge Dictionary (2002 – CD-Rom) does register a reasonably accurate account of what a linguist specializes in but only in the second part of the following two-part Boolean definition: "someone who is learning a foreign language or can speak it very well, or someone who has a specialist knowledge of the structure and development of languages." (Needless to point out that the first part of this definition gets it even more hopelessly wrong than the entry in the other two dictionaries). When the lay person is confronted with the sort of things linguists routinely say about language (for instance, the claim that all human languages are equally complex in their structural configurations, provided one considers them in their totality), their reaction is usually one of stultified incredulity, followed by a dismissive shrug of their shoulders, indicative of their disapproval of the way specialised knowledge has distanced itself from common sense views and developed its own "convoluted" lines of reasoning (RAJAGOPALAN, 2002a). In fact linguistics stands apart from probably every other academically consolidated discipline in one respect: the kind of authority that it commands with the public at large. Physicists and biologists have no problem in getting the admiring attention from the lay public. Members of the lay public fondly nurture stories about the eccentric scientist – usually a chemist or a biologist – engrossed in research in a crowded and dingy laboratory, teeming with gurgling test tubes, Kipp's apparatuses emitting strange-smelling gases and what have you. The fact that no one outside a close-knit group of peers has the remotest clue as to what the fellow is up to is considered no problem; rather, that is just what really makes him so charming.

Even radio and television weather-forecasters are listened to, albeit with some distrust, since most people do know that meteorology is as yet far from being an exact science. So too many newspaper and magazine readers are often caught taking a sneak look at the kind of things the astrologer has to say about what their zodiac signs have in store for them, even though many of them may not have any faith whatsoever in the scientific pretensions of astrology or may not be willing to admit in public their real convictions on the matter. When it comes to linguistics, however, the ordinary person is often unwilling even to admit that he or she needs the help of a science to become wiser about what language is and what it is not. Instead, the lay person is often found boasting that he or she knows what language is all about. The only uncertainties they have are about the correctness of specific usages (for which they willingly turn to a traditional grammarian who typically has a ready-made answer to each and every one of their queries). On their part, professional linguists prefer to continue to ignore the lay persons, justifying their reaction on the grounds that theirs is a science and, like every other science, linguistics too is not for the uninitiated. As one of the discipline's most important representatives and, by all means, the one responsible for bringing the name of the discipline to the attention of wider public, put it, [...] the search for theoretical understanding pursues its own paths, leading to a completely different picture of the world, which neither vindicates nor eliminates our ordinary ways of talking and thinking. (CHOMSKY, 1995, p. 10). Notice that Chomsky's remark is very carefully worded. He is careful, as the majority of linguists are not, to stop short of claiming that scientific understanding is necessarily at loggerheads with public understanding. The truth remains nevertheless that many linguists tacitly assume that the knowledge that they have accumulated through painstaking research over the years shows how hopelessly muddle-headed the ordinary person is in respect of language and its intricacies. Whereof the usual air of contempt vis-à-vis what is collectively dismissed as 'folk linguistics' (RAJAGOPALAN, 2003a; forthcoming 1). But, as experience has shown, linguists have had a heavy price to pay and, by and large, continue to do so, for their principled decision not to have any trucks with the lay persons. The 'dogs-may-bark-but-thecaravan-goes-on' attitude assumed by many has often made them largely marginalized and inconsequential in public debates over languagerelated issues. Historically, linguists have gone about their business in utter disregard for public opinion. Yet, all too frequently, they are found grumbling, like Achilles in his tent, that their authority is not recognised the way it should be by the wider public. They lament the state of affairs but seldom have any concrete suggestions towards addressing it. The following words by Leonard Bloomfield in his inaugural address to the Linguistic Society of America speak volumes for themselves:

Our schools are conducted by persons who, from professors of linguistic science down to teachers of the classrooms, know nothing of the results of the linguistic science, not even the relation of writing to speech or standard language to dialect. In short, they do not know what language is and yet must teach it, and in consequence waste years of every child's life and reach a poor result. (BLOOMFIELD, 1925, p. 2).

As Geoffrey Nunberg was to remark years later, Bloomfield, Fries, Hall, and their contemporaries spoke to educators with all the arrogance of an adolescent science that was jealous of its intellectual prerogatives. As a result, their educational pronouncements now sound as high-handed and in some cases as irresponsible as many of the dogmas they were intended to counter. (NUNBERG, 1989, p. 586).

Given the continued stand-off between the two, it comes as no surprise that professional linguists all too frequently find themselves set aside in policy decisions over linguistic matters. As it happens, the policy makers in these cases are veteran politicians who tend to be much more attentive to the vox populi than expert opinion. This has been attested to time and time again in countries across the globe. The present paper is an attempt to focus on the language issue as it is currently unfolding in Brazil. Thanks to a legislative bid some years ago by a member of the House of Representatives by name Aldo Rebelo to curb the wide-spread use of English in the day-to-day life of average citizens, large segments of the country's population have suddenly become interested in language-related issues. The bill has already passed muster in the lower house and has just been returned by the upper house, the Senate, in a completely unrecognisable form. The avowed aim of the original bill and the one that was born out of its ashes is to protect the country's national language, Portuguese, against what it sees as the merciless onslaught of English, by common consent the lingua franca of the globalised world.

The original version of the bill was full of rhetoric embellished with fanfare and verbal pyrotechnics – of the kind that directly appeals to popular sentiments of nationalism and what Fishman (1968) has called 'nationism', i.e. the desire to legislatively intervene in the destiny of a national language with a view to furthering certain nationalist agendas. The country's linguists, initially stunned and stupefied as well as somewhat embarrassed at having been caught with their pants down, soon regained their breath (and their wits) and almost unanimously (there were some occasional discordant voices) condemned what they rightly saw as a xenophobic attempt to stifle the natural development of a language and mould its destiny with perilously chauvinistic objectives in mind. Notable among the discordant voices just referred to is that of Carlos Vogt, a linguist of considerable prestige, who wrapped up a paper entiled "Português, língua universal " (Portuguese, universal language): Safeguarding [...] the Portuguese language is safeguarding ourselves as well as our rich cultural diversity. In this regard, the bill put forward by Congressman Aldo Rebelo, under scrutiny in (Brazil's) national congress since 1999, could turn out to be an important legal instrument with which to stregthen the conditions for our linguistic and cultural identity. (VOGT, 2002, p. 29). But Vogt's remark is far from being representative of the stance taken by the overwhelming majority of linguists in Brazil (or, for that matter, by our colleagues in other countries, as and when they too find themselves embroiled in public controversies involving language). The position typically adopted by professional linguists all over the world is that the phenomenon of language is best approached independently of social, cultural or even emotional/sentimental connotations it might evoke in the minds of ordinary people. As a result of the hew and cry as well as tremendous pressure brought to bear upon the legislators by academic associations such as the Brazilian Association of Linguistics (ABRALIN), Brazilian Association of Applied Linguistics (ALAB), and others, the Rebelo bill was drastically altered by the Upper House of the Brazilian national congress and is now awaiting presidential approval. Perhaps, one most important spinoff from the imbroglio created by the entire episode is a sudden awakening on the part of Brazil's academic linguists. The following remark by Faraco, one of the country's leading linguists, is clearly indicative of this new sense of awareness:

Linguists are faced with the challenge of approaching these questions as fundamentally political questions and think about ways of making their voices heard, thus contributing to the beginning of an urgently needed cultural war among contending discourses that address the language of Brazil. (FARACO, 2001, p. 31). As it happens, however, it is becoming increasingly clear that the rigmarole is far from over. The popular resentment against the arrogant march of English into their daily lives has gained fillip from unexpected quarters precisely at the moment when it looked as if linguists had at long last gained the upper hand. A self-styled group called "Brazilian Linguists for Democracy" has suddenly sprung up and started to claim the right to speak on behalf of the vox populi. In what is best described as a vertable verbal Blitzkrieg, its advocates have forced their way into an Internet discussion group called Comunidade Virtual de Linguagem, which has been functioning for some time and which is used by professional linguists, graduate students and – as the rules laid down by its founding members state – anyone who has any interest in linguistic matters (where the qualifier is loosely defined so as to accommodate the maximum number of potential candidates to membership). (Incidentally, the more vociferous members of this selfstyled "task force" have since been denied access to the chatroom on charges of failure to comply with basic rules of decency). The scenario as it is currently unfolding has the linguist once again in the dock, being pinned down by accusing fingers and obliged to respond to charges of social irrelevance and pointless erudition. If the current trend continues to progress the way it has for some time, Brazil's professional linguists will in all likelihood soon find themselves suddenly catapulted to square one (that is to say, if they haven't been so catapulted already), as in a game of "Snakes and Ladders". No matter what sort of ugly or catastrophical denouement awaits the ongoing drama, one thing is increasingly becoming clear. The average person in the street remains mostly impervious to the arguments of the linguists which they find far too academic and often counter to their own much-cherished 'common sense'. What has gone awry here? Could it be the case that linguists have revealed themselves to be hopelessly wanting in basic skills of mass communication?

In an attempt to address these questions, I suggest that there is an urgent need to rethink some of the basic principles that have governed our characteristic attitude (as linguists, that is) to public opinion. For there to be a genuine dialogue between the two parties, linguists and lay persons – or, for that matter, any two parties – there has to be some amount of give-and-take on the part of either side (RAJAGOPALAN, forthcoming-1, 2). Now, for reasons already spelled out earlier, this is by all means easier said than done. Given that the science of language, Linguistics, was itself founded on an inaugural decision to ignore the ordinary person's point of view and to start afresh on a "clean slate", no frank exchange of views between the two sides will be possible unless and until linguists agree to give up or at least strategically suspend one of the founding principles of their discipline. This is by no means an easy task, especially in view of the fact linguistics itself probably inherited the proverbial distrust of public opinion from a tradition extending to earlier times. This is especially the case in Germany, the one culture that saw the rise of interest in language in the eighteenth century. As Hennigsen (1989) points out,

Hegel, who was interested in the unfolding of meaning in the process of universal history, treated [the] Volkgeist (the people's mentalité] somewhat disparagingly by relegating it to lower levels of meaning that lacked in conceptual clarity. Vox populi, the voice of the people, held no promise for him of any truth of any aspect of the process of human history. Truth would emerge from the negation of this commonsensical type of knowledge. (HENNINGSEN, 1989, p. 46).

What Henningsen's remark goes to show is that any decision to break the ice and engage in a meaningful dialogue with the lay person is bound to be an uphill task. The first step in this direction is a most urgently needed realisation on the part of the linguist that linguistics, like any other body of knowledge, is invested with the marks of its own discursive origins. This is by no means something peculiar to linguistics. All disciplines – tout court – begin their march towards academic recognition as discourses. And linguistics is no exception to this rule. It always begins with a group of early enthusiasts who gather informally. Through their diligent discursive practices aimed at carving out an intellectual territory for themselves, they set about the task of laying down the basic ground rules which will from then on delimit the emergent field and mark it off from its neighbouring disciplines. Philosophy began like this in ancient Greece around the figure of a bearded, bald-headed, short statured man of exceptional intellectual acumen and power of persuasion who regularly gathered a group of enthusiastic followers in a marketplace, the Plaka, in the centre of the ancient city of Athens. Centuries later, this practice was continued in Oxford where J.L. Austin founded the school of Ordinary Language Philosophy during his famous Saturday Morning Lectures.

The important point about informal chats resulting in the founding of great academic disciplines is that dialogism is invariably and inevitably present in the early discursive practices of every discipline. It is not for nothing that the founding texts of Western philosophy are called Dialogues. Plato, the author, knew full well the rhetorical power of dialogic interaction. But one misses the whole point if one concludes that the use of dialogue by Plato only served a rhetorical purpose. The truth is that the new discipline that his works inaugurated, namely Philosophy, would not have taken the form it did, if it had not been for the Socratic method of elenchus that Plato so effectively demonstrated in those early works. Elenchus works by eliciting self-contradiction in one's interlocutor's thought. It is the symbolic presence of the interlocutor that gives the technique of elenchus its extraordinary appeal to readers by far removed from its original enunciatory context. Elenchus takes place within the dialogic format. Dialogue in turn calls forth real-life communication in progress. And successful communication in turn is only possible when the interlocutors not only recognise each other's presence but address themselves to each other's doubts, scepticisms, anxieties and so on. What this goes to prove is that, in its inception at least philosophy was very much a pragmatic enterprise (RAJAGOPALAN, 2002d). Not only was its early diffusion carried out through face-to-face verbal interaction, the very structure of its reasoning was dialogic through and through. It was verbal fencing, where the one who could muster the right argumentative skills won the duel. True, all this was swept aside by philosophers of succeeding generations who preferred to conduct the business of philosophy as a mostly solitary business. Descartes famously retreated to his self-imposed "solitary confinement" in appalling conditions in a single-room accommodation at Ulm, where the only "luxury" (or sign of modern civilisation) was the presence of a stove that would keep the inside temperature from dipping to sub-zero levels. Kant too was mostly a solitary figure, with all the eccentricities that usually go with people who shun the company of fellow humans. One might say that, in its modern version, Philosophy has mostly been conducted as an occupation of solitary meditation by hermit-like persons who preferred to communicate to the world outside in the form of monologues, treatises and so on. The popularly cherished image of the eccentric scientist – a chemist or a biologist locked in an inhospitable laboratory for days on end as discussed earlier – harks back to and is modelled on such prototypical figures. But the appearance of monologue in many philosophical discourses only helps camouflage their essentially dialogic origins. Like Socrates and Plato, who were anxious to debate the views of the Sophists, so too was Descartes concerned to lay to rest the rampant scepticism of many of his contemporaries regarding the possibility of ever attaining philosophical certainty. Likewise, Kant's work, especially of the so-called 'critical' period, has been widely recognised as engaging in a silent dialogue between two unlikely predecessors, Descartes and Hume, both of whom he greatly admired. What has all this to do with the pragmatic underpinnings of philosophy? The pragmatic dimension comes to the fore as soon as it is recognised that philosophy is a discursive practice through and through – even when philosophical texts succeed in concealing it. By insisting on seeing philosophy as a body of knowledge more geometrico (the model here is Euclid's Geometry), one not only sidesteps its discursive origins but also momentarily leaves in suspension its inalienably pragmatic mode. What is true of philosophy is true of linguistics as well. This is hardly surprising, given that it is philosophy that most theoreticallyoriented disciplines have traditionally modelled themselves on. Like philosophy, linguistics too was down to earth, and goal-oriented in its origins. Some of the very ancient works of grammar such as Panini's trail-blazing Asthadhayi (? fourth century B.C.) were undertaken with a keen interest in language maintenance and standardisation of the Sanskrit language across the several kingdoms in the Asian subcontinent where the language was spoken. It was a teaching grammar, with a very precisely defined purpose, a fact that many linguists today tend to overlook even as they recognise the scientific brilliance that went into its making (RAJAGOPALAN, 2003b).

What all this discussion about the dialogic character of academic disciplines such as philosophy and linguistics clearly shows is that concern with those who were not part of the in-group was paramount in the minds of the early practitioners of each of them. Their respective discourses were aimed at convincing – indeed, winning over the hearts and minds of – the barely initiated as well as the stubbornly sceptical. In fact, as Socrates recognised all too readily, that is the only way new knowledge can spread. What Bacon called argumentum ad baculum may work for some time (and for the wrong reason) but is unlikely to sway the minds of people over a long period of time. One thing that has clearly emerged from the ongoing controversy over language in Brazil is that professional linguists have been dismally wanting in the rhetorical skills needed to sway public opinion in their favour. Instead, their opinions frequently strike the general public as arrogant and standoffish. I have discussed some of these views at length elsewhere (RAJAGOPALAN, 2002a) and will not repeat them here. But the gist of the argument presented there is this: when confronted with public opinion, we linguists have typically reacted by exclaiming that such views lack any kind of scientific backing or rigour. We tend to dismiss them outright as childish or unscientific. Rather than address the anxieties of ordinary persons for what they are worth, we characteristically question the academic or scientific credentials of those who voice them. To put it differently, we tend to use ad hominem arguments in order to fight our way through adverse public opinion. The reaction from the public to such abrasive tactics is perfectly predictable. To begin with, it is just as abrasive. As noted at the beginning of this paper, members of the wider public usually have very little idea of what modern linguistics is really all about. Professional linguists' unwillingness to explain their science in a manner accessible to those who are uninitiated in their "craft", coupled with their often dismissive attitude to what those who are uninitiated generally think or believe, understandably leads the general public to conclude that linguistics itself is a body of knowledge with very little practical consequence. It is by no means enough if we continue to simply insist that linguistics has a lot to contribute to the general welfare. No doubt convictions do move mountains (as the saying teaches us), but this only happens if we convince those around us of the kind of things we claim we are ourselves convinced of. Rev.

The lesson to learn from the discussion thus far is therefore fairly straightforward: if we linguists are at all to make any headway in our efforts to influence public opinion and bring the weight of our accumulated wisdom to have any bearing whatsoever on policy decisions involving language and so on, it is absolutely necessary that we adopt new ways of communicating with lay people. Rather than treat them as mere providers of raw data on which to base our studies, we should approach them as our genuine interlocutors. Among other things, this entails the need to put all the emphasis on the right strategies of argumentation, taking into consideration the fact that our interlocutors do have a right to their own opinions, no matter how weird or bizarre they may appear to us at first glimpse (RAJAGOPALAN, 2002b). Furthermore, there is an equally urgent need to recognise that true dialogue can only begin to take place if we are willing to listen to what they, our interlocutors, have to say, instead of dismissing their views as pre-scientific or muddle-headed even before they have had a chance to express themselves freely . Here is where some of the lessons from pragmatics might prove to be of great help. Pragmatists are in a much better position to break the communicational gridlock referred to above, given that, when all is said and done, pragmatics is precisely about communicating with others. If, from a historical point of view, linguistic pragmatics has been, rightly or wrongly, entrusted with the task of taking care of unsolved (and unsolveable) problems left over by the other putatively "nobler" members of the Peircean triad (namely, syntax and semantics), it may well turn out to be case that the greatest challenge awaiting it today is to bridge the biggest of all the communicational gaps it has thus far been called upon to confront – that between the linguists and the lay persons. In other words, pragmatics may turn out to be our last hope for clearing up long-standing mutual suspicions vis-à-vis the public at large – or, at the very least, making a rapprochement possible somewhere down the road (RAJAGOPALAN, 2002c, d).

ACKNOWLEDGEMENT

I wish to thank the CNPq for funding my research (Process no. 306151/88-0).

REFERENCES

1. AITCHISON, J. Misunderstandings about language: a historical view. Journal of Sociolinguistics, 5/4, p. 61-620, 2001.

2. BLOOMFIELD, L. Why a linguistic society. (text of the lecture delivered on the occasion of the founding of the Linguistic Society of America). Language,1.1, p. 1-5, 1925.

3. CHOMSKY, N. A. Language and nature. Mind. v. 104, n. 413, p. 1-61, 1995.

4. FARACO, C.A. Guerras em torno da língua. Folha de São Paulo, São Paulo, 2001. Caderno Mais, p. 30-31.

5. FISHMAN, J. Nationality-nationalism and nation-nationism. In: FISHMAN, J.; FERGUSON, C. A.; DAS-GUPTA, J. (Ed.). Language Problems of Developing Nations. New York: Wiley, 1968. p. 98-112.

6. HENNINGSEN, M. The politics of purity and exclusion: literary and linguistic movements of political empowerment in America, Africa, the South Pacific, and Europe. In: IN JERNUDD, B. H.; SHAPIRO, M. J. (Ed.) The Politics ofLanguage Purism. New York: Mouton de Gruyter, 1989. p. 31-52.

7. HUTTON, C. Law lessons for linguists? Accountability and acts of professional classification. Language & Communication. 16.3, p. 205-

214, 1996.

8.   JOHNSON, S. Who's misunderstanding whom? Sociolinguistics, public debate and the media. Journal of Sociolinguistics, 5.4, p. 591-610, 2001.

9.   NUNBERG, G. Linguists and the official language movement. Language. 65.6, p. 579-595, 1989.

10.   RAJAGOPALAN, K. National languages as flags of allegiance; or the linguistics that failed us: a close at emergent linguistic chauvinism in Brazil. Journal of Language & Politics. v. 1, n. 1, p. 115-147, 2002a.

11.   RAJAGOPALAN, K. Resenha do livro FARACO, C. A. (Org.). Estrangeirismos: Guerras em Torno da Língua. D.E.L.T.A, v. 18, n. 2,. p. 339-344, 2002b.

12.   RAJAGOPALAN, K. Sobre a especificidade da pesquisa no campo da pragmática. Cadernos de Estudos Lingüísticos, v. 42, p. 89-98, 2002c.

13.   RAJAGOPALAN, K. Por uma pragmática voltada à prática lingüística. In: ZANDWAIS, Ana (Org.). A relação entre pragmática e enunciação. Porto Alegre, R.S.: Ed. Sagra Luzzatto, 2002d. p. 22-35.

14.   RAJAGOPALAN, K. Politics of language and the ambivalent role of English in Brazil. World Englishes, v. 22, n. 2, p. 91-101, 2003a.

15.   RAJAGOPALAN, K. The philosophy of applied linguistics. In: DAVIES, A.; ELDER, C. (Ed.). Handbook of Applied Linguistics. Blackwell Publishers,2003b. p. 397-420.

16.   RAJAGOPALAN, K. The language issue in Brazil: when local knowledge clashes with expert knowledge. In: CANAGARAJAH, S. (Org.). Local Knowledge, Globalization, and Language Teaching. Forthcoming-1. NewJersey: Lawrence Erlbaum Publishers.

17.   RAJAGOPALAN, K. Emotion and language politics: the Brazilian case. Journal of Multilingual & Multicultural Development. Forthcoming-2.

18.   RAJAGOPALAN, K. Social aspects of pragmatics. In: MEY, J.L. (Ed.). Pragmatics. Encyclopedia of Language and Linguitics. Forthcoming-3. UK: Elsevier.

19.   VOGT, C. Português, língua universal. Scientific American – Brasil, 1.1, p. 29, 2002.

Chapter 6

METAPHOR IN APPLIED LINGUISTICS: FOUR COGNITIVE APPROACHES

Gerard Steen

Department of English Language and Culture Vrije Universiteit; The Netherlandssa

ABSTRACT

This article presents some considerations into metaphor in language and thought– 'the topic and title of the first conference of its kind in Brazil'. The paper focuses on the discussions presented in the round table, which were mostly directed to the empirical research on metaphor in Applied Linguistics. This integrative and retrospective reflection on the papers presented will be conducted from the perspective of the debate into the relationship between metaphor in language and in thought. This central issue is at the core of my proposal for four different approaches to metaphor, based on the interdependence between language and thought as system and as use: 1) metaphor in language as system; 2) metaphor in thought as system; 3) metaphor in language as use and 4) metaphor in thought as use. It is within the framework of these categories that metaphors should be studied, with a certain degree of autonomy, so that their interdependence can be better understood.

FOUR COGNITIVE APPROACHES TO METAPHOR

It is my privilege to offer some integrative and prospective remarks about "metaphor in language and thought", the topic and title of the first conference of its kind in Brazil. When I was originally preparing for this task, I did so from the perspective of the book I am currently writing with Ray Gibbs, entitled *Finding metaphor in language and thought* (Steen and Gibbs in preparation). The tentative structure of our book formed the guideline for the series of workshops we offered during the conference, and it was my intention for the present contribution to review the main claims we had been making. However, the continued high-quality discussions at the conference itself have made it unnecessary to go over these grounds again. What I will do instead, therefore, is make a connection with the main concern of most of the participants at the conference, doing empirical metaphor research in applied linguistics.

The conference organization lying in the hands of Mara Sofia Zanotto and her colleagues from LAEL at PUC São Paulo, it is no surprise that applied linguistics turned out to be the focus of discussion. The presence of Lynne Cameron and Jacob Mey as other keynote speakers only reinforced this tendency. That is why I will make some comments about metaphor in applied linguistics from my more general concern with metaphor in language and thought.

Only fairly recently have students of metaphor been joined by applied linguists. The collection of chapters edited by Cameron and Low (1999a) is the most important testimony to this development. It is the first book publication coming out of a series of originally applied-linguistics conferences called «Researching and applying metaphor», or RAAM, which was founded by Cameron and Low. Other results of this conference series may be encountered in*Metaphor and Symbol* (Volume 14, Number 1, 1999) and *Journal of Pragmatics* (Steen in press). More metaphor research of an applied linguistic nature has been reviewed by Cameron and Low (1999b).

When applied linguists study metaphor, they are typically concerned with metaphor in language as use (e.g. Cameron and Low 1999a: xiii; Low and Cameron 2002: 84). This includes ordinary discourse (any kind of communication by means of language, typically in some institutional context), language learning and language teaching of various kinds, and more general practices of language counseling and advice, such as text design. Part of this endeavor, moreover, is concerned with intervening in language use: as Cameron has claimed, linguistics is applied not just to describe the world of language use, but to change it.

These comments leave a lot of overlap between applied linguistics and discourse analysis, which I think is as it should be. There are important differences between these two areas of study too, especially when it comes to*applying* knowledge of language and discourse in practice, such as education, communication, and so on. But I think these issues are ultimately irrelevant to the purposes of the present paper.

However, these observations are meaningless unless we know what does not qualify as «language as use». I propose that language as use ought to be contrasted with language as system, and that language itself ought to be differentiated from thought. The complete set of cognitive approaches to metaphor, then, consisting of combinations of single perspectives, looks like this:

- metaphor in language as system
- metaphor in thought as system
- metaphor in language as use
- metaphor in thought as use

Even though some scholars may be worried about the artificiality of these distinctions, I think that it is useful to explore them, simply because many linguists keep making an appeal to different combinations of them (approaches) when they characterize their own practice. Thus, the same distinctions may be recognized in Cameron and Low›s (1999a) preface describing the general field of metaphor studies. Ray Gibbs (1999a), in his analysis of the experience of literal and figurative meaning (language and thought as use), treats intentions as more important than the meanings of words or utterances themselves. George Lakoff (1994) has written about conceptual systems as related to cognitive processing as well as to linguistic systems and their use. And Ray Jackendoff›s (2002) new addition to the development of a conceptual semantics shows that these distinctions are important for non cognitive-linguistic work on meaning outside metaphor and applied linguistics, too. As long as it is recalled that these are distinct perspectives on language and thought, not hard-and-fast distinctions between language and thought themselves, it may be useful to differentiate between these approaches as diverging ways of conceptualizing the object of study.

Various disciplines have made contributions to each of these approaches. Cognitive linguistics is involved in all of them, whereas applied linguistics is mostly concerned with the third and fourth approaches, as is, for instance, discourse analysis. One reason for distinguishing between approaches as opposed to disciplines is that disciplines may include more than one approach whereas it is essential for some purposes to be precise about which approach one is taking. This also enables researchers to combine aspects from more than one discipline (e.g. applied linguistics, discourse analysis, pragmatics, and cognitive linguistics) for the purposes of pursuing just one approach (e.g. metaphor in language as use).

The more positive definition of language as use is no trivial matter, as may be gleaned from the various definitions of discourse discussed by Schiffrin, Tannen, and Hamilton (2001) in their *Handbook of discourse analysis*. Moreover, any empirical approach to language use, I would argue, cannot ignore the cognitive and social role of discourse genres as a means for managing and monitoring the many aspects of language use, including metaphorical language use (Steen 1999; 2002a; 2002b). Genre functions as an explanatory concept for many aspects of metaphor in language use, but the notion of genre itself is no simple definitional matter either. And finally there is the problem of the definition of metaphor as opposed to non-metaphor in language as use. Cameron (1999b: 114) has discussed several criteria for defining and especially identifying metaphor in language use, and they can produce rather different results regarding what counts as a metaphorical stretch of language.

There are hence at least three fundamental theoretical problems in any applied-linguistic study of metaphor:

- the definition of language as use
- the definition of genre as a cognitive or social device for monitoring language use
- the definition of metaphor in language as use

The fourfold distinction between cognitive approaches to metaphor may now be used to discuss the definition of language as use. In making a distinction between the four approaches, I would like to suggest that it is possible and even useful to adopt a restricted approach to language as language use, by momentarily backgrounding language as system, or backgrounding thought as conceptual system and its use. Let me begin with an illustration.

Cameron (1999b: 114) suggests that *salary* "can be said to be metaphorical because it originally referred to salt given to Roman soldiers". What I would like to argue is that this fact is irrelevant to the study of language as use, simply because very few contemporary language users have access to this fact. What is more, I suggest that applied linguists should ignore it for the study of language as use while at the same time admitting that, for other purposes, *salary* may have to be regarded as metaphorical or metonymic in approaching language as a (diachronic) system (e.g. Geeraerts 1997). Thus, *salary* may be figurative in one approach (language as system) whereas it may be literal in another approach (language as use).

Applied linguists do not have to take everything on board that has come out of other approaches to metaphor, because some of these findings may simply be irrelevant to their approach of metaphor given their conceptualization of language as use. However, by the same token it may be perfectly possible for applied linguists to utilize other information about metaphor that has come from work done in other approaches that is relevant for the study of metaphor in language use. Thus, much of the cognitive-linguistic work on metaphor in language and thought may be said to embody an approach to language as system, especially a lexical system, and thought as system, especially a conceptual system. It would be obnoxious for the study of metaphor in language use to ignore all findings from these lines of research. In fact, it has been precisely these findings which have now triggered an interest in their application in applied linguistics, which studies the use of these systems in actual discourse. As a result, many of the findings of these other approaches have to be taken seriously in the study of metaphor in language use and play the role of assumed background knowledge in applied-linguistic research. I will offer one or two illustrations in a moment.

This is the point of making and using the distinctions introduced above. A bird›s eye view of the study of metaphor shows that applied linguists momentarily assume some status quo in general and cognitive linguistics (regarding language as system) and cognitive linguistics (regarding thought as system). True, this is a status quo that applied linguists have to reconstruct for their own purposes, but they have to do so with maximal respect for the original approaches. The selection and organization of that status quo then facilitates examination of how parts of these two postulated systems affect the on-going use of metaphorical language in concrete situations of discourse. This is part of the excitement of doing this type of interdisciplinary research.

It may not be too difficult to accept such a picture of the division of labor for the three approaches mentioned just now. However, it may be a little harder for some to agree to the claim that if applied linguists focus on metaphor in language as use, they should also momentarily take for granted what is known about metaphor in thought as use. Many applied linguists (as well as discourse analysts, pragmaticians, and cognitive linguists) study the use of the language system and the use of the conceptual system in combination with each other, since they often deal with language use as an expression of more encompassing cognitive processes and social interaction. Cameron›s starting point for her workshops at the conference, that «metaphors indicate understandings and attitudes,» is a perfect illustration. However, I would like to insist that this still presupposes a careful distinction between, on the one hand, (linguistic) «metaphor,» and, on the other hand, «understandings and attitudes» (thought). Otherwise it would be hard to examine their relation in a controlled fashion.

I would therefore like to advocate the same argument as above, and suggest that we see the approach of metaphorical thought-as-process (or use of a conceptual system) as one distinct approach to doing empirical metaphor research, even when we examine metaphor in language use. And when we do look at metaphorical thought as a process in its own terms, we need to take on board not just the work done in cognitive linguistics, but the complete tradition of psycholinguistics and cognitive and social psychology, as well as the many useful distinctions and findings it has produced. We have to assume (or construct) some state of play in that tradition in the same way as we do for general linguistics and cognitive linguistics with respect to language as system and thought as system, respectively. As Cameron (1999a: 12-13) has noted, «Theoretical clarity is also needed in the relation *assumed between* [my emphasis, GS] language and thought, as this will underlie inferences that are made between linguistic evidence and thinking.»

For instance, when applied linguists make assumptions about metaphor as thought, they have to be aware of such processing distinctions as those proposed by Gibbs (1994), between comprehension and subsequent processing of the product of comprehension, as in recognition, interpretation, and appreciation (cf. Gibbs 1999b). Comprehension refers to the thought process concerned with the immediate appropriation of an utterance by an addressee, until the point of the utterance is understood. This is often referred to as the «click of comprehension.» However, after this first moment of comprehension, people may continue to process the mental product of this comprehension process and think about the utterance *as* a metaphor (metaphor recognition), or assign an evaluation to the effort they have had to put into comprehending and perhaps interpreting it (metaphor appreciation). My own work on metaphor understanding in literature is concerned with these 'later' thought processes of recognition, interpretation, and appreciation (Steen 1994), and any conclusion about these optional late processes should not be confused with information about obligatory comprehension processes.

Applied linguists also need to be aware of three radically different operations that are possible for metaphor processing in natural discourse (Steen 1994):

- disambiguation of polysemy that is historically motivated by metaphor
- retrieval of a pre-stored metaphorical mapping
- on-line construction of a metaphorical mapping

The first scenario, for instance, makes it possible for an applied linguist to observe that a metaphor may be present in the language used, but that it does not have to be there in the on-line cognitive process of the language user (parts of the conceptual system used).

Moreover, these forms of metaphor processing need to be distinguished from metaphoric processing. Metaphoric processing is a mode of cognition that is not dependent on the presence of linguistic metaphors in discourse per se but on some other conventions of a genre (Steen 1994; Gibbs 1999b). Looking at metaphor as thought hence includes people›s construction of metaphoric cognitive representations for literary allegories or perhaps scientific or educational models, which are text genres that many scholars would say do not contain metaphoric language. Again, one approach does not lead to the same ordering of the study of metaphor as another approach.

We have also emphasized that different individuals may exhibit the various cognitive operations of metaphor processing in varying degrees (cf. Steen and Gibbs 1999). For instance, children may acquire some conceptual metaphors wholesale from their language learning without necessarily having to re-experience all the cultural and embodied events that originally gave rise to conceptual metaphors. Moreover, Gibbs (1999c) has argued that this may be a phenomenon that concerns every individual›s relation to all of the metaphorical cultural patterns they participate in.

Applied linguists also have to take into account that, within individuals, cognitive processing of metaphorical language may take place at different levels of semantic depth and detail. Some processes require longer and deeper chains of cognitive operations on metaphorical expressions than others (Steen 2001). Thus, if metaphorical thought is defined as people›s performing a complete mental mapping across domains, it may not be clear whether language users may also be said to think metaphorically if they only construct some kind of metaphorical proposition, or some comparison statement, or an analogy, and leave it at that. Again, the presence of metaphorical language in use does not lead in a direct fashion to a clear-cut situation regarding metaphorical thought in cognitive processing. Metaphorical talk does not necessarily equal metaphorical thought.

It is true that applied linguists need not limit their attention to metaphor in language as use, but may also be concerned with metaphor in cognitive processes, or with metaphor in cognitive processes plus metaphor in language use. Cameron (1999a: 8) has made a similar observation: «Researchers need to decide early in the process whether metaphor is being considered as a phenomenon of language, or of thought, or both, « However, I believe that applied linguists always need to study the language as use in order to arrive at an examination of thought as process (or its products) if they want to study that (too). That is the reason I have emphasized the role of metaphor in language as use.

The advantage of adopting the systematic distinctions between the four approaches to metaphor in language and thought is the following. Researchers do not have to feel that they are inconsistent when, for their own purposes, something does not count as metaphorical whereas for other purposes it does. I have exemplified this in various ways, concerning *salary*, polysemy disambiguation, and metaphorical thought by means of metaphoric processing, or by means of comparison or analogy. What is more, applied linguists do not have to feel that their approach should be able to deal with all of the issues of metaphor research from their intentionally limited and focused standpoint. There is a decided benefit in saying that some research operates with one approach whereas other research operates with a different approach: it may and hopefully will eventually be possible to see these approaches as complementary. Distinct approaches investigate a multidimensional object from different sides and consequently see the object from a different angle. The bird's eye view of science will then be able to integrate these approaches into one whole.

However, this picture also suggests that this will only be possible if researchers are willing to adopt related distinctions of the field, according to for instance language and thought as well as system and use, as I am suggesting. Moreover, they should also be willing to adopt consistent definitions for the phenomenon under study across the four approaches, the third fundamental problem for any applied– linguistic study of metaphor that I mentioned above. For instance, many students of metaphor today regard it as a case of non-literal mapping across conceptual domains (Lakoff 1993; Lakoff and Johnson 1999). As soon as this definition is shifted, either in the direction of blending theory (Fauconnier and Turner 2002; cf. Grady et al. 1999) or in the direction of class-inclusion theory (Glucksberg 2001; Glucksberg and Keysar 1993), this has implications for the definitions and their applications, in all four approaches. Working with a systematic distinction between these approaches facilitates the precise discussion of these shifts and implications for different research projects.

In sum, the general nature of the cognitive approach to metaphor I am advocating resides in the assumption that language and thought are two related forms of cognition which need to be studied in their own terms in order to establish the precise nature of their relationship. Their study also has different shapes depending on whether they are seen as systems or as the use of those systems. This situation makes it possible to distinguish between four relatively autonomous approaches to metaphor as cognition.

The main property of the generally cognitive approach to metaphor is the move away from the emphasis on linguistic autonomy that has traditionally characterized much work in linguistics and pragmatics. We would like to endorse the novel claim and research program in cognitive linguistics that assumes and explores the interdependence between language and thought as system and use (Steen and Gibbs 1999). However, I also feel that this program has tended to obscure some of the real distinctions of metaphor in cognition by conflating the four approaches too much. For instance, it is not always clear whether the cognitive-linguistic claim that we understand love in terms of a journey applies to our generalized conceptual system or to a concrete on-line process of cognition. That is why we wish to use the distinctions between the approaches in order to examine their interrelations in a more precise and controlled fashion. This strategy assumes that we can offer provisional definitions of each of the four approaches – which is what I have attempted to do in a sketchy fashion – in order to facilitate the research into the relationships between the approaches afterwards. The next section will demonstrate how this cognitive approach to metaphor may help address some of the questions raised by the papers presented at the conference.

METAPHOR IN LANGUAGE AND THOUGHT

When we adopt the cognitive approach to metaphor outlined above, we can see that the papers at the conference on metaphor in language and thought can be grouped together in various ways as a reflection of their close relation to one approach or another. In what follows, I will restrict my attention to the plenary papers and the symposia. I am not doing this because the other papers were inferior, because they were not; but simply because the general papers were accessible to everybody.

Philosophical Approaches

One general characteristic of the cognitive approach is its scientific as opposed to philosophical nature. True, the cognitive approach does have implications for philosophy, as has been pointed out by Lakoff and Johnson (1999). However, it is not inherently tied to a particular philosophy of the world, knowledge, or scientific knowledge itself. Lakoff and Johnson (1980; 1999) have argued for a close relationship between the cognitive approach to metaphor and their philosophy called "experientialism", which includes "embodied realism" as its epistemology. However, there are many researchers working in cognitive science who do not subscribe to this particular brand of philosophy. It is therefore of fundamental importance to keep these philosophical discussions alive, as was also demonstrated by the papers by Helena Martins as well as by Kanavillil Rajagopalan.

Rajagopalan raised the issue of the literalization of metaphor, and presented the claim that metaphor and literalness themselves are metaphorical notions. I wonder whether he is referring to the same notion of literalness as Lakoff (1986) or Gibbs (1993) here, who do not believe that there is a metaphorical element in their definitions, but that is just an aside. The interesting issue for the applied linguist, or for the cognitive researcher of metaphor in general, is the question how Rajagopalan's discussion has a bearing on doing empirical cognitive research. For even though there may be fundamental problems with the notion of literalness or metaphor, these problems have not led to an overall rejection of the notions themselves. The practical goal of doing research into metaphor, including its fundamentally problematic aspects, requires that one cuts the knot at a particular moment in order to get going with the empirical work.

What this means for the applied linguist is that researchers should not continue to hesitate forever in actually cutting the knot an injunction which emphasizes the difference between the cognitive-scientific approach and the philosophical one. However, what this also means is that applied linguists should always be prepared to go back to the moment when they did cut the knot, in order to re-examine the assumptions they made in distinguishing between metaphor and non-metaphor, including literal, language and thought. It is one job of philosophers to keep asking questions about these assumptions and act as kind of academic hecklers. Turning the perspective round, however, it is the job of applied linguists and other empirical researchers to gather evidence that has a bearing on these questions, so that we do not keep going round in circles. This is precisely what the Pragglejaz metaphor identification project attempts to do in terms of theoretical and operational definitions for metaphor identification (Steen 2002c).

Helena Martins drew our attention to the widespread cognitive-linguistic assumption that metaphors are based in relatively stable and established conceptual systems, the thought-as-system approach I distinguished above. She discussed how this approach affects our view of metaphor novelty or conventionality, making novel metaphor "a possible but relatively rare phenomenon." She argued for a Wittgensteinian, "non-superlative" re-consideration of the role of conceptual systems, situating them in our language-infused human practices rather than anywhere else. As a result, novel metaphor can only be observed against the background of specific and concrete contexts of language use.

For the cognitive researcher, there does not seem to be an issue here of choosing for or against Wittgenstein. Instead, Martins' argument throws into relief how the approach to language and thought as cognitive systems is not sufficient for a sophisticated view of the actual workings of metaphor during use. What is needed is a further refinement of these system-oriented approaches, according to whether the systems are seen as either abstract, theoretical constructs, which are studied in their own right by cognitive linguists; social constructs carried by groups or cultures, which are studied by anthropologists or cultural sociologists; or individual constructs put to use by real people in their concrete human practices (e.g. Gibbs 1999c). As with the notions of literal and metaphorical discussed above, philosophical work on language and thought as systems can be made productive for theoretical modeling in the service of empirical research.

Language as System

When we turn from the philosophical papers to the cognitive-scientific papers presenting work on metaphor in language as a system, the distance with the applied-linguistic work on metaphor is diminished. For our present purposes, these are examples of papers that address an aspect of the status quo in one approach, language as system. This status quo regarding language as system is necessarily assumed and placed in the background as provisionally unproblematic by the applied linguist who is interested in metaphor in language as use. Of course, these "language-as-system" papers pursue their own ends in terms of their own traditions. But for the applied linguist who adopts a cognitive approach to metaphor, these are papers representing a different approach to metaphor, functioning as an auxiliary in the applied linguistic research.

We may now illustrate one of the benefits of this attempt to order the field of cognitive research on metaphor. In accepting that applied linguists take on board a set of assumptions about work done on metaphor in language as system, it becomes clear that such metaphor research is embedded in linguistic traditions of their own. For instance, when we look at the papers by Margarida Basilio and Heronides Moura, applied linguists need to come to terms with a model of the language system that can accommodate the relations between metaphor in morphology (Basilio) and metaphor in the lexicon (Moura). The selection of such a model is not unproblematic. By implication, it is important for applied linguists to be explicit about what they are taking on board for the temporary purpose of their investigation, and what not.

Let us take Moura's paper as a case in point. His work on polysemy in the lexicon is situated in the generative tradition represented by Pustejovsky (1995). This model works with rather elaborate representations of lexical items, including accounts of their argument structure, event structure, qualia structure, and lexical inheritance structure. Moura's main point is that this "richer lexical representation would make it possible for the semantic theory to describe the creative use of words, including regular polysemy and metonymy." And it is not just that "regular polysemy is predictable from the lexicon's structure", but it is "predictable from the lexicon's structure only, regardless of *a previous cognitive process*" (my emphasis, GS).

The basic question asked by Moura concerns the role of the lexicon as an independent contributor to the creation of meaning. He contrasts this to the more important role assigned to the encyclopedia in the cognitive-linguistic approach. However, what is facilitated by the adoption of a more neutral bird's eye view of all these approaches is to raise the question of the concrete and precise relation between the two approaches.

In particular, the generativist view highlights meaning as produced by the lexical system of the dictionary, whereas the cognitive-linguistic view highlights meaning as produced by the conceptual system of the encyclopedia. I hasten to add that these are all too blatant generalizations in themselves, as may be understood from the exchange between Taylor (1996) and Jackendoff (1996; cf. 2002). However, what is at issue is Moura's argument "that the linguistic system has a role in the production of figurative meanings, and that this role is associated with systematic lexical relations, " I would prefer to see this as one possible hypothesis. If regular polysemy is held to follow from the lexicon's structure only, this view follows from a set of initial assumptions about the role of the lexicon that differs from the assumptions of at least some cognitive linguists, such as Taylor. A bird's eye view of the cognitive approaches to metaphor, however, raises the question why the generative account of the lexicon could not alternatively be developed to account for the conceptual system, to the effect that it is not words but concepts that display the kind of structure or information postulated by Pustejovsky. Another question would ask why the two systems, linguistic and conceptual, could not work in concert, instead of attributing all responsibility for the creation of meaning to the linguistic system. In fact, this turns out to be Moura's position, too, who wishes to see the lexicon as a constraint on conceptual metaphor (personal communication, 7 March 2003). Applied linguists who favor the cognitive-linguistic approach might prefer a view of language in which the lexicon has a more limited role to play, and if they do, they should not incorporate Moura's view of the lexicon in their own view of language as system without further ado.

The adoption of the more specific standpoint of the applied linguist who starts out from language as use raises another question. How are the linguistic and conceptual systems as reconstructed by Moura (or Taylor) involved in the "creative use of words" as understood by the applied linguist, the discourse analyst, the pragmatician, and many cognitive linguists? Only if there is perfect correspondence between the structure of the abstract lexicon of the ideal native speaker on the one hand and the individuals' lexical repertoires on the other, can it be claimed that the structure of the lexicon as proposed by Moura directly accounts for the creation of meaning in concrete use. This is an assumption that not many psycholinguists and psychologists would be prepared to make.

These questions are of equal importance for the study of the lexical constructions discussed by Margarida Basilio. She analyzes *swordfish* and *beija-flor* as metaphorical compounds, the former depending on an image mapping between the form of a sword and the form of a fish, while the latter is slightly more complex. The compound *beija-flor* can be glossed as "kiss-flower", and means "humming bird". The claim is that there is a metaphorical mapping between the relation between the humming bird and a flower on the one hand and one person kissing another person on the other hand. My question about this type of analysis would be whether the mapping perceived as relevant for language as a morphological or lexical system should also be invoked for the analysis of language as use or thought as use. In other words, how plausible would it be to claim that these mappings are part of language use defined in some psychological manner? Do language users always retrieve or construct these linguistic or conceptual mappings in their minds when they lexically access these words? And how can this be determined? The distinction between the two approaches raises questions about metaphor in language and thought that require further empirical and theoretical research.

Let me finally explicate the connection with applied linguistics. Under what view of applied linguistics would it be interesting to have to deal with the metaphorical mapping detected in *beija-flor*? Well, it might be interesting for developing teaching programs in second or foreign language learning. But does it require an applied linguist to find and describe this type of mapping? Or does it make more sense that this type of metaphorical meaning is more relevant to a description of language as a system, which is then assumed as part of the input for the curriculum? I prefer the latter view of the division of labor, because it is eventually the general systematicity in the language system that decides how an expression will be presented for learning in education. Findings from a language as system approach are needed or presupposed by the applied linguist who then wishes to include them into a language teaching program that may be studied as language as use.

The relation between the perspective on language as system and language and thought as use is also important for the paper on blending by Maria Salomão. In fact she also includes the fourth approach, which deals with cognition as conceptual system, and discusses a number of metaphors in a typically cognitive-linguistic mix of all four approaches. That is, she makes assumptions about language as system and use, and about thought as system and use, and produces an argument based on all of these assumptions. In this case, Salomão concludes that blending theory may be a better candidate for dealing with novel metaphor than conceptual metaphor theory (cf. Grady, Oakley, and Coulson 1999).

My problem with this kind of mixed approach is that so many assumptions are made for so many approaches at the same time. For instance, to turn to the "thought-as-system" approach that is part of Salomão's project, how secure is the postulation of conceptual metaphors like LIFE IS A JOURNEY? Lakoff and Johnson (1999) have recently adopted the distinction between primary and complex metaphor advanced by Grady (1997). LIFE IS A JOURNEY is a complex metaphor that may be analyzed as arising through the combination of a number of primary metaphors, including PURPOSES ARE DESTINATIONS. However, it is one thing to claim that our conceptual system has primary metaphors which may be combined to produce complex metaphors during use, but it is another claim to state that our conceptual system has both primary as well as complex metaphors in conventionalized and fixed forms. At this moment, it seems to me that we simply know too little to make either assumption at the exclusion of the other or even further alternatives (cf. Murphy 1996, 1997; Vervaeke and Kennedy 1996). Moreover, when we shift the perspective from these systems to cognitive processing, it is not necessarily the case that the analyses offered by blending theorists actually capture what is going on in the minds of individual language users (Gibbs 1999c; 2000). It is therefore important to be explicit about which assumptions from which approach are accepted when a judgment has to be made regarding the overall conclusion of the paper that conceptual metaphor theory cannot deal with novel metaphor as well as blending theory. Focusing on one approach while backgrounding the others seems to be a research strategy that makes this type of monitoring of assumptions more manageable. It temporarily fixes a status quo in one or more alternative approaches while critically examining the claims of one provisionally central approach.

Language as Use

Cognitive linguists often focus on all four approaches at the same time, but applied linguists regularly combine two out of four in that they typically address language and thought as use. Apart from Lynne Cameron's series of workshops on metaphor-led discourse analysis, this combination of approaches was also evident from the papers by João Telles on (teacher) counseling and Maria Isabel Asperti Nardi on librarian training. Both Telles and Nardi address thought processes through the careful analysis of language use, but they also pay attention to language awareness and other aspects of language use as opposed to thought process.

The relation between approaching metaphor as part of language as use versus as part of thought as the use of a conceptual system is also important for Cameron's work. Her metaphor-led discourse analysis produces a list of expressions that qualify as metaphorical talk. However, Cameron is careful not to make unwarranted inferences about the presumably related metaphorical thought processes. If cognitive linguists have a tendency to see the linguistic patterns as evidence for underlying conceptual processes, applied linguists like Cameron are more skeptical or perhaps neutral about these postulated connections and ask for further validation (cf. Low 1999).

Cameron's approach to language as use is socio-cultural. Her approach to language as use is from one specific vantagepoint, namely as the process of interaction between individuals engaged in the discourse. A broad indication of this type of approach might be interactional sociolinguistics or conversation analysis of the kind represented by Gumperz, Schegloff, and others, although I am not sure whether Cameron would like to call herself that. My point is that this particular type of approach looks at language as use by focusing on the interaction patterns in the behavior of the language users. That is the decisive framework which facilitates Cameron's analysis of metaphorically used words as, for instance, "stepping stones" in an educational setting, or as "a rope bridge flung across a gorge" of affective distance between a perpetrator and a victim in a criminal setting. That is also the framework for deciding how metaphors in the language can be taken as indications of perspectives and attitudes of speakers, which is strictly speaking a matter of metaphor as thought. Cameron is aware of this and is careful to use the wording "metaphors *suggest* perspectives and attitudes": she remains true to her language as use approach, and the relation with thought as the use of a conceptual system is only one of possible implications for further research.

Another way in which Cameron is careful is in her alignment with a competing definition with language as use, which I would like to call, for want of a better term, the «textual» approach to language as use. This concerns the conceptualization of language use as a semiotic structure that exceeds the level of the sentence, and has to do with the analysis of relational, referential and topical coherence, discourse type, discourse form, and discourse content. These phenomena are all studied by Cameron from her interactional or socio-cultural perspective, and this perspective affects how observations are made about these textual aspects of metaphor in language use. For instance, it is not just observed that metaphors occur at the end of an episode of talk, but it is also observed that they function as summaries. Moreover, this is an observation that accords with previous findings of other interactional sociolinguists (e.g. Drew and Holt 1998), so that the interpretation of this phenomenon seems to have relatively high validity. When Cameron finds other textual patterns that are relatively novel in the metaphor literature, she is careful to hedge her conclusions by stating, for instance, that «There *may* be patterns in the dynamics of Topic and Vehicle utterances in episodes around metaphors." In my opinion, this displays a high level of sensitivity to the nature and limitations of the application of one perspective (the interactional one) to these data. It rightly alerts us to the need for further research in this area, with other data and with another perspective on language as use (the textual one), before any firm conclusions about this aspect of metaphor in language as use may be drawn.

Moving on to other plenary applied-linguistic paper at the conference, there is Nardi›s research on the interpretation, by a number of librarian trainees, of the metaphor *industrialists of information*. This paper takes us into the approach of metaphor as part of thought, and more specifically, thought as the use of a conceptual system. The first phase of Nardi's study is concerned with each student's process of metaphor comprehension and interpretation (Gibbs 1994), and she uses individual verbal protocols to track these cognitive processes (cf. Steen 1994; Cameron 2002).

What is interesting is that the procedure then involves a shift, from eliciting individual text processing to guiding the socially negotiated interpretation of the metaphor by the same subjects in an event of group reading. These are two rather different moments in the study. The first involves language use as a backgrounded and expressive medium of metaphorical thought, and may be seen as concerned with the process of metaphor interpretation. The second moment places language use much more in the foreground, as a constitutive interactional tool between students for understanding their own thought, while trying to construct a more detailed collaborative interpretation of the metaphor. Labeling this interaction process as "the socioconstruction of the interpretation of the target metaphor," in my view, is only applicable to the second phase: the first phase involves the participants' individual interpretation of the target metaphor and may be seen as a cognitive psychological study.

Nardi also points out the implications of the group interpretation of the target metaphor in students' understanding of their emergent model of the practice of librarianship. She affords insight into one moment of the process of understanding and constructing a detailed model of the future librarians' practice and of a new professional identity and self-image. The result of this process, a professional's completed self-image, is the main target of João Telles's study of a secondary school teacher's notions of teaching and language. He addresses the story of his participant about her development as a teacher, and interprets her story as a variant of the awakening of sleeping beauty.

My emphasis on the distinction between language as use versus thought as use may be helpful here in that it facilitates dealing with the tenacious relation between the teacher's words in the interviews on the one hand (language use) and the sleeping beauty theme behind the words that is reconstructed by the analyst on the other hand (thought as use). Since this connection is not self-evident, one may think of conducting further interviews which can clarify whether the participant does indeed see herself as a sleeping beauty who has awakened, and if so, in what respects, precisely. The distinction between approaches might make it easier to accept that further interviewing entails taking a step back from the original verbal data (language as use), which might otherwise remain the center of interest for an applied-*linguistic* study of this teacher's metaphors. Another differentiation that might follow from the proposed distinctions is the one between this self-image as a retrospective reconstruction of a personal past as opposed to this self-image as data about the genuine development itself. The latter could only be achieved if there were previous verbal protocols, through which the development of the story of sleeping beauty might be traced in a longitudinal fashion.

Tony Berber›s work, finally, on metaphor in early applied linguistics writing, starts at the opposite end of the scale. It starts out with patterns of metaphorical usage in a large corpus of written texts, and thereby backgrounds the thought that may lie behind any single incidence of a potentially metaphorical collocation. Instead, Berber aims to find recurrent possible underlying metaphors, which means that he is addressing conventional metaphor in the lexicon. If anything, his study lies on the border between language as use and language as system.

Apart from suggesting metaphorical senses for key lexical items, Berber›s work also suggests conventional metaphorical mappings, such as TEACHING IS CONSTRUCTION. The latter need to be tested for their validity in independent research on metaphor in conceptual systems, with the appropriate theories and methodology of this approach. This is precisely what ought to be done with all of the conventional metaphors proposed by cognitive linguistics, and this is precisely why the above-mentioned distinction between the four approaches is needed.

CONCLUSION

I have tried to show how the various general papers at the conference adopt different positions towards finding metaphor in language and thought. Some stop short of doing the actual empirical research and present philosophically fundamental queries regarding the theoretical conceptualization of the whole undertaking (Rajagopalan and Martins). I have argued that applied linguists need to remain aware of these issues, but should not hesitate in proceeding to formulate their own theoretical and operational standpoints for research.

Others emphasize that metaphor can also be approached as part of language regarded as a symbolic system, with such distinct levels of linguistic organization as morphology and the lexicon (Moura and Basilio). These research traditions, I have claimed, often come with their own assumptions about the role of language as a system during language use and cognitive process. It is not always unproblematic to adopt the findings or approaches of these traditions into a research project utilizing another approach, such as language as use. Therefore it takes some caution in deciding which aspects of these approaches to language as system should be taken on board in an applied linguistics project. However, at the same time, applied linguists cannot do without such assumptions about the language system, so that they are simply forced to make a choice about their language as system assumptions at some point.

The same holds true for assumptions about thought as a conceptual system, and thought as the use of that conceptual system during cognitive processing. We have seen how the findings of these approaches do play a role in applied linguistic research of various kinds, with reference to work by Cameron, Telles, Nardi, and Berber. My main point here has been to insist that most of the findings of applied linguists concern language as use. Such findings may allow for formulating implications for thought as use or language and thought as system, but these implications are tentative. They are hypotheses for further research that should be pursued within the framework of these alternative approaches themselves.

I wish to close this paper with a reference to the one plenary paper that I have not mentioned. Jacob Mey suggested that metaphors should not merely be approached as arising from language or thought and then taken as influences on our activities and environment. He proposed that we should turn this perspective round. Mey sees metaphors as pragmatic acts, or types of activities that have a special effect on our understanding. My own attitude to this proposal is that this may say something about the origin of some metaphors, but that it still requires or at least does not pre-empt an analysis of the cognitive and linguistic effects of these activities along the lines that I have suggested. It is true that a fully behavioral orientation to metaphor and the ways it is expressed demands attention to pragmatic acts, but it is also true that pragmatic acts cannot be accounted for solely from a social or interactional perspective. Therefore I should like to stick to the importance of the four approaches distinguished in this paper as the more central starting points for any study of metaphor in language and thought.

AUTHOR'S NOTE

I am grateful to Mauricio Carvalho, Heronides Moura, and Solange Vereza for their useful comments and suggestions.

REFERENCES

1. CAMERON, L. 1999a. Operationalising 'metaphor' for applied linguistic research. In L. CAMERON & G. LOW (Eds.),*Researching and applying metaphor* (pp. 3-28). Cambridge: Cambridge University Press.

2. _____. 1999b. Identifying and describing metaphor in spoken discourse data. In L. CAMERON & G. LOW (Eds.),*Researching and applying metaphor* (pp. 105-132). Cambridge: Cambridge University Press.

3. CAMERON, L. 2002. *Metaphor in educational discourse.* London and New York: Continuum.

4. _____ & LOW, G. 1999. Metaphor. *Language Teaching, 32,* 77-96.

5. _____ & LOW, G. (Eds.). 1999. *Researching and applying metaphor.* Cambridge: Cambridge University Press.

6. DREW, P., & HOLT, E. 1998. Figures of speech: figurative expressions and the management of topic transition in conversation. *Language in society, 27,* 495-522.

7. FAUCONNIER, G., & TURNER, M. 2002. *The way we think: Conceptual blending and the mind's hidden complexities.* New York: Basic Books.

8. GEERAERTS, D. 1997. *Diachronic prototype semantics: A contribution to historical lexicology.* Oxford: Oxford University Press.

9. GIBBS, R. W., jr. 1993. Process and products in making sense of tropes. In A. Ortony (Ed.), *Metaphor and thought, second edition* (pp. 252-276). Cambridge: Cambridge University Press.

10. _____. 1994. *The poetics of mind: figurative thought, language, and understanding.* Cambridge: Cambridge University Press.

11. _____. 1999a. *Intentions in the experience of meaning.* Cambridge: Cambridge University Press.

12. _____. 1999b. Researching metaphor. In L. CAMERON & G. LOW (Eds.), *Researching and applying metaphor* (pp. 29-47). Cambridge: Cambridge University Press

13. _____. 1999c. Taking metaphor out of our heads and putting it into the cultural world. In R. W. GIBBS, jr. & G. J. STEEN (Eds.), *Metaphor in cognitive linguistics* (pp. 145-166). Amsterdam: John Benjamins.

14. _____. 2000. Making good psychology out of blending theory. *Cognitive Linguistics, 11*(3/4), 347-358.

15. GLUCKSBERG, S. 2002. *Understanding figurative language.* New York: Oxford University Press.

16. GLUCKSBERG, S., & KEYSAR, B. 1993. How metaphors work. In A.

ORTONY (Ed.), *Metaphor and thought, second edition* (second ed., pp. 401-424). Cambridge: Cambridge University Press

17. GRADY, J. E. 1997. *Foundations of meaning: Primary metaphors and primary scenes.* Unpublished Ph D, University of California, Berkeley, Berkeley.

18. _____, OAKLEY, T., & COULSON, S. 1999. Blending and metaphor. In R. W. GIBBS, jr. & G. J. STEEN (Eds.),*Metaphor in cognitive linguistics* (pp. 101-124). Amsterdam: John Benjamins.

19. JACKENDOFF, R. 1996. Conceptual semantics and cognitive linguistics. *Cognitive Linguistics, 7*(1), 93-129.

20. _____. 2002. *Foundations of language: Brain, meaning, grammar, evolution.* Oxford: Oxford University Press.

21. LAKOFF, G. 1986. The meanings of literal. *Metaphor and Symbolic Activity, 1*(4), 291-296.

22. _____. 1993. The contemporary theory of metaphor. In A. ORTONY (Ed.), *Metaphor and thought* (second ed., pp. 202-251). Cambridge: Cambridge University Press.

23. _____. 1994. What is a conceptual system? In W. F. OVERTON & D. S. PALERMO (Eds.), *The nature and ontogenesis of meaning* (pp. 41-90). Hillsdale, NJ: Lawrence Erlbaum.

24. _____ & Johnson, M. 1980. *Metaphors we live by.* Chicago: Chicago University Press.

25. _____ & JOHNSON, M. 1999. *Philosophy in the flesh: The embodied mind and its challenge to western thought.* New York: Basic Books.

26. LOW, G. 1999. Validating metaphor research projects. In L. CAMERON & G. LOW (Eds.), *Researching and applying metaphor* (pp. 48-65). Cambridge: Cambridge University Press.

27. _____ & CAMERON, L. 2002. Applied-linguistic comments on the metaphor identification project. *Language and Literature, 11*(1), 84-90.

28. MURPHY, G. 1996. On metaphoric representation. *Cognition, 60*, 173-204.

29. _____. 1997. Reasons to doubt the present evidence for metaphoric representation. *Cognition, 62*, 99-108.

30. PUSTEJOVSKY, J. 1995. *The generative lexicon.* Cambridge, MA: MIT Press.

31. SCHIFFRIN, D., TANNEN, D., & HAMILTON, H. E. (Eds.). 2001. *The handbook of discourse analysis.* Oxford: Blackwell.

32. STEEN, G. J. 1994. *Understanding metaphor in literature: an empirical approach*. London: Longman.

33. _____. 1999. Genres of discourse and the definition of literature. *Discourse Processes, 28*(2), 109-120.

34. _____. 2001. A rhetoric of metaphor: linguistic and conceptual metaphor and the psychology of literature. In D. H. SCHRAM & G. J. STEEN (Eds.), *The Psychology and Sociology of Literature: In Honor of Elrud Ibsch* (Vol. 35, pp. 145-164). Amsterdam: John Benjamins.

35. _____. 2002a. Metaphor in Bob Dylan›s ‹Hurricane›: Genre, language, and style. In E. SEMINO & J. CULPEPPER (Eds.), *Cognitive stylistics: language and cognition in text analysis* (pp. 183-210). Amsterdam: John Benjamins.

36. _____. 2002b. Poetics and linguistics again: the role of genre. In S. CSABI & J. ZERKOWITZ (Eds.), *Textual secrets: the message of the medium* (pp. 42-51). Budapest: School of English and American Studies, Eotvos Lorand University Budapest.

37. _____. 2002c. Metaphor identification: A cognitive approach. *Style, 36*(3), 386-407.

38. _____ (Ed.). (In press). *Researching and applying metaphor across languages*. Special issue of *Journal of Pragmatics*.

39. _____ & GIBBS, R. W., jr. 1999. Introduction. In R. W. GIBBS, jr. & G. J. STEEN (Eds.), *Metaphor in Cognitive Linguistics* (pp. 1-8). Amsterdam: John Benjamins.

40. _____ & GIBBS, R. W., jr. (In preparation). *Finding metaphor in language and thought*. Amsterdam: John Benjamins.

41. TAYLOR, J. 1996. On running and jogging. *Cognitive Linguistics, 7*(1).

42. VERVAEKE, J., & KENNEDY, J. M. 1996. Metaphors in language and thought: Falsification and multiple meanings. *Metaphor and Symbol, 11*(4), 273-284.

Chapter 7

INCORPORATING LINGUISTIC KNOWLEDGE FOR LEARNING DISTRIBUTED WORD REPRESENTATIONS

Yan Wang[1], Zhiyuan Liu[1], Maosong Sun[1,2]

[1] State Key Laboratory of Intelligent Technology and Systems, Tsinghua National Laboratory for Information Science and Technology, Department of Computer Science and Technology, Tsinghua University, Beijing, China

[2] Jiangsu Collaborative Innovation Center for Language Competence, Jiangsu, China

ABSTRACT

Combined with neural language models, distributed word representations achieve significant advantages in computational linguistics and text mining. Most existing models estimate distributed word vectors from large-scale data in an unsupervised fashion, which, however, do not take rich linguistic knowledge into consideration. Linguistic knowledge can be represented as either link-based knowledge or preference-based knowledge, and we propose knowledge regularized word representation models (KRWR) to incorporate these prior knowledge for learning distributed word representations. Experiment results demonstrate that our estimated word representation achieves better performance in task of semantic relatedness ranking. This indicates that our methods can efficiently encode both prior knowledge from knowledge bases and statistical knowledge from large-scale text corpora into a unified word representation model, which will benefit many tasks in text mining.

INTRODUCTION

The performance of text mining is heavily dependent on word representation. The most widely used methods of word representation are vector space models (VSM) [1], which represent word meanings with vectors, with each dimension corresponding to semantic or syntactic information of words. VSM can be easily used to conduct similarity measures by computing distances between vectors, and thus are widely adopted in various applications such as information retrieval, text classification and question answering.

The basic idea of learning word representations is assuming contextual information of words provides a good clue to word meaning, and similar words tend to share similar distributions of contextual information. For instance, distributional semantic models (DSM) [2] use vectors to record contexts (e.g., co-occurring words) in which target words appear in a large corpus. It has long been known that simple co-occurrence counts do not work well for DSM. Techniques such as reweighting, smoothing and dimension reduction have been proposed to enhance performance [2]. However, these optimization techniques require heavily manual tuning. Moreover, DSM is non-trivial to be extended to higher level representation of sentences or documents.

By contrast, prediction-based methods are developed to build word representation. These methods estimate word vectors so as to maximize the predictive probability of the contexts when observing a target word in the corpus. Among these methods, neural language models (NLM) [3] are the most attractive due to their impressive characteristics.

- The dimension of word vectors in NLM is relatively lower (usually ranging from 10 to 2000). Its capability of representation grows at exponential speed with the increase of vector dimension. Since word meanings are represented as a vector of real values, it is named as *distributed word representation* or *word embedding*.

- The representation in continuous vector space brings easy measurement of similarity between two words, and complicated smoothing techniques are not necessary.

- Both syntactic and semantic properties of words are encoded into the unified word representations from large-scale corpora, which can be easily adopted by multi-task applications.

With these advantages, distributed word representation has shown its power with promising performance in many applications [4, 5].

A large-scale corpus is required for sufficient estimation of word vectors in distributed representation [3]. In the big data era, computational efficiency is becoming increasingly crucial, and many distributed representation methods based on neural networks heavily suffer from high computational complexity. To address the computational efficiency issue, recently two simple and powerful models have been proposed for learning distributed representation [6]: Continuous Bag-of-Words Model (CBOW) and Continuous Skip-gram Model. By discarding non-linear hidden layer, both the models manage to learn from large-scale corpora efficiently.

Most existing methods for distributed word representation are unsupervised and only learn from text corpora. As a matter of fact, people have constructed a variety of knowledge bases about words and languages. Seeing that tremendous linguistic knowledge is ready in these knowledge bases, it is fairly intuitive for us to consider incorporating the prior knowledge in word representation learning from text corpora.

We can gain great advantages by incorporating external prior knowledge into word representation learning.

- Prior knowledge provides more useful information from knowledge bases beyond statistics from corpora. For example, after knowing that both *car* and *automobile* refer to the same meaning in the real world, we conclude that they are synonyms. Although these two words share the same meaning, their context might not be so similar because they are often used in different linguistic styles. Hence, the prior knowledge may, to some extent, fix the bias of word vectors learned from corpora. The bias may be caused for various reasons, such as the domains of corpora, or statistical insufficiency of those low-frequency words.

- Many specific domains, such as some scientific research areas, usually maintain rich domain knowledge bases. When entering these domains, especially when domain-specific corpora are not sufficient enough compared to general corpora, the domain-specific prior knowledge will provide essential help to learn good domain-specific word representation. It will be of great significance for domain adaptation of text mining applications.

Moreover, knowledge bases are usually constructed manually and thus are more reliable than statistical methods. Various types of knowledge bases have been manually developed by human experts. Here are some typical ones:

- **WordNet** [7] is a lexical knowledge base for English, which groups English words into set of synonyms named as *synsets*. For example, the above-mentioned *car* and*automobile* lie in the same synset. Besides, WordNet also records semantic relations between these synsets, such as part-of and hypernym relations.

- **Word Association Network (WAN)** [8] is a dictionary produced from a word game. In this game, a person is shown a randomly-picked word, and is asked to write those words that he/she arises in mind. WAN records the association relations from given words to their associated words. For example, people may tend to associate with *Christmas* when given the word *gift*.

- **PPDB** [9] is a database of paraphrase rules extracted automatically by comparing millions of paraphrase pairs. This database classifies paraphrase rules into four classes including lexical rules, one-to-many rules, phrasal rules and syntactic rules. Each of the lexical rules contains two words (w_i, w_j) indicating that w_j can replace w_i when paraphrasing. Almost for each lexical rule (w_i, w_j), there is an inverse rule (w_j, w_i). So we can extract many word pairs that share the same semantic meanings.

Knowledge bases usually contain complicated and heterogenous information. It is unnecessary and impossible to take all of them into consideration. In this paper, we consider the semantic relevance information between words provided by knowledge bases for word representation learning. The semantic relevance knowledge can be represented as either link-based knowledge or preference-based knowledge:

- **Link-based Knowledge.** We can use links to represent semantic relevance between words, i.e., a link between two words indicating they are relevant and no link indicating irrelevant. For example, we can transform either synsets in WordNet or associations in WAN into link-based knowledge. Moreover, we can also assign weights to links as relatedness between words.

- **Preference-based Knowledge.** The preference-based knowledge does not assign absolute relatedness score between words, and only records preference ranks according to relatedness. Take WAN for example, for a given word, we can rank associated words according to the number of people mentioning them, and provide preference-based knowledge of word pairs.

Link-based knowledge and preference-based knowledge are two distinct types of word knowledge, and require different techniques to incorporate into word representation.

In some cases, link-based knowledge can be transformed into preference-based knowledge. For example, we could simply rank word pairs according to their relatedness scores in link-based knowledge, or pick any linked word pairs against any unlinked pairs to build preference-based knowledge. It is usually difficult for people to objectively and sophisticatedly determine the absolute relatedness scores of word pairs in isolation. People may concern more about the preference among word pairs. Hence, it may be more reliable to consider preference-based knowledge instead of weighted link-based knowledge.

The transformation apparently does not work all the time. Take synsets in WordNet for example, we only know the words in a synset are relevant to each other, but do not know which pairs are more relevant than another. Moreover, link-based knowledge does provide relevant word pairs, but does not indicate all remaining pairs are irrelevant. Hence, we cannot simply regard linked word pairs preferred thank all unlinked pairs.

In this paper, we take prior word knowledge into distributed word representation, and propose a unified framework named as **Knowledge Regularized Word Representation (KRWR)**. In principle, KRWR works for all methods of distributed word representation, but since it is impossible to investigate the effectiveness of all representation models, we only take CBOW as the typical model for study because of its efficiency on big data and recent popularity. Experiments on real-world data sets demonstrate the learned word vectors can successfully encode prior knowledge, which will greatly benefit a collection of text mining applications.

CBOW Model

The architecture of Continuous Bag-of-Words Model proposed in [6] is similar to the feed-forward neural-network language model (NNLM). It is named as a bag-of-words model because all words within the context window are projected to the same position in projection layer, without considering the order of words. The non-linear hidden layer in NNLM is removed to accelerate training process.

In CBOW model, each word corresponds to a unique vector, represented as a column in a word matrix $W \in \mathbb{R}^{K \times V}$, where K is the dimension of a word vector, and V is the size of word vocabulary. Given each window in a sentence, the sum of contextual word vectors is used as features to predict the target word. The framework of CBOW model is demonstrated in Fig. 1.

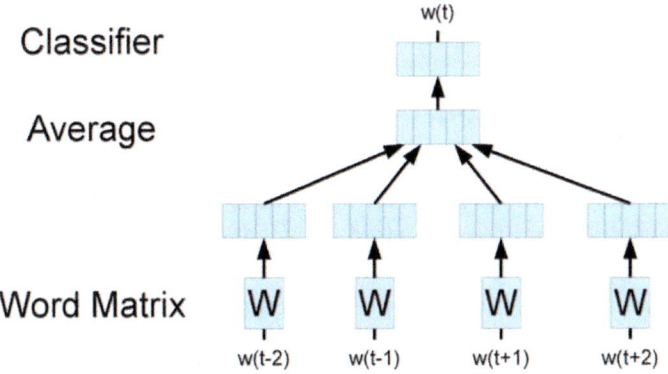

Figure 1: CBOW model.

Formally, given a sequence of words, $D = (w_1, \ldots, w_T)$, the objective function of the CBOW model is to maximize the average log-likelihood,

$$L(D) = \sum_{t < |T|} \log \Pr \left(w_t | w_{t-s}, \ldots, w_{t-1}, w_{t+1}, \ldots, w_{t+s} \right)$$

(1)

where the windows size is $2s+1$. The prediction task is a typical multi-class classification problem.

We denote the context $(w_{t-s},\ldots,w_{t-1},w_{t+1},\ldots,w_{t+s})$ as w_c. The prediction probability can be typically defined with a *softmax* fashion as follows,

$$\Pr(w_t|w_c) = \frac{\exp(g(w_t, w_c))}{\sum_i \exp(g(w_i, w_c))} \tag{2}$$

where $g(w_t,w_c)$ indicates the un-normalized log-probability for each output word w_t. In CBOW model, the probability is simply defined as

$$g(w_t, w_c) = \vec{w}_t \cdot \vec{w}_c \tag{3}$$

where $\vec{w}$ indicates the distributed embedding vector for a word w, and the operator $\cdot$ is the dot product of two vectors. For implementation, *hierarchical softmax* [10] is adopted to softmax for training, and we follow the work in [6] and build a binary Huffman tree as the structure of hierarchical softmax. The training complexity is $T\times K+K\times\log(V)$, where T is the window size, K is the dimension of word vectors and V is the size of vocabulary.

In this paper, we present our method based on the CBOW model, i.e. Knowledge Regularized CBOW (KCBOW), and implement based on an open source project *word2vec* [6, 11] (https://code.google.com/p/word2vec/). Note that, our work can be easily extended to other methods of distributed word representation.

Prior Knowledge Construction in KCBOW

As mentioned in the introduction section, from knowledge bases including but not limited to WordNet, WAN and PPDB, we can extract either link-based knowledge or preference-based knowledge. Link-based knowledge and preference-based knowledge are related to each other but not identical. We take WordNet and WAN for example, to demonstrate the construction of prior knowledge.

Link-Based Knowledge Construction

In WordNet, each synset indicates a unique word sense, usually including several words with identical or similar semantic meanings. There are also multiple types of relations between synsets, such as part-of and hypernym. In Fig. 2, we demonstrate a small miniature of topology in WordNet, by taking the word *bank* as our focus. From the figure, we observe that the word *bank*, as a polysemous word, appears in multiple synsets (represented with dashed circles) and connects them together. Meanwhile, the relation hyponym/hypernym between synsets (represented with arrow) also connects synsets together.

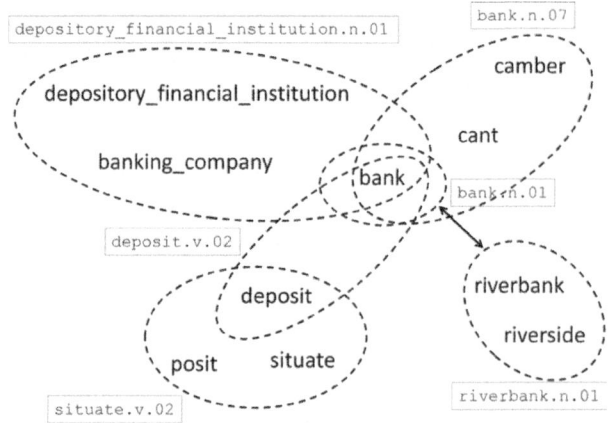

Figure 2: A small miniature of topology in WordNet.

The word *bank* is related to many other words by synsets (represented with dashed circles) and hyponym/hypernym relationship (represented with arrow).

Based on synsets and relations, we can build a word graph and construct link-based knowledge as shown in Fig. 3. In this graph, two connected words are considered to be semantically related with each other.

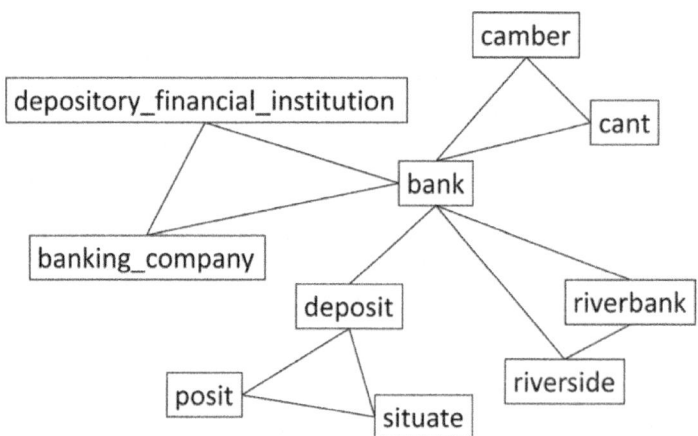

Figure 3: Link-based knowledge is constructed according to the topology as shown in Fig. 2.

Formally, we construct a prior knowledge matrix $P \in \mathbb{R}^{V \times V}$, in which $P_{ij} = p(w_i, w_j)$ is the relatedness between the ith word and the jth word in vocabulary. According to Fig. 3, we can simply set $p(w, v) = 1$ if there is a link between the word w and w, and otherwise $p(w, v) = 0$. We can also employ other sophisticated measures to compute semantic relatedness between words according to the topology of WordNet, such as the shortest-path method, et al. However, these measures are not guaranteed to be always correct, and hence in this paper we select the above-mentioned simple version.

Preference-Based Knowledge Construction

Preference-based knowledge provides a different perspective as compared to link-based knowledge. The preference-based knowledge is essential for the following two reasons: (1) Under some circumstances, link-based knowledge is not available or sufficient. (2) Sometimes we may care more about the preference order by relatedness of word pairs, instead of the absolute relatedness scores of word pairs in isolation. Take WAN for example, each word may be associated to tens or hundreds of words in different number of times. We cannot well distinguish which word pairs should be linked together and which are not. In this case, it is more appropriate for us to construct preference-based knowledge according to the number of association times instead of link-based knowledge.

We construct preference-based knowledge P from WAN as follow. For a word w_s in a WAN, suppose the associated word list is $\{(w_1, c_1), \ldots, (w_L, c_L)\}$, where c_i is the association count indicating how many people associates the word w_i given the word w_s, and L is the list size. For each two words w_i and w_j in this list, if $c_i > c_j$, we can get the preference-based knowledge $w_i > w_j$, meaning that the word w_c prefers to be more related to w_i compared to w_j. We can thus get a preference-based knowledge fact $(w_s, w_i, w_j) \in P$, indicating $w_i > w_j$ with respect to the target word w_s. Note that, if two words are equally associated to the target word, we will not build preference-based knowledge for them. We exclude triples in which two words are equally associated to the target word.

Take the word *bank* for example, in WAN its top-3 association words are $\{(money, 115), (account, 5), (robber, 5)\}$. According to the list, we can build the following preference-based knowledge (*bank, money, account*) and (*bank, money, robber*).

The idea of preference-based knowledge is, to some extent, related to the framework of learning to rank in information retrieval [12, 13]. Link-based knowledge and preference-based knowledge can transfer to each other: (1) For any $p(w_s, w_i) > p(w_s, w_j)$ in link-based knowledge, we can construct a preference-based knowledge fact (w_s, w_i, w_j). (2) For any (w_s, w_i, w_j) in preference-based knowledge, we can simply construct link-based knowledge $p(w_s, w_i)$ $= m$ and $p(w_s, w_j) = n$ guaranteeing $m > n$. However, the transformation usually introduces noise and loses information. For example, the transformation in Type (1) may lose the scoring information of $p(w_s, w_i)$ and $p(w_s, w_j)$, and the setting of m, n in Type (2) will introduce much noise.

In summary, link-based knowledge and preference-based knowledge provide us distinct perspectives to prior knowledge, and in the following section, we will show how to learn distributed word representation with the prior knowledge.

Learning Word Representation with Prior Knowledge

We propose a new framework for learning distributed word representation by incorporating prior knowledge as a regularizer. The idea of the regularization is straightforward: words which are semantically relevant to each other should have similar vectors. Formally, we define a regularized likelihood as follows,

$$O(D, P) = (1 - \lambda)L(D) + \lambda R(D, P), \tag{4}$$

where $L(D)$ is the log-likelihood of the word sequence D, and $R(D,P)$ is a harmonic regularizer defined on prior knowledge P, and λ is the harmonic factor, with a range $[0, 1]$. The learning algorithm will aim to maximize $O(D,P)$. When $\lambda = 0$, optimizing $O(D,P)$ is identical to maximizing $L(D)$, and when $\lambda = 1$, the optimization of $O(D,P)$ will only depend on prior knowledge.

Learning with Link-Based Knowledge

For link-based knowledge, we define $R(D,P)$ as follows,

$$R(D, P) = \sum_{w, v \in V} p(w, v) \log r(w, v), \tag{5}$$

where $p(w,v)$ indicates the prior relatedness between the words w and v, and $r(w,v)$ is the relatedness measured with distributed representation vectors of w and v. The relatedness $r(w,v)$ can be measured with various methods. For example, we can define $r(w,v)$ with softmax probability,

$$r(w, v) = \frac{\exp(g(w, v))}{\sum_{v'} \exp(g(w, v'))}. \tag{6}$$

In this case, $r(w,v) \neq r(v,w)$, and thus we will consider the cases in both sides in Eq. (5). In the following sections, this regularizer is referred to as Softmax Probability Regularizer (SPR).

We can also adopt Euclidean distance to measure the relatedness, i.e.,

$$r(w, v) = \exp\left(-\parallel \vec{w} - \vec{v} \parallel_2^2\right).$$

(7)

We refer to this regularizer as Euclidean Regularizer (ER). Note that, Euclidean distance is not compatible with hierarchical softmax used for optimizing $L(D)$.

The prior relatedness between w and v may be asymmetric, i.e., $p(w,v) \neq p(v,w)$; meanwhile$r(w,v) \neq r(v,w)$. Hence, we formalize $R(D,P)$ as follows,

$$R(D, P) = \frac{\lambda}{2} \sum_{w,v \in V} \left(p(w, v) \log r(w, v) + p(v, w) \log r(v, w)\right).$$

Take the format of SPR for example, we finally have the objective function as follows,

$$O(D,P) = (1 - \lambda) \sum_{t < |T|} \log \frac{\exp(\vec{w}_t \cdot \vec{w}_c)}{\sum_i \exp(\vec{w}_i \cdot \vec{w}_c)}$$
$$+ \frac{\lambda}{2} \sum_{w,v \in V} \left(p(w, v) \log \frac{\exp(\vec{w} \cdot \vec{v})}{\sum_{v'} \exp(\vec{w} \cdot \vec{v'})} + p(v, w) \log \frac{\exp(\vec{w} \cdot \vec{v})}{\sum_{w'} \exp(\vec{w'} \cdot \vec{v})}\right).$$

(8)

Learning with Preference-Based Knowledge

With preference-based knowledge, we consider the preference relations between two word pairs. Given a preference fact $(w_s, w_i, w_j) \in P$, we want to make sure $r(w_s, w_i) > r(w_s, w_j)$. That is, we want to make sure w_s is more related with w_i as compared to w_j. In this paper, we propose two methods to define $R(D,P)$ for preference-based knowledge.

It is straightforward for us to model preference-based knowledge using a margin-based ranking criterion, defined as follows,

$$R(D, P) = \sum_{(w_s, w_i, w_j) \in P} \left[r(w_s, w_i) - r(w_s, w_j) - \gamma\right]_-,$$

(9)

where $r(w,v)$ is the semantic relatedness between the words w and v measured with distributed representation vectors of w and v, $[x]_-$ denotes the negative part of x, and γ is a hyper-parameter indicating the margin. The regularizer is named as Margin Regularizer (MR). As mentioned in the last section, $r(w,v)$ can be calculated with either softmax probability or Euclidean relatedness. In empirical experiments, we find that the performance of MR with softmax probability is poor as compared to the other methods. Hence, we only show the results of using Euclidean relatedness for MR.

Alternatively, inspired by the idea of Negative Sampling [11], for a preference-based knowledge fact $(w_s, w_i, w_j) \in P$, we can also distinguish the more related word w_i from w_j using logistic regression, and thus define $R(D,P)$ as follows,

$$R(D, P) = \sum_{(w_s, w_i, w_j) \in P} \log \sigma(\vec{w}_s \cdot \vec{w}_i) + \log \sigma\left(-\vec{w}_s \cdot \vec{w}_j\right),$$

$$(10)$$

where $\sigma(x)=1/(1+\exp(-x))$ is the sigmoid function. Following negative sampling, we use inner product between two word vectors to indicate their relatedness. The regularization is named as Negative Sampling Regularizer (NSR).

There are two differences between MR and NSR: (1) They use different methods to measure semantic relatedness between two words, MR with Euclidean distance and NSR with inner product. (2) MR set a margin between two word pairs, which enhances the discrimination ability of MR as compared to NSR. Meanwhile, the performance of MR is sensitive to the setting of the margin.

Similar to the modeling method of link-based knowledge, we can incorporate $R(D,P)$ with existing representation modeling method $L(D)$ into $O(D,P)$. In the following section, we will introduce the methods for parameter estimation.

Parameter Estimation

We learn KCBOW models using stochastic gradient descent (SGD). In $O(D,P)$, $L(D)$ and $R(D,P)$ are learned with different data sets, but aim at learning a unified distributed word representation. For the $L(D)$ part, we apply the idea in [6, 11] and adopt both hierarchical softmax and negative sampling for optimization. For $R(D,P)$, we propose two schemes for learning: joint optimization and post optimization.

Joint Optimization (JO). In *word2vec*, word representation is learned using the asynchronous version of stochastic gradient descent (ASGD), with multiple threads, using different training data and updating shared word vectors. It is thus straightforward for us to perform joint optimization of $L(D)$ and $R(D,P)$ with multiple threads. Each thread is assigned to optimize either $L(D)$ or $R(D,P)$ with thread-specific data, and update shared word vectors.

Post Optimization (PO). As mentioned in the previous section, Euclidean distance is not compatible with hierarchical softmax used for optimizing $L(D)$, and thus cannot perform joint optimization. We hence propose post optimization for ER and MR. That is, after the learning of $L(D)$ or the joint optimization of $O(D,P)$, we take the learned word representation as a new starting point, and begin to optimize $R(D,P)$ according to ER (Eq. (7)) and MR (Eq. (9)). However, this may cause overfitting. Therefore, we may modify Eq. (7) and Eq. (9) to avoid overfitting, defined as follows,

$$R'(D, P) = R(D, P) - \delta \left(\| \vec{w}_s - \vec{w}_s' \| + \| \vec{w}_i - \vec{w}_i' \| + \| \vec{w}_j - \vec{w}_j' \| \right) \tag{11}$$

where $\vec{w}_s', \vec{w}_i' \text{ and } \vec{w}_j'$ are original word vectors learned before post optimization, and δ ranges from 0.0 to 1.0. By adding the second formula in Eq. (11) as a penalty, we prevent the optimization from moving word vectors too far away from original learned vectors. Obviously, other optimization methods for $R(D,P)$ can also be used in post optimization, by simply adding the penalty formula.

Note that, for SPR and ER of link-based knowledge and MR of preference-based knowledge, we can perform both joint optimization and post optimization, whereas for NSR of preference-based knowledge, we can only perform post optimization.

Model initialization plays an important role in deep learning. In joint optimization, we initialize all dimensions of vectors with random small real numbers. In post optimization, we first randomly initialize the vectors before pre-training CBOW and then take these pre-trained vectors to initialize the regularization process.

Experiments and Analysis

In this section, we first introduce the datasets and construction of prior knowledge, then describe the evaluation tasks, metrics and results, and analyze the influence of some parameters. At the end of this section, we evaluate our models with the task of semantic relatedness ranking to demonstrate that, incorporating prior knowledge is critical to improve the quality of distributed word representation.

Datasets

We select July 2013 snapshot of Wikipedia (http://dumps.wikimedia.org/enwiki/20130708/) and extract all articles with Wikipedia Extractor (http://medialab.di.unipi.it/wiki/Wikipedia_Extractor) as training corpora of distributed word representation. The vocabulary consists of about 185 thousand words which appear more than 100 times in the corpora. There are 1.36 billion tokens in the training corpora in total. All tokens are transformed to lower case.

During the training process, we ignore those tokens that are not included in the vocabulary.

In our experiments, we select three datasets to construct link-based knowledge and preference-based knowledge, including WordNet, WAN and PPDB.

WordNet (http://wordnet.princeton.edu/) [7] is a large English lexical knowledge base. In WordNet, nouns, verbs, adjectives and adverbs are manually grouped into sets of synonyms (synsets), with each expressing a distinct concept. Synsets are connected with each other according to their semantic and lexical relations. WordNet contains about 150 thousand words organized in about 120 thousand synsets. In this paper, we extract link knowledge from WordNet version 2.1 with the help of JWI (http://projects.csail.mit.edu/jwi/). We consider two relations in WordNet to construct link-based knowledge: (1) It is straightforward that, for each pair of words in the same synset, they are linked since they share the same word sense. However, there are usually not many words in each synset on average. It is not sufficient to construct link-based knowledge using only synsets. (2) We also consider relations between synsets to construct link-based knowledge. To be specific, if synset S_i and S_j are linked by a certain kind of relation, then we add links between all pairs (w,v) if and only if $w \in S_i$ and $v \in S_j$.

The University of South Florida Free Association Norms [8] (http://w3.usf.edu/FreeAssociation/) is a large WAN database, involving more than 6,000 participants. 5,019 words are selected as cues and three quarters of a million responses are collected. This database offers 72,000 word pairs and a sample of it is shown in Table 1. #G is the size of participant group given the cue word, and #P is number of participants who produce the target. For example, given cue word *bank*, 115 out of 144 participants produce the response of *money*. This dataset can construct both link-based knowledge and preference-based knowledge. We select triples $\{(w_s,w_i,w_j)\}$ that meet the criteria $(\#P_s(i)-\#P_s(j))/\#G > 0.02$ to construct knowledge.

Table 1: Sample of University of South Florida Free Association Norms

Cue	Target	#G	#P
bank	money	144	115
bank	account	144	5
bank	robber	144	5
bank	teller	144	4
bank	loan	144	2
bank	vault	144	2

doi:10.1371/journal.pone.0118437.t001

PPDB [9] (http://www.cis.upenn.edu/~ccb/ppdb/) is a paragraph dataset with over 220 million English paraphrase pairs, consisting of 73 million phrasal and 8 million lexical paraphrases. PPDB is organized in six packages ranging from S (Small) to XXXL (3-eXtreme Large), with different trade-off between precision and coverage. We choose the lexical rules of XL, XXL and XXXL packages as link-based knowledge. There are overlaps among the three packages.

For all datasets, we abandon the links and triples containing words not included in our vocabulary. For each of the datasets, we randomly select around 1/25 of links or preference triples to construct testing sets, and the rest form training sets. The actual number of links in each set is listed in Table 2.

Table 2: Number of Links in Different Datasets

Dataset	Training Set (thousand)	Testing Set (thousand)
XL	125	5
XXL	598	30
XXXL	2640	100
WN	2000	80
WAN	68	3

doi:10.1371/journal.pone.0118437.t002

To better distinguish different datasets, we assign each dataset a name. In this section, the datasets with name of XL, XXL and XXXL correspond to packages from PPDB. WN and WAN refer to WordNet and the University of South Florida Free Association Norms, respectively. Datasets with suffix "-Train" refer to the training sets with which we train the model, and those with suffix "-Test" refer to the testing sets. For link-based knowledge, we construct datasets named XL-Train, XL-Test, XXL-Train, XXL-Test, XXXL-Train, XXXL-Test, WN-Train, WN-Test, WAN-Train, WAN-Test. For preference-based knowledge, we have WANP-Train and WANP-Test datasets, which consist of about 263,000 and 10,000 triples respectively.

Evaluation Tasks and Metrics

To demonstrate that our model can efficiently encode the prior knowledge, we use the training sets to learn distributed word representation, and evaluate the models on testing sets. Since a training set and the corresponding testing set are extracted from the same knowledge source, a model that successfully encodes the prior knowledge in training set should be more consistent with the prior knowledge in testing set than the model trained without prior knowledge.

For link-based knowledge, we evaluate models by measuring the relatedness of word pairs in testing sets. The relatedness of a pair of words is calculated using the inner product of two word vectors. We assume the words in each pair in both training set and testing set are related with each other, hence a higher average relatedness of word pairs measured with our models indicates more consistency between the learned model and the testing link-based knowledge.

For preference-based knowledge, we evaluate models in the fashion of classification. For each triple (w_s, w_i, w_j), if a learned model meets $\vec{w}\ s\cdot\vec{w}\ i > \vec{w}\ s\cdot\vec{w}\ j$, then the model correctly classifies the triple. In this way, we can use the accuracy of a model on a set of triples to measure the performance.

Parameter Settings

We use hierarchical softmax and negative sampling with 12 threads to train CBOW model as our baseline. In all of the following experiments, the dimension of each word vector is 500, and the window size is 15. The learning rate of SGD decreases linearly from a fixed initial value to 0.

It is obvious that a model will learn prior knowledge more sufficiently if running more SGD iterations in regularization threads. In experiments, the ratio of threads for learning $L(D)$ and $R(D,P)$ is set between 5:1 and 10:1 to get the best performance. That is, when five to ten threads are used for learning $L(D)$, we will set one thread for learning $R(D,P)$ with prior knowledge. Since the number of iterations in regularization threads exerts greater influence on the result, we focus on controlling the iterations of regularization threads instead of setting λ to balance $L(D)$ and $R(D,P)$ in Joint Optimization. We leave further discussion about the influence of iteration times in section 4.5.

There is a technical trick when training Euclidean Regularizer to improve performance. During each iteration of post optimization, we do not optimize each single link in isolation. Instead, for each word, we find all other words that link to this word and calculate the average vector of all word vectors as the center of all these words. We optimize the Euclidean distance between the target word and this center rather than the sum of distances between the target word and linked words. This will reduce the influence of noisy links in prior knowledge.

Experiment Results

With WN-Train dataset, we train different models with different optimization methods to compare the performance. The average relatedness achieved by various models are shown in Table 3. In this table, JO-SPR indicates Softmax Probability Regularizer trained by Joint Optimization, PO-SPR means Softmax

Probability Regularizer trained by Post Optimization, and PO-ER means Euclidean Regularizer trained by Post Optimization.

Table 3: Average Relatedness of Different Methods

Method	WN-Train	WN-Test
CBOW	0.084	0.083
JO-SPR	0.432	0.423
PO-SPR	0.153	0.153
PO-ER	**0.465**	**0.464**

doi:10.1371/journal.pone.0118437.t003

From the table, we observe that, the models of JO-SPR and PO-ER achieve much higher consistency with the testing link-based knowledge than the original CBOW model. This indicates that, these models have successfully encoded the given knowledge into distributed word representations. It seems that PO-SPR is not so good as the other two models.

Afterwards, we use JO-SPR to train with different datasets to demonstrate that our model could learn from any set of link-based knowledge, from small sets such as WAN-Train, to large sets such as WN-Train and XXXL-Train. We also merge all training sets and train our model with the mixture of all link-based knowledge. The results of average relatedness on link-based knowledge are shown in Table 4. In this table, the column "Single Set" means that the JO-SPR model is trained using the training set of one dataset, and then evaluated on the training set itself or the corresponding testing set. The column "Multiple Sets" means that the JO-SPR model is trained using the link-based knowledge from all training sets and then evaluated on each dataset.

Table 4: Average Relatedness on Different Datasets

Dataset	CBOW	Single Set	Multiple Sets
XL-Train	0.199	0.321	0.286
XL-Test	0.199	0.271	0.282
XXL-Train	0.141	0.254	0.218
XXL-Test	0.142	0.224	0.213
XXXL-Train	0.090	0.206	0.143
XXXL-Test	0.091	0.189	0.139
WN-Train	0.084	0.432	0.278
WN-Test	0.083	0.423	0.273
WAN-Train	0.161	0.241	0.192
WAN-Test	0.161	0.205	0.189

doi:10.1371/journal.pone.0118437.t004

On each data set, the JO-SPR model significantly outperforms CBOW. Our model can learn link-based knowledge from all kinds of sources. On relative small datasets like XL-Train, the average relatedness of the JO-SPR model on XL-Test is apparently lower than that on XL-Train, as compared to large datasets. This indicates that the JO-SPR model exhibits more severe overfitting on small datasets, because the regularization threads will execute more iterations for a small prior knowledge. This issue will be discussed in detail in the next subsection.

On the other hand, when we combine knowledge from different sources together for learning a unique model, as shown in the column "Multiple Sets", there will be much less overfitting. Our model performs nearly identical on both training sets and testing sets. Meanwhile, the performance on each dataset is consistently lower than that of training with only the corresponding training dataset. The reasons are: (1) datasets from different sources are not completely consistent with each other; and (2) the average number of iterations for each link is diluted so the learning process might be not so sufficient.

To better visualize the performance on different datasets, the results on testing sets are also shown in Fig. 4. The improvement of our model on average relatedness depends on the datasets. Especially on WN-Test, the average relatedness of our model is about 5 times as compared to the original CBOW model, which indicates that the links in WordNet is more consistent inherently. It is not surprising because WordNet is built by several experts with more stable criteria and thus contains less noise.

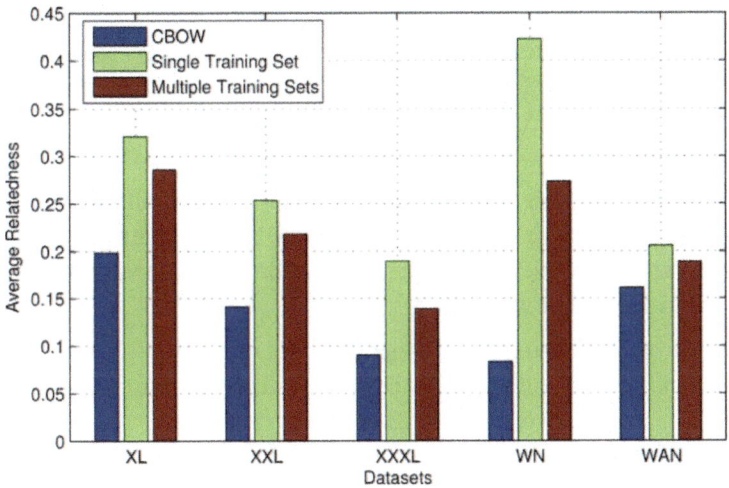

Figure 4: Average relatedness.

To learn preference-based knowledge, we train Negative Sampling Regularizer with Joint Optimization (JO-NSR) and Margin Regularizer with Post Optimization (PO-MR). The results of preference classification accuracy are shown in Table 5. JO-NSR shows great improvement in accuracy as compared to the original CBOW model, and PO-MR can fit the data with significant accuracy. In Section 4.6, we will demonstrate that PO-MR model has drawback of overfitting.

Table 5: Preference Classification Precision of Different Methods

Method	WANP-Train	WANP-Test
CBOW	0.628	0.628
JO-NSR	0.746	0.717
PO-MR	0.942	0.914

doi:10.1371/journal.pone.0118437.t005

INFLUENCE OF ITERATION TIMES IN JOINT OPTIMIZATION

For the JO scheme, the number of iterations in SGD directly influences the consistency between learned vectors and prior knowledge. We take two strategies to control the number of iterations and explore its influences.

- Change the numbers of threads for learning from raw corpora and prior knowledge, respectively. Since the overall computation of learning from raw corpora is almost constant, hence creating more threads for regularization will lead to more regularization iterations.

- Let the threads for learning from prior knowledge sleep for a short period (typically from 10 ms to 500 ms) every 1000 iterations. This strategy can reduce the number of regularization iterations arbitrarily.

Considering that different datasets are of different scale, it is more reasonable to control the relative iteration times rather than absolute iteration times. Take JO-SPR with link-based knowledge for an example, we control the number of iterations divided by the number of links, i.e., the iteration times per link, as the independent variable.

We train with link-based knowledge from datasets of XXXL and WAN separately and evaluate the average relatedness of both training set and testing set of XXXL and WAN. The results are shown in Fig. 5. As the increase of iteration times per link, the average relatedness increases at first, then decreases after the peak is achieved. The reason is that, too many iteration times will lead to overfitting on training sets and make the average relatedness on testing sets drop.

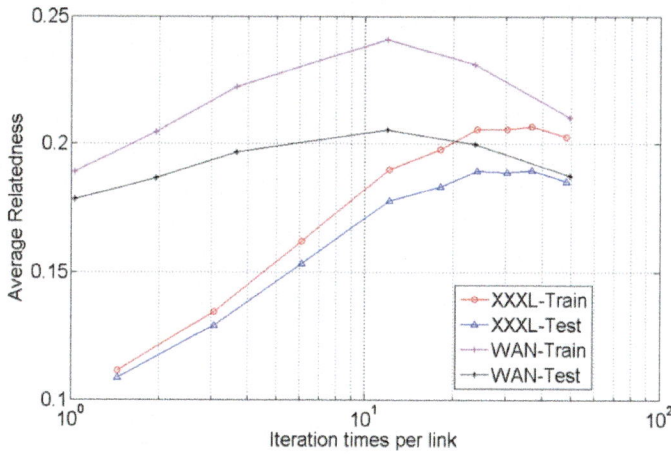

Figure 5: Influence of iterations per Link.

Another observation is that higher average relatedness on training set is accompanied by larger divergence in average relatedness between training set and testing set. It is important to realize trade-offs between fitting the knowledge and ensuring the generalization. This is a common issue that should be taken into consideration for most statistical learning algorithms.

Semantic Relatedness Ranking

In the previous subsections, we have demonstrated that our models can successfully incorporate the prior knowledge into distributed word representations. However, the previous evaluation is not enough, because the goal of incorporating prior knowledge is to obtain high quality word representations rather than just fitting knowledge bases. Therefore, we further investigate the performance of word representations for semantic relatedness ranking after incorporating prior knowledge.

Semantic relatedness ranking is a classical task to evaluate quality of word representations. The evaluation dataset usually contains a list of word pairs. For each word pair, human annotators are asked to determine how semantically related they are, and the annotations are considered as gold standard. Given the evaluation dataset, word representation models can also compute the semantic relatedness of these word pairs. Then the Spearman's rank correlation coefficient (Spearman's ρ) between human and model rankings could be used to measure the quality of word representations.

Wordsim-353 [14] is a widely-used dataset for semantic relatedness ranking. It has been used to evaluate many different word representation systems. Word representation with multiple prototypes [15] aims to build multiple distinct vectors for all senses of a word, which is expected to be more discriminative than traditional word representation methods. Tiered clustering [16] proposes a mixture model to derive multiple prototype representations for word senses, which can also be used to measure word relatedness. The two methods both achieve a score of about 0.77. WN30G [17] utilizes WordNet to determine the semantic relatedness between word pairs and achieves a Spearman's ρ of 0.66. ESA [18] is another knowledge-based method that learns distributional representations of words with the favor of Wikipedia and achieves a score of 0.75.

In Table 6, we list the Spearman's ρ of some previous work and our models. For our models, we also consider mixing various knowledge sources. The mixing method is straightforward, i.e., we incorporate one type of knowledge in joint optimization and incorporate another type of knowledge in post optimization. In Table 6 we use JO-SPR and PO-ER to mix two types of knowledge, including XXXL + WN and WAN + WN.

Table 6: Spearman's ρ on Wordsim-353 Dataset

Model	Knowledge	WS353
Multiple Prototypes	-	0.770
Tiered Clustering	-	0.769
WN30G	WordNet	0.660
ESA	Wikipedia	0.750
CBOW	-	0.734
JO-SPR	XL	0.756
JO-SPR	XXL	0.754
JO-SPR	XXXL	0.765
JO-SPR	WN	0.746
JO-SPR	WAN	0.758
PO-ER	WN	0.764
JO-NSR	WANP	0.734
PO-MR	WANP	0.707
JO-SPR, PO-ER	XXXL, WN	**0.778**
JO-SPR, PO-ER	WAN, WN	**0.784**

doi:10.1371/journal.pone.0118437.t006

From Table 6 we observe that JO-SPR combined with PO-ER achieves the best Spearman's of 0.784, outperforming both pure unsupervised learning method and traditional knowledge-based methods. From the table, we conclude that: (1) Link-based knowledge is helpful to enhance the quality of distributed word representations, and different datasets bring improvements in different degrees. (2) Preference-based knowledge does not directly contribute to improvements in this task. Perhaps information depicted by preference-based knowledge is too detailed, and cannot have a good coverage over the evaluation dataset. (3) It is acceptable that JO-NSR learns preference-based knowledge without hurting the overall quality of word representation. But for PO-MR the strong tendency of fitting knowledge is harmful in the task due to overfitting. (4) Better representations can be produced by mixing various knowledge sources with different methods into one single model. According to our experiments, the combinations of JO-SPR trained with XXXL or WAN dataset and PO-ER trained with WN dataset beat all other models trained with single datasets. This indicates that, appropriate combinations of knowledge sources may significantly improve the quality of distributed word representations.

In experiments, we have tried to decrease the ratio of threads for learning $L(D)$ and $R(D,P)$ to emphasize the role of prior knowledge. We find that when the thread ratio comes to 9:6, the performance on wordsim-353 reduces to less than 0.4. The reason may be that, the coverage of prior knowledge is not extensive enough to provide sufficient information for learning good representation itself, and thus can only work as supplementary information.

We also analyze the variances of word-pair ranking lists obtained by CBOW and our model of JO-SPR (XXXL) + PPO-ER (WN). We regard the human-annotated rankings of word pairs as gold standard. Our model makes 193 out of 353 word pairs closer to the gold standard rankings. If we only consider the 123 word pairs with the most significant ranking variances (the ranking change is over 35, i.e., about 10% of the whole list), there are 74 of them become closer to gold standard rankings.

The incorporation of prior knowledge may also bring some noise. This noise hurts word representation learning by either making some related words far from each other, or making some unrelated words close to each other. Take the word pair *lad* and *brother* for example. In gold standard, the ranking of the word pair is 262, and CBOW ranks the word pair in 280, but our model ranks the pair in 36. The reason is that, the knowledge in PPDB-XXXL believes the two words are related to each other, and the word *lad* is infrequent in our text corpus. Hence our model tends to learn word representation of *lad* according to the prior knowledge. Take another word pair *tennis* and *racket* for example. The rankings by gold standard, CBOW and our model are 87, 47 and 167. Our model underestimate the relatedness of the two words simply because the prior knowledge does not mention any relatedness information for the word pair.

Note that, the rankings in gold standard are not always reliable. For example, the word pair *precedent* and *antecedent* is ranked in 192 by gold standard. In fact, the two words are related to each other. Since both words are infrequent and their word vectors cannot be sufficiently learned from text corpus, hence CBOW only ranks them in 187. Due to the favor of prior knowledge, our model successfully identifies their relatedness and ranks them in 30.

In summary, the prior knowledge may either enhance or conflict with word representations learned from text corpus. We should find appropriate prior knowledge to incorporate in learning word representations.

RELATED WORK

Word Representation

There have been various approaches for word representation, including one-hot representation, distributional representation and distributed representation.

In one-hot representation, the length of word vectors is identical to the size of the vocabulary. For the vector of a specific word, only one dimension is on, indicating the corresponding word. The representation is usually used as the basis of document representation, e.g., bag-of-words model [1], which usually suffers from sparsity issue.

As mentioned in the introduction section, distributional representation assumes similar words tend to share similar contextual distributions [2]. Since simple co-occurrence-based distributional representation does not work well, techniques such as reweighting, smoothing and dimension reduction have been proposed. Typical models include self-organizing semantic map [19–21] and latent semantic analysis (LSA) [22]. Besides, clustering techniques based on contextual information have also been proposed for distributional representation, such as Brown Clustering [23].

Most methods for distributional representation are unsupervised. It have been empirically verified that prediction-based distributed representation generally outperforms distributional representation [24, 25]. Distributed representation estimates word vectors so as to maximize the probability of the contexts given target word. Statistical language models based on neural networks, as the representative distributed representation methods, have been widely used in various applications including POS-tagging, entity recognition, syntactic parsing and semantic role labeling [3–5, 24, 26–29]. The characteristics of *word2vec* for modeling implicit relations of words have also been used to extract semantic hierarchies of words from plain texts [30].

Computational complexity of above-mentioned distributed representation models are usually high, which make these models not feasible for large-scale corpora in big data era. To address this issue, Continuous Bag-of-Words Model (CBOW) and Continuous Skip-gram Model [6, 11], which discard non-linear hidden layer and manage to learn large-scale corpora efficiently. To our knowledge, there has been few work on incorporating prior knowledge into distributed word representation.

Learning with Prior Knowledge

Prior knowledge has been considered in model learning in many tasks. The most related one is latent topic modeling with prior knowledge. For example, document networks are considered as a regularizer in topic models [31]. Similarly, Dirichlet Forest is employed to encode Must-Links and Cannot-Links among words given by domain knowledge for topic modeling [32]. Moreover, First-Order Logic is used to encode domain knowledge for topic modeling [33].

In this paper, we also adopt regularization-based method to incorporate prior knowledge for distributed word representation. Different from the version in topic modeling, we propose specific objective functions and optimization techniques in consideration of the characteristics of word representation models. In experiments we have demonstrate the effectiveness of our methods.

The word representation model in [24] provides semi-supervised framework to learn word representation. However the supervision comes from a small amount of labeled text. This type of knowledge is indirect, because it only contains the expected function or usage of words, rather than word meanings and relations among words.

Conclusion and Future Work

In this paper, we propose a unified framework to incorporate prior knowledge into distributed word representation. It is expected that, prior knowledge can compensate for information that is not contained in text corpora. We consider two types of knowledge, i.e., link-based knowledge and preference-based knowledge. For the two types of knowledge, we propose specific objective functions and incorporate them into word representation learning as a regularizer. We further present joint optimization and post optimization for parameter estimation.

In experiments, we demonstrate that this is a promising way to improve the quality of distributed word representation. Considering that accessible corpora may be insufficient both in amount and quality for representation learning of all words, especially in some domain-specific situations, utilization of prior knowledge is a practical solution to obtain better word representation and benefit other NLP tasks. Moreover, this work is a general framework, which can be easily extended to other distributed representation methods.

Essentially, word representation learning is a type of representation learning. What we are trying to emphasize is that, prior knowledge of words can really help word representation models to better capture semantic meanings of words. As for a specific NLP task, such as relation inference, annotated data should be the most direct knowledge to leverage. Word representations learned with indirect prior knowledge such as WordNet are expected to provide better initialization for further optimization.

The methods proposed in this paper is an encouraging start of learning distributed word representation with prior knowledge. There are many challenging topics for further exploration, and we list some as future work:

Types of prior knowledge. In this paper, we mainly focus on incorporating word knowledge. We can explore more complicated prior knowledge, such as the world knowledge in Wikipedia. Complicated entity relations in large-scale knowledge graphs may provide more useful information for word representation [34, 35].

- Representation of prior knowledge. In this paper we represent prior knowledge into two types. We can also design more expressive representation scheme, such as the first-order logic.

- Word representation methods. We may consider incorporate prior knowledge into other distributed word representation methods. For example, distributed representation of multiple word prototypes [15] can also be combined with prior knowledge. With synsets in WordNet, we can learn multiple word prototypes and disambiguate word senses in corpora simultaneously.

ACKNOWLEDGMENTS

The authors would like to thank the handling editor and anonymous reviewers for their valuable and insightful comments.

AUTHOR CONTRIBUTIONS

Conceived and designed the experiments: ZYL MSS. Performed the experiments: YW ZYL. Analyzed the data: YW ZYL. Contributed reagents/materials/analysis tools: ZYL. Wrote the paper: ZYL. Proofreading: ZYL.

REFERENCES

1. Manning CD, Raghavan P, Schütze H (2008) Introduction to information retrieval, volume 1. Cambridge university press Cambridge.

2. Turney PD, Pantel P (2010) From frequency to meaning: Vector space models of semantics. Journal of artificial intelligence research 37: 141–188.

3. Bengio Y, Schwenk H, Senécal JS, Morin F, Gauvain JL (2006) Neural probabilistic language models. In: Innovations in Machine Learning,

Springer. pp. 137–186.

4.   Collobert R, Weston J (2008) A unified architecture for natural language processing: Deep neural networks with multitask learning. In: Proceedings of ICML. pp. 160–167.

5.   5.Collobert R, Weston J, Bottou L, Karlen M, Kavukcuoglu K, et al. (2011) Natural language processing (almost) from scratch. JMLR 12: 2493–2537.

6.   Mikolov T, Chen K, Corrado G, Dean J (2013) Efficient estimation of word representations in vector space. Proceedings of ICLR.

7.   Miller GA (1995) Wordnet: a lexical database for english. Communications of the ACM 38: 39–41. doi: 10.1145/219717.219748.

8.   Nelson DL, McEvoy CL, Schreiber TA (2004) The university of south florida free association, rhyme, and word fragment norms. Behavior Research Methods, Instruments, & Computers 36: 402–407. doi: 10.3758/BF03195588.

9.   Ganitkevitch J, Van Durme B, Callison-Burch C (2013) PPDB: The paraphrase database. In: Proceedings of NAACL-HLT. Atlanta, Georgia: Association for Computational Linguistics, pp. 758–764.

10. Morin F, Bengio Y (2005) Hierarchical probabilistic neural network language model. In: Proceedings of AISTATS. volume 5, pp. 246–252.

11. Mikolov T, Sutskever I, Chen K, Corrado GS, Dean J (2013) Distributed representations of words and phrases and their compositionality. In: Proceedings of NIPS. pp. 3111–3119.

12. Liu TY (2009) Learning to rank for information retrieval. Foundations and Trends in Information Retrieval 3: 225–331. doi: 10.1561/1500000016.

13. Li H (2011) Learning to rank for information retrieval and natural language processing. Synthesis Lectures on Human Language Technologies 4: 1–113. doi: 10.2200/S00348ED1V01Y201104HLT012.

14. .Finkelstein L, Gabrilovich E, Matias Y, Rivlin E, Solan Z, et al. (2001) Placing search in context: The concept revisited. In: Proceedings of WWW. pp. 406–414.

15. Huang EH, Socher R, Manning CD, Ng AY (2012) Improving word representations via global context and multiple word prototypes. In: Proceedings of ACL. pp. 873–882.

16. Reisinger J, Mooney R (2010) A mixture model with sharing for lexical semantics. In: Proceedings of EMNLP. pp. 1173–1182.

17. Agirre E, Alfonseca E, Hall K, Kravalova J, Paşca M, et al. (2009) A study on similarity and relatedness using distributional and wordnet-

based approaches. In: Proceedings of HLT-NAACL. pp. 19–27.

18. Gabrilovich E, Markovitch S (2007) Computing semantic relatedness using wikipedia-based explicit semantic analysis. In: Proceedings of IJCAI. volume 7, pp. 1606–1611.

19. Ritter H, Kohonen T (1989) Self-organizing semantic maps. Biological cybernetics 61: 241–254. doi: 10.1007/BF00203171.

20. Honkela T, Pulkki V, Kohonen T (1995) Contextual relations of words in grimm tales analyzed by self-organizing map. In: Proceedings of ICANN. volume 2, pp. 3–7.

21. Honkela T (1997) Self-organizing maps in natural language processing. Ph.D. thesis, Helsinki University of Technology Espoo, Finland.

22. Landauer TK, Foltz PW, Laham D (1998) An introduction to latent semantic analysis. Discourse processes 25: 259–284. doi: 10.1080/01638539809545028.

23. .Brown PF, Desouza PV, Mercer RL, Pietra VJD, Lai JC (1992) Class-based n-gram models of natural language. Computational linguistics 18: 467–479.

24. .Turian J, Ratinov L, Bengio Y (2010) Word representations: a simple and general method for semi-supervised learning. In: Proceedings of ACL. pp. 384–394.

25. Baroni M, Dinu G, Kruszewski G (2014) Dont count, predict! a systematic comparison of context-counting vs. context-predicting semantic vectors. In: Proceedings of ACL. pp. 238–247.

26. Mnih A, Hinton GE (2008) A scalable hierarchical distributed language model. In: Advances in neural information processing systems. pp. 1081–1088.

27. Socher R, Lin CC, Ng A, Manning C (2011) Parsing natural scenes and natural language with recursive neural networks. In: Proceedings of ICML. pp. 129–136.

28. Socher R, Bauer J, Manning CD, Ng AY (2013) Parsing with compositional vector grammars. In: Proceedings of ACL.

29. Guo J, Che W, Wang H, Liu T (2014) Revisiting embedding features for simple semi-supervised learning. In: Proceedings of EMNLP. pp. 110–120.

30. Fu R, Guo J, Qin B, Che W, Wang H, et al. (2014) Learning semantic hierarchies via word embeddings. In: Proceedings of ACL. pp. 1199–1209.

31. Mei Q, Cai D, Zhang D, Zhai C (2008) Topic modeling with network regularization. In: Proceedings of WWW. pp. 101–110.

32. Andrzejewski D, Zhu X, Craven M (2009) Incorporating domain knowledge into topic modeling via dirichlet forest priors. In: Proceedings of ICML. pp. 25–32.

33. Mei S, Zhu J, Zhu J (2014) Robust regbayes: Selectively incorporating first-order logic domain knowledge into bayesian models. In: Proceedings of ICML. pp. 253–261.

34. Bordes A, Usunier N, Garcia-Duran A, Weston J, Yakhnenko O (2013) Translating embeddings for modeling multi-relational data. In: Proceedings of NIPS. pp. 2787–2795.

35. Lin Y, Liu Z, Sun M, Liu Y, Zhu X (2015) Learning entity and relation embeddings for knowledge graph completion. In: Proceedings of AAAI.

Chapter 8

LANGUAGE PROBLEMS IN APPLIED LINGUISTICS: LIMITING THE SCOPE

A. Effendi Kadarisman

Universitas Negeri Malang Jalan Semarang 5 Malang 65145, Indonesia

ABSTRACT

This article critically discusses the paradigmatic shift in applied linguistics, resulting in a claim that countless real-world language problems fall within its scope, but in reality they weaken the discipline and make it lack a focus. Then it takes a closer look at the nature of these language problems, and picks out, for analysis, real examples of writing problems in ELT in Indonesian context. It further argues that, by focusing primarily on problems in ELT and SLA, applied linguistics reaffirms its well-defined position and underscores its significant contributions to both disciplines. Finally, it concludes the discussion by adding some notes on the question of autonomy in both applied linguistics and in ELT in Indonesia.

INTRODUCTION

In applied linguistics (AL) today the term 'language problem' has become a key concept. Davies (2004) argues that the discipline is primarily devoted to seeking "a practical answer to a language problem" (p. 19). Along this line of argument, McCarthy (2001, p. 1), citing Brumfit (1991, p. 46), states that applied linguistics tries to offer solutions to "real-world problems in which language is a central issue"; and hence it is appropriately called "a problem-driven discipline" (p. 3). Similarly, Cook and Wei (2009, p. 3) use the term "realworld language problems", and note that the International Association of Applied Linguistics specifies the term as "practical problems of language and communication" (p. 1). Likewise, Davies and Elder (2004) use a similar term "social problems involving language" (p. 1).

A problem arises when applied linguistics tries to encompass all kinds of real-world language problems. This huge and unlimited scope of AL may suggest, on the one hand, that AL has become a very powerful discipline, taking up everything concerning language and any of its related problems. On the other hand, it implies that AL lacks a focus; for when it deals with everything, it eventually deals with nothing (Hult, 2008, p. 12). 'Language problems' in AL thus present themselves as puzzling phenomena, which deserve serious attention and need further investigation. Accordingly, the present article raises five inter-related questions. Why do language problems in AL seem to be limitless and endless? What is the nature of language problems in AL? What does ELT in Indonesian context look like, particularly in dealing with writing problems? What is the actual role of AL vis-à-vis ELT and SLA? What is the nature of AL relationship with theoretical linguistics? Answers to these five questions are the major concerns of this article; and they are presented in order.

PARADIGMATIC SHIFT: FROM LINGUISTICS APPLIED TO APPLIED LINGUISTICS

The seemingly endless 'language problems' making up the boundless scope of AL are probably the effect of paradigmatic shift in the discipline. Applied linguists today (see, e.g., Davies and Elder, 2004; McCarthy, 2001; Widdowson, 1984) claim that AL is not simply the application of linguistic theories, principles, methods, or techniques for the purpose of solving language problems at hand. On the contrary, AL is now an autonomous and independent discipline (Rajagopalan, 2004). Although the word 'linguistics' stands, syntactically, as the head being modified by 'applied' in the given name 'applied linguistics', AL is no longer under the shadow of linguistics, let alone an offshoot of it. In fact, (theoretical or context-free) linguistics is only one of the numerous disciplines (such as sociolinguistics, pragmatics, discourse analysis, psychology, sociology, education, and many more) to which AL relates in a collaborative, not a dependent manner (Cook and Wei, 2009; Spolsky, 2008). Along this line of argument, Davies and Elder (2004), following Widdowson (2000), have distinguished between Linguistics Applied (LA) and Applied Linguistics (AL). The former, also termed 'applications of linguistics', refers to "the assumption that the [language] problem can be reformulated by the direct and unilateral application of concepts and terms deriving from linguistic enquiry itself" (p. 9). In my opinion, one best example of LA can be seen in the direct application of Bloomfieldian linguistic principles in the field of FL teaching, producing the well-known Audiolingual Method (ALM), summarized in Table 1. As shown in this table, the relationship between the linguistic principles and their application in the ALM is quite straightforward. All the three principles and their applications are self-explanatory and need no further explanation.

Table 1: Bloomfieldian Principles and their Application in the ALM

Linguistic Principles	Application in the ALM
Language is primarily speech.	Teach speech before writing.
Language is a set of habits.	Do drilling as the best way of forming FL habits.
Every language is different.	Do contrastive analysis as the basis for material development and predicting errors.

The first scholarly attempt to build the ALM began with the work of Fries (1945) and reached its peak in the work of Lado (1964). Lado's book Language Teaching bears the sub-title A Scientific Approach, which implicitly refers to the claim that linguistics is a science in the sense that physics or chemistry is a science (Bloomfield, 1933, p. 33). One important characteristic of a science is providing "high precision" in describing its objects of investigation. Thus 'scientific approach' means linguistics-based approach and hence provides 'guidance of high precision' as how to conduct FL teaching. By and large, Lado's Language Teaching can be seen as the 'holy bible' for the ALM. It succinctly outlines linguistic and psychological principles of language learning and language teaching (see chapters 4 and 5). It defines 'learning a second language' as "acquiring the ability to use its structure within a general vocabulary under essentially the conditions of normal communication among native speakers at conversational speed" (p. 38). Overall, the book is a complete manual of FL teaching geared toward helping the learners to achieve structural and lexical mastery as the basis for communicative ability. In other words, according to the ALM, mastering a second language begins with mastering language form and moves toward proficiency in language function. The well-known instructional materials faithfully based on the ALM are English 900 series, which had world-wide circulation during the 1970s. In Indonesia, during the 1970s through the early 1980s Student Book and its Supplementary Reader (volumes 1, 2, 3, respectively) for senior high schools were also ALM-based materials. In sum, despite its failure owing to the wrong linguistic and psychological assumptions (Brown, 2001, pp. 23-24), the ALM is probably one best example of LA (Linguistics Applied) in the field of FL teaching.1 By contrast, while LA can be seen as direct application of linguistic principles to solve a given problem, AL requires "intervention [as] a matter of mediation"; [it] has to relate and reconcile different representations of reality, including that of linguistics without excluding others" (Davies and Elder, 2004, p. 9). An excellent example is given by Widdowson (1984, p. 14) in his critique of Chomsky's (1957, p. 87) famous examples:

(1)   Flying planes can be dangerous.

This sentence is syntactically ambiguous, interpretable in two different ways:

- It can be dangerous to fly planes
- Planes which fly can be dangerous.

While paraphrase (2.b) is syntactically acceptable, it is, according to Widdowson, pragmatically vacuous. What a plane does is of course fly; and why should it be dangerous? He further goes on providing a pragmatically acceptable interpretation

- Planes can be dangerous when they fly
- Planes can be dangerous when flying
- Planes can be dangerous flying
- Flying planes can be dangerous.

The series of paraphrases in (3) make up a brilliant argument. While sentence (1) by Chomsky is syntactically ambiguous but somewhat meaningless pragmatically, paraphrase (3.d) by Widdowson, which has gone through a long derivation from (3.a), is not only syntactically ambiguous but also pragmatically meaningful. This is a great example of providing 'a different representation of reality'. Widdowson (1984, pp. 9-10) further notes the major difference between linguistic analysis and native speaker's intuition. In linguistic analysis, accurate description is the ultimate goal, allowing 'no tolerance for vague notion, imprecision, and ambiguity'. Conversely, 'communicative behavior' which represents native speakers' communicative competence 'is [often] vague, imprecise, and ambiguous'. This can be seen through the difference between 'syntactic ambiguity' and 'pragmatic indeterminacy'. Syntactic ambiguity can always be resolved by drawing different tree structures and providing paraphrases, revealing that a given syntactic construction (in natural language data) may be ambiguous in two or three different ways—as illustrated by Flying planes can be dangerous in (1). On the other hand, pragmatic indeterminacy, as the term suggests, may have countless interpretations depending on the given context. Consider the following utterances by A and B in dialogue (4).

A: Will you?

B: Of course.

The question and answer in elliptical forms here imply that the 'speaker meanings' are determined by a previous 'text', that is, a previous verbal communication by both interlocutors A and B. Now the reader can imagine unlimited numbers of previous conversations which allow the generation of both utterances in (4) and at the same time determine their communicative intents. For the sake of economy, Table 2 gives a summary contrasting between LA and AL, or between the old and new paradigms pertaining to applied linguistics. As shown in Table 2, LA, which belongs to the old paradigm, is a dependent discipline subsumed under theoretical linguistics, whose primary task is applying linguistic principles to solve language problems, particularly those in the area of FL teaching and learning. In contrast, AL, which claims to have set up a new paradigm, relates to linguistics in a collaborative manner; and hence it is an autonomous problem-driven discipline. It is concerned with realworld language problems and tries to offer the best possible solutions by relating them, either directly or indirectly, not only to linguistics but also to other relevant disciplines. Briefly, the paradigmatic shift from LA to AL is not only a liberating move from affiliation to autonomy, but also an exploding coverage of the subject matter: from the limited problems in the area of FL teaching and learning to a boundless scope covering practically all kinds of language problems.

Table 2: Comparing Linguistics Applied with Applied Linguistics

Parameter	APPLIED LINGUISTICS	
	Old Paradigm (LA)	New Paradigm (AL)
relation to theoretical linguistics	hierarchical or affiliated	partnership or collaborative
status as a discipline	dependent	independent or autonomous
name and method	*Linguistics Applied* = applying linguistic principles to solve FL teaching and learning problems	*Applied Linguistics* = identifying problems and finding solutions in a systematic way (problem-driven discipline)
scope of subject matter	limited to / focused on FL teaching and learning	any real-world language-related problem

A cautionary note is necessary here. The term 'LA' (as an old paradigm) is given by present-day applied linguists to justify that AL is an independent discipline, going far beyond the applications of linguistics and hence no longer under its domination. Former scholars such as Fries (1945) and Lado (1964), however, never saw themselves that way, but rather conceived themselves and were admitted by other contemporary and forthcoming scholars as pioneers in the field of FL teaching. By analogy, one often considers oneself 'a good guy' by pointing a finger at (frequently dead) enemies and calls them 'bad guys'. The derogatory term LA is probably needed to promote the position of AL and makes it look promising academically.

A CLOSER LOOK AT LANGUAGE PROBLEMS IN APPLIED LINGUISTICS

This section provides an answer to the second question: What is the nature of language problems in AL? Before answering this question, it is necessary to take a look at the 'lists of possible problems' making up the scope of AL, as proposed, for example, by Cook (2003), Davies and Elder (2004), and McCarthy (2001). Cook (2003, pp. 7-8) identifies three headings as follows: (1) language and education; (2) language, work, and law; and (3) language, information, and effect. The first heading includes (a) first-language education; (b) second- and foreign-language education; (c) clinical linguistics; and (d) language testing. The second heading includes (a) workplace communication; (b) language planning; and (c) forensic linguistics. The third heading includes (a) literary stylistics; (b) critical discourse analysis; (c) translation and interpretation; (d) information design; and (e) lexicography. Davies and Elder (2004, p. 1) present the language problems in a series of questions. They are problems in the areas of (a) language teaching; (b) speech pathology; (c) translation and interpretation; (d) language testing; (e) bilingual program; (f) literacy; (g) discourse analysis; (h) medium of instruction; (i) second language acquisition; and (j) legal language. McCarthy (2001, p. 1) gives a list of 14 problems—in the following areas: (a) speech therapy; (b) foreign language teaching; (c) legal language; (d) advertising; (e) report writing; (f) historic naming; (g) language testing; (h) literary studies; (i) lexicography; (j) machine translation; (k) language planning; (l) international navigation; (m) primate/animal communication; and (n) medical sociology. Then McCarthy adds "the list could continue, and … is quite likely to grow even bigger over the years" (p. 2). Under critical examination, the three long lists of language problems above teach us three important lessons. First, as noted earlier, AL has become so ambitious that it tries to claim that every language-related problem is within the confines of its subject matter. This has been criticized by Cook and Wei (2009), saying, "definitions of applied linguistics now are more like lists of the areas that make it up" (p. 1). In other words, AL has no focus of scholarly interest, making "the applied linguist a Jack of all trades", one who "knows a little about many areas" (p. 2). If so, then AL seems to have failed to become a field of specialization.

Secondly, it is doubtful that people encountering all of those language problems listed above will come and consult with applied linguists for the best possible solutions. Many areas listed above are academic disciplines of their own; discourse analysis, critical discourse analysis, lexicography, and forensic linguistics are sub-fields of linguistics. And language planning is much closer to sociolinguistics than to AL. Under the umbrella of 'language education', foreign language teaching, language testing, and second language acquisition are autonomous disciplines; and so is translation. Advertising probably needs more insight from stylistics than from AL; and stylistics is part of literary studies. Briefly, each of these well-established disciplines has produced scholars of its own, whose expertise is much needed when problems arise in the discipline. A Jack of all trades can never compete against an expert. Third and finally, the three lists have two things in common: foreign language teaching (FLT) and second language acquisition (SLA)2 . In fact, they constitute the home base for AL. Despite its claim for such a broad coverage in subject matter, it is these two areas that have been in close contact with AL. Cook and Wei (2009) observe, "The International Association of Applied Linguistics Congress in 2008 had nine papers on first language acquisition compared with 161 on second language acquisition and 138 on foreign language teaching" (p. 1). Clearly, SLA and FLT made up the backbone for the congress. The close connection between FLT and AL is further confirmed by Hult (2008), "The predominant notion of applied linguistics is that it serves the needs of language teaching, particularly ELT" (p. 14). In brief, the nature of countless language problems in AL is that they are conceived rather imaginary than real. The real problems AL has been dealing with in earnest are problems in FLT and SLA. In is in these two areas that AL has been most successful (Cook & Wei, 2009, p. 3). The following section will take a closer examination of EFL teaching and learning in Indonesia, and pick out examples of naturally occurring classroom problems.

ELT IN INDONESIAN CONTEXT: A CLOSER LOOK AT WRITING PROBLEMS

The term 'problem' is in itself problematic. As Cook and Wei (2009) puts it, "in one sense it means a research question posed in a particular discipline; in another sense it is something that has gone wrong which can be solved" (p. 2). A more careful scrutiny should reveal that, between 'something wrong' and 'research question', there are other possible interpretations of 'problem'. Thus 'problem' has multifarious meanings, ranging from the most negative to the near-neutral. I would propose that the semantic range includes (a) error; (b) controversial issue; (c) difficulty; (d) challenge; and (e) curious phenomenon. 'Error' represents 'something wrong', and 'curious phenomenon' represents 'research question', which is near-neutral.3 Between them lie 'controversial issue', 'difficulty', and 'challenge'. Each of these meanings requires some explanation. Before we proceed further, it should be noted in passing that in the field of ELT, teaching and learning are equally important. In fact, the present trend in education suggests moving from the teacher-centered to the learner-centered perspective (Brown, 2001), implying that learning should shape and give direction to teaching rather than the other way around (pp. 46-47). In effect, learning problems often need to be taken into account before teaching problems. Going back to the term 'error', for instance, most likely we are dealing with learning errors, and not teaching errors. Recall that 'error' lies in the extreme negative side of the semantic range presented above. And what is error? "Errors are the flawed side of learner speech or writing" (Dulay et al., 1982, p. 138). In other words, they are target language forms produced by an L2 learner which deviate from the standard norms. Obviously, errors are learning problems, since the learner has done something wrong and needs correction. Here, errors reflect difficulty of target language learning. At the same time, however, errors are also teaching problems; they challenge the teacher with how to help the learner correct the errors. During the heyday of audiolingualism, errors had to be avoided at all costs, or else they would become part of the new language habits (Brown, 2011, p. 23). However, since the publication of Corder's (1967) "The Significance of Learners' Errors", they have been considered natural and inevitable part of FL learning. These two different opinions of errors make them a controversial issue. So errors have now come up as a curious phenomenon which needs serious investigation. This brief discussion of errors makes it clear that errors as language problems fall within all five categories in the semantic range. Errors can be something wrong and difficulty on the part of EFL learners; they can be a challenge for EFL teachers; and they may show up as a controversial issue as well as a curious phenomenon (a research problem) for L2 researchers. The learning and teaching problems can be very complex in nature; they may interrelate, mutually influence, or affect each other.

In their discussion of errors, Dulay et al. (1982) propose two types of classifying errors: linguistic category taxonomy and surface strategy taxonomy (pp. 138-199). Under the former, errors can be grammatical or lexical errors. Under the latter, errors can be errors of omission, addition, double markings, regularization, and misformation. To illustrate, below is a sentence from a narrative written by an Indonesian high school student.4 The errors in (5) are shown by putting the words in italics.

(5)   If they *fallen* down, certainly *not save*, *beside* the road is cliff.

        To help identify the errors, a revised version of this sentence is given in

(6)   If they fall down, certainly they will not be safe; on the right/left side of the road is a cliff.

By referring to (6) as the standard from, we can use the linguistic category taxonomy and identify the errors in (5): fallen is a grammatical error in verb form; save is a lexical error, a verb used in place of an adjective (safe); and beside is another lexical error, used in place of on the right/left side of. Using the surface category taxonomy, we can say that fallen is a misformation error. The intended sentence Certainly not save contains errors of omission and misformation; and the sentence beside the road is cliff contains an error of omission. What do these errors reveal? If we take a psycholinguistic perspective and look at (5) as a partial manifestation of the learner's interlanguage (see

Selinker, 1972), then we can say that those basic grammatical and lexical errors tell us that the learner (a boy) is still at the elementary level. His interlanguage or transitional competence is barely adequate for him to convey his message in good English. All of his errors are learning problems for him. For the teacher, these problems pose a challenge: how s/he should help the learner correct the errors. Obviously, the learner needs to improve his interlanguage competence; and it means that more intensive teaching is required. For L2 researchers, the errors require in-depth analysis—which reminds us of Contrastive Analysis and Error Analysis. The former explains the nature of negative transfer; the latter tells us that the errors indirectly reflect the level of the learner's transitional competence. In a nutshell, errors can be learning, teaching, and research problems. Now I would like to move ahead and dwell on a controversial issue, a doubtful grammaticality judgment on a particular form. Overall, this derives from a personal account of teaching Advanced Applied Linguistics to doctoral students at the School of Graduate Studies (PPs), State University of Malang (UM) during the second semester of the 2011/12 academic year. One brilliant student in the class wrote an excellent essay entitled "Making their Voices Heard: Introducing the Joy of Poetry Writing through Peer Analysis". In this essay, there was a sentence containing a phrase 'quality poems' that was puzzling to me.

(7)   Given sufficient exposure to quality poems, the students might in turn develop an ability to produce their own piece of poems (italics added).

In my opinion, the phrase was not grammatical. So, I corrected it, changing the phrase into "high-quality poems". The following week, the student came up to me with two sentences (written by English native speakers) containing phrases similar to hers. Getting more bewildered, I wrote an email to four American colleagues— three linguists (Thomas Conners, Ph.D., Thomas Hunter, Ph.D., and William O'Grady, Ph.D) and one expert in SLA (Margaret DuFon, Ph.D.).

Therefore, this is the story of 'quality poems'; it is a 'controversial issue' in prescriptive grammar, a 'difficulty' that gives a 'challenge' to me as an instructor. Two native speakers judge it correct; but one native speaker considers it wrong. Personally, I feel relieved because Dr. Thomas Hunter goes along and agrees with me. At least, my grammaticality judgment is not as bad as I thought it was. This story relates to ultimate attainment in FL learning or L2 acquisition. Saville-Troike (2006, p. 17) argues that the ultimate attainment is called 'multilingual competence', significantly different from 'native competence' as the ultimate attainment in L1 acquisition. I completely agree with this statement. Upon reflection, I am fully aware that my multilingual competence in English can never compete against my native competence in Indonesian. Whenever I am in doubt about correct grammar or usage in English, I always seek help from my native-speaker colleagues. To sum up, EFL teaching and learning problems in Indonesian context require serious attention from applied linguists. The two illustrative examples selected in writing errors and grammaticality judgment are meant to demonstrate that naturally occurring problems (even when limited to the classroom context) can be very complex in nature, and truly challenging to ELT and AL scholars. Of course, there are dozens or even hundreds of other real teaching and learning problems which need equally serious attention and investigation, and eventually well thought-out solutions. The urgent point now is that AL should stop claiming that any language-related problem falls within its scope, and go back attending to problems in ELT and SLA.

Applied Linguistics in Indonesia: Elt and Sla as Major Concerns

The claim for countless and ever-growing language problems as constituting AL subject matter has been prevalent in recent textbooks: Cook's (2003) Applied Linguistics, Cook and Wei's (2009) Contemporary Applied Linguistics, Davies and Elder's (2004) The Handbook of Applied Linguistics, McCarthy's (2001) Issues in Applied Linguistics, and Spolsky and Hult's (2008) The Handbook of Educational Linguistics. Thus the claim that AL scope has been continually expanding occurs in the international sphere. Therefore, the aims of the critique launched in this article are twofold: first, to point out that the ambitious claim of AL in the global sphere is more pretentious than realistic; and secondly, to keep the current practice of AL in Indonesia that has remained faithful in serving the needs primarily of ELT and secondarily of SLA. In support of the second aim, the 5th Conference on Applied Linguistics (CONAPLIN), held at Indonesia University of Education (UPI) in September 2012, can be taken as a useful reference. The theme of the conference was "Language Teacher Development in a Globalized World"; and as noted in the leaflet and cited in Table 3, the conference covers eight areas of specialization.5 Table 3 tells us that Language Teaching, with its seven sub-topics, is the most dominant area of the conference, followed by Language Acquisition, which of course includes SLA. To keep the 'applied' nature of AL, the next two areas are Applied Psycholinguistics and Applied Sociolinguistics (italics added), suggesting that it is the application or practical sides of both disciplines that are the major concerns. Discourse Analysis and Corpus Studies constitute part of macro-linguistics, or the study of language in context, reminding us that solving a real-world language problem is always framed in a particular 'context'. As for Translation and Interpretation, applied linguists are well aware that the act of translating and interpreting always involves linguistic aspects pertaining to both the source language and the target language, telling us that this act is partly 'applications of linguistics' is the real sense of the term. Finally, Literary Studies and Social Praxis, placed at the end of the list, looks more like an addendum: who knows there are language-related problems creeping around in literature or in the society that need attention from applied linguists.

Table 3: Areas of Specialization in CONAPLIN 5

1. Language Teaching	2. First, Second and Foreign Language
a. Teaching Strategies and Techniques	Acquisition
b. Teacher Training and Cultivation	3. Applied Psycholinguistics
c. Trends and Challenges in Language Teaching	4. Applied Sociolinguistics
	5. Discourse Analysis
	6. Corpus Linguistics
d. Language Teaching Assessment	7. Translation and Interpretation
e. Language Teaching Policies	8. Literary Studies and Social Praxis
f. Curriculum and Material Development	
g. Language for Specific Purposes	

This highlight on CONAPLIN 5 ties together three things. First, it is true that AL in Indonesia is primarily concerned with ELT and SLA. Secondly, there is overlap between AL and linguistics, as seen in the inclusion of (Applied) Psycholinguistics, (Applied) Sociolinguistics, Discourse Analysis, and Corpus Linguistics. They are well-known disciplines in linguistics, and are usually also included in linguistics conferences. Finally, the eight areas in CONAPLIN 5 may probably remind us of 'language problems' in AL. Definitely, these eight areas are not language problems. However, potentially there are countless topics of interest in each area, to be selected and developed into conference papers. Referring back to the five meanings of 'problem' discussed earlier (i.e., error, controversial issue, difficulty, challenge, curious phenomenon), a topic of interest sounds much like a curious phenomenon; but it is slightly different. A curious phenomenon is considered 'near-neutral', since it invites investigation; but a topic of interest invites discussion, and so it is considered 'neutral'. This is like doing a hair-splitting business; but for the purpose of achieving descriptive adequacy, the distinction is necessary. After obtaining good support from CONAPLIN 5, I would like to find more support from the university where I teach. Now going back home and looking at the recent Catalog, English Department (2012), State University of Malang (UM), I feel relieved to find out that in the curriculum of each study program, AL goes hand in hand nicely, mostly with ELT and occasionally with SLA (noted in the course descriptions, to be discussed shortly), as shown in Table 4.

Applied Linguistics (shown in italics in Table 4) is there in the S1, S2, and S3 curricula at the English Department at UM; it is a compulsory course only in the S2 curriculum, but an elective course in both S1 and S3 curricula. In both curricula of the two S1 programs the official name of the course is 'Applied Linguistics', in the S2 curriculum 'Critical Review on Applied Linguistics', and in the S3 curriculum 'Advanced Applied Linguistics'. In the study programs of all levels, Applied Linguistics goes together with TEFL and SLA— with varied names for the last two courses.7 Notice that the official name for the S1, S2, and S3 study programs is ELT (English Language Teaching), with the S1 study program in English Language and Literature being a different program. Interestingly, all the three courses (AL, TEFL, and SLA) are offered in the study programs of all levels, including the S1 program in English Language and Literature, albeit as elective courses. When students at this S1 study program graduate and want to teach English, the Department has already provided them with some theoretical knowledge and practical skill of how to teach English as a foreign language.

Table 4: Applied Linguistics, TEFL, and SLA in the S1, S2, and S3 Curricula (cited partially) of English Department UM

No.	Study Program	Course	Credit Hours	Offering Status
1	S1 in ELT	*Applied Linguistics*	2	elective
		TEFL	4	compulsory
		Second Language Acquisition	2	elective
2	S1 in English Language & Literature	*Applied Linguistics*	2	elective
		TEFL	2	elective
		Second Language Acquisition	2	elective
3	S2 in ELT	Critical Review on *Applied Linguistics*	2	compulsory
		Methods of TEFL	2	compulsory
		Critical Review on SLA Research	2	compulsory

Of greater importance are course descriptions for AL offered at the three levels (S1, S2, and S3) of the programs (only relevant parts of the course descriptions contained in the Catalogue are cited here, mostly through paraphrases). For both S1 study programs (p. 42), AL provides students with adequate knowledge of the relationship between research findings in linguistics and English language teaching and learning. Obviously, this is practicing AL of the old paradigm. For the S2 study program (p. 55), AL is also concerned with the application of linguistic principles in FL teaching and learning, but the contents of the course include, among others, reorientation and redefinition of AL as a problem-driven discipline. Here we see that AL has moved one step ahead toward autonomy, although still showing strong dependence on theoretical linguistics. For the S3 study program (p. 60), AL seeks to point out how linguistic theories influence and give shape to TEFL and SLA. Reorientation of AL is explicitly mentioned, from a theory-affiliated discipline to a problem-driven discipline. Moreover, the major concern is to keep its primary goal: bridging the gap between theoretical linguistics and TEFL as well as SLA. Here we see that AL has become more autonomous, while keeping harmonious relationship with linguistics. The discussion of the three course descriptions for AL8 boils down to three major points. First, in the study programs of all levels, AL has been designed to serve the needs of TEFL/ELT and to some extent SLA, suggesting that AL at the English Department at UM has been in the right direction. Secondly, as it redefines itself, AL has gained more freedom and become a problem-driven discipline (italics added). It is the term "problem" here that has led (or misled) the discipline to claim that any language-related problem falls within the scope of AL. All the arguments presented earlier should be more than adequate in proving the falsity of the claim. Third and last, it is interesting to observe that AL—as going up through the S1, S2, and S3 course descriptions—seems to have been moving on toward much greater autonomy. Now, a crucial question arises. How much autonomy does AL need? This question needs long answers; and they will be given in the following section. Upon reflection, referring to CONAPLIN 5 and the curricula of S1, S2, and S3 study programs in ELT at the English Department at UM, it is true that AL in Indonesia has been on the right track; it has been in good service to ELT and SLA. There is no need for AL in Indonesia to grab every language-related problem and make it part of its subject matter. Within ELT and SLA alone, there are innumerable problems waiting for AL to attend to. Recall that 'language problem' has a huge range of meanings: error, controversial issue, difficulty, challenge, curious phenomenon, and topic of interest. Accordingly, AL in Indonesia may make considerable progress by focusing on naturally occurring problems in ELT and SLA, which may become more abundant owing to the possibility that each problem may get multiplied by more than one interpretation.

QUESTION OF AUTONOMY IN APPLIED LINGUISTICS (AND ELT IN INDONESIA)

Let us go back to the question: how much autonomy does AL need? Or, in other words, how does AL relate to theoretical linguistics? This question has brought up different answers, settling down eventually to three types of relationship: minimum dependence on linguistics, mutual need between AL and linguistics, and (moderate or strong) reliance on linguistics. The first position is stated clearly by Cook and Wei (2009), "Linguistics nowadays plays a minimum role in applied linguistics" (p. 2). In fact, linguistics is only one of the contributing disciplines. They further point out that "applied linguists have explored psychological models such as declarative/procedural memory and emergentism, mathematical models such as dynamic systems theory or chaos theory, early Soviet theories of child development such as Vygotsky, French thinkers such as Foucault and Bourdieu— nothing seems excluded" (Cook & Wei, 2009, p. 2). It seems that they have some feeling of dislike toward linguistics; and it turns out to be true. According to Cook and Wei (2009), "indeed some practitioners radiate hostility toward linguistics, preferring to draw on almost any other area" (p. 3). These scholars have unintentionally dispelled the word 'linguistics' from 'applied linguistics', hence making the discipline in limbo. Most probably, this first position is the position of AL that takes every language-related problem into the confines of its subject matter; and this is a favorable position for the Jack of all trades applied linguists. The second position is best represented by McCarthy (2001, p. 4-5), following earlier steps taken by Widdowson (1980, 1984). McCarthy argues that AL as a problem-driven discipline relates to 'linguistics as a partner', not a mother discipline. Scholars of both disciplines have different responsibilities. The responsibility of linguists is to build theories of language that are verifiable, and to offer models, descriptions, and explanations of language that satisfy not only intellectual rigor but intuition, rationality, and common sense. On the other hand, the responsibility of applied linguists is not simply to 'apply linguistics' but—by looking critically at theories, models, and descriptions of language—to work toward 'relevant models' of their own that best suit the purpose of solving language problems at hand. "The applied linguist is a gobetween", noted Cook and Wei (2009, p. 3), whose primary task is "provide an interface between linguists and practitioners where appropriate, and to be able to talk on equal terms to both parties" (McCarthy 2001, p. 5). Although sharing different intellectual responsibilities, McCarthy continues, scholars of both disciplines "should adopt a critical position vis-à-vis the work of their peers, both within and across the two communities" (p. 5). Partnership and equal footing between both disciplines as suggested by McCarthy could be an ideal relationship; but the bare facts should not be overlooked: "theories, models, and descriptions of language" precede 'relevant models' designed by applied linguists. This suggests that, so long as AL derives its own models either directly or indirectly from research findings in linguistics, the claim for the equal footing remains an aspiring ideal rather than an accomplished fact. The strong reliance on linguistics is proposed by The International Association of Applied Linguistics (AILA 2009), which proclaims that "applied linguistics is an interdisciplinary field of research and practice dealing with practical problems of language and communication that can be identified, analysed or solved by applying available theories, methods or results of Linguistics or by developing new theoretical and methodological frameworks in Linguistics to work on these problems" (Cook & Wei, 2009, p. 1). In this definition, AL looks like a daughter discipline, whose job is to solve language problems by applying linguistics or inventing a linguistics-based framework. This position of strong dependence is probably rejected by most present-day applied linguists. On the other hand, the moderate reliance on linguistics can be seen in the work of Cook (2003), who defines AL as "the academic discipline concerned with the relation of knowledge about language to decision making in the real world" (p. 5). He states that at present there is a difficult relationship between AL and linguistics. Both context-free linguistics (best represented by generative linguistics) and context-bound linguistics (as represented particularly by sociolinguistics, functional linguistics, and discourse analysis) have moved along at the conceptual level: trying to describe and explain, and eventually build a theory or draw general principles of language. This is of course so far apart from the AL decision-making business in dealing with real-world language problems (Cook, 2003, pp. 9-10). And yet, despite the different goals of both disciplines, Cook still believes in the significant role of linguistics. He states that LA methodology is by necessity complex; "it must refer to the findings and theories of linguistics, choosing among different schools and approaches, and making these theories relevant to the problem at hand" (Cook, 2003, p. 10). On the one hand, this scheme is very similar to what Widdowson (1984) calls 'relevant models', which take into account not only linguistic descriptions but also native speakers' intuition. On the other hand, the scheme is in accord with McCarthy's (2001) proposal for "theoretical stance" without making "theoretical allegiance" (pp. 5-7). Theoretical stance means that AL should build its own 'theory' or systematic way of approaching L2 learning and teaching problems, whereas theoretical allegiance refers to choosing one particular linguistic theory with the belief that it is the 'best theory' for FL teaching. In the past, theoretical allegiance showed up in the global sphere (with its massive influence in Indonesia during the 1970s and early 1980s) in the adoption of Bloomfieldian linguistics together with behaviorist psychology as foundations for the Audiolingual Method. Then, scholars came to realize that L2 acquisition is a lot more than habit formation through drilling; for L2 in the making is in fact an independent and dynamic language system of its own, called 'interlanguage' (Selinker, 1972) or 'transitional competence' (Corder, 1967). Notice that the term 'competence' here originates from Chomsky (1965, p. 4), carrying with it a strong flavor of mentalism that is in total opposition to behaviorism. And mentalism has indeed succeeded in its attack on behaviorism, and pushing it off the stage.

Criticizing behaviorism and audiolingualism today is like killing a dead horse; but from this lesson a relevant question arises: does 'theoretical allegiance' that has failed with audiolingualism take place today? Strangely enough, it does; and it does occur in Indonesia. The 2004 curriculum for Indonesian high schools, under the big umbrella of communicative language teaching (CLT), has adopted the so-called systemic functional linguistics genrebased approach (SFL GBA), which relies heavily on Hallidayan linguistics. With audiolingualism, the prominent activity was drilling; with the GSA, the center of ELT is genre or text. But there is an important difference. The Audiolingual Method was so well outlined and straightforward that EFL teachers knew exactly what they were required to do. By contrast, the GBA, which seems to require the teachers to understand Hallidayan basic linguistic principles before doing the teaching, has caused much confusion.9 Emilia's (2011) book, Pendekatan Genre-Based dalam Pengajaran Bahasa Inggris: Petunjuk untuk Guru (Genre-Based Approach in English Language Teaching: A Guide for the Teachers) is an excellent helping hand, which has done its best to sweep out the confusion and try to put the teachers back in confidence. But this generous intellectual help does not negate the fact that ELT in Indonesia has been trapped by the strong belief that a particular linguistic school can offer a 'best approach'. Moreover, AL and SLA were not there yet during the formation of audiolingualism; but in the first decade of the 21st century, when the GBA was adopted in Indonesia, all insights from highly well-developed AL, SLA, and TEFL were there at our disposal, but seemed to have been ignored. So, the question of autonomy now turns from LA to ELT: how much autonomy does ELT in Indonesia need? It does not need autonomy. Just as audiolingualism was happy thriving under the domination of Bloomfieldian linguistics, the GBA is equally happy struggling under the shadow of Hallidayan linguistics. This GBA incidence makes the question of autonomy in ELT in Indonesia somewhat irrelevant. Some autonomy is there for EFL teachers to plan and implement the teaching-learning process; but the freedom is within the confines of Hallidayan linguistics. In other words, the practice of ELT in Indonesia is still much under the cast of linguistic shadow. Will the newly introduced 2013 curriculum change the present state of ELT Indonesia? We are all in the position of 'wait and see'. From the off-side notes on ELT in Indonesia, let us go back to the question of autonomy in AL. While AL scholars have been so busy defining the position of AL vis-à-vis linguistics, theoretical linguists, to the best of my knowledge, are never aware of this AL hectic business. What they know is that AL is there as a sub-field of linguistics, just as other subfields (such as psycholinguistics, neurolinguistics, and forensic linguistics) are there making up linguistics a much richer, constantly growing discipline. In fact, the tension or sometimes hostility has been there in linguistics between scholars of different schools or persuasions. During the 1960s there was a devastating attack by generative linguists on the Bloomfieldian school, claiming that it lacked descriptive and explanatory adequacy (Chomsky, 1965, pp. 4- 8). Then there were 'linguistics wars' (Harris, 1995) between Chomsky and his former students, founders of generative semantics. For Chomsky, the most prominent part of linguistic theory was (and still is) syntax; but for his students it was semantics. The wars lasted for about a decade, with Chomsky coming out victorious. Next, sociolinguists such as Hudson (1970) and Hymes (1972, 1974) launched serious criticism of Chomsky for ignoring language use in social context; but, since Chomsky believes that language is a mental, not a social fact, he never gives any response to them. Another cause of resentment against Chomsky comes from proponents of linguistic relativity (see, e.g., Gumperz & Levinson, 1996) and linguistic particularity (Becker, 1995), especially for his insistence on linguistic universality, culminating in the theory of Universal Grammar (UG) which is so abstract in nature and detached away from actual language use (Chomsky, 1981, 1995). This list may go on and on; but it should stop at this point. At this point, it is Chomsky who has been at the center of linguistic turbulence for nearly four decades, and has remained a legend— adored as an angel, but also loathed as a devil (Harris, 1995, p. 77).

At this point, applied linguists should be well aware that their hectic business of defining AL position has no effect whatsoever on linguistics. In fact, the negative effect fires back on itself. A number of books bearing the name Applied Linguistics can be difficult or very difficult for (prospective) EFL teachers to read. This is because, in discussing the position of AL, the authors assume that the readers have adequate knowledge about linguistic aspects they criticize. To illustrate, going back to Widdowson's (1984, p. 14) attack on Chomsky's example "Flying planes can be dangerous" discussed earlier in this article, I have found out that none of my EFL students, even at the doctoral level, understands the point Widdowson has eloquently made. Obviously, they lack syntactic knowledge on which Chomsky builds his argument for the necessity of the deep structure underlying the ambiguity of the sentence. Another example is McCarthy's (2001) furious attack on 'sentence grammar', preferring implicitly to teach 'discourse grammar' (pp. 50-53). Putting a provocative sub-heading "Sentence: Friend or Foe", McCarthy argues along the way pointing out that sentences as linguistic units are inadequate for expressing speaker meanings in actual verbal communication. He sums up his argument, saying, "In language pedagogy, the sentence may be less than useful, even irrelevant, in performing mundane speech acts such as greetings, suggestions, thanks, and apologies, not to mention in the extended performance of spoken collaborative tasks" (McCarthy, 2001, p. 53). Briefly, for McCarthy the sentence is the enemy. This provocative argument must be confusing to EFL teachers; for when they teach grammar in their daily routines, they teach sentence grammar. What is wrong with sentence grammar? Upon careful examination, what McCarthy says is nothing but an echo of arguments in pragmatics and sociolinguistics. Referring to pragmatics, he gives prominence to speaker meaning (illocutionary force) rather than sentence meaning (locutionary force). Referring to sociolinguistics, he believes more in communicative competence proposed by Hymes (1972) rather than in linguistic competence proposed by Chomsky (1965). When applied linguists have strong passion to carry over controversial issues in linguistics into AL, the result is confusion on the part of the practitioners.

To conclude this section, the real issue is not how much autonomy AL needs, but rather, how well the applied linguist understands linguistic theories, methods, and descriptions; and how well they are able to make the best use of these findings for the purpose of solving the problem at hand. Recall that a problem may have a huge range of meanings; and understanding the nature of a given problem will help provide the best possible solution. From my own experience of learning the two disciplines, as my knowledge of linguistics develops, my understanding of AL and its directions goes deeper and becomes better. At the same time, from the personal experience of teaching AL through the years and looking carefully at its controversial issues, I have come to realize why parts of pure linguistics incite disappointment, frustration, or even resentment on the part of the applied linguists. Overall, the term 'linguistics' in 'applied linguistics' can be either a curse or a blessing, depending on how applied linguists relate the two disciplines. The shift of paradigm from LA to AL is a historical construct invented by the 'good guys'. It is useful as an academic discourse, but of little value when AL has to come down to the actual problem-solving business. The claim for the ever-expanding scope of AL gives more disadvantage than advantage, since the discipline will fail to produce real professionals and produce only Jack of all trades applied linguists. So, going back to the essentials is necessary: focusing on real language problems in ELT and SLA. In this respect, AL in Indonesia has all along been on the right tract, without neglecting the necessary exposure to the international sphere to keep itself well-informed. CONAPLIN at UPI has set up a good example of doing AL in the country. It focuses on language problems in ELT and SLA, while allowing other closely related disciplines to offer topics of interest to enrich the scholarly discussion. Looking at the seven sub-disciplines of ELT at the 5th CONAPLIN (i.e., (a) teaching strategies and techniques; (b) teacher training and cultivation; (c) trends and challenges in language teaching; (d) language teaching assessment; (e) language teaching policies, (f) curriculum and material development; and (g) language for specific purposes), the real need becomes clear—not the specific knowledge of linguistics, but the broad knowledge of language and other relevant disciplines.

The 'quality poems' example presented in the third section of this article is meant to tell the reader that there is nothing trivial in scholarship. Only by treating a minor problem in a serious manner can we solve bigger problems satisfactorily. Similarly, I am fully aware that both side-track notes in the last section may weaken the coherence of the essay. But their significant value is more important than the rhetorical structure of the essay. The adoption of the genrebased approach that bewilders Indonesian EFL teachers is deplorable, because it shows that the practice of AL in Indonesia has at one time stumbled on the stone of ignorance. From the heated debates among theoretical linguists arguing for the 'best theory', applied linguists should learn a good lesson. Now there is no need to define AL position against linguistics, since it has turned out to be an energy-consuming, time-wasting, and fruitless attempt. In fact, it has backfired and made some AL books and reading materials less accessible to (prospective) EFL teachers. The right way of doing AL expectedly yields a systematic attempt to correct learning errors, settle controversial issues, face challenges, overcome difficulties, conduct research on curious phenomena, select and discuss topics of interest, and make right decisions on issues concerning ELT and SLA problems. By doing so, AL has clearly defined itself as a problem-driven discipline, not a problem-inciting discipline. Keeping and blowing up trivial issues on its relationship with linguistics would not make AL gain better academic standing, but would make it part of annoying language problems!

ACKNOWLEDGEMENTS

I would like to thank, first, Nurenzia Yannuar, an M.A. degree holder in Linguistics and a colleague at the English Department, State University of Malang, for proofreading and suggesting improvements of the earlier draft, and, secondly, an anonymous reviewer for suggesting important revisions and correcting errors of the submitted manuscript. Any possible shortcomings and deficiency, however, are my responsibility alone.

REFERENCES

1. Allen, H. B. (1964). Readings in applied English linguistics. New York: Appleton-Century-Croft. Becker, A. L. (1995). Beyond translation: Essays toward a modern philology. Ann Arbor: The University of Michigan Press.

2. Bloomfield, L. (1933). Language. Chicago/London: The University of Chicago Press.

3. Brown, D. H. (2001). Teaching by principles: An interactive approach to

language pedagogy (Second Edition). New Jersey: Prentice Hall Regents.

4. Brumfit, C. C. (1991). Applied linguistics in higher education: Riding the storm. BAAL Newsletter, 38, 45-9.

5. Catalog, English Department (2011). Malang: Faculty of Letters, State University of Malang.

6. Chomsky, N. (1957). Syntactic structures. The Hague: Mouton. Chomsky, N. (1965). Aspects of the theory of syntax. Cambridge, Massachusetts: The MIT Press.

7. Chomsky, N. (1981). Lectures on government and binding. Mouton: The Gruyter. Chomsky, N. (1995). The minimalist program. Cambridge, Massachusetts: The MIT Press.

8. Cook, G. (2003). Applied linguistics. Oxford: Oxford University Press. Cook, V., & Wei, L. (2009). Applying linguistics and language teaching in the twenty-first century. In V. Cook & L. Wei (Eds.), Contemporary Applied Linguistics: Language Teaching and Learning (Vol 1), (pp. 1-9). New York: Continuum.

9. Corder, S. P. (1967). The significance of learner's errors. In J. C. Richards. (Ed.), Error analysis: Perspectives on second language acquisition (pp. 19-30). London: Longman.

10. Davies, A. (2004). Introduction to part I: Linguistics applied (L-A). In A. Davies & C. Elder (Eds.), The handbook of applied linguistics (pp. 19-24). Malden, MA: Blackwell Publishing.

11. Davies, A., & Elder, C. (2004). General introduction, applied linguistics: Subject to discipline? In A. Davies & C. Elder (Eds.). The handbook of applied linguistics (pp. 1-15). Malden, MA: Blackwell Publishing.

12. Dulay, H., Burt, M., & Krashen, S. (1982). Language two. Oxford: Oxford University Press.

13. Emilia, E. 2011. Pendekatan genre-based dalam pengajaran bahasa Inggris: Petunjuk untuk guru [Genre-based approaches in English teaching: Guidelines for teachers]. Bandung: Rizqi Press.

14. English 900: A basic course (volumes 1, 2, 3, 4, 5, 6). (1964). New York: Collier Macmillan International, Inc.

15. English for the SLTA series: Students' book I, II, III, and supplementary reader I, II, III. (1981). Jakarta: Balai Pustaka.

16. Fries, C. C. (1945). Teaching and learning English as a foreign language. Ann Arbor: The University of Michigan Press.

17. Gass, S. M., & Selinker, L. (1994). Second language acquisition: An introductory course. Hillsdale, New Jersey: Laurence Erlbaum

Associates,Publishers.

18. Gumperz, J. J., & Levinson, S. C. (1996). Rethinking linguistic relativity. Cambridge: Cambridge University Press.

19. Harris, R. A. (1995). The linguistics war. New York/Oxford: Oxford University Press.

20. Hudson, R. A. (1970). Sociolinguistics. Cambridge: Cambridge University Press.

21. Hult, F. M. (2008). The history of educational linguistics. In B. Spolsky & F.

22. M. Hult (Eds.), The handbook of educational linguistics (pp. 10-24). Malden, MA: Blackwell Publishing.

23. Hymes, D. (1972). On communicative competence. In J. B. Prides & J. Holmes (Eds.), Sociolinguistics (pp. 269-85). Harmondsworth: Penguin.

24. Hymes, D. (1974). Foundations in sociolinguistics: An ethnographic approach. Philadelphia: University of Pennsylvania Press.

25. Lado, R. (1964). Language teaching: A scientific approach. New York: McGraw-Hill, Inc.

26. McCarthy, M. (2001). Issues in applied linguistics. Cambridge: Cambridge University Press.

27. Rajagopalan, K. (2004). The philosophy of applied linguistics. In A. Davies & C. Elder (Eds.), The handbook of applied linguistics (pp. 397-420).Malden, MA: Blackwell Publishing.

28. Saville-Troike, M. (2006). Introducing second language acquisition. Cambridge: Cambridge University Press.

29. Selinker, L. (1972). Interlanguage. In J. C. Richards (Ed.), Error analysis: Perspectives on second language acquisition (pp. 31-54). London: Longman.

30. Spolsky, B. (2008). Introduction: What is educational linguistics? In B. Spolsky & F. M. Hult (Eds.), The handbook of educational linguistics (pp. 1-9). Malden, MA: Blackwell Publishing.

31. Widdowson, H. G. (1980). Models and fictions, Applied Linguistics 1(2), 165-70.

32. Widdowson, H. G. (1984). Applied linguistics: The pursuit of relevance. In H.G. Widdowson (Ed.), Explorations in applied linguistics, 2 (pp. 7-20).Oxford: Oxford University Press.

33. Widdowson, H. G. (2000). On the limitations of linguistics applied. Applied Linguistics, 21(1), 3-25.

Chapter 9

A COMPARATIVE STUDY OF EVIDENTIALITY IN RAS IN APPLIED LINGUISTICS WRITTEN BY NS AND CHINESE WRITERS

Linxiu Yang

Foreign Languages School, Shanxi University, Taiyuan, China

ABSTARCT

This paper is devoted to a comparative study of evidentiality in RAs (Research Articles) of NS (Native speakers) and Chinese writers. It examines whether cultural factors influence the writer's choice concerning evidentiality and the interpersonal functions of evidentiality. First, it illustrates the necessity of the comparative study. Second, it presents the findings, including the similarities and the differences. Third, the pedagogical implications are pointed out.

INTRODUCTION

As a pervasive linguistic phenomenon in almost all languages, evidentiality has recently been arousing the interest of linguists and has become a hot research topic in linguistics. It has been studied from various perspectives (e.g. Chafe, 1986; Palmer, 1990, 2001; Mushin, 2000, 2001; Halliday & Matthiessen, 2004; Hu, 1994a, 1994b; Fang, 2005; Tang, 2007; Yang, 2009, 2010). Each has its own interest, purpose and research focus and sheds light on evidentiality. To further the study of evidentiality in RAs written by the writers from different cultural background, this paper makes a comparative study of evidentiality in RAs in applied linguistics written by NS and Chinese speakers. The study shows that the use of evidentiality in RAs is both universal, cultural, and language-specific.

Definition of Evidentialitiy in the Current Study

Evidentiality has become a hot research topic in linguistics. However, there has been no consensus yet on what evidentiality is and what kind of linguistic category it is. The disagreements mainly occur in the following aspects. The first is whether evidentiality is a grammatical category or a semantic one. The second is what the semantic scope of evidentiality is. As to the issue of whether evidentiality is a grammatical category or a semantic one, studies have shown that it is language-specific. In about a quarter of the world's languages, every statement is required to specify the type of source on which it is based—for example, whether the speaker sees it, hears it, infers it from indirect evidence, or learns it from someone else. This linguistic category, whose primary meaning is information source, is called "evidentiality". In Boas' (1938: p. 133) words, "while for us definiteness, number, and time are obligatory aspects, we find in another language location near the speaker or someone else, [and] source of information— whether seen, heard, or inferred—as obligatory aspects." From Boas' words, it can be seen that in some languages, evidentiality is an obligatory category. As to how to express evidentiality, different languages demonstrate different evidential systems. Tariana, an Arawak language, spoken in the multi lingual area of the Vaupes in northeast Amazonia, has a complex evidential system. In this language, one cannot (cannot) simply say "Jose played football". Instead, speakers have to specify whether they see the event happen, hear it, or know about it because somebody else tells them, etc. This is achieved through a set of evidential markers fused with tense. Omitting an evidential in Tariana will result in an ungrammatical and highly unnatural sentence. Look at the following examples.

a)   Juse ifida di-manika-ka.

"   Jose has played football (we saw it)";

b)   Juse ifida di-manika-mahka.

    "Jose has played football (we heard it)";

c)   Juse ifida di-manika-nihka.

    "Jose has played football (we infer it from visual evidence)";

d)   Juse ifida di-manika-sika.

"   Jose has played football (we assume this on the basis of what we already know)".

(Adapted from Aikhenvald, 2004: p. 2). The examples above illustrate that the evidentiality is obligatory in the language of Tariana. To mark the information source, some markers are used, such as ka, mahka, nihka and sika, which are termed as evidentials or evidential markers in evidential studies. These instances show that in Tariana evidentiality is a grammatical category and it is expressed through affixes or clitics. However, this is only one of the understandings concerning evidentiality and evidentials. If evidentiality is defined from the formal perspective, it seems that evidentiality only occurs in some languages, but is not universal. For example, in the languages of English, Chinese, German and so on, there are no grammaticalised evidential systems. In these languages, there are no affixes or clitics to express evidentiality. Thus, concerning evidentiality, there exist different research orientations. While some linguists still show great enthusiasm for describing the grammatical evidential systems of some languages, more researchers agree that evidentiality is not a grammatical form, but a semantic category. It is agreed that the semantics of evidentials are universal and exist in almost all the languages in the world. The differences exist in whether it is obligatory or optional and how the semantics are construed in grammatical, lexical or other forms. For example, Japanese pre sents a quite complex system of evidential coding. It has both grammaticalised and non-grammaticalised evidentials (Mushin, 2001). Unlike Tariana and Japanese, the evidential category in English is not grammaticalised (Lazard, 2001). Yet, English has a rich repertoire of evidential devices (Chafe, 1986). It has a broad range of devices such as verbs, adverbs, adjectives, nouns and so on. According to Chafe (1986: p. 261), the difference between some Indian languages and English in evidentiality is not a matter of evidential vs. number of evidentials. It is partly a question of how evidentiality is expressed: is it by suffixes, adverbs or something else? Studies have also shown that some linguists still stick to the grammaticalised evidentials and exclude other realization forms of evidentiality.

However, more researchers tend to take evidentiality as a semantic one and study various forms in different languages. In English, if evidentiality is taken as a grammatical category, just as in some Indian languages, it appears unnecessary to study evidentiality, for there seems to be no grammaticalised evidentials. In fact, many researchers have been studying evidentiality in English (e.g. Chafe, 1986; Palmer, 1990, 2001; Mushin, 2000, 2001; Halliday & Matthiessen, 2004; Hu, 1994a, 1994b; Fang, 2005; Tang, 2007), which shows that the notion of evidentiality as a semantic one has been broadly accepted. This paper also takes evidentiality as a semantic notion. The previous discussion has shown that evidentiality has been accepted as a semantic notion. This has been one of the important research orientations in evidential studies.

The second issue concerning evidentiality is the semantic scope of evidentiality. It is claimed (Aikhenvald, 2004) that evidentiality is an obligatory grammatical category in the language of Tariana, having the primary function of indicating the source of information. This view is considered to be the narrower understanding of evidentiality in evidential studies. Bussemann (1996: p. 157), one of the linguists who hold the narrow view on evidentiality, defines evidentiality as "the structural dimension of grammar that codifies the source of information transmitted by a speaker with the aid of various types of constructions". Aikhenvald (2003: p. 19) also overtly declares the narrow view of evidentiality. She defines the term "evidentiality" in its strict grammatical sense. She holds that the gratuitous extension of evidentiality to cover every way of expressing uncertainty, probability and one's attitude to the information is one of the current misconceptions concerning evidentiality. She thinks that this extension will be unhelpful and quite uninformative and that this approach obscures the status of evidentiality distinct from modality, mood and tense. Those who hold the narrow definition of evidentiality mainly put their focuses on some highly-inflectional languages and concentrate on the detailed descriptions of the grammatical evidential systems. However, this is only one side of the coin.

There is another understanding that with the indication of information source as the core meaning, evidentiality may also be related to the degree of the speaker's certainty of the information. Compared with the previous one, this is a broad view of evidentiality. First, it does not confine evidentiality to a grammatical one. Instead, it treats evidentiality as a semantic notion and whatever forms of evidentials are within the scope of research. Second, evidentiality, in addition to indicating the information source, may acquire other meanings of reliability, probability, possibility, etc. Third, the semantics of evidentiality is universal, and is expressed in different languages. Some languages have grammaticalised systems to indicate evidentiality, but others do not.

In some languages, evidentiality is obligatory, but in others it is not. Chafe (1986) is the leading figure who defines evidentiality in its broadest sense. He defines evidentiality as "attitude toward information". Under the broader definitions, both grammatical evidentials and lexical ones are taken into consideration. Therefore, evidential studies are not only confined to those languages with grammatical evidential systems, but also extended to almost all the languages in the world. In sum, in this paper we take evidentiality as a semantic notion to indicate the information source and, at the same time, the speaker's degree of commitment to the factual status of the information.

Literature Review and the Necessity of a Comparative Study

Studies of evidentiality began in the early part of the 20th century, and the leading figures are Boas (1911), Sapir (1921), and Jakobson (1957), to name just a few. The initial stage of evidential studies focused on some highly inflectional languages and more efforts were made to describe the grammaticalised evidential systems. Since then, there has been a surge of interest in the topic of evidentiality. The publishing of a collection of papers on evidentiality under the title Evidentiality: The linguistic coding of epistemology

(Chafe & Nichols, 1986) has become a milestone. Thereafter, evidentiality has been approached from different perspectives by various scholars. Chafe (1986) studies evidentiality in a broad way and defines "evidentiality" in "the broadest sense".

His definition of evidentiality concerns the speaker's attitude toward knowledge with sources of information embodied in it. He notes the reliability of evidentials, but the defect is that he does not pay enough attention to context. In his study, Chafe also shows that evidential use is one of the differences between spoken and written languages by comparing evidentiality in academic writings and conversations. Palmer (1990, 2001) takes evidentiality as a type of modality, a sub-category of propositional modality.

He treats evidential modality as a different term from epistemic modality, but he also admits the overlap between the two. He also talks about the reliability of evidence in some languages and frames the hierarchy of evidentials. Mushin's study (2000, 2001) focuses more on the epistemological considerations of the evidence in presenting information. The most important point in Mushin's study is that the adoption of a particular epistemological stance in presenting information depends not only upon the source of information, but also upon the overall communicative goals, which proves that the information source sometimes does not coincide with the actual evidential choice. There are many factors which will influence the speaker's adoption of evidentials.

Aikhenvald & Dixon (2003) and Aikhenvald (2004) treat evidentiality in its narrowest sense and pay much attention to evidential systems in different languages, especially in some less-known languages in the world. They only focus on the grammatical evidentials, and lexical ones are outside the scope of their research. In their research, they point out the relationship between evidentiality and genre convention. They also mention the pragmatic implications and effects of evidentials and point out that the irregular evidential use will bring about unexpected stylistic effects, which sheds light on the evidential study at the genre and discourse level.

Nuyts (2001) also touches upon evidentiality in his study of epistemic modality from the cognitive-pragmatic perspective. In his study, he admits that evidentiality and epistemic modality are sometimes conflated, yet he still treats epistemic modality as a different category from evidentiality. He holds that evidentiality concerns the speaker's indication of the nature (the type and quality) of the evidence invoked for (assuming the existence of) the state of affairs expressed in the utterance, but it does not involve any explicit evaluation in terms of the truth of the state of affairs. According to his study, evidentiality can be taken as one of the qualification categories differentiating the divergent expressions of epistemic modality.

In Systemic Functional Linguistics (SFL), evidentiality is not studied as an independent category. In fact, Halliday & Matthiessen (2004: p. 605) mention for the first time "evidentiality" in the third edition of "Introduction to Systemic Functional Linguistics". In their opinion, when "a proposition is assessed as being projected by somebody other than the speaker", "this kind of assessment is known as evidentiality". Halliday's understanding of evidentiality only concerns certain types of evidentiality, but not all the types. Although SFL does not conduct a detailed study of evidentiality, the theoretical framework can be adopted to interpret evidentiality from a functional and social perspective just as Fang (2005) and Tang (2007) have done.

In China, some scholars have studied evidentiality from different perspectives. The first type is the introduction of the linguistic phenomenon of evidentiality. The second is the application of the theories of evidentiality to analyse certain texts, such as Hu (1994a) and Tang (2007). Fang (2005, 2006) talks about the nature of evidentiality from the perspective of SFL and points out that the study of evidentiality in SFL can elevate the evidential studies up to a metatheoretical level. Zhu (2006) devotes much to the Chinese evidentials and shows the unique expressions of the semantics of evidentiality in Chinese. Tang (2007) discusses the discoursal features of evidentiality in English news reports of an epidemic situation update.

These researches have been of great help for people to better understand the linguistic phenomenon of evidentiality from wide perspectives. In spite of the achievements made in the previous studies on evidentiality, research in this area is still in its infancy and much work still needs to be done for improvement and supplement. For instance, the study of the evidential use in academic discourse is far from enough. More comparative study between different cultures is needed. In particular, the necessity of the comparative study lies in the following two points: First, the comparative study is theoretically significant. Through the comparative study of evidentiality in RAs in applied linguistics produced by NS and Chinese writers, the study seeks to show that evidentials chosen by the RA writer will be influenced and bounded by cultural characteristics.

The study reveals that while the semantics of evidentiality is universal, evidentials the speaker/writer chooses in the same genre or context may be different. The differences may be attributed to cultural differences, to some degree, if not all. Therefore, this study, in theory, will show that evidential uses in the genre of RAs are culturally bounded. Second, the comparative study is pedagogically significant. RAs are perhaps one of the academic genres that have attracted the greatest attention, not only because of the vast number of articles published annually, but also because of the need to help the researchers and postgraduate students to succeed in the construction of texts appropriate for submission of scientific journals.

Much of the success involves academic socialization, that is, an understanding of the rules and strategies of the academic community (Belcher & Braine, 1995; Swales, 1990), which is materialized in the linguistic choices made in the texts. Unfortunately, these linguistic choices do not appear to be clear to the non-native and novice writers of RAs in English. Particularly in the foreign language contexts, the researchers often suffer from the reiterated frustration of having their papers returned for language reasons.

For non-native writers, they need to know not only the cultural and rhetorical aspects of writing an article but also the use of grammar and lexis to construct sentences appropriate for the RA. The current research holds that evidentiality is a strong discourse strategy to fulfill the various interpersonal functions. However, it does not stop at the semantic level. Instead, it goes further to examine the grammar and lexis to realize the semantics of different evidential strategies. The latter one is more pedagogically significant. The functional grammar (Halliday, 1994, 2004), which relates form to meaning and context, is the basis of this research to relate the semantics and functions of evidentiality with linguistic forms. From the detailed quantitative analysis of the corpora, the study finds the specific differences of evidentiality used by NS and Chinese RA writers.

Therefore, the help for non-native writers is more practical. In this regard, this comparative study is mainly pedagogically significant and it will help the Chinese writer to step toward success in publication in English. In sum, the comparative study aims to examine whether the cultural factors will influence evidential adoptions in RAs. It tries to raise the RA writer's awareness of how evidentiality can help the writer in the construction and attainment of persuasion.

DATA AND METHODOLOGY

English RAs of applied linguistics are chosen as the data. In spite of disciplinary differences as an influencing factor, the exploration of evidential use in different disciplines is beyond the scope of the current study. The corpus consists of 100 RAs in applied linguistics amounting to about 670,000 words. For the comparative study, 50 RAs published by NS writers and 50 produced by Chinese writers are selected. The articles come from the Internet (www. elsevier.com) and the journals in the libraries of Xiamen University. The English journals selected for this study are: Journal of English for Academic Purposes (2004-2008), Journal of English for Specific Purposes (2004- 2008), and Journal of Pragmatics (2004-2008) (see Appendix 1). The data of RAs are confined to the same period because of the fact that genres are quite stable in a certain period of time. On the other hand, they are also in a state of constant evolution, as Fairclough (1992) notes, "a genre implies not only a particular text type, but also particular processes of producing, distributing and consuming text… Changes in social practice are both manifested on the plane of language in changes in the system of genre, and in part brought about by such changes". The genre of RAs also may change over time. Therefore, in order to examine the linguistic features of RAs, the study chooses RAs published during the same time for the validity of the research results. The 50 RAs produced by Chinese writers in applied linguistics come from the journal Teaching English in China from 2004 to 2007.

The data-coding of this research is done manually at the preliminary stage to identify and count all the potential lexical and discourse-based items that indicate different evidential types. The material for data-coding includes the body of the articles, i.e. the complete text of the articles, excluding abstracts, notes, linguistic examples, tables, and figures. Then, Microsoft Office Excel is adopted to deal with the data and draw the figures accordingly. In addition, in order to take the context of evidentials into consideration to find the concordance patterns, a concordance software is also adopted. This quantitative approach is meant to identify the frequency of occurrences and to produce comparable data. The statistical results are the basis for later illustration of evidentiality as a discourse strategy to fulfill the various interpersonal functions. The frequency of occurrence of each group of items is calculated in permillage (This passage should use the past tense).

Findings of the Comparative Study

The quantitative results reveal some similarities and differences between the two (specify what two things explicitly here). In this part, the similarities and differences are elaborated, from which the common characteristics and different academic conventions concerning evidentiality can be clearly shown.

Similarities Found in the Comparative Study

After the close examination in the comparative study, the similarities are summarized as follows.

First, the semantics of evidentiality is universal in both of the two corpora. Look at the Figure 1.

As is shown in Figure 1, the writers in both corpora use a significant number of evidentials ($f = 11.83$ for NS and $f = 10.54$ for Chinese), which shows that evidentiality is a pervasive linguistic phenomenon in RAs, with no significance between the two groups of writers. It also shows the universality of the semantics of evidentiality in RAs across languages. In both the corpora, the writer adopts various evidential types and also respective linguistic forms to show how he or she acquires the information and in what degrees he or she makes commitment to the factual status of the information. All the evidential types in our classifications occur in both of the corpora. One more common characteristic is that in both corpora, there is an unbalanced adoption among different evidential types. The most frequently used evidentials are reporting evidentials and identials ependent relationship between the generic st iagrammed as follows. tu Table 1. types and generic structures of RAs in the two corpora (with Other-reporting Self-reporting Belief Sensory Inferring nferring evidentials. Belief evidentials and sensory ev are less common in both corpora. This unbalanced adoption tendency reveals the typical way in which the RA writer constructs knowledge. Second, the interd ructures and evidential types exist in both of the corpora. Consider the Tables 1-3 and Figure 2. Table 1 and Figure 2 show that in different generic structures evidential types occur with different frequencies. For instance, Introduction adopts the most evidentials and Data and Method the least, with Findings and Discussion part and Conclusion part in the middle. It is also found that certain generic structures demand certain types of evidential types and certain types of evidentials prefer certain generic structures. For example, other-reporting evidentials are mainly adopted in the introduction, while the inferring evidential strategy is adopted in the

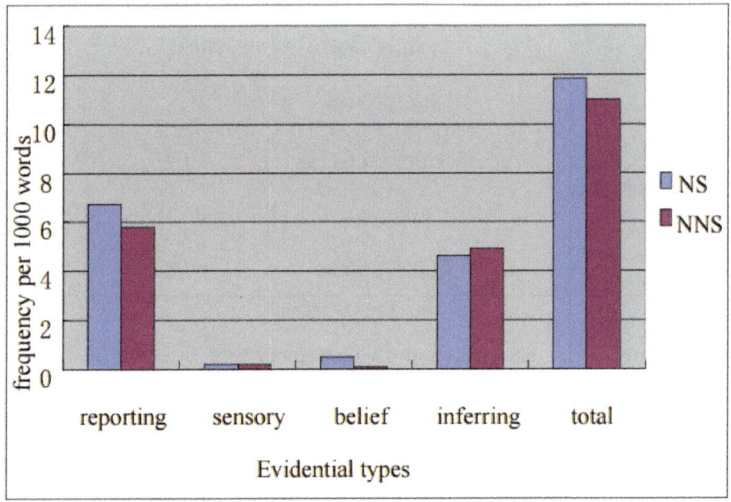

Figure 1: Frequencies of evidential types in NS and Chinese corpora.

Table 1: Evidential types and generic structures of RAs in the two corpora (with frequency per 1000 words)

	Other-reporting		Self-reporting		Belief		Sensory		Inferring	
	NS	NNS	NS	NNS	NS	NNs	NS	NNS	NS	NNS
Introduction	9.65	8.50	2.16	1.08	0.32	0	0	0	3.09	3.45
Data and method	1.87	1.80	0.54	0.44	0.07	0	0	0	1.95	1.87
Findings and discussion	3.08	2.98	2.07	1.98	0.344	0.01	0.27	0.34	4.44	4.64
Conclusion	1.87	1.90	3.57	3.45	1.33	0.02	0	0	7.67	6.86

Table 2: Realizations of evidential types in NS and Chinese corpora

Evidential types	Evidentials	Frequencies	
		NS	NNS
Sensory	See	0.17	0.15
Belief	I/we suggest, argue, think; it can be suggested, argued, assumed, etc.	0.27	0.24
	Author + date	2.06	2.12
Reporting	Verbal	2.18	2.13
	Non-verbal	0.38	0.29
	Modal verbs	4.18	3.98
	Relational process	1.07	0.97
Inferring	Adjectives	0.33	0.37
	Modal adjunct	0.08	0.97

Table 3: Reporting verbs used in NS and Chinese corpora

	Frequently adopted other-reporting verbs
NS	Find, argue, point out, suggest, claim, show, assume, think, hold, note, reveal, observe, indicate
Chinese	Claim, find, note, indicate, argue

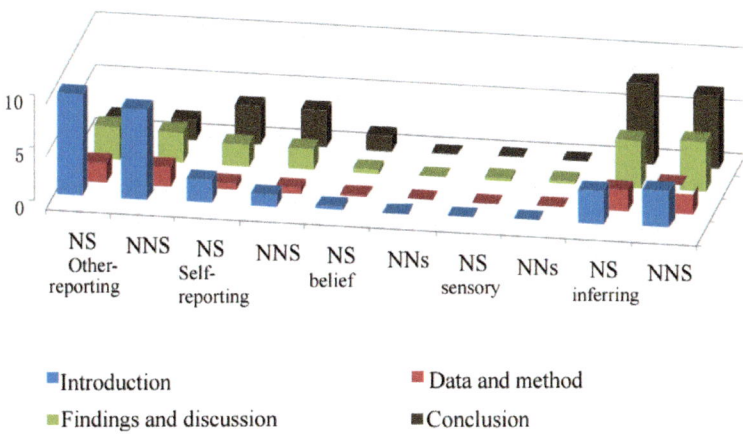

Figure 2: Evidential types in generic structures of RAs by NS and Chinese writers.

Discussion and Conclusion parts

The infrequently used evidential strategies only occur in certain generic structures. For example, the sensory evidentials are only used in the Findings and Discussion parts. This close relationship between the generic structures and evidential types reveals that the sub-purposes and nature of different generic structures will affect the writer's adoption of evidential types.

Third, the linguistic realizations of evidentiality bear the similar characteristics in both of the corpora, as shown in the following table. As seen from Table 2, verbal forms are the most frequent realization of evidentiality in both corpora except the author + date convention.

As for the inferring evidential type, the frequently used form is the modal verb and as for the reporting evidential type, reporting verbs are most often used. Fourth, in both of the corpora, evidentiality can be taken as a discourse strategy to realize the interpersonal functions discussed in the current research. This means that evidentiality is not just a means to denote the information, but more importantly, it is a rhetorical device. It has more functions than indicating information source. The writer's evidential choice will have interpersonal and discourse implications, and in turn, the negotiation of the interpersonal relationship is one of the important motivations for evidential choice. This is the common characteristic of evidentiality in RAs with no difference across cultures.

In sum, the similarities in evidential use in RAs of NS and Chinese writers show the universality of semantics of evidentiality in RAs. The writer adopts different evidentials to denote the construction of knowledge in different generic structures of RAs. Evidentiality can help the writer do more than indicating the information source.

Differences found in the Comparative Study

In addition to the similarities, differences concerning evidentiality as a discourse strategy to fulfill the interpersonal functions are summarized as follows. First, differences exist in the use of reporting evidential type. Figure 1 has shown that reporting evidential type is the most important evidential type in both of the corpora. However, the difference lies in the degree of the writer's awareness of adopting this evidential type to fulfill the interpersonal functions discussed in the previous sections. As has been mentioned, when reporting the prior work and other researchers' work, the writer will at the same time show his evaluation of and stance toward the reported sources and the reported information. The choice of reporting verbs reveals the writer's stance. Reporting verbs can be used to represent the reported information as true or as false. The verbs also allow the writer to ascribe a view to the reported authors as positive, neutral, tentative or critical. However, the study has found the differences in the two corpora concerning the reporting of evidential type. Look at the Table 3. As seen in Table 3, there are some differences in reporting verbs choice. Compared with the Chinese writer, the NS writer has more choices in reporting verbs. They can choose from more different reporting verbs to select the most appropriate one. It is unclear whether the language proficiency may cause the NS writer to choose within a broader range, but it seems to be certain that the Chinese writer may not have clear awareness of the discursive implications and the interpersonal functions of the reporting verbs. Sometimes, what they need is just to find a verb and they seem not to consider whether this verb will help them to get a certain discourse or interpersonal purposes. It is also found that the Chinese writer more frequently chooses reporting verbs such as claim, which is one of the important means for distancing from a dialogic perspective as discussed above. By using this type of reporting verb, the writer will leave limited room for the reader to join in the dialogue and admit little dialogistic space for alternative viewpoints. Therefore, it can be concluded that, although the NS and Chinese writer both admit the importance of the prior literature and show significant respect for previous research, the Chinese writer seems to have less power in choosing appropriate reporting verbs to help him or her to fulfill the interpersonal functions. He is much more inclined to impose attitudes towards the previous work upon his reader. The writer's authorial identity is unreasonably exaggerated. In addition to the differences in the choice of reporting verbs, it is also found that in choos ces also exist.

As stated above, to report others' work, the writer can choose between human and inhuman sources, or between specific and unspecific. In this regard, it is found that the specific human source, such as Hyland argues that... is common in both the corpora. Compared with the NS writers, the Chinese writer adopts more unspecific sources for the otherreporting type.

Third, as mentioned above, in the use of inferring evidential type, the writer tends to choose low value of modality to show lower degrees of certainty. This hedging strategy has rhetorical functions. For instance, it can lessen the writer's responsibility for the truth and factual condition of the information or it can broaden the dialogic space to allow for alternative positions from the reader, or it is a politeness strategy to avoid the face-threatening acts to both the writer and to the reader, and so on. For whatever reasons, choosing a low degree of certainty to present information is more often used by the writer than to choosing a higher degree of certainty by using the modal must. However, our examination has shown that the Chinese writer tends to use a high degree of certainty more often than the NS writer. This has the negative effect because the information will sound too imposing for the reader to accept.

CONCLUSION

It is hoped that this study will be helpful for EAP courses and academic writing. The researchers' need to publish i h has generated a growing demand for academic writing courses. To satisfy this need, it is necessary to develop awareness of the different linguistic resources used by the writers who succeed in publishing. While experienced writers may understand that writing is a context-rich, situational and constructive act, many learners see reading and writing as merely an information-exchange process. Thus, to help students to move beyond this simple, ideational view to a more complex, interpersonal model should be a teaching priority. Unfortunately, the teaching practices of RAs seemed to be based on traditional normative principles rather than on solid empirical evidence from analysis of actual language use. In this sense, the current research provides some solid empirical evidence on the writer's adoption of evidentiality and the findings may have implications for the teaching of academic writing as well as deepening and broadening the writer's understanding of evidentiality in academic discourse.

In sum, writing with awareness of the relationship between evidentiality and its functions may enable the writer to construct the appropriate text in terms of evidentiality, and eventually lead to the ultimate goal of successful publication. It is suggested that in future EAP teaching and writing, raising awareness of the functions of evidential choice is the most important. The writer needs to be aware that each of his choices of evidentiality will have different discursive implications and will help them to achieve their ultimate goal more easily. The genrebased pedagogy concerning evidentiality is also necessary. Learning from the published writings will be very helpful for the students to improve their own writings.

This comparative study lays a foundation for future research and provides an orientation for further study. There are more areas to be further studied. First, the functions of evidentiality can be studied; Second, because of the genre convention, evidential use in other genres, even evidential use across genres, is worthy of more research; Third, evidential use in different languages may vary, which is believed to be an interesting topic in evidential study.

ACKNOWLEDGEMENTS

This work was supported by Chinese Educational Bureau [grant number: 11 YJC740128] and Social Science Grant by Shanxi Province [grant number: 1005123].

REFERENCES

1.   Aikhenvald, A. (2004). Evidentiality. Oxford: Oxford University.
2.   Aikhenvald, A., & Dixon, R. (2003). Studies in evidentiality. Amsterdam: John Benjamins Publishing Company.
3.   Barton, E. L. (1993). Evidentials, argumentations, and epietemological stance. College English, 55, 745-769. doi:org/10.2307/378428
4.   Boas, F. (1911). Handbook of American Indian Languages. Washing ton DC: Government Printing Office.
5.   Boas, F. (1938). Language. In F. Boas (Ed.), General anthropology. Boston: D.C. Heath and Company.
6.   Bussmann, H. (1996) Routledge dictionary of language and linguistics. London: Routledge.
7.   Chafe, W. (1986). Evidentiality in English conversation and academic writing. In W. Chafe, & J. Nichols (Eds.), Evidentiality: The linguistic coding of epistemology. Norwood, NJ: Ablex.
8.   Chafe, W., & Nichols, J. (1986). Evidentiality: The linguistic coding of epistemology. Norwood, NJ: Ablex.
9.   Fairclough, N. (1992). Discourse and social change. Cambridge: Polity Press.
10.   Fang, H. M. (2005). A Systemic-functional approach to evidentiality. Ph.D. Thesis, Shanghai: Fudan University.

11. Halliday, M. A. K. (1985). An introduction to functional grammar. London: Arnold.

12. Halliday, M. A. K. (1993). The construction of knowledge and value in the grammar of scientific discourse: Charles Darwin's the origin of the species. In M. A. K. Halliday, & J. R. Martin (Eds.), Writing science. Literacy and discursive power. London: The Falmer Press.

13. Halliday, M. A. K., & Matthiessen, C. M. I. (2004). An introduction to functional grammar. London: Arnold.

14. Hu, Z. L. (1994a). Evidentiality, reporting and argumentation. Foreign Languages Studies, 2, 22-28.

15. Hu, Z. L. (1994b). Evidentiality in language. Foreign Languages Teaching and Studies, 1, 9-15.

16. Jakobson, R. (1957). Shifters, verbal categories, and the Russian verb. Massachusetts: Harvard University Press.

17. Lazard, G. (2001). On the grammaticalization of evidentiality. Journal of Pragmatics, 33, 358-368. doi:10.1016/S0378-2166(00)00008-4

18. Mushin, I. (2001). Evidentiality and epistemological stance: Narrative retelling. Amsterstam: John Benjamins Publishing Company.

19. Mushin, I. (2000). Evidentiality and deixis in narrative retelling. Journal of Pragmatics, 32, 927-957. doi:10.1016/S0378-2166(99)00085-5

20. Nuyts, J. (2001). Epistemic modality, language and conceptualization: A cognitive-pragmatic perspective. Amsterdam: John Benjamins Publishing Company.

21. Palmer, F. (1990). Modality and the English modals. London: Longman.

22. Palmer, F. (1986). Mood and modalit. Cambridge: Cambridge University Press.

23. Sapir, E. (1921). Language: An introduction to the study of speech. New York: Harcourt, Brace and Co.

24. Swales, J. (1990). Genre Analysis: English in academic and research setting. Cambridge: Cambridge University Press.

25. Tang, B. (2007). Systemic-functional approach to discourse features of evidentiality in English News reports of epidemic situation update. Ph.D. Thesis, Shanghai: Fudan University.

26. Yang, L. X. (2009). Evidentiality in English research articles. Ph.D. Thesis, Xiamen: Xiamen University.

27. Yang, L. X. (2010). Genre perspective on evidentiality. In Chellenges to Systemic Functional Linguistics: Theory and Practice. Sydney: Macquarie University Press.

Chapter 10

CUE COMPETITION BETWEEN ANIMACY AND WORD ORDER: ACQUISITION OF CHINESE NOTIONAL PASSIVES BY L2 LEARNERS

Jia Wang[1], Caihua Xu[2]

[1]Department of Linguistics and Translation, City University of Hong Kong, Hong Kong, China

[2]College of Chinese Language and Culture, Beijing Normal University, Beijing, China

ABSTRACT

Based on the Competition Model (Bates & MacWhinney, 1978; MacWhinney, 2005; MacWhinney, 2012) , the present study investigates L2 cue strategies in the acquisition of Chinese notional passives by English-speaking and Japanese-speaking learners. Two experiments were conducted to examine both the comprehension and production of Chinese notional passives. The main findings included: 1) L2 learners' acceptability of notional passive increased with improved Chinese proficiency but even advanced learners showed significant difference from Chinese native speakers; 2) L2 learners produced more notional passive sentences than bei-passive sentences and advanced learners showed no difference from Chinese native speakers; 3) Cross-linguistic influence seemed to affect L2 learners' comprehension and production of Chinese notional passives. The results support the universality of animacy cue proposed by Gass (1987) but also suggest that word order and pragmatic factors may affect L2 learners' cue strategies. The study also evidences the contribution of the input to the development of L2 cue strategies, which is in line with the predictions of the Competition Model.

INTRODUCTION

This study explores how L2 learners of Chinese make use of cues in their acquisition of Chinese notional passive, specifically, the use of animacy cue and word order cue in English-speaking and Japanese-speaking learners of Chinese. By conducting both a comprehension and a production experiment, we examine how the L2 learners' cue strategies develop with increasing Chinese proficiency. Our study also tests whether the learners' L1 backgrounds play a role in their cue strategies.

Chinese Notional Passive and Previous Studies

Passive voice is almost universal in the world's languages but it is represented in various forms. In inflecting languages as well as agglutinating languages, passive construction is usually indicated by compulsory morphological markings on the verb. By contrast, in Chinese, an isolating language, the verb used in an active sentence and a passive one are the same morphologically. Moreover, a wide range of devices are employed to express passive meaning in Chinese (Chao, 1968; Huang, 1999; Lu, 2004; Xiao et al., 2006). According to a corpus- based study by Xiao et al. (2006), Chinese passives fall into two types: one is the marked passive, which makes use of a morpheme, such as bei (the most typical one), jiao, rang; the other is the unmarked passive, which can also refer to notional passives (i.e., the patient is in preverbal position) and lexical passives (i.e., using lexical words such as ai, "suffer"). Examples of marked passives and notional passives are as follows:

1) marked passive: 杯子 被 (他) 打 碎 了。

   beizi bei (ta) da sui -le

   cup marker (he/him) break pieces particle

   The cup was broken into pieces (by him).

2) notional passive: 杯子 打 碎 了

   beizi da sui -le

   cup break pieces particle

   The cup was broken into pieces.

In terms of functions, bei passives emphasize the dynamic event itself and the unexpected or undesirable influence on the patient, while notional passives describe the stable and objective state resulted from the action (Xiao et al., 2005; Qu, 2006). The frequency of bei passives and notional passives also vary across different stylistic contexts. Based on a quantitative survey of contemporary Chinese passive constructions, Song et al. (2007) observed that bei passives are more frequently used in formal contexts and notional passives are more frequently used in informal context. The present study is mainly focused on the acquisition of notional passives by English- speaking and Japanese-speaking learners of Chinese (L2).

For notional passive sentences in Chinese, the semantic role of the initial noun is the patient of the action denoted by the predicate. In English, the semantic role of the initial noun is also the patient, as exemplified in 3), where "the glass" was acted upon by the action "break". In Japanese, passives fall into two categories: direct passive and indirect passive, as seen in example 4) (cf. Seino & Tanaka, 2006: 326-328). Similarly, the initial noun "Taro" in direct passive example is also the patient of the action "hit", and "the mother" in the indirect passive example is adversely affected by the event, i.e., "son's death", so its semantic role can also be considered as "patient" or "affected". Therefore, Chinese notional passives share the same semantic structure as English and Japanese passives.

3)   English passive: The glass was broken by John.

4)   Japanese passive:

a)   Direct passive: Taro-ga Jiro-ni nagur-are-ta.

      Taro-NOM Jiro-by hit-Passive-Past "Taro was hit by Jiro"

b)   Indirect passive: Sono hahaoya-wa musuko-ni shin-are-ta.

the mother-TOP son-by die-Passive-Past "unfortunately for the mother, the son died"

Despite the similarity, Chinese notional passives are different from passives in English and Japanese in that the verb in Chinese passives remain its bare form whereas the verb is usually changed morphologically in English and Japanese passive constructions. Respectively speaking, in English, "be + done (past participle)" is used in passive sentences, and the verb has to have an additional suffix (except for irregular verbs); in Japanese, the suffix "rareru" should be attached to the stem of vowel-stem verbs and "areru" should be attached to the stem of consonant-stem verbs in passive sentences (Seino & Tanaka, 2006) . It is also worthy to note that Chinese notional passives, without any passive marker, are head-final, structurally parallel with Japanese active sentences (SOV) but quite different from English (SVO). Therefore, it would be interesting to explore how English or Japanese speaking L2 Chinese learners will perform in the comprehension and production of Chinese notional passives.

Previous studies on the acquisition of L2 Chinese passives have found that many errors seem to be related to notional passives. Li (1996) analyzed the writings of L2 Chinese learners from different L1 backgrounds and found that the most common error was the misuse of the bei marker instead of notional passive or lexical passive. Liu (2000) and Wang (2006) reached the same conclusion through the analysis of the writings by Japanese speaking and Korean speaking learners, respectively. Huang et al. (2007) revealed the same tendency by analyzing English speakers' Chinese writings. A more recent study by Feng (2011) adopted an English-to-Chinese translation task and found that English native speakers tended to correspond to the passive marker bei with the passive marker in English so they translated English passive sentences into Chinese bei sentences instead of notional passive sentences. For example:

5)   The gift has been sent to him.

6)   bei passive: 礼物 已经 被 寄 给 他 了。

       gift already bei send to him particle

7)   notional passive: 礼物 已经 寄 给 他 了。

       gift already send to him particle

In the above example, the notional passive construction is actually more appropriate because the action of "sending a gift" does not have an undesirable effect on the "gift". If, for example, the gift was sent to him by mistake, which is unexpected and undesirable, we could use the bei passive. Therefore, the choice between the notional passive and the bei passive depends on the context.

The studies reviewed above adopt the methodology of error analysis and inform us that the acquisition of Chinese notional passives seems to pose difficulty for L2 learners of Chinese. From an empirical approach, the current study examines the acquisition of Chinese notional passives through controlled experiments within the framework of the Competition Model. The findings of this study will shed light on our understanding of L2 learners' cue strategies in their comprehension and production of such passive constructions.

The Competition Model and Second Language Processing

The Competition Model (henceforth, CM), proposed by Bates and MacWhinney (Bates & MacWhinney, 1978; 1981; 1989) , simulate the procedures learners employ in language acquisition. As a functionalist model, the CM focuses on cross-linguistic variation in the multiple-to-multiple mapping between form and function, so competition will arise when a given form maps onto several functions or a given function maps onto several forms. Learners' task is to discover the particular form-function mappings that characterize the target language. The basic concept of the CM is "cue", represented by various linguistic features, such as stress (phonological cues), verb agreement (morphological cues), preverbal position (word order cues) and noun animacy (semantic cues), and so on. According to Bates and MacWhinney (1989) , the primary determinants of cue strength is cue validity, which is the combined product of availability (how often it is present to enact a certain function) and reliability (how often it can be assigned with a certain function when it is present). As stated above, passive voice in Chinese can be represented by notional passives, marked bei passives or lexical passives, so the cue of the passive marker bei is not always available; however, when bei appears in a sentence, it consistently denotes passive meaning. Therefore, passive marker bei in Chinese is low in availability but high in reliability. MacWhinney (2002) has pointed out that availability is more important than reliability for children. We predict that this might be also true for L2 learners especially beginners with limited L2 input.

According to the CM, cues are assigned with different strengths across languages. L2 learners prefer to rely on their L1 settings of cue strength at the beginning of language learning and gradually shift to L2 settings with increasing L2 proficiency (Bates & MacWhinney, 1987). This has been confirmed in a number of cross-linguis- tic studies on bilinguals (Harrington, 1987; McDonald & Heilenman, 1991; Hernandez, Bates, & Avila, 1994; Su, 2001; Morett & MacWhinney, 2013) . However, there remains controversy over the task of agent identification over unnatural stimuli such as "the logs arechopping the boy (animacy cue in competition with word order cue)". McLaughlin and Harrington (1989) suggested that participants had to resort to a particular problem- solving strategy rather than sentence processing strategy under such situations. Gibson (1992) also commented that the use of ungrammatical stimuli invalidated the results of the experiments based on the CM. Responding to Gibson's criticism, MacWhinney and Bates (1994)argued that results from previous Competition Model experiments did not show sharp discontinuity between grammatical and ungrammatical stimuli.

In view of these disputes, the present study will make an attempt to test the applicability of the CM through grammaticality judgment and sentence completion tasks. In the example 2) above, the noun "beizi (cup)", occupies the preverbal position, which usually indicates the role of agent, but it is inanimate, so there is a competition between word order and animacy cues. If the word order cue wins, then the noun will be assumed to be the agent and fulfill the action of "breaking something", which is implausible; instead, the cup is usually broken by someone, taking the role of a patient. Therefore, if L2 learners relied on word order cue, they would not accept notional passives with basic world knowledge. By contrast, in marked bei passive, if L2 learners could resort to the cue of the passive marker bei, they would get the meaning of the sentence easily.

Although many studies have confirmed the transfer of L1 processing strategies in L2 acquisition, some studies suggested the existence of a universal cue that is primary to other cues. For example,Gass (1987) found that semantic cues seemed to have a prepotency in language processing. The study found that English-speaking learners of L2 Italian almost did not transfer their L1 syntactic strategies, but Italian-speaking learners of L2 English did transfer their lexical-semantic strategies (animacy cues). Further support comes from Sasaki (1991) 's study of English and Japanese bilinguals and Liu, Bates and Li (1992) 's study of English and Chinese bilinguals. In response to this issue, MacWhinney (1987) argued that an interpretation based on semantic strategy might be a last resort, used when learners fail to find reliable grammatical cues, rather than a universal strategy. Never- theless, MacWhinney (2008) maintained that animacy cues seemed to be nearly universal because all other things being equal, almost all languages preferred animate subjects. Therefore, more evidence is necessary to test the universality of the animacy cues.

Another issue of our concern is about sentence production. According to MacWhinney (1987) , competition among the cues that represent the properties of ideas will arise when ideas and intentions are to be converted into lexical items in production. In a more recent work, MacWhinney (2005) also described sentence production as involving message formulation, lexical activation, morphosyntactic arrangement, and articulator planning. Each step was called an "arena" for competition between items; for example, in the arena of message formulation, different communicative goals compete and winning goals are typically initialized and topicalized. To our knowledge, however, no studies within the framework of the Competition Model have been reported to elicit empirical data on sentence production. The present study will look into the issue of cue strategies in L2 sentence production.

THE PRESENT STUDY

Research Questions

By examining L2 learners' comprehension and production of Chinese notional passives, this study seeks to investigate Chinese cue strategies of L2 learners. To sum up, we attempt to explore the following questions:

1) Which kind of cue strategies will L2 learners adopt in the comprehension of Chinese notional passives?

2) Which kind of cue strategies will L2 learners adopt in the production of Chinese passives?

3) Will there be cross-linguistic influences in the acquisition of Chinese notional passives by L2 learners?

4) How will L2 learners' acquisition of notional passives develop with increasing Chinese proficiency?

Research Method

Two offline experiments were conducted to explore the above questions through examining the comprehension and production of Chinese notional passives. There was a break of two weeks between the two experiments.

Experiment One

Participants

A total of 111 college students participated in the study. They were recruited from a university in Beijing. They comprised of two main groups: L2 learners of Chinese (n = 91) as the experimental group and Chinese native speakers (CH; n = 20) as the control group. L2 learners of Chinese were further divided into two groups: English native speakers (EN); Japanese native speakers (JA). L2 learners were from four different levels of Chinese courses which therefore served as the evidence for their relative proficiency. There were 46 EN-subjects: 11 at elementary level, 13 at post-elementary level, 13 at intermediate level, and 9 at advanced level. There were 45 JA-subjects: 13 at elementary level, 10 at post-elementary level, 13 at intermediate level, and 9 at advanced level.

Materials and Procedure

A grammaticality judgment test was adopted to explore L2 learners' comprehension of notional passives. Four types of sentences were included: active sentences (n = 8), notional passives (n = 8), agentless bei-passive (n = 8) and non-sentence (n = 24). Notional passive sentences are target items; active sentences, with SVO structure, served as a control baseline by which we mean L2 learners are expected to acquire active before passive; agentless bei passives, which have the passive marker, functions as comparison with unmarked notional passives; non-sentences, with wrong word order, served as distractors. All the participants were prompted to rate the sentences on a 1 - 5 scale (1 for definitely ungrammatical; 2 for possibly ungrammatical; 3 for not sure; 4 for possibly grammatical; 5 for definitely grammatical). The results were collected as the raw data for subsequent statistical analysis. Therefore, three variables under investigation were sentence type, L1 background, and Chinese proficiency.

Each subject received 48 test stimuli printed in random order on a sheet. The experimenter was present throughout the whole experiment. The sample materials of each sentence type are shown in Table 1.

Experiment Two

Participants

Considering the task difficulty of sentence production, we did not invite participants at the elementary level in Experiment one to participate in experiment two; students at the other 3 levels (n = 67) were invited. Another group of native Chinese students (n = 36) participated in the experiment as the control group.

Materials and Procedure

Paired pictures were used to elicit sentence production. A pilot test was conducted to choose pictures that could successfully elicit notional passives from native Chinese speakers. In order to elicit passive sentences, the subject/ topic was designated under each group of pictures. As shown in the following target pictures in Figure 1, "蛋糕 (dan4gao1)", which means "cake", was designated as the subject, so the participants had to complete the sentence starting with "蛋糕". We also used other types of pictures that did not usually elicit passive sentences as distractors, as shown theFigure 1. The order of target items and distractor items were randomized. There were a total of 20 groups of pictures: 10 target pictures aiming to elicit passive sentences and 10 distractors to elicit other types of sentences. The participants were required to complete the sentences according to the given pictures. Pinyin (the Phonetic form of Mandarin Chinese) was acceptable when participants did not know how to write the characters.

RESULTS

Results of Experiment One

After excluding an outlier whose mean score was beyond two standard derivations in the JA group at elementary level, we obtained the results of the grammaticality judgment task (GJT), as shown in Table 2.

Performance of L2 Chinese Learners

EN group: ANOVA on the data of L2 learners in the EN group showed a significant main effect of sentence type, $F(3, 126) = 390.81$, $p < 0.001$, and every level ranked the four sentence types as follows: Active > Notional passive > Agentless bei-passive > Non-sentence. There was also a significant main effect of L2 proficiency, $F(3, 42) = 4.39$, $p < 0.01$, but the interaction between sentence type and L2 proficiency was not significant, F(9, 126) = 1.60, p > 0.05. Post-hoc analysis revealed that over the judgment of notional passives and active sentences, the difference between neighboring levels was not significant, p > 0.05, but over the judgment of agentless bei passives, advanced L2 learners had a significantly higher acceptability than intermediate L2 learners, p < 0.05. From the mean scores of the GJT, we found that L2 learners across four proficiency levels all accepted active sentence (the scores were 4.66 - 4.92, near 5 "definitely correct"). As for notional passives, L2 learners also tended to consider such a structure acceptable (the average scores were 3.82 - 4.42, around 4, "probably correct"), but they were not as determinate as they were toward active sentence. If they had relied on word order cue, the inanimate noun in preverbal position would be regarded as the agent, which is contradictory to common sense (for example, "coffee" cannot perform the action of "drinking" instead it was drunk by someone), and they would reject the notional passive. Therefore, we presume that L2 learners in EN group made use of animacy cue in the comprehension of Chinese notional passive. However, their indeterminacy suggests that they were still sensitive toward word order cue. By contrast, over the judgment of the agentless bei passive, L2 learners showed much more indeterminacy (the average scores were 2.71 - 3.69, around 3, "not sure"), which indicates that the cue of passive marker posed certain difficulty for them.

Table 1: Examples of test materials in experiment one

Type	Examples		
Notional passive	早饭/做/好/了。	Breakfast/make/good/-le	The breakfast is ready.
Agentless *bei*-passive	杯子/被/打/碎/了。	Cup/hit/broken/-le	The cup was broken.
Active sentence	他/喜欢/北京。	He/like/Beijing	He likes Beijing.
Non-sentence	老师/他/是。	Teacher/he/-to be	?

Table 2: Means of GJT (standard derivations in brackets)

L2 proficiency	L1 background	Agentless *bei*-sentence	Notional passive	Active sentence
Elementary	EN(11)	3.10 (0.59)	3.82 (0.49)	4.66 (0.30)
	JA(12)	3.00 (0.48)	4.04 (0.69)	4.50 (0.32)
Post-elementary	EN(13)	3.20 (0.94)	4.09 (0.32)	4.58 (0.54)
	JA(10)	3.21 (1.22)	3.91 (0.57)	4.44 (0.60)
Intermediate	EN(13)	2.71 (.85)	3.92 (0.56)	4.89 (0.22)
	JA(13)	2.79 (.35)	3.98 (0.55)	4.70 (0.38)
Advanced	EN(9)	3.69 (.90)	4.42 (0.87)	4.92 (0.17)
	JA(9)	3.51 (.61)	4.57 (0.32)	4.87 (0.22)
\	CH(20)	4.81 (.30)	4.79 (0.29)	4.98 (0.06)

Figure 1: Examples of target pictures (left) and distracters (right) in experiment two.

JA group: ANOVA on the data of L2 learners in the JA group of the four levels showed a significant main effect of sentence type, $F(3, 120) = 318.03$, $p < 0.001$, and every level ranked the four sentence types as follows: Active > Notional passive > Agentless bei-passive > Non-sentence. We also found a significant main effect of L2 proficiency, $F(3, 40) = 3.00$, $p < 0.05$; the interaction between sentence type and L2 proficiency was not significant, $F(9, 120) = 1.87$, $p > 0.05$. Post-hoc analysis did not find significant difference between different proficiency levels on the judgment of notional passive and agentless passive but on the judgment of notional passives, the judgment between advanced level and post-elementary level was marginally significant, $p \approx 0.05$. The mean scores also indicated that L2 learners in the JA group accepted active sentence (the average scores were 4.44 - 4.87, near 5 "definitely correct") and also notional passive but they showed a little indeterminacy over notional passives (the average scores were 3.91 - 4.57, around 4, "probably correct"). Just as the EN group, L2 learners in the JA group also made use of animacy cue in their comprehension of notional passives and their sensitivity toward word order cue resulted in the indeterminacy. Moreover, also similar to the the EN group, L2 learners in the JA group were also quite uncertain over the grammaticality of the agentless bei passive (the average scores were 2.79 - 3.51, around 3, "not sure"), suggesting that the passive marker bei is also a hamper for the JK group.

Comparison between EN and JA groups: From the analysis of the L2 learners' performances above, we found L2 learners in the EN group and the JA group were quite similar in that they made use of animacy cue in the comprehension of Chinese notional passives but both groups were a little sensitive to word order cue. Moreover, both groups showed indeterminacy in the cue of the passive marker bei. To confirm our observation, we conducted a one-way ANOVA on the data from the two groups. The results indicated that both groups indeed showed no significant difference in the acceptability of notional passives from elementary to advanced proficiency ($F(1, 22) = 0.79$, $p > 0.05$; $F(1, 22) = 0.93$, $p > 0.05$; $F(1, 25) = 0.08$, $p > 0.05$; $F(1, 17) = 0.24$, p

> 0.05). Similarly, the EN and JA groups at all proficiency levels showed no significant difference in the judgment of the agentless bei passive ($F(1, 22) = 0.20$, $p > 0.05$; $F(1, 22) = 0.003$, $p > 0.05$; $F(1, 25) = 0.17$, $p > 0.05$; $F(1, 17) = 0.26$, $p > 0.05$). These findings suggest that English-speaking and Japanese-speaking learners had similar performance in the comprehension of Chinese notional passives and agentless bei passives.

Comparison between L2 Chinese learners and Chinese Native Speakers

EN and CH: A one-way ANOVA analysis was conducted on the data of the EN group and native Chinese speakers, as illustrated in Figure 2. It was found that L2 learners from elementary level to intermediate level all had a significantly lower acceptability of notional passives than natives ($F(1, 30) = 48.97$, $p < 0.001$; $F(1, 32) = 42.03$, $p < 0.001$; $F(1, 32) = 33.83$, $p < 0.001$), but the difference between the EN group and natives was not significant at the advanced level, $F(1, 28) = 3.03$, $p > 0.05$, which indicates that with increased proficiency, L2 learners in EN group became native-like in the comprehension of notional passive and their use of animacy cue. Over the judgment of active sentence, it is also not until advanced level that L2 learners showed no significant difference from natives, $F(1, 28) = 2.41$, $p > 0.05$. However, over the judgment of agentless bei passives, L2 learners in the EN group across all proficiency levels showed significantly lower acceptability than natives, ($F(1, 30) = 116.48$, $p < 0.001$; $F(1, 32) = 51.54$, $p < 0.001$; $F(1, 32) = 198.94$, $p < 0.001$; $F(1, 28) = 25.72$, $p < 0.001$). This lends more support to previous analysis of their difficulty in the acquisition of the passive marker bei.

JA and CH: A one-way ANOVA analysis was also conducted on the data from the JA and Chinese native groups, as illustrated in Figure 3. Results indicated that the JA group had significantly lower acceptability of notional passives than native Chinese from elementary to intermediate level ($F(1, 31) = 18.34$, $p < 0.001$; $F(1, 29) = 32.17$, $p < 0.001$; $F(1, 32) = 37.98$, $p < 0.001$), however, there was no significant difference between advanced JA and natives, $F(1, 28) = 3.35$, $p > 0.05$. Over the judgment of active sentences, the development pattern was the same: L2 learners had significantly lower acceptability than native Chinese ($F(1, 31) = 43.57$, $p < 0.001$; $F(1, 29) = 16.58$, $p < 0.001$; $F(1, 32) = 22.30$, $p < 0.001$; $F(1, 28) = 4.24$, $p < 0.05$). Similarly, L2 learners had significantly lower acceptability of agentless bei passives than natives across all proficiency levels, ($F(1, 31) = 175.72$, $p < 0.001$; $F(1, 29) = 31.52$, $p < 0.001$; $F(1, 32) = 320.43$, $p < 0.001$; $F(1, 28) = 62.54$, $p < 0.001$), which also confirmed our analysis above that L2 learners in the JA group also had difficulty in acquiring the passive marker bei.

To summarize so far, the results from Experiment one demonstrated that L2 Chinese learners from both EN and JA group could make use of animacy cue in their comprehension of notional passive but this was influenced by their sensitivity toward word order cue; with increasing Chinese proficiency, both EN and JA became native-like in their use of animacy cue. We also found that L2 learners have difficulty in acquiring the cue of the passive marker bei and even at higher proficiency their acquisition was significantly different from native Chinese speakers. Then how do L2 learners make use of cues in production? Let's turn to the results from Experiment two.

Results of Experiment Two

Recall that an inanimate noun, such as "蛋糕 (cake)", was designated as the subject under each group of pictures in Experiment two. As expected, most of the sentences produced were passive sentences, which could be categorized into 3 types: notional passives, bei-passives, and others. The percentage of each type was demonstrated in Figure 4. Examples of each type are as follows:

8)   Notional passive: 蛋糕吃(完)了。(The cake was eaten up.)

9)   Bei passive: 蛋糕被(孩子)吃完了。(The cake was eaten up (by the boy)).

10)   Others: 蛋糕?有了。(There is no cake left.)

First, let's look at the results from the control group. There were nearly twice the number of notional passives (61%) as for bei-passives (31%), indicating that native Chinese speakers preferred notional passives to bei passives in the given context of the present study. Similarly, the results of L2 learners showed that both groups at every proficiency level all preferred notional passives to bei passives and they even showed stronger reliance on the use of notional passives compared to native speakers, which is suggestive of their use of animacy cue. Moreover, L2 learners produced much less bei passives than native Chinese, but at the Advanced level, the ratio of notional passives dropped a little and the ratio of bei-passives increased (from less than 5% to around 15%), which indicates that the use of the passive marker bei is difficult for L2 learners but their acquisition of this cue improves with increasing Chinese proficiency.

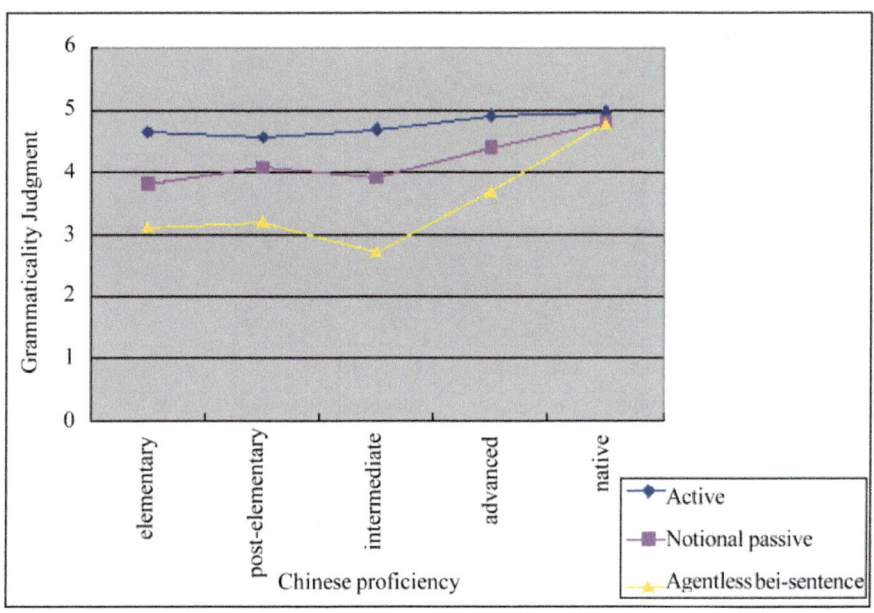

Figure 2: Comparison between L2 learners in EN group and Chinese native speakers.

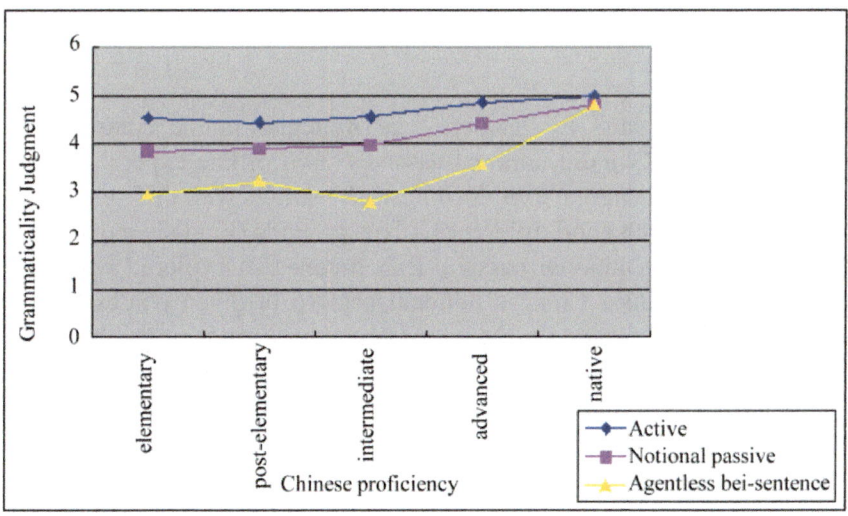

Figure 3: Comparison between L2 learners in JA group and Chinese native speakers.

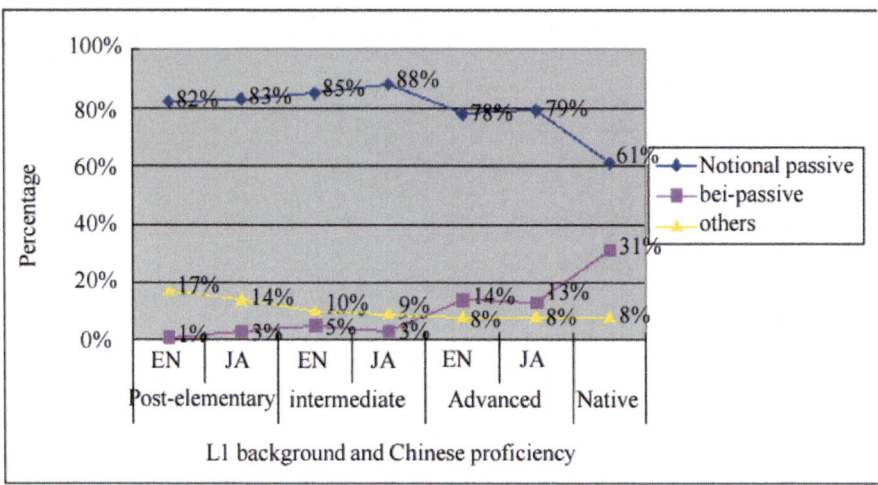

Figure 4: Results of sentence production in experiment two.

The results of Experiment two are compatible with our findings in Experiment one: L2 learners could make use of animacy cue and acquire notional passives quite easily but they had difficulty in acquiring the cue of the passive marker bei.

DISCUSSION

This study investigated L2 learners' cue strategies in the comprehension and production of Chinese notional passives. Two offline experiments were conducted: Experiment one examined how L2 learners with different Chinese proficiencies (4 levels) and different L1 backgrounds (English and Japanese) interpreted Chinese notional passive. Experiment two explored whether L2 learners could produce Chinese notional passive in given contexts. It was found that L2 learners could make use of animacy cue in their comprehension of notional passives and their performance became native-like with increased Chinese proficiency. In production, L2 learners showed even stronger reliance on the use of notional passives compared to native Chinese speakers. By contrast, L2 learners showed difficulty in their use of the passive marker bei in the comprehension and accordingly they produced quite a limited number of bei passive sentences.

The Universality of Animacy Cue

Our results showed that animacy cue is accessible to L2 learners from the very beginning (elementary level), evidenced by their high acceptability of notional passives. This lends support to Gass (1987)'s claim that animacy cue is universal and also echoes the findings of Sasaki (1991) that English-speaking learners of Japanese tended to drop L1 word order cue and resorted to L2 animacy cue. We consented to MacWhinney (2008)'s argument that since nearly all languages preferred animate subjects under normal circumstances, animacy cue is nearly universal. In Chinese notional passives, the subject position is occupied by an inanimate noun, such as "蛋糕 (the cake)", and the verb-complement phrase, such as "吃完 (eat up)", which obviously acts upon the initial noun but the actor (agent) is not told. It turned out thatL2 learners made use of animacy cue and perceived the meaning of the notional passive correctly; otherwise, if they had used word order cue and regarded the inanimate noun as the subject (agent), they would not have accepted notional passive. As pointed out in MacWhinney (2002), children might have difficulty in understanding passive but by the age of four or five, they would have no problem by turning to cues such as "by", "past participle", and etc. In the case of notional passives, although there is neither a passive marker nor morphological inflection on the verb, adult L2 learners could also make use of animacy cue to comprehend the sentence with their basic world knowledge.

Effects of Word Order and Pragmatic Cues

Although L2 learners made use of animacy cue and accepted notional passives, they still showed indeterminacy to some extent compared with native Chinese, which can be seen from the result that their acceptability of notional passive was significantly lower than natives before they reached advanced proficiency. We presume that this may be due to their sensitivity toward word order cue. As is shown from the results in Experiment one, L2 learners acquired active sentences quite early and easily, which provides evidence for their strong awareness of Chinese basic word order SVO. Therefore, when confronted with a notional passive sentence with the word order OV, they might think that the subject is missing or the object should appear after the verb. Within the framework of the Competition Model, there exists competition between animacy cue and word order cue in the comprehension of Chinese notional passives by L2 learners. Even though animacy cue won out at last, word order cue still affected L2 learners' comprehension of notional passives.

In sentence production, L2 learners relied on notional passives instead of the marked bei passive. Compared with Chinese native speakers, they produced much less bei passives. This seems to be inconsistent with previous findings that L2 learners tend to overgeneralize passive marker bei (Li, 1996; etc.). One possible reason, we speculate, is that L2 learners are oversensitive to the restriction of the Chinese bei passive that bei is usually used in undesirable contexts, which is often stressed during the instruction of passive structures. In the present study, the contexts provided by the pictures were neutral, such as a boy ate up the whole piece of cake, a girl drank up the coffee, and etc. Therefore, L2 learners may avoid using the bei passive in a non-negative context. It was found that L2 learners across four proficiency levels produced about 80% of notional passives but only about 5% of bei passives at intermediate proficiency; even when they reached advanced proficiency, there was still only 13% - 14% bei passive. By contrast, native speakers produced almost a third of bei passives (31%). Recall that L2 learners showed a high degree of indeterminacy in accepting agentless bei passive in comprehension. By scrutinizing the test materials and the data, we found that L2 learners had a higher acceptability of bei passives that bear a negative meaning, such as "钱包被偷走了 (The purse was stolen)", the average judgment of which was 4.20 by the English-speaking group and 4.12 by the Japanese-speaking group, but they tended to reject those with neutral meaning, such as "车被开走了 (The car was driven away)", the average judgment of which was 2.65 by English-speaking group and 2.72 by Japanese-speaking group. In a study by Wu and Zhou (2005) , a typical context was used to elicit bei passive from L2 learner of Chinese, that is, "someone was hit by a car", which is negative under normal circumstances. It was found that L2 learners produced a high percentage of bei passive, indicating L2 learners' sensitivity to the pragmatic factors. Comparing our study with Wu and Zhou's, we may also speculate that one possible reason why animacy cue could win over the cue of passive marker bei in production is that L2 learners were quite aware of the pragmatic cue: undesirable context.

Input and Development of L2 Cue Strategy

The role of input cannot be underestimated in second language acquisition. We found that L2 learners' acquisition of notional passives was a slow and gradual process. With increasing Chinese proficiency, L2 learners became native-like in their comprehension of notional passives at the advanced proficiency, which indicated that they made better use of animacy cue and were affected less by word order. The Competition Model states that what control language learning are the distributional properties of the input, and cues with high reliability and availability are acquired first(MacWhinney, 2002) . As mentioned above, notional passives are frequently used in Chinese, especially in informal spoken contexts. Besides, it has been found that animacy cue is the strongest cue second to the passive marker bei (Li et al., 1993). As for word order cue, it is not quite reliable in that Chinese varies in SVO, OSV and SOV. Therefore, with more exposure, L2 learners could make better use of animacy cue and became less sensitive to the word order cue.

In addition, Li, Bates, and MacWhinney (1993) also found that the passive marker bei was the strongest cue for native Chinese speakers. It was explained that native Chinese had received enough input of bei sentences even though they are not so frequently used in Chinese. However, for L2 learners, the low availability of bei sentences may lead to their persistent difficulty in acquiring the passive marker bei even until advanced proficiency, apart from the influence of pragmatic factors we analyzed above.

L1 Transfer on Cue Strategies

The results of the present study showed there were no significant differences between the two groups: English speaking learners and Japanese speaking learners, which seems to indicate that there is no L1 transfer on the cue strategies by L2 learners. However, we observed that L2 learners from both groups were affected by word order cue in their comprehension of notional passive before advanced proficiency as discussed. Apart from intra-linguistic interference from L2 Chinese analyzed above, there might also be inter-linguistic interference, that is, L1 transfer. For English-speaking learners, they might transfer their L1 syntax-based strategy such as word order cue or morphological cue (inflections) into their comprehension of notional passives: notional passives have OV order but no morphological inflections are required on the noun or the verb; therefore, L1-English learners showed indeterminacy over the grammaticality of notional passive before they reached advanced proficiency. For Japanese-speaking learners, unexpectedly, they did not show any advantage over L1-English learners since their L1 cue strategy is semantic-based (Sasaki, 1991) . We assume that L1 transfer, if it occurred, was counteracted by the inter-linguistic interference from Chinese word order cue. As seen from their high acceptability of Chinese active sentence, L1-Japanese learners were well aware of the main word order of Chinese SVO, which differentiates from their L1 word order SOV. As predicted by the Competition Model, L2 learners start with L1 cue strategies in their L2 processing, and this has been confirmed in many cross-linguistic studies based on the model (Harrington, 1987; Su, 2001; McDonald & Heilenman, 1991; Hernandez, Bates, & Avila, 1994) . Although the present study failed to find a strong effect of L1 transfer, it offered more evidence for the universality of animacy effect, which may overwhelm the cross-linguistic influence.

CONCLUSION

The present study finds that L2 learners of Chinese can make use of animacy cue in their acquisition of Chinese notional passives, thus providing more evidence for the universality of semantic cue. However, we also find that the cue strategies are also affected by word order, pragmatic factors, L1 transfer and most importantly, L2 input. It must be pointed out that this study adopts an offline methodology without recording the response time so a more vivid and nuanced picture of L2 language processing is not demonstrated. Despite the limitation, the findings of our study display a comprehensive analysis of L2 learners' cue strategies in the comprehension and production of Chinese notional passives. Research in the future may replicate the present study with online tasks so as to further explore factors that may affect L2 cue strategies in second language acquisition.

ACKNOWLEDGEMENTS

We appreciate the editors and the anonymous reviewers for their hard work and valuable comments to enhance this paper. Thanks go to Dr. CHAN Yuet Hung Cecilia for her valuable suggestions during the preparation of the manuscript. Thank Daniel Lee and Phuong Nguyen for their help in revising the paper. All remaining errors, if any, remain our own.

REFERENCES

1.   Bates, E. , & MacWhinney, B. (1978). Competition, Variation and Language Learning. In B. MacWhinney (Ed.), Mechanisms of Language Acquisition (pp. 157-194). Hillsdale, NJ: Erbaum.

2.   Bates, E., & MacWhinney, B. (1981). Second Language Acquisition from a Functionalist Perspective: Pragmatic, Semantic, and Perceptual Strategies. In H. Winitz (Ed.), Annals of the New York Academy of Sciences Conference on Native and Foreign Language Acquisition (pp. 190-214). New York: New York Academy Press.

3.   Bates, E. A., & MacWhinney, B. (1989). Functionalism and the Competition Model. In B. MacWhinney, & E. Bates (Eds.), The Cross Linguistic Study of Sentence Processing (pp. 3-76). New York: CUP.

4.   Chao, Y.-R. (1968). A Grammar of Spoken Chinese. Berkeley: University of California Press.

5.   Feng, J. (2011). Analysis of the Issue of Generalization in the Acquisition of Chinese Notional Passive by English Native Speakers. Journal of Language and Literature Studies, 4, 163-164.

6.   Gass, S. M. (1987). The Resolution of Conflicts among Competing Systems: A Bidirectional Perspective. Applied Psycholinguistics, 8, 329-350.

7.   Gibson, E. (1992). On the Adequacy of the Competition Model. Language,

68, 812-830.

8. Harrington, M. (1987). Processing Transfer: Language-Specific Processing Strategies as a Source of Interlanguage Variation. Applied Psycholinguistics, 8, 351-377.

9. Hernandez, A. E., Bates, E. A., & Avila, L. X. (1994). On-Line Sentence Interpretation in Spanish-English Bilinguals: What Does It Mean to Be "In Between"? Applied Psycholinguistics, 15, 417-446.

10. Huang, C. T. J. (1999). Chinese Passives in Comparative Perspective. Tsinghua Journal of Chinese Studies, 29, 423-509.

11. Huang, Y., Yang, S., Gao, L., & Cui, X. (2007). The L2 Acquisition of the Chinese Bèi-Construction. Chinese Teaching in the World, 80, 76-90.

12. Li, D. (1996). Waiguoren xuehanyu yufa pianwu fenxi (Error Analysis of the Grammar of Foreigners Learning Chinese). Beijing: Beijing Language and Culture University Press.

13. Liu, H., Bates, E., & Li, P. (1992). Sentence Interpretation in Bilingual Speakers of English and Chinese. Applied Psycholinguistics, 13, 451-484.http://dx.doi.org/10.1017/S0142716400005762

14. Lu, J. M. (2004). Some Issues of Passive Sentences of Mandarin Chinese. Chinese Linguistics, 8, 9-15.

15. MacWhinney, B. (2005). Extending the Competition Model. International Journal of Bilingualism, 9, 69-84. http://dx.doi.org/10.1177/1367006905 0090010501

16. MacWhinney, B. (2002). The Competition Model: The Input, the Context, and the Brain. Pittsburgh: Department of Psychology, Carnegie Mellon University, Paper 219.http://repository.cmu.edu/cgi/viewcontent.cgi?arti cle=1214&context=psychology

17. MacWhinney, B. (2012). The Logic of the Unified Model. In Handbook of Second Language Acquisition (pp. 211-227). London: Routledge.

18. MacWhinney, B. (2008). A Unified Model. In N. C. Ellis, & P. Robinson (Eds.), Handbook of Cognitive Linguistics and Second Language Acquisition (pp. 341-372). New York: Erlbaum.

19. MacWhinney, B., & Bates, E. (1994). The Competition Model and UG. Pittsburgh, PA: Department of Psychology, Research Showcase at Carnegie Mellon University.

20. McDonald, J. L., & Heilenman, L. K. (1991). Determinants of Cue Strength in Adult First and Second Language Speakers of French. Applied Psycholinguistics, 12, 313-348.http://dx.doi.org/10.1017/ S0142716400009255

21.   McLaughlin, B., & Harrington, M. (1989). Second-Language Acquisition. Annual Review of Applied Linguistics, 10, 122- 134. http:// dx.doi.org/10.1017/S0267190500001240

22.   Morett, L. M., & MacWhinney, B. (2013). Syntactic Transfer in English-Speaking Spanish Learners. Bilingualism: Language and Cognition, 16, 132-151.http://dx.doi.org/10.1017/S1366728912000107

23.   Qu, C. X. (2006). Chinese Discourse Grammar. Beijing: Beijing Language and Culture University Press.

24.   Sasaki, Y. (1991). English and Japanese Interlanguage Comprehension Strategies: An Analysis Based on the Competition Model. Applied Psycholinguistics, 12, 47-73.http://dx.doi.org/10.1017/S0142716400009371

25.   Seino, T., & Tanaka, S. (2006). The "Passive" Voice in Japanese and German: Argument Reduction versus Argument Extension. Linguistics, 44, 319-342.http://dx.doi.org/10.1515/LING.2006.012

26.   Song, W. H., Luo, Z. J., & Yu, J. C. (2007). A Quantitative Analysis of the Occurrence Ratio of Agent in Contemporary Chinese Passive Constructions. Studies of the Chinese Language, 02, 113-124.

27.   Su, I. R. (2001). Transfer of Sentence Processing Strategies: A Comparison of L2 Learners of Chinese and English. Applied Psycholinguistics, 22, 83-112.http://dx.doi.org/10.1017/S0142716401001059

28.   Wu, M. J., & Zhou, X. B. (2005). The Comparison of Learning Difficulty on Chinese Bei-Sentence and Passive Sentence in Meaning. Chinese Language Learning, 01, 62-65.

29.   Xiao, R., McEnery, T., & Qian, Y. (2006). Passive Constructions in English and Chinese: A Corpus-Based Contrastive Study. Languages in Contrast, 6, 109-149.http://dx.doi.org/10.1075/lic.6.1.05xia

30.   Wang, Z. L. (2006). Xiandai hanyu beidong biaoshu litihua yanjiu (A Comprehensive Study on Chinese Passive). Dalian: Liaoning Normal University Press.

Chapter 11

THE ARCHAEOLOGICAL RECORD SPEAKS: BRIDGING ANTHROPOLOGY AND LINGUISTICS

Sergio Balari[1], Antonio Benítez-Burraco[2], Marta Camps[3], Víctor M. Longa[4], Guillermo Lorenzo[5], and Juan Uriagereka[6]

[1]Departament de Filologia Catalana and Centre de Lingüística Teòrica, Universitat Autònoma de Barcelona, Edifici B, 08193 Barcelona, Spain

[2]Departamento de Filología Española y sus Didácticas, Universidad de Huelva, Campus de El Carmen, 21071 Huelva, Spain

[3]Department of Anthropology, Center for the Advanced Study of Human Paleobiology, The George Washington University, Washington, DC 20052, USA

[4]Departamento de Literatura Española, Teoría da Literatura e Lingüística Xeral, Universidade de Santiago de Compostela, Campus Norte, 15782 Santiago de Compostela, Spain

[5]Departamento de Filología Española, Universidad de Oviedo, Campus El Milán, 33011 Oviedo, Spain

[6]Department of Linguistics, University of Maryland, 1102 Marie Mount Hall, College Park, MD 20742, USA

ABSTRACT

This paper examines the origins of language, as treated within Evolutionary Anthropology, under the light offered by a biolinguistic approach. This perspective is presented first. Next we discuss how genetic, anatomical, and archaeological data, which are traditionally taken as evidence for the presence of language, are circumstantial as such from this perspective. We conclude by discussing ways in which to address these central issues, in an attempt to develop a collaborative approach to them.

INTRODUCTION

The emergence of human language is generally seen as one of the major transitions in the evolution of the organic world [1]: the defining characteristic of the human species [2–4] or at any rate a crucial twist within it [5–7]. The issue is not without controversy, as linguistic abilities have been argued to be present in other species of hominids. Relevant evidence ranges from genetic data [8, 9] to the presence/absence of some sort of "symbolic culture" [10–13]—and considerations concerning the anatomy of the organs of speech and hearing abound as well [14–22]. Far from attempting to settle the chronological issue, our goal is to put forth some theoretical considerations that may be useful in evaluating the existing evidence, suggesting new avenues of research. Our perspective, often referred to as biolinguistic, goes back to ideas by Eric Lenneberg, Noam Chomsky, Massimo Piattelli-Palmarini, and others [23–27], which extend from Linguistics to other areas of Cognitive Science [28, for an overview].

In Section 2, we present the biolinguistic conception of language. To avoid a dreadful terminological matter, we will refrain from using the common term "language" and will use instead the expression Faculty of Language when referring to the object that may have evolved, in roughly the sense that organs evolve within organisms. In Sections 2.1 through 2.3, we review what is customarily taken to be evidence for the presence of language, demonstrating how this is questionable when interpreted from the perspective of a mental faculty. We argue that the biolinguistic perspective, with its conception of the Faculty of Language, may help Evolutionary Anthropology in the quest for our origins—especially those of our unique cognitive capacities. More specifically, in Section 3 we offer an example of how the biolinguistic perspective may contribute to progress in research, showing how a shift in focus helps us make significant headway.

LANGUAGE: THE BIOLINGUISTICS' VIEW

The Faculty of Language may be defined as a natural system of computation that resides in the mind/brain of all members of the human species. Our definition uses the term "human" simply because (so far) no conclusive evidence exists of the presence of the Faculty of Language in any other extant or extinct species. As a result, the Faculty of Language (as present in humans) provides the only frame of reference for us to test scientific hypotheses concerning one putative such faculty in Neanderthals, or any other species. Being computational, this faculty must be studied as an information processing system based on the application of certain symbol manipulating capabilities [29, 30]. Being natural, it should be understood as an organ that is part of a larger organ system—the nervous system [31]. This faculty is also contingently taken to interface other parts of the mind/brain, intuitively related to "meaning" and "sound" (or "gesture") [32].

To emphasize this point, we see as accidental properties of the Faculty of Language the fact that, in humans, it interfaces other cognitive systems, in particular a Conceptual-Intentional and a Vocal-Auditory component. This collection of systems (the Faculty of Language + Conceptual-Intentional components + Vocal-Auditory components) is often labeled as "the Faculty of Language in the broad sense," following Hauser et al.'s convention [33]. Factually, how central the Conceptual-Intentional interface may be to the human Faculty of Language is open to debate, but the interface with the Vocal-Auditory system is certainly contingent [34, 35]. As decades of research into human sign languages demonstrate, these share the structural properties of human vocal languages [36–38]. So the externalization of "linguistic thought" does not privilege the Vocal-Auditory system, and it can also interface Gestural-Visual components.

The fact that (some) Faculty of Language interfaces are contingent is important. Our definition does not exclude the (metaphysical) possibility of a Faculty of Language system that shares definitional properties as outlined above but only some of the contingent properties we normally associate to the faculty in the human sense. Our conception allows, also, for a natural computational system with powers analogous to the linguistic ones to be studied here, but which is interfaced with entirely different mental subsystems. In the hypothetical, the faculty in question might implement "functions" that are entirely different from those traditionally attributed to human language. Underlying these assumptions is Chomsky's distinction between "competence" and "performance" [32]: a system of knowledge (the Faculty of Language) versus the (various) ways in which this system may be put to use. Inasmuch as these properties of the Faculty of Language are contingent, the natural system of computation itself should be seen as functionally unspecific [31].

Those qualifications constrain the range of hypotheses to test with respect to the origins of the Faculty of Language. In particular, considerations about "systems of communication"—or comparable such "functions" ascribed to language in a vague sense—become orthogonal to the faculty itself. Language as humans experience it serves multiple purposes: to communicate thoughts, to be sure, but also to assert the mere presence of an interlocutor, to lie, to joke, to express beauty, to frighten into submission, to "talk to oneself," to call a distant star or a number that affects no imaginable communicative act, to describe instances of nondenumerable expressions in mathematics, and surely many other purposes that any reader can fathom. Any of those is a "function of language", though none of them seems more natural than the others. Importantly for our purposes, the idea that language is "tailored to communication" (or any of the other "functions" alluded to) has provided no particular insight into the Faculty of Language as understood by linguists of our persuasion.

The qualifications above also entail that language, when rigorously understood, is far from a skill to be learned by repetitive training, like skiing or scuba-diving. This is particularly the case for "first languages," as acquired by children up to puberty. It is an open question whether a "second language" acquired by an adult—often through explicit teaching and rarely to native fluency—may indeed be a skill, subject to variations in ease and rapidity of acquisition, final performance, improvement, decay without practice, and so forth. This unfortunately confounds the matter of interest here. For it may well be that English, definable in some abstract sense as a set of instructions one could (ideally) get in training school for immigrants, has relatively little to do with English in the mind of a native English-speaking preschooler. For perspective, one can train a human to hang glide, by taking advantages of the air currents a condor uses. However, it would seem unjustified to assimilate the mental faculty behind the condor's (natural) flight to the skills necessary to succeed at human (artificial) hang gliding (this is not to imply that learning a second language does not employ the Faculty of Language in some sense—after all, only humans learn second languages, even if they do not do it to perfection. The point is raised simply to emphasize the difference between an observable behavior and its underlying causes). If we are interested in the evolution of a natural entity like the Faculty of Language, we cannot satisfy ourselves with vague considerations about whatever mental capacity allows humans to learn languages as adults—we have to go after the natural system in children.

That said, it is also important to distinguish the process of acquiring English (any first language) from the innate developmental process leading to the Faculty of Language in an individual. To use another bird analogy, one thing is for a zebra finch to acquire his (paternal) song (as opposed to a different acquirable song by another conspecific) and a very different thing is for that same zebra finch to develop the mind/brain "circuitry" that makes the achievement possible. Now just as the development of acquisition and performance brain circuits is a well-understood prerequisite for successful bird-song behavior [39], so too the development of the Faculty of Language seems to be a precondition for the acquisition of a given human language.

Having set aside contingent properties of the Faculty of Language, it is worth emphasizing its intrinsic characteristic: combinatory power. In short, the Faculty of Language, as a natural computational system, appears to be roughly equivalent to the family of systems traditionally classified as (mildly) context-sensitive in the Chomsky Hierarchy of grammars [40–43]. In a nutshell, this means that the system is capable of constructing complex expressions with (i) a hierarchical structure and (ii) dependencies among nodes in the hierarchy that are not expressible as hierarchical nodes, thus requiring a more powerful computation (see Section 3 on this). It is commonly held that no other natural computational system has the same power of the Faculty of Language [33]. Hauser et al. refer to this system as "the Faculty of Language in the narrow sense," meaning both that it is the core component of the Faculty of Language in the Broad Sense and that it seems to be an evolutionary novelty [33, 44].

Given this set of assumptions, we would like to examine next the evidence that is customarily adduced for the presence of linguistic abilities in a given species. Our interpretation of the data differs substantially from the traditional one in Evolutionary Anthropology and suggests a slight shift in focus. We will concentrate on the sorts of evidence that are most often discussed in relation to language origins: genetic, anatomical, and archeological considerations, in that order.

Genes for Language?

Molecular biology currently benefits from methodological tools capable of elucidating the differences, at the molecular level, between human beings and other organisms. As a consequence, it can also establish a precise chronological dating of relevant evolutionary changes. Moreover, the progressive optimization of techniques devoted to the analysis of the so-called fossil DNA has opened the way to the possibility of directly measuring the molecular evolution of such genes, yielding a much more accurate temporal perspective of the nature, pace, and magnitude of changes [45, 46]. This extraordinary methodological turn has made it possible for the first fragments of nuclear genes from Homo neanderthalensis to be cloned and sequenced [8, 47–49].

At this molecular level, FOXP2, generally regarded as the "gene of language" [50–54], has been the focus of much attention. This is the case due to two crucial facts: (i) the occurrence of two nonsynonymous changes in the sequence of the protein encoded by it [55], and (ii) the almost certainty that the corresponding Neanderthal gene also contains both substitutions. This suggests that the two modifications in point were not selected in correspondence with the emergence of Homo sapiens (around 200,000 years before present [55]), but in fact much earlier: within a common ancestor of our species and Homo neanderthalensis (c. 500,000 years before present [8]). The latter scenario has led different authors to speculate about the presence of a fully human Faculty of Language—or rather "language" in some general sense—in the second species [9, 56].

Interest in such comparative analyses has extended to other genes whose mutations appear to cause specific language impairments (these are conditions disjoint from neurological dysfunctions, mental retardation, broad cognitive deficits, a hearing impairment, or an inadequate exposition to linguistic stimuli during development). For instance, different substitutions in both DYX1C1 and ROBO1, two genes associated to dyslexia [57–59], have been positively selected in the human lineage: in the first case, after the separation of the evolutionary lines leading, respectively, to humans and the rest of higher primates [57] and, in the second case, between 12 and 16 million years ago [58]. As a complete genetic characterization of the Faculty of Language cannot be made with the exclusion of genes that, when mutated, impair other cognitive capacities besides language, the catalogue of genes of interest is expected to increase in the near future [60, 61].

All these findings point to new and exciting avenues of research concerning the evolution of the Faculty of Language. However, conclusions on this area are undermined by a very common, but unfortunately untenable, assumption that the existence of full-fledged linguistic abilities in other hominids can be automatically inferred from the presence of the human variant of any of these genes.

To begin with, even if many genes have presently been cloned from people affected by specific language disorders [60, 62, 63], paradoxical situations routinely arise. (i) Sometimes relevant genes are also expressed in brain regions not related to language processing, and even in tissues outside the nervous system. (ii) Sometimes such genes are mutated in people affected by other cognitive (i.e., non specifically linguistic) disorders or are simultaneously linked to diverse language impairments. (iii) In some individuals affected by a particular language disorder, the sequence of such "language genes" is normal (phenocopy), while (iv) the linguistic competence of some of the individuals endowed with an anomalous variant of one of these genes is not impaired at all (null-penetrance) or is just mildly impaired (reduced penetrance). Moreover, (v) the identity of such genes differs (to a certain extent) from one population to another or depending on the subtype of the disorder (for a review of different cases, see [60, 63]).

A second point of concern is how genes actually contribute to the regulation of the development and functioning of the neural substrate of the Faculty of Language. Several considerations are worth bearing in mind. (i) Genes do not directly determine language; they just synthesize biochemical products, which will be engaged in particular physiological functions. (ii) Ordinarily, the same gene plays different roles (i.e., contribute to different physiological functions) in diverse moments and body tissues during ontogeny (pleiotropy). Simultaneously, (iii) many genes usually contribute (each to a different extent) to the same biological process (polygenism). Finally, (iv) the extent to which a particular gene product contributes to such a biological process heavily depends on the precise balance it keeps, in a particular moment and place, with the biochemical products encoded by the remaining genes involved.

Other parameters besides genes themselves also contribute to the initial "wiring" of the neural substrate of the Faculty of Language. These include maternal factors (in essence, protein gradients inherited via the egg cytoplasm) and regulatory elements belonging to all levels of biological complexity between genes (and their products) and brain areas [64] (concretely, the metabolome, different subcellular organelles, the diverse brain cells, the synaptic activities, and diverse specific brain circuits). Furthermore, information relating to the structural features and functional properties of the neural substrate of language could plausibly be generated as a consequence of the developmental process itself [65, 66]. Plus they could depend on general laws that apparently regulate the self-organization of biological systems [67, 68]. All these additional nongenetic factors, robustly appearing and acting at certain developmental stages, can be plausibly regarded as innate. Consequently, what can be deemed "innate" clearly transcends what can be regarded as "genetic" [69].

A third concern relates to the fact that complex regulatory mechanisms probably determine just the basic interconnection patterns among the diverse types of differentiated neurons involved (and, thereafter, the basic histological organization of the main anatomic macrostructures which conform the neural substrate of language). In itself, however, this need not produce fully operative computational devices, understood in more or less customary cognitive terms [70]. Frankly, no one has a clear picture as to how such systems may arise in nature in general, let alone minds/brains [71]. Another way of stating this important issue, emphasizing the distance between what happens at measurable brain levels and what is understood in more abstract mind terms, is that any brain prewiring must be compulsorily implemented by the feedback effect exerted by neural activity during language processing. Only in such a way is the ultimate cytoarchitecture of the neural substrate of the Faculty of Language achieved, with fully operative neural structures somehow resulting.

A fourth and crucial point to consider is that an increasing body of evidence suggests that most of the molecular changes occurred along our speciation have affected the transcriptome rather than the genome (and, consequently, the relevant protein sequences) [72–76]. These changes would essentially have carried the following: (i) modifications in the expression levels of different genes (and generally in the corresponding protein stocks) [72] and (ii) modifications in the spatiotemporal expression profiles of others, with the subsequent creation of new combined expression patterns; these are probably the basis for the appearance of new structural and functional compartmentalisations at the brain level and eventually of new cognitive capacities [77].

At the same time, both kinds of changes would have fundamentally been the result of the modification of the following: (i) the cis regulatory regions of gene expression (i.e., noncoding regions located proximal to coding sequences on the same DNA strand), as witnessed by the high number of positive selection signals observed in noncoding regions of genes associated with brain development and function [78, 79], (ii) the levels and/or modulating properties of certain transcription factors, components of signal transduction pathways, and noncoding RNAs (ncRNAs) [80] and (iii) the splicing patterns of mRNA of certain genes [81, 82], which could have affected on average around 6 to 8 percent of human exons, as compared with the chimpanzee [82]. Indeed, alternative splicing (i.e., the synthesis of different functional RNAs from the same primary transcript) is more frequent in the brain tissue than in any other [83]. Finally, it is also worth bearing in mind that other innate information storage systems, including mitochondrial DNA and epigenetic mechanisms, appear to exhibit a number of significant differences between humans and higher primates [84].

The case of FOXP2 leads to some particularly illustrative conclusions. The introduction of the human variant in mice produces interesting phenotypic alterations [85], while the human protein brings about in vitro and in vivo a variation in the transcriptional regulation pattern of the FOXP2 factor, as compared to what happens in the chimpanzee [86]. Nevertheless, we mostly lack information about the sequence (and evolutionary history) of the regulatory regions of the gene. Very probably, significant mutations in these regions have occurred throughout the evolution of our species, with effects on the biological activity of the FOXP2 protein probably surpassing those caused by the mutations accumulated in the coding sequence of the gene. Moreover, we also lack enough information about the sequences targeted by the gene [87] in other hominids (including Neanderthals) which have also been subject to positive selection during our recent evolutionary history. In other words, presently we are in the dark even about the existence of alternative expression patterns relatively to that of our species.

Advances in the molecular understanding of language are certainly fast and promising—but still inconclusive and relatively informative (connections between molecular and linguistic data are generally indirect and rather unclear. E.g., the protocadherin 11 gene pair (PCDH11X/PCDH11Y) has been suggested as a putative determinant of language via its role in cerebral asymmetry [88]. Cerebral asymmetry and right-handedness have recently been attributed to Neanderthals and pointed out as an additional clue in favor of the existence of complex linguistic capabilities in this species [89]. However, the relation between cerebral lateralization and language is not an implicational one [90–

92]. Furthermore, the relation between lateralization and the peculiarities of the Faculty of Language qua computational system is unclear, if it exists at all [93]). There is, however, one thing we can be sure of: we cannot simply infer the presence of the Faculty of Language from just the existence of the human variant of a group of interesting genes, given all other relevant uncertainties.

On Speech and Hearing

Since Lieberman and Crelin's analysis of the Neanderthal vocal tract [14], the debate on the speech capabilities of extinct hominid species has thrived, generally based on anatomical studies [15–19, 94]. This line of research has recently been complemented through the important finding, by the team working at Sierra de Atapuerca, of the ear ossicles of a Homo heidelbergensis. These have made possible to determine relevant features of this and other species' hearing capabilities [20–22]. In this section, we would like to review these matters, although not attempting to be exhaustive—for example, we set aside studies focusing on anatomical features like the neural canal. Right from the onset we want to say that, in our view, it is unfortunate that this interesting debate should have been twisted into one on the presence of full-fledged linguistic abilities. Given our discussion above, an inference from a modern speech and hearing apparatus to the Faculty of Language, as presently understood by linguists, is unwarranted. In what follows we unpack our arguments as explicitly as this context permits.

First, it is a contingent fact that some humans externalize their "linguistic thoughts" through a Vocal-Auditory interface; other humans achieve the same result through a Gestural-Visual interface. Thus the presence of a modern anatomy of the vocal tract and of the middle ear, per se, does not sanction an inference of the presence of the Faculty of Language (as they are soft organs, the outer and inner ear do not fossilize, so we can only extrapolate their structure in extinct species from comparative studies with other, closely related, extant species. Needless to say, the inner ear plays a determining role in the way the auditory signal is processed [95,96]). On similar logical grounds, absence of the modern anatomy of the vocal tract would not allow us to infer absence of the Faculty of Language. For perspective, we would not conclude, if examining a human being who is incapable of gestural-visual abilities, a corresponding absence of linguistic abilities—on the basis of the fact that in other individuals the relevant interface does exist. Patently, correlations of this sort are weak. A being with a thoroughly modern Vocal-Auditory interface but no Faculty of Language is as easy to imagine as a being with archaic Vocal-Auditory interface but Faculty of Language "plugged" into some different externalization system (or none whatsoever). There is no a priori reason to dismiss these reasonable theoretical possibilities (see [97–99], for some evolutionary implications).

Secondly, one must carefully separate the perception of sounds as such from the categorization of such stimuli in linguistic terms. A given organism may be able to produce/perceive sounds like, say, [u] or [i], without this entailing that this sounds are interpreted as vowels by the organism in point (these are the sounds that, for a human subject, correspond to the vowels appearing in the English words "booed" and "bead", resp. Note that English [u] and [i] are always long vowels and thus with a slightly extended duration than the corresponding short vowels found in other languages like Spanish. However the linguistic quality of these sounds is the same in both languages), without this entailing that these sounds are interpreted as vowels by the organism in point. In essence, vowels are linguistic units that, together with consonants, constitute the building blocks of syllables. The latter, in turn, are the basic constituents in the phonological structure of words and phrases, the basis for their characteristic rhythmic structure (rhythmical feet being still higher-order units) and so on. Thus a linguistic symbol is not just a sound, but an element in an intricate system of values that satisfy the famous slogan (attributed both to Saussure and to Meillet) that "chaque fait linguistique fait partie d'un ensemble oùtout se tient." The distinction is not just pedantic. Human babies in prelinguistic stages are able to perceive categorically vocalic sounds like [u] or [i] [100], but so are other mammals, primates included [101–105]. However, no one should attribute the category "vowel" to these nonlinguistic beings— unless one is ready to argue that, for these creatures too, relevant such percepts arrange themselves into a system of interrelated values.

From a biolinguistic perspective, the state of affairs just described means that human languages have their phonetic/phonological structure adjusted to production/perception capabilities of the species. However, perceptual capabilities as such are probably quite ancient. In all likelihood, they are associated to the evolution of the mammalian inner ear and its ability to perform the spectral analysis of complex waveforms in order to individuate their most intense harmonics. Moreover, the data on the perceptual capabilities of mammals are a clear indication that a perfect adjustment between production and perception is not something to be expected in all cases. It is observed in chimpanzees, whose vocalizations appear to contain sounds like human [a], [o], and [u], but nothing comparable to [i] or [e], which, given the sensitivity of their middle ear, are hard to discriminate for them [104]. That case contrasts with that of chinchillas, who perceive but do not produce a variety of the categories that enter the linguistic repertoire in some form [106]. More to the point of our concerns here, we simply do not know what may have happened in earlier hominid species and whether they could or could not discriminate sounds that they were not able to produce accurately [22, 61].

Lieberman [107] argued that if we were to find any evidence for the Faculty of Language in Neanderthals, and they externalized Faculty-of-Language expressions through the Vocal-Auditory interface, we would be able to predict that their phonetic inventory was smaller than ours. Lieberman furthermore suggested that this would be a phonetically less efficient system than ours. However, in point of fact anatomical evidence cannot tell us much about the Faculty of Language. All it can tell us is that human hearing capabilities antedate the apparition of Homo sapiens, whereas the modern configuration of the vocal tract seems to be a novelty of this species (note, moreover, that some of the features considered to be critical for the evolution of speech are not as uniquely human as has often been assumed. Thus, a descended larynx may be a human novelty as compared to other primates—but it is also observed in other mammals [108, 109]). Until we have additional, solid, evidence that this change might have had something to do with the emergence of a fully articulated language with a Faculty of Language interfacing a Vocal-Auditory system, the rest is sheer speculation (see [110, 111], for some interesting proposals about how research in this area might proceed).

An Archeological Approach to Language

Archaeologists studying the Paleolithic tend to agree that the transition to the Upper Paleolithic is one of the most complex, often elusive, research topics in this field [112]. Chronologically located at c. 40,000 years before present, it is a process that includes the demise of Neanderthals and not only the appearance of anatomically modern humans in Europe but their survival and their expansion into Eurasia—including areas that had never been inhabited before by older hominid species. Despite over forty years of studies and a few unquestionable advances, a clear and precise idea of how this phenomenon took place still escapes us. Predictably, language and other abilities considered modern are central to the debate of the demise of Neanderthals and the endurance of anatomically modern humans (who are assumed to have had the same type of cognitive development level and faculties as present-day humans [6]). Far too often, it has been presupposed that these qualities are what ultimately made the difference between the fates of the two species (see [113], among others).

Until a decade ago, a hypothetical revolution that would have taken place with the arrival of anatomically modern humans in Europe was seen as the spark lighting the intense changes the archaeological record of this period reveals [114]. A thorough revision of the African record [115] put an end to speculation, as it showed that every single "revolutionary characteristic" had been independently developed in that continent before being brought into

Europe as part of a new-to-the-area "toolkit"—for over 100,000 years. With that result in mind, any analysis that attempts to shed light on the origins of language simply cannot be done on European data alone but must be based on much older remains, unearthed in African soil, where relevant traits first appeared. A simple linguistic argument for this view stems from the fact that the basic structure of natural languages (e.g., in their logical form) is roughly the same in all inhabited continents [116]. All existing evidence points to the direction that an underlying Faculty of Language, no matter how abstract, emerged in a focal African point and was subsequently carried to the confines of the planet.

Needless to say, the origins of the Faculty of Language cannot be directly studied by Archaeology as commonly understood, because of the lack of fossil evidence in this regard. At the same time, Archaeology aims at shedding light on how ancient humans lived and how they adapted to the environment and survived. Some of the ways in which this must have happened seem so intrinsically connected with the use of language that, no matter how invisible their fossil remains may have been, they ought to be taken into account when reconstructing the past. This is why a variety of archaeological projects have focused on this topic. We will concentrate now on the aforementioned set of innovations that left marks or remains in the record: a collection of traits also studied for other periods, involving economy, subsistence, technology, and so forth.

A word of clarification is relevant at this point. One traditional aspect in which archaeology may relate to linguistics, and vice versa, involves the sociocultural aspect of language, especially as encoded in lexical structures. What linguists call a lexicon—which can be defined as a repository of linguistic idiosyncrasies atomized into words—is undeniable a cultural artifact, aside from a fundamental cognitive component that the Faculty of Language interfaces with. Plainly, the way in which humans live affects how they record their living history through their words. In the process skills, traditions, instructions and other forms of "know how" repository may have been coded. It takes little reflection to realize that such explicit or implicit instructions would have such effects as cutting production time for tools or allowing for elaborate living dwellings, let alone artistic or metaphorical creations. In this regard, more or less sudden innovation in any of the latter—some of which do leave fossil records—can be seen as an indirect argument for a lexicon. Inasmuch as the lexicon presupposes a Faculty of Language, this then also constitutes indirect evidence for such a mental organ (see [117], where the argument is presented in a less meticulous fashion).

In the sections below we look into the traits that have been identified as "modernity indicators," all part of the archeological record. We will examine their relation to the Faculty of Language, as well as their implications for anatomically modern humans, their expansion out of Africa, and their survival.

Technology

Lithic industries constitute by far the largest corpus of remains in the archaeological record of the Paleolithic period. Accordingly, there is a large number of remains that can be grouped under the label of "technological markers". We will focus on three types that appeared at different moments during the Middle Stone Age. Among these are microliths (c. 70 ka), points (c. 250 ka), and blades (c. 280 ka) [115].

Middle Stone Age lithic industries represent a radical change from previous industries, both morphologically and technologically: relevant assemblages include smaller tools and new types, such as blades and microliths. Both were thought to have been part of composite tools, formed by a nonlithic section into which several lithic pieces would be inserted. Points were vastly represented across the African Continent during the Middle Stone Age; during that time they constitute a clear case of regional artifact style, a modernity indicator. These were also hafted to shafts, to be used as projectiles [118].

Composite tools imply aspects that cannot be related to older types of tools. These include forward planning (standardized microliths as replacement of similar older pieces broken during use) and the preparation and complementation of different types of materials that had to be worked in different ways and in separate stages, very likely well before needed. These traits are typically attributed to a stage of cognitive development that can perhaps be related to the Faculty of Language.

Complex bone technology appears in the African record at around 110 ka, during the Middle Stone Age. It contains impressive pieces like the Katanda harpoons and points from D. R. Congo [119]. These materials are dated well before the appearance of the split base points that signal the presence of the earliest Aurignacian in Western Europe. McBrearty and Brooks [115] consider that the African bone-working tradition has its origins much earlier in the Pleistocene. The Middle Stone Age levels show that its development was widespread in that continent.

Bone tools and artifacts manufactured using ivory, antler, and shell supports (organic technology) are considered modernity markers. Complex organic technology is one of the innovations that signal the onset of the Upper Paleolithic in Europe. It is at this point that we have the first evidence that relevant materials are worked using techniques that are different from those used to produce lithic tools. Previous attempts to use bone exist, but relevant artifacts are crudely worked [120, 121]. Of course, the innovation highlighted here relates not so much to the type of materials employed but to the way in which the materials were worked to make tools. Several techniques (polishing, sawing, and abrasion) started at that time to manufacture organic tools. Split-base bone points are an example of artifacts manufactured using such methods.

The abovementioned types of tools have implications within economic parameters. While some saw Middle Stone Age populations as mostly scavengers [122], it is now clear that they hunted. Moreover, their use of points indicates that they had no need to get close to game, which boosted survival rates at the same time that it improved productivity. Chase identifies a specific type of hunting practice as exclusive to anatomically modern humans [117], which is the driving of large game into enclosures or towards cliffs. European examples date from the Middle Pleistocene onwards, and some are related to Mousterian lithic assemblages [123, 124]. The latter would not even imply the use of projectiles, since the animal's fall would cause their certain death. According to this author, sophisticated language was needed to coordinate and organize this kind of hunting technique, though of course the argument remains indirect.

McBrearty and Brooks [115] also highlight the appearance of fishing and shell-fishing at around 110 and 140 ka, respectively, in the African record. These activities would have increased the number of resources available to human groups, at the same time that they opened marine coastal regions to exploitation and colonization.

The exodus of anatomically modern humans out of Africa, whatever its causes, can be traced back to the moment we see the introduction and systematic use of new resources into the Middle Stone Age diets. This was clear from the Lower Stone Age onwards. Once out of Africa, this expansion led anatomically modern humans to the colonization and occupation of Eurasian regions that had never before been explored. From early on this process witnessed the improved adaptability of relevant populations, who were able to survive in a broad array of environments and landscapes—on vastly improved resources. This prevented episodes of food crises leading to starvation and disease, which would have likely caused high mortality rates in previous periods.

The geographical expansion in turn brought the appearance of long distance networks, as well as new possibilities emerging from ties among groups living in different areas and exploiting different environments. Resources opened for those populations: not only in terms of alliances created by marriage—thus broadening the gene pool—but also arriving from foreign territories, as the case for new raw materials. More importantly, concepts and ideas, technologies and beliefs traveled too. Given the richness of what was shared, developed, and maintained, it seems unlikely that most of this sharing could have happened without lexical encoding, therefore presupposing the Faculty of Language [125]. We turn our attention to this in the next section.

Symbols and Culture

Material remains interpreted as symbolic, ritualistic, or nonfunctional have often been the focus of studies trying to shed light on the question of the origins of language—a highly complex system of symbolic combination. Some proposals have caused heated debates, as they revolved around objects of unclear use and significance, whose putative symbolic nature can only be presumed. Surely the use of bona-fide symbols implies a particular cognitive (or even neural) evolution—and perhaps this is related to some aspects of the Faculty of Language [117]. However material culture remains, especially those extremely rare ones, can only offer a very partial view of the minimum cognitive abilities of the people who made such objects [115, 126].

   McBrearty and Brooks characterize symbolic behavior as "the ability to represent objects, people, and abstract concepts with arbitrary symbols, vocal or visual, and reify such symbols in cultural practice." We return shortly to the issue of whether such an ability entails or is presupposed by the Faculty of Language. The most commonly undisputed signs of symbolism in this sense, in the extant archaeological record, appear in Africa at around 250–300 ka. This is during the Acheulian-Middle Stone Age boundary, the latter being a period during which both Homo helmei and early Homo sapiens were present in Africa [115]. Within the extensive list of archaeological traits that start appearing at that time, the following are those classified as symbolic:

- regional artifact styles;
- self-adornment objects (ornaments are defined by Mellars as "small objects for which [there is] no obvious functional explanation" [127]. Note that Chase [117] cautions against this direct relationship and offers an ethnographical list of perforated, grooved and serrated artefacts with practical functions), like beads (from c. 82 ka) and other perforated pieces;
- use of pigment—processed (from c. 280 ka onwards);
- notched and incised objects—organic and inorganic materials (from c. 105 ka);
- image and representation—also called "naturalistic art" (from c. 45 ka in Africa);

• burials with grave goods, ochre, and ritual objects [128].

A cautionary note is due here. Although McBrearty and Brooks label the list above "modern human behaviors," so far very few anatomically human moderns remains have been found in association with symbolic artifacts. The same is true about any components of assemblages to which these remains are commonly assigned (Middle Stone Age in Africa and early Upper Paleolithic/ Aurignacian in Europe) (physically, the makers of the early Aurignacian are poorly known [6], but fossils from Moravia and the Czech Republic link those to anatomically modern humans rather than to other, older, populations). Finally, there are cases of Neanderthal remains associated to Chatelperronian objects—for example, Saint-Césaire, Poitou-Charentes (France) [129, 130], some of which would qualify as symbolic artifacts according to some definitions.

It is also noteworthy that, in some instances where allegedly symbolic material has been found in relation with Neanderthal remains, bona-fide symbolism has been ruled out as a falsifiable explanation. For instance, while anatomically modern human burials can certainly be considered ritualistic, Neanderthal burials are often described as merely hygienic [131–133]. In a different instance, ochre was found in the latest Mousterian level and the earliest Upper Paleolithic level at l'Arbreda Cave in Serinyà, Banyoles (Spain): to its excavators for the last few decades, this ochre is a sign of symbolic behavior during the earliest Upper Paleolithic at the site. However, these researchers do not understand what the same type of remains mean in the Mousterian layer below [134]. Thus, curiously, the very same ochre found in that layer is not related to symbolic activities [135].

One more interesting debate concerns what happened at around 40 ka, when the aforementioned modern behaviors enter the European scene [136]. Then Neanderthals, who for over 200 ka had developed assemblages entirely devoid of symbolic artifacts, appear to start producing objects of the relevant kind. Did Neanderthals suddenly get the Faculty of Language, or some such symbolic engine? A large number of researchers have preferred to see this situation as a case of acculturation of Neanderthals at the hands of innovative and versatile anatomically modern humans [135].

To sum up, considerable disagreement exists among experts, and a lot of work still needs to take place before the fossil evidence yields more information about the Faculty of Language [117]. But a more serious cautionary note should be added from the perspective of linguistics, concerning the validity of taking the vestiges of symbolic behavior or "symbolic culture" as unquestionable evidence for the presence of the kinds of complex abilities commonly associated to the Faculty of Language.

Factually, a collection of cultural practices correlate with the presence of anatomically modern humans, and a number of these fall under the rubric of symbolic behavior or culture. Given this correlation, the following is often assumed as a valid inference:

- Symbolic Culture → the Faculty of Language.
- This inference is often supplemented by its converse:
- the Faculty of Language → Symbolic Culture.
- In essence, this presupposes that a Symbolic Culture is only possible with language and that a Symbolic Culture is a necessary consequence of language. Thus,
- the Faculty of Language → Symbolic Culture.

However, these inferences are invalid, based as they are on a false premise that the use of linguistic symbols is a special case of symbolic behavior. We need to clarify this.

We do not question the idea that a Symbolic Culture may indeed be characterized as an instance of bona-fide symbolic behavior. This basically means that relevant practices partake of signification systems established between different entities, through the relations they stand in with respect to other entities within the system (the most explicit formulation of this idea is to be found in Renfrew [137] and Noble and Davidson [7]. It has never been challenged neither by evolutionary anthropologists nor by archaeologists). The problem is that the Faculty of Language does not respond to this characterization for two different reasons: first, the Faculty of Language is not a behavior, symbolic or otherwise, but a natural system of computation. Second, the semantics of natural languages does not seem to be the product of the kinds of relations that make cultural symbols meaningful.

As pointed out by Eco [138], cultures can only be understood as complex and opaque systems of significations. They are complex because the meaning of each particular component depends on the relations it establishes with the other components of the system. They are opaque because we will hardly be able to know the meaning of a particular symbol unless we know how it is used (this is, e.g., one of the arguments for what Renfrew [137] calls the cognitive-processual approach to archaeology and against what he calls the interpretive approach). So in order to properly understand the meaning of a particular element of the symbolic culture of a group of, say, early humans we should know how it was used in its context (how its use related to that of other elements of the same cultural set). It is highly doubtful that the same general conditions extend to natural languages, pace Wittgenstein [139] and Ryle [140] (although Wittgenstein's work is perhaps the main reference for Anthropology and Archaeology [141]).

The linguistic point is simple. Once we know the meaning of given words (DOG, UNICORN, BROWN, GREEN, etc.) we automatically gain access to the meanings of combinations thereof (BROWN DOG, BROWN UNICORN, GREEN DOG, etc.). This is so even without previous familiarity with the situations in which these symbols might be appropriate. In short, the semantics of natural languages possesses two well-established properties that no cultural system of symbols exhibits: compositionality and productivity. The only known explanation for these linguistic conditions is through the action of a computational system capable of dealing with hierarchical structures.

The contrast is thus clear. While the meanings of the elements making up a Symbolic Culture are opaque until we enter in contact with that Symbolic Culture (to participate in/observe/be informed of the practices in which these elements become meaningful), nothing of this sort applies to the meanings of linguistic complex expressions. These we naturally grasp as we hear them, even with no prior exposition and in the absence of corresponding entities or situations. Nothing of this comes as a surprise once we accept that Symbolic Culture and the Faculty of Language are very disparate entities: Symbolic Cultures are systems of complex and intricate culturally acquired behaviors, while the Faculty of Language is a natural component of the mind/brain of certain organisms (for detailed presentations of this argument see Fodor [30, 142–144]. Wittgenstein was aware of the consequences of the argument and, therefore, tried to show that the semantics of utterances is in fact not compositional [145]. Such a view has not been very influential in semantic studies [30, 146, 147]).

From all this it follows that "meaning" in a cultural system of symbols (or "meaning$_{SC}$") is probably quite different from "meaning" in a natural language (or "meaning$_{FL}$"). A crucial consequence of this is that the capacity of dealing with meaning$_{SC}$ does not presuppose or entail the capacity of dealing with meaning$_{FL}$. The putative connection between the two in humans is a contingent fact on which we cannot base reliable generalizations. The logic is corroborated by the fact that nonhuman apes appear to be able to acquire symbolic systems, at least under experimental conditions [148]—and perhaps even in the wild [149]. No primate, however, has ever been able to acquire/develop a full-fledged "language," or even rudimentary versions thereof involving some serious combinatorial syntax.

A BIOLINGUISTIC VIEW ON THE NEANDERTHAL/ MODERN DIVIDE

Linguistic Complexity

Once again, the Faculty of Language is a natural computational system, capable of constructing complex expressions with a hierarchical structure and nuanced dependencies holding at arbitrarily long distances. The hierarchical structure of linguistic expressions is illustrated by the simple fact that the sentence "The boy says that he likes apples" contains the sentence "He likes apples", and could be contained within the sentence "Everybody knows that [...]." This means that linguistic utterances are not mere concatenations or linear arrangements of symbols but are instead hierarchically organized sets of units, as the following bracketing representation shows:(4)[Everybody knows [that the boy says [that he likes apples]]].

As for long-distance dependencies, note for example that (4) contains a subject pronoun (he) optionally coreferring with the subject noun phrase (the boy) in the middle sentence. This preferred (though not obligatory) reading is captured by coindexation:(5)[Everybody knows [that the boy$_i$ says [that he$_i$ likes apples]]].

Further dependences exist in this sentence under the form of subject/verb agreement ("everybody knows", "the boy says," and "he likes"). Arbitrarily large amounts of linguistic material can be introduced in between the verb and its subjects, without this having effect in the robustness of the dependency. Thus observe that(6)Everybody in this (large (but still very (very) charming)) house knows that the boy with the red hat (that was a present form good old Santa) says that he uncontrollably (and in fact even morbidly) likes apples.

In addition, linguistic expressions can contain more subtle forms of long-distance dependences, technically known as "displacement" relations. This point can be illustrated with Wh-interrogative sentences, in which question words show up far away from the position where they receive interpretation as verbal arguments, as in (7) (where "e" represents the "empty position" left behind by question word after "moving"):(7)[What$_i$ does everybody know [that the boy says [that he likes e$_i$]]].

The ones just reviewed are well-established linguistic facts [28, 150]. They are, in a nutshell, the reasons behind the characterization of the Faculty of Language as a "Type 1" system in terms of its computational complexity, using as a reference point the Chomsky Hierarchy of formal grammar [40–43], which we review next.

Formal Complexity

The said hierarchy defines different classes of "formal languages" (or corresponding grammars), arranged in an increasing scale of complexity. In these mathematical constructs, a "formal language" is understood as a set of strings of symbols generated under certain general admissibility conditions. Crucially, for a system of these characteristics to work, a finite collection of rules, describing the admissible strings in the language, can be produced and result in a computation that halts at some point (it should be easy to see, given the characterization of a "formal language" just introduced, that this mathematical notion is not synonymous to the biolinguistic notion of language defined at the outset of this paper. The notions are however related in some abstract sense [151]).

This ensures that, given the rules of a language (technically, its grammar), some computational device exists capable of mechanically generating any of the strings of the language in question. However, since the arrangement of symbols in a string may be more or less intricate, in definable ways, some languages may require more or less complex devices to generate them. The complexity of a language-generating device (an automaton) is essentially defined in terms of the amount and sophistication of its memory resources. Simply put, more complex languages can only be generated by automata with the appropriate memory resources. This distinction is what underlies the traditional classification of languages, grammars, and corresponding automata from Type 3 (or "finite-state", the simplest ones) to Type 0, the most complex.

The Chomsky Hierarchy therefore provides a useful frame of reference to determine the complexity of Turing-computable problems (the architecture of relevant automata was defined by Alan Turing by theoretically imagining a logical processor writing operational steps on an infinite tape, one step at a time. When one speaks of "memory" within this system, one is basically referring to the ability to designate sections of the writing tape not so much for the purposes of carrying the computation forward but rather with the purpose of storing instructions to be used at later computational times. Different memory regimes determine, in the end, the overall complexity of the "formal languages" so characterized). Any such problem, inasmuch as it is computationally tractable, may be expressed by way of a "formal language" in the Hierarchy—success in this task being just a matter of identifying the critical properties of the problem. Type 3 languages are so simple that they can be described by an automaton with no memory (strings in this type of language are in fact like beads arranged in a linear fashion, with no further internal structuring).

Next up in the hierarchy, we find Type 2 or context-free languages. These need an automaton with enough memory to keep track of what structure is being built, while some embedded substructure is being further constructed. Context-free languages already provide a good measure of complexity for natural languages, since most of their structures fall within the computational capabilities of a "push-down" automaton. This is so called because it contains a simple memory "stack," such that the last item stored into the "stack" is the first one to come out, the top of said "stack" always being involved when recalling items from memory.

Push-down automata may actually describe some long-distance dependencies: those that happen to be "nested" within one another, as in the English example in (8a) (part of the sentence "Peter says that John wants to let Mary read the book"). However, natural language dependencies are known to also be "crossed-serial." One relevant example is the translation of (8a) into a language like Dutch:(8a)

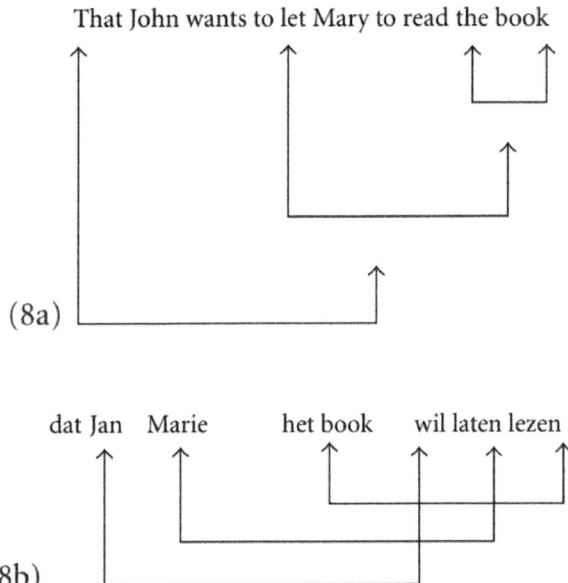

Push-down automata are not equipped to deal with the sorts of dependencies in (8b). This is so because no simple "stack" regime can allow the computation to, at the same time, establish a dependency between two items in the computation and to continue holding an item in between those two in active memory—for subsequent computation. "Stacks" are too simple minded a memory: the entire set of stored items has to be active up to the very last item in storage, and this last item must be the first to be recalled.

A more powerful kind of automaton is needed to generate cross-serial dependencies, either with allowable manipulations within the "stack" (not just at the top) or a different sort of memory procedure. It is this property of natural languages that makes them characterizable as Type 1, or context-sensitive, within the scale of computational complexity defined by the Chomsky Hierarchy (see Table 1 for a summary). Indeed, most theoretical discussion in the last half century has ultimately centered around the issue of precisely how (and when) linguistic structures happen to be of this complex sort.

Table 1: The first three levels of complexity of the Chomsky Hierarchy, with a formal example of the kinds of structures each generates. A context-free grammar may keep track of the number of symbols in every subset so long as it deals with a maximum of two correlated subsets, If the same number of symbols in three (or more) correlated subsets is required within a given "formal language", a context-sensitive grammar is required to describe it [152]

Level of complexity	Language	Sample string
Type 3, finite-state	$a^*b^*c^*$	aabbbbccc
Type 2, context-free	$a^n b^n c^*$	aaabbbcc
Type 1, context-sensitive	$a^n b^n c^n$	aaabbbccc

Is the Complexity of Knots Relevant to the Archaeology of Language?

From our evolutionary perspective, an interesting question arises in light of the formal facts just reviewed. One way to determine whether a given hominid species had the Faculty of Language (as presently exhibited by us) would be to test their computational capabilities—in order to determine how high they were within the Chomsky Hierarchy. Obviously this is not doable in any direct fashion, since the fossil record does not contain direct linguistic evidence of the right sort. Nevertheless, there may well be an indirect manner to proceed that could take advantage of fossilized remains, by seeking traces of language in domains that, while not being directly defined as linguistic, may presuppose a "technical intelligence" that could well be, in some sense at least, parasitic on the Faculty of Language [153]. The prospect is realistic inasmuch as, as emphasized at the outset, this faculty interfaces with other cognitive systems and, through these, with general cognition and the mechanisms underlying behavior [33, 154].

From this perspective the key is to observe relevant aspects of the fossil record with a "grammatical lens," thus asking what sort of algorithm would computationally describe a given rule-governed behavior. If such an algorithm happens to be low within the Chomsky Hierarchy, not much can be surmised from the exercise, since behaviors thus described are common in animal cognition. But if the opposite is the case, and a hypothesized algorithm to describe a given behavior happens to fall high within the Chomsky Hierarchy, the result would potentially be significant. This is so because it is very rare to find bona-fide complex computational behaviors in the natural world. When or if such behaviors are isolated and properly described, three possibilities emerge for them: (i) that they correspond to a mental capacity that is totally unrelated to the Faculty of Language, (ii) that they depend, instead, on some interface with the computational procedure that the Faculty of Language presupposes, or (iii) that the said behaviors obey the conditions of a faculty that actually underlies both the Faculty of Language and whatever is responsible for the inferred behavior.

The idea of connecting artifactual properties with the presence of language (in some sense) is not new. But such exercises are rarely accompanied by rigorous criteria for evaluating the validity of underlying correspondences [155]. The foregoing discussion is aimed at addressing this methodological concern. A proposal originally made by Uriagereka et al. [156, 157], concerning the capacity to tie knots, is a model story of what we are arguing for. It involves a unique behavior within apes, whose computational description falls high within the Chomsky Hierarchy and whose results are inferable from the fossil record.

Particular knotting techniques (say, "clove hitch," "Eskimo bowline," and so on) are cultural practices. What interests us, instead, is the fact that, underlying these technical traditions, a certain natural capacity exists that, so it seems, is not accessible to other primates. One way to assess the complexity of knot tying is to resort to their mathematical characteristics. Knot-theory is the branch of topology that deals with the nature and properties of knots. From this perspective knots are conceptualized as elastic, closed, and tangled strings. The most basic knot (the unknot) is like a circle (i.e., a string joined by its two ends) lying on a single plane. More complex knots are constructed by crossings of the string, such that some parts thereof lie on more than one plane. The minimal knot is a string with three crossings (the so-called threefoil knot). An important area of knot-theory is to determine whether a complexly tangled string is the unknot, and if not what kind of knot it is (the "unkotting problem"). Formal details aside, the task of determining whether any given string is knotted is known to have a complexity comparable to the one needed to process an expression in a natural language (for given knots the computational complexity can be greater than that needed to process linguistic expressions, which moves us into obscure issues dealing with mathematical intuition in humans. Still, for our point to be relevant it is enough to think of simple knottings of the sort routinely used at work in human societies. For an introduction to knot-theory see [158], and [159] for complexity issues).

When actually making a knot, humans must, at a certain point in time, relate a portion in the knot with the background "figure". Intuitively, this is an operation in which both grouping and long distance-like relations are implied [156, 157, 160]. If so (un)tying knots (or determining whether a tangled string is knotted) seems to require an underlying computational system of Type 1 (or even a more powerful system). Once again, such a system is context-sensitive, which is to say capable of keeping track of the computational history until the overlapping(s) needed for knotting take(s) place. The process as a whole can be modeled by storing some (arbitrary) elements A, B, C, in that order, in some computational stack, to then proceed to relate element A at the bottom of the stack to some element D in the current state of the computation (the crossing). This could be represented as in (9a), which is to be compared to (9b):(9a) [D₁ [C [B A₁]]](9b)[What₁ does everybody know [that the boy says [that he likes e₁]].

Abstracting away semantically irrelevant symbols, the formal parallel with a long-distance dependency should be clear.

Again, the correspondence itself could signal the existence of a grammar for knots. However, these sorts of dependencies are exceedingly rare within the primate world. It seems more plausible to ascribe the parallelism in (9) either to the bona-fide Faculty of Language (extended in the appropriate cognitive direction [161]) or to a deeper cognitive system underlying both that faculty and some putative system specific to knots. If either of the latter conditions holds, finding structures of the sort in (9a) in the fossil record would argue for the Faculty of Language being in place by that time.

One last important clarification is in order: being able to learn a specific motor sequence to tie a knot is not sufficient evidence for inferring complex cognitive capacities. The scarce literature on knot-tying abilities in humans has only focused on how people learn to tie a knot either by instruction or by imitation [162, 163]. This may tell us something about how a cultural practice may have been transmitted, but it says nothing about the process of inventing new knots, which humans have been doing for millennia. Similar confusions often arise in the literature on animal behavior, for example when attempting to demonstrate whether birds can parse nested dependencies [164]. As has been noted by many [165, 166], training a bird to successfully identify a couple of such dependencies may tell us nothing about the ability involved in creating any new such expression. Full creativity has always been what is most puzzling about human language.

Setting the Record Straight

Knots are not directly attested in Anatomically Modern Humans until 27 ka B.P., by means of weaving, both in clothing and clothing representations [167]. However, they can be inferred long before that, from purposefully perforated ornaments (beads, teeth, shells, etc.) and small projectile technology (arrow heads, arches, and harpoons), the oldest evidence of which is about 90–75 ka ([168–170], and [171] for an even earlier date). Those dates, of course, are tantalizingly close to what is presumed to be in the range of the emergence of the Faculty of Language.

From this perspective, a very intriguing issue is whether Neanderthals (or, for that matter, other hominids) were capable of knotting behaviors. Perforated shells dated at 50 ka and older, found at the Aviones site, Spain, have been presented as an indication that Neanderthals shared some of these practices with Anatomically Modern Humans [13]. The case merits serious examination, but the fact that the perforations in point are not deliberate (that is, they are indisputably due to natural causes) makes one wonder to what extent the relevant ornament was used in a deliberate way as a carefully crafted and prominently worn piece of jewelry, possibly a mark of social status.

Possibilities to interpret the relevant data, even from a biolinguistic point of view, are multiple. However, the most promising seem to be two. The first is that the Faculty of Language is an anatomically modern human evolutionary novelty among primates. By and large, this possibility fits well with the strong contrast between the material culture of anatomically modern humans and Neanderthals [4, 6, 12, 128, 172–176]. The extremely diversified and dynamic character of the former could be a reflection of the open-endedness productivity of the Faculty of Language, a consequence of its computational properties [177]. Note that a computational system of Type 2 is enough for genuine "recursion" (or systematic and unlimited nested embedding) [33, 178]. This is the formal property that explains why sentences have no upper limit of components and, therefore, that there is no upper number of possible utterances a language allows [179]. However, recursion is still insufficient to deal with the real complexity of human languages. The qualification is in order because it could even be the case that Neanderthals had achieved one level of complexity without reaching the other see [180–183] for perspective. The second hypothesis is that the Faculty of Language is a feature shared by both anatomically modern humans and Neanderthals, already present in their common ancestor (i.e., a sapiens synapomorphy).

The latter position would rationalize Krause et al.'s finding concerning the antiquity of the FOXP2 genetic variant [8]. It also would explain the abilities underlying the ornaments of Aviones site (see above; [13]) particularly if some independent proof is found of their use as beads tied together by some sort of thread. This hypothesis would be consistent with the possibility that there might exist other Type 1 computational systems in nature—beyond the human Faculty of Language. One case to examine seriously involves species of weaver birds that tie knots as a part of their nest construction techniques. Some of these knots are (near) equivalents of human knots [184, 185] (some apes in captivity have been reported to tie simple knots [186]). The jury is of course out on whether this means that the birds in point have the cognitive equivalent of a Faculty of Language, albeit with nest-building consequences instead of anything familiar to humans. Key to answering that question would be to determine the level of complexity the birds can attain in their knot-tying abilities. Patently, some of their relevant knots are more complex than others, and the question is whether any or all of them can be produced by the compilation of a motor skill (for example, the knots used in Michel and Harkins' experiment [162] are simple (the sheepshank, the butterfly knot, and the "magic" slip-knot), and yet only 37% of their subjects were able to learn to tie the three of them by just attending demonstrations, i.e., observing the necessary motor sequence to tie them).

Clarifying either position should also help us understand the late cultural achievements of Neanderthals: whether they constitute an acculturation effect from contacts with anatomically modern humans [12, 187], an independent cultural development [11, 130], an intraspecific "last minute" evolutionary event, or even the result of interbreeding [49]. It is good to have new tools to address such open questions.

CONCLUSIONS

In presenting the biolinguistic approach to the study of language, this paper has developed some ideas on how that approach may contribute to the study of human history. For the brand of linguistics we represent, the communicative or even symbolic aspects of language are not as central as its formal properties. Only by focusing on these properties are we able to draw a clear picture of the computational resources necessary to generate a human language. The natural cognitive computational system capable of deploying these resources—the Faculty of Language, an organ of our minds/brains—is thus our main subject of inquiry. Given this basic assumption, we have explored how research on Evolutionary Anthropology can be complemented: by qualifying or reassessing the interpretation of the existing data. It is our hope that future research will benefit from the perspective offered here, by strengthening the interdisciplinary stance that the inquiry into the origins of our species necessarily requires. When we need to date remains, we turn to Physics and Chemistry; when studying hominid remains, we ask palaeobiologists and geneticists—and experts on nutrition are consulted when palaeodiets are the focus. Similarly, when aiming at progress in the study of language and its origins, linguistics should prove to be useful. We hope it has been.

ACKNOWLEDGMENTS

This work has been carried out through the project Biolingüística: evolución, desarrollo y fósiles del lenguaje(FFI2010-14955) from the Ministerio de Ciencia e Innovación (Spain) and partially cofunded by FEDER funds (EU). It also received partial support from the Generalitat de Catalunya through Grant 2009SGR1079 to the Centre de Lingüística Teòrica of the UAB. The authors want to express their gratitude to two anonymous IJEBreviewers for their helpful comments.

REFERENCES

1.   J. Maynard-Smith and E. Szathmáry, The Major Transitions in Evolution, Oxford University Press, Oxford, UK, 1995.

2.   D. Bickerton, Language and Species, The University of Chicago Press, Chicago, Ill, USA, 1990.

3.   T. J. Crow, "Schizophrenia as the price that Homo sapiens pays for language: a resolution of the central paradox in the origin of the species," Brain Research Reviews, vol. 31, no. 2-3, pp. 118–129, 2000.

4.   S. Mithen, The Singing Neanderthals, Weidenfield and Nicholson, London, UK, 2005.

5.   R. Klein and B. Edgar, The Dawn of Human Culture, John Wiley & Sons, New York, NY, USA, 2002.

6.   R. Klein, The Human Career, University of Chicago Press, Chicago, Ill, USA, 3rd edition, 2009.

7.   W. Noble and I. Davidson, Human Evolution, Language and Mind. A Psychological and Archaeological Inquiry, Cambridge University Press, Cambridge, UK, 1996.

8.   J. Krause, C. Lalueza-Fox, L. Orlando et al., "The derived FOXP2 variant of modern humans was shared with Neandertals," Current Biology, vol. 17, no. 21, pp. 1908–1912, 2007.

9.   E. Trinkaus, "Human evolution: Neandertal gene speaks out," Current Biology, vol. 17, no. 21, pp. R917–R919, 2007.

10.   F. d›Errico, C. Henshilwood, G. Lawson et al., "Archaeological evidence for the emergence of language, symbolism, and music—an alternative

multidisciplinary perspective," Journal of World Prehistory, vol. 17, no. 1, pp. 1–70, 2003.

11. F. D›Errico, "The invisible frontier. A multiple species model for the origin of behavioral modernity,"Evolutionary Anthropology, vol. 12, no. 4, pp. 188–202, 2003. ··

12. P. Mellars, "The impossible coincidence. A single-species model for the origins of modern human behavior in Europe," Evolutionary Anthropology, vol. 14, no. 1, pp. 12–27, 2005. ··

13. J. Zilhão, D. E. Angelucci, E. Badal-García et al., "Symbolic use of marine shells and mineral pigments by Iberian Neandertals," Proceedings of the National Academy of Sciences of the United States of America, vol. 107, no. 3, pp. 1023–1028, 2010. ·

14. P. Lieberman and E. S. Crelin, "On the speech of the Neanderthal man," Linguistic Inquiry, vol. 2, pp. 203–222, 1971.

15. P. Lieberman, "On the evolution of language: a unified view," Cognition, vol. 2, no. 1, pp. 59–94, 1973. ·

16. J. L. Heim, L. J. Boë, and C. Abry, "La parole à la portée du conduit vocal de l'homme de Neandertal,"Comptes Rendus—Palevol, vol. 1, no. 2, pp. 129–134, 2002. ··

17. L. J. Boë, J. L. Heim, K. Honda, and S. Maeda, "The potential Neandertal vowel space was as large as that of modern humans," Journal of Phonetics, vol. 30, no. 3, pp. 465–484, 2002.

18. P. Lieberman, "Current views on Neanderthal speech capabilities: a reply to Boe et al. (2002)," Journal of Phonetics, vol. 35, no. 4, pp. 552–563, 2007.

19. L. J. Boë, J. L. Heim, K. Honda, S. Maeda, P. Badin, and C. Abry, "The vocal tract of newborn humans and Neanderthals: acoustic capabilities and consequences for the debate on the origin of language. A reply to Lieberman (2007a)," Journal of Phonetics, vol. 35, no. 4, pp. 564–581, 2007. ··

20. I. Martínez, R. M. Quam, M. Rosa, et al., "Auditory capacities of human fossils: a new approach to the origin of speech," in Proceedings of the 2nd ASA-EAA Joint Conference Acoustics, pp. 4177–4182, Acoustical Society of America, The European Acoustics Association and Société Française d'Acoustique, Paris, France, 2008.

21. I. Martínez, J. L. Arsuaga, R. Quam, J. M. Carretero, A. Gracia, and L. Rodríguez, "Human hyoid bones from the middle Pleistocene site of the Sima de los Huesos (Sierra de Atapuerca, Spain)," Journal of Human

Evolution, vol. 54, no. 1, pp. 118–124, 2008.

22. I. Martínez and J. L. Arsuaga, "El origen del lenguaje: la evidencia paleontológica," Munibe (Antropologia-Arkeologia), vol. 60, pp. 5–16, 2009.

23. R. Berwick and N. Chomsky, "The biolinguistic program: the current state of its evolution and development," in The Biolinguistic Enterprise: New Perspectives on the Evolution and Nature of the Human Language Faculty, A. M. Di Sciullo and C. Boeckx, Eds., pp. 19–41, Oxford University Press, Oxford, UK, 2011.

24. C. Boeckx and M. Piattelli-Palmarini, "Language as a natural object— linguistics as a natural science,"Linguistic Review, vol. 22, no. 2–4, pp. 447–466, 2005.

25. L. Jenkins, Biolinguistics, Cambridge University Press, Cambridge, UK, 2000.

26. E. Lenneberg, Biological Foundations of Language, John Wiley & Sons, New York, NY, USA, 1967.

27. C. Boeckx and K. Grohmann, Eds., The Cambridge Handbook of Biolinguistics, Cambridge University Press, Cambridge, UK, forthcoming.

28. C. Boeckx, Language in Cognition. Uncovering Mental Structures and the Rules Behind Them, Willey-Blackwell, Malden, Mass, USA, 2009.

29. H. Putnam, "Brains and behavior," in History and Philosophy of Science, Section L, American Association for the Advancement of Science, 1961, reprinted in N. Block, ed., Readings in Philosophy of Psychology. Volume One, pp. 24–36, Harvard University Press, Cambridge, Mass, USA, 1980.

30. J. A. Fodor, The Language of Thought, Crowell, New York, NY, USA, 1975.

31. N. Chomsky, Language and Mind, Harcourt Brace, New York, NY, USA, 1968.

32. N. Chomsky, Aspects of the Theory of Syntax, MIT Press, Cambridge, Mass, USA, 1965.

33. M. D. Hauser, N. Chomsky, and W. T. Fitch, "Neuroscience: the faculty of language: what is it, who has it, and how did it evolve?" Science, vol. 298, no. 5598, pp. 1569–1579, 2002.

34. N. Chomsky, "Approaching UG from below," in Interfaces + Recursion = Language? Chomsky's Minimalism and the View from Syntax– Semantics, U. Sauerland and H. M. Gärtner, Eds., pp. 1–29, Mouton de

Gruyter, New York, NY, USA, 2007.

35. N. Chomsky, "Some simple evo devo theses: how true might they be for language," in The Evolution of Language. Biolinguistic Perspectives, R. K. Larson, V. Déprez, and H. Yamakido, Eds., pp. 45–62, Cambridge University Press, Cambridge, UK, 2010.

36. D. Brentari, Ed., Sign Languages, Cambridge University Press, New York, NY, USA, 2010.

37. K. Emmorey, Language, Cognition, and the Brain. Insights from Sign Language Research, Lawrence Erlbaum, Mahwah, NJ, USA, 2002.

38. C. Neidle, J. Kegl, D. MacLaughlin Jr., et al., The Syntax of American Sign Language: Functional Categories and Hierarchical Structure, MIT Press, Cambridge, Mass, USA, 2000.

39. E. D. Jarvis, "Learned birdsong and the neurobiology of human language," Annals of the New York Academy of Sciences, vol. 1016, pp. 749–777, 2004.

40. N. Chomsky, "Three models for the description of language," IRE Transactions on Information Theory, vol. 2, pp. 113–124, 1956.

41. N. Chomsky, "On certain formal properties of grammars," Information and Control, vol. 2, pp. 137–167, 1957.

42. N. Chomsky, "Formal properties of grammars," in Handbook of Mathematical Psychology. Vol. II, R. D. Luce, R. R. Bush, and E. Galanter, Eds., pp. 323–418, John Wiley & Sons, New York, NY, USA, 1963.

43. A. K. Joshi, "Tree adjoining grammars: how much context-sensitivity is required to provide reasonable structural descriptions?" in Natural Language Parsing. Psychological, Computational, and Theoretical Perspectives, D. R. Dowty, L. Karttunen, and A. M. Zwicky, Eds., pp. 206–250, Cambridge University Press, Cambridge, UK, 1985.

44. W. T. Fitch, M. D. Hauser, and N. Chomsky, "The evolution of the language faculty: clarifications and implications," Cognition, vol. 97, no. 2, pp. 179–210, 2005. · ·

45. A. Cooper and R. Wayne, "New uses for old DNA," Current Opinion in Biotechnology, vol. 9, no. 1, pp. 49–53, 1998.

46. M. Hofreiter, D. Serre, H. N. Poinar, M. Kuch, and S. Pääbo, "Ancient DNA," Nature Reviews Genetics, vol. 2, no. 5, pp. 353–359, 2001.

47. J. P. Noonan, G. Coop, S. Kudaravalli et al., "Sequencing and analysis of Neanderthal genomic DNA," Science, vol. 314, no. 5802, pp. 1113–1118, 2006.

48. H. A. Burbano, E. Hodges, R. E. Green et al., "Targeted investigation of the neandertal genome by array-based sequence capture," Science, vol. 328, no. 5979, pp. 723–725, 2010.

49. R. E. Green, J. Krause, A. W. Briggs et al., "A draft sequence of the neandertal genome," Science, vol. 328, no. 5979, pp. 710–722, 2010.

50. K. E. Watkins, N. F. Dronkers, and F. Vargha-Khadem, "Behavioural analysis of an inherited speech and language disorder: comparison with acquired aphasia," Brain, vol. 125, no. 3, pp. 452–464, 2002. ·

51. G. F. Marcus and S. E. Fisher, "FOXP2 in focus: what can genes tell us about speech and language?"Trends in Cognitive Sciences, vol. 7, no. 6, pp. 257–262, 2003. · ·

52. F. Vargha-Khadem, D. G. Gadian, A. Copp, and M. Mishkin, "FOXP2 and the neuroanatomy of speech and language," Nature Reviews Neuroscience, vol. 6, no. 2, pp. 131–138, 2005.

53. L. D. Shriberg, K. J. Ballard, J. B. Tomblin, J. R. Duffy, K. H. Odell, and C. A. Williams, "Speech, prosody, and voice characteristics of a mother and daughter with a 7;13 translocation affecting FOXP2,"Journal of Speech, Language, and Hearing Research, vol. 49, no. 3, pp. 500–525, 2006. · ·

54. S. E. Fisher and C. Scharff, "FOXP2 as a molecular window into speech and language," Trends in Genetics, vol. 25, no. 4, pp. 166–177, 2009.

55. W. Enard, M. Przeworski, S. E. Fisher et al., "Molecular evolution of FOXP2, a gene involved in speech and language," Nature, vol. 418, no. 6900, pp. 869–872, 2002. · ·

56. F. d'Errico, "The archaeology of language origin," in Proceedings of the 7th International Conference on the Evolution of Language (EVOLANG7 ‹08), A. Smith, K. Smith, and R. Ferrer i Cancho, Eds., pp. 413–414, World Scientific, 2008.

57. M. Taipale, N. Kaminen, J. Nopola-Hemmi et al., "A candidate gene for developmental dyslexia encodes a nuclear tetratricopeptide repeat domain protein dynamically regulated in brain," Proceedings of the National Academy of Sciences of the United States of America, vol. 100, no. 20, pp. 11553–11558, 2003. · ·

58. K. Hannula-Jouppi, N. Kaminen-Ahola, M. Taipale et al., "The axon guidance receptor gene ROBO1 is a candidate gene for developmental dyslexia," PLoS Genetics, vol. 1, no. 4, article e50, 2005. ·

59. L. M. McGrath, S. D. Smith, and B. F. Pennington, "Breakthroughs in the search for dyslexia candidate genes," Trends in Molecular Medicine, vol.

12, no. 7, pp. 333–341, 2006.

60. A. Benítez Burraco, "Genetics of language. Roots of specific language deficits," in The Cambridge Handbook of Biolinguistics, C. Boeckx and K. K. Grohmann, Eds., Cambridge University Press, Cambridge, UK, forthcoming.

61. S. Balari, A. Benítez-Burraco, V. M. Longa, and G. Lorenzo, "The fossils of language: what are they, who has them, how did they evolve?" in The Cambridge Handbook of Biolinguistics, C. Boeckx and K. K. Grohmann, Eds., Cambridge University Press, Cambridge, UK, forthcoming.

62. S. D. Smith, "Genes, language development, and language disorders," Mental Retardation and Developmental Disabilities Research Reviews, vol. 13, no. 1, pp. 96–105, 2007.

63. A. Benítez-Burraco, Genes y Lenguaje: Aspectos Ontogenéticos, Filogenéticos y Cognitivos, Reverté, Barcelona, Spain, 2009.

64. J. Choudhary and S. G. N. Grant, "Proteomics in postgenomic neuroscience: the end of the beginning,"Nature Neuroscience, vol. 7, no. 5, pp. 440–445, 2004.

65. S. Oyama, The Ontogeny of Information. Developmental Systems and Evolution, Duke University Press, Durham, NC, USA, 2000.

66. S. Oyama, P. Griffiths, and R. D. Gray, Eds., Cycles of Contingency. Developmental Systems and Evolution, MIT Press, Cambridge, Mass, USA, 2001.

67. S. Kauffman, At Home in the Universe: The Search of the Laws of Self-Organization and Complexity, Oxford University Press, New York, NY, USA, 1995.

68. S. Kauffman, Investigations, Oxford University Press, New York, NY, USA, 2000.

69. P. Bateson and M. Mameli, "The innate and the acquired: useful clusters or a residual distinction from folk biology?" Developmental Psychobiology, vol. 49, no. 8, pp. 818–831, 2007.

70. F. Ramus, "Genes, brain, and cognition: a roadmap for the cognitive scientist," Cognition, vol. 101, no. 2, pp. 247–269, 2006.

71. C. R. Gallistel, The Organization of Learning, MIT Press, Cambridge, Mass, USA, 1990.

72. W. Enard, P. Khaitovich, J. Klose et al., "Intra- and interspecific variation in primate gene expression patterns," Science, vol. 296, no. 5566, pp. 340–343, 2002. · ·

73. P. Khaitovich, W. Enard, M. Lachmann, and S. Pääbo, "Evolution of

primate gene expression," Nature Reviews Genetics, vol. 7, no. 9, pp. 693–702, 2006.

74. J. M. Sikela, "The jewels of our genome: the search for the genomic changes underlying the evolutionarily unique capacities of the human brain.," PLoS Genetics, vol. 2, no. 5, article e80, 2006. · ·

75. E. J. Vallender, N. Mekel-Bobrov, and B. T. Lahn, "Genetic basis of human brain evolution," Trends in Neurosciences, vol. 31, no. 12, pp. 637–644, 2008.

76. A. Varki, D. H. Geschwind, and E. E. Eichler, "Human uniqueness: genome interactions with environment, behaviour and culture," Nature Reviews Genetics, vol. 9, no. 10, pp. 749–763, 2008.

77. M. B. Johnson, Y. I. Kawasawa, C. E. Mason et al., "Functional and evolutionary insights into human brain development through global transcriptome analysis," Neuron, vol. 62, no. 4, pp. 494–509, 2009. · ·

78. S. Prabhakar, J. P. Noonan, S. Pääbo, and E. M. Rubin, "Accelerated evolution of conserved noncoding sequences in humans," Science, vol. 314, no. 5800, article 786, 2006.

79. R. Haygood, O. Fedrigo, B. Hanson, K. D. Yokoyama, and G. A. Wray, "Promoter regions of many neural- and nutrition-related genes have experienced positive selection during human evolution,"Nature Genetics, vol. 39, no. 9, pp. 1140–1144, 2007.

80. J. S. Mattick, "Challenging the dogma: the hidden layer of non-protein-coding RNAs in complex organisms," BioEssays, vol. 25, no. 10, pp. 930–939, 2003. · ·

81. P. Gagneux and A. Varki, "Genetic differences between humans and great apes," Molecular Phylogenetics and Evolution, vol. 18, no. 1, pp. 2–13, 2001. · ·

82. J. A. Calarco, Y. Xing, M. Cáceres et al., "Global analysis of alternative splicing differences between humans and chimpanzees," Genes and Development, vol. 21, no. 22, pp. 2963–2975, 2007.

83. G. Yeo, D. Holste, G. Kreiman, and C. B. Burge, "Variation in alternative splicing across human tissues,"Genome Biology, vol. 5, no. 10, p. R74, 2004. ·

84. A. Mochizuki, Y. Takeda, and Y. Iwasa, "The evolution of genomic imprinting," Genetics, vol. 144, no. 3, pp. 1283–1295, 1996. ·

85. W. Enard, S. Gehre, K. Hammerschmidt et al., "A humanized version of FOXP2 affects cortico-basal ganglia circuits in mice," Cell, vol. 137, no. 5, pp. 961–971, 2009.

86. G. Konopka, J. M. Bomar, K. Winden et al., "Human-specific transcriptional regulation of CNS development genes by FOXP2," Nature, vol. 462, no. 7270, pp. 213–217, 2009.

87. E. Spiteri, G. Konopka, G. Coppola et al., "Identification of the transcriptional targets of FOXP2, a gene linked to speech and language, in developing human brain," American Journal of Human Genetics, vol. 81, no. 6, pp. 1144–1157, 2007.

88. T. H. Priddle and T. J. Crow, "The protocadherin 11X/Y gene pair as a putative determinant of cerebral dominance in Homo sapiens," Future Neurology, vol. 4, no. 4, pp. 509–518, 2009. · ·

89. D. W. Frayer, I. Fiore, C. Lalueza-Fox, J. Radovčić, and L. Bondioli, "Right handed Neandertals: Vindija and beyond," Journal of Anthropological Sciences, vol. 88, pp. 113–127, 2010. ·

90. J. L. Bradshaw and N. C. Nettleton, "The nature of hemispheric specialization in man," Behavioral and Brain Sciences, vol. 4, no. 1, pp. 51–63, 1981. ·

91. C. Cantalupo and W. D. Hopkins, "Asymmetric broca›s area in great apes: a region of the ape brain is uncannily similar to one linked with speech in humans," Nature, vol. 414, no. 6863, article 505, 2001. · ·

92. C. Cantalupo, D. L. Pilcher, and W. D. Hopkins, "Are planum temporale and sylvian fissure asymmetries directly related? A MRI study in great apes," Neuropsychologia, vol. 41, no. 14, pp. 1975–1981, 2003.

93. A. Benítez-Burraco, "La lateralización cerebral y el origen del lenguaje," Estudios de Lingüística. Universidad de Alicante, vol. 21, pp. 35–52, 2007.

94. S. Martelli, A. Serrurier, A. Barney, et al., "3-d morphometric and acoustic analysis of chimpanzee and human vocal tracts, and their use in the reconstruction of Neanderthal vocal tracts and their acoustic potential," in Proceedings of the 8th International Conference on the Evolution of Language (EVOLANG8 ‹10), A. D. M. Smith, M. Schuwstra, B. de Boer, and K. Smith, Eds., pp. 449–450, World Publishing, 2010.

95. B. C. J. Moore, An Introduction to the Psychology of Hearing, Academic Press, London, UK, 3rd edition, 1989.

96. J. O. Pickles, An Introduction to the Physiology of Hearing, Academic Press, London, UK, 2nd edition, 1988.

97. M. C. Corballis, From Hand to Mouth. The Origins of Language, Princeton University Press, Princeton, NJ, USA, 2002.

98. G. W. Hewes, "Primate comunication and the gestural origin of language,"

Current Anthropology, vol. 14, pp. 5–24, 1973.

99. W. C. Stokoe, Language in Hand. Why Sign Came Before Speech, Gallaudet University Press, Washington, DC, USA, 2001.

100. J. Mehler, P. Jusczyk, G. Lambertz, N. Halsted, J. Bertoncini, and C. Amiel-Tison, "A precursor of language acquisition in young infants," Cognition, vol. 29, no. 2, pp. 143–178, 1988. ·

101. P. K. Kuhl and J. D. Miller, "Speech perception by the chinchilla: identification functions for synthetic VOT stimuli," Journal of the Acoustical Society of America, vol. 63, no. 3, pp. 905–917, 1978.

102. P. K. Kuhl and D. M. Padden, "Enhanced discriminability at the phonetic boundaries for the voicing feature in macaques," Perception and Psychophysics, vol. 32, no. 6, pp. 542–550, 1982. ·

103. P. K. Kuhl and D. M. Padden, "Enhanced discriminability at the phonetic boundaries for the place feature in macaques," Journal of the Acoustical Society of America, vol. 73, no. 3, pp. 1003–1010, 1983. ·

104. S. Kojima and S. Kiritani, "Vocal-auditory functions in the chimpanzee: vowel perception,"International Journal of Primatology, vol. 10, no. 3, pp. 199–213, 1989.

105. S. Kojima, I. F. Tatsumi, S. Kiritani, and H. Hirose, "Vocal-auditory functions of the chimpanzee: consonant perception," Human Evolution, vol. 4, no. 5, pp. 403–416, 1989. ·

106. J. Bartl, Läutausserungen der Chinchillas im Sozialverband, doctoral dissertation, Ludwig-Maximilians-Universität, Fachbereich Veterinarmedizin, München, Germany, 2006.

107. P. Lieberman, "Hominid evolution, supralaryngeal vocal tract physiology, and the fossil evidence for reconstructions," Brain and Language, vol. 7, no. 1, pp. 101–126, 1979. ·

108. W. T. Fitch, "The phonetic potential of nonhuman vocal tracts: comparative cineradiographic observations of vocalizing animals," Phonetica, vol. 57, no. 2–4, pp. 205–218, 2000. ·

109. W. T. Fitch and D. Reby, "The descended larynx is not uniquely human," Proceedings of the Royal Society B, vol. 268, no. 1477, pp. 1669–1675, 2001. ·

110. B. Samuels, "The third factor in phonology," Biolinguistics, vol. 3, pp. 355–382, 2009.

111. B. Samuels, M. D. Hauser, and C. Boeckx, "Do animals have Universal Grammar? A case study in phonology," in The Oxford Handbook of Universal Grammar, I. Roberts, Ed., Oxford University Press, Oxford,

UK, forthcoming.

112. M. Camps and P. R. Chauhan, Sourcebook of Paleolithic Transitions: Methods, Theories, and Interpretations, Springer, New York, NY, USA, 2009.

113. R. DeSalle and I. Tattersall, Human Origins, What Bones and Genomes Tell Us about Ourselves, TAMU Press, College Stattion, Tex, USA, 2008.

114. P. Mellars, "Cognitive changes and the emergence of modern humans in Europe," Cambridge Archaeological Journal, vol. 1/1, pp. 63–76, 1991.

115. S. McBrearty and A. S. Brooks, "The revolution that wasn›t: a new interpretation of the origin of modern human behavior," Journal of Human Evolution, vol. 39, no. 5, pp. 453–563, 2000. ·

116. J. Uriagereka, Syntactic Anchors: On Semantic Structuring, Cambridge University Press, Cambridge, UK, 2008.

117. P. G. Chase, The Emergence of Culture. The Evolution of a Uniquely Human Way of Life, Springer, New York, NY, USA, 2006.

118. A. Brooks, J. Yellen, L. Nevell, and G. Hartman, "Projectile technologies of the African MSA," inTransitions before the Transition. Evolution and Stability in the Middle Paleolithic and Middle Stone Age, E. Hovers and S. Kuhn, Eds., pp. 233–255, Springer, New York, NY, USA, 2006.

119. J. E. Yellen, A. S. Brooks, E. Cornelissen, M. J. Mehlman, and K. Stewart, "A middle stone age worked bone industry from Katanda, Upper Semliki Valley, Zaire," Science, vol. 268, no. 5210, pp. 553–556, 1995. ·

120. J. Gonzalez Echegaray, L. G. Freeman, B. Madariaga, et al., Cueva Morín. Excavaciones 1969, Patronato de las Cuevas Prehistoricas de la Provincia de Santander, Santander, Spain, 1973.

121. L. G. Freeman, "More on the Mousterian: flaked bone from Cueva Morín," Current Anthropology, vol. 24, pp. 366–377, 1983.

122. L. R. Bindford, The Faunal Remains From Klasies River Mout, Academic Press, New York, NY, USA, 1984.

123. M. A. Levine, "Mortality models and the interpretations of horse population structure," in Hunter-Gatherer Economy in Prehistory: A European Perspective, G. Bailey, Ed., Cambridge University Press, Cambridge, UK, 1983.

124. P. A. Mellars, "The chronology of the South-West French Mousterian: a review," in L'Homme de Neandertal, Vol. 4, La Technique, L. Bindford and J.-P. Rigaud, Eds., pp. 97–120, Université de Liège, Liège, Belgium, 1988.

125. R. I. M. Dunbar, "Coevolution of neocortical size, group size and

language in humans," Behavioral and Brain Sciences, vol. 16, no. 4, pp. 681–735, 1993.

126. T. Wynn, "Piaget, stone tools and the evolution of human intelligence," World Archaeology, vol. 17, no. 1, pp. 32–43, 1985. ·

127. P. Mellars, "The character of the Middle-Upper Palaeolithic transition in South-West France," in The Explanation of Culture Change, C. A. Renfrew, Ed., pp. 255–276, Duckworth, London, UK, 1973.

128. P. Mellars, "Archaeology and the origins of modern humans: European and African perspectives," inThe Speciation of Modern Homo Sapiens, T. J. Crow, Ed., pp. 31–47, British Academy, London, UK, 2002.

129. F. Levêque, "Les donées du gisement de Saint-Césaire et la transition Paléolithique moyen/supérieur en Poitou-Charentes," in El Origen del Hombre Moderno en el Suoreste de Europa, V. Cabrera Valdés, Ed., pp. 263–286, Universidad Nacional de Educación a distancia,, Madrid, Spain, 1993.

130. F. d›Errico, J. Zilhão, M. Julien, D. Baffler, and J. Pelegrin, "Neanderthal acculturation in western Europe? A critical review of the evidence and its interpretation," Current Anthropology, vol. 39, supplement 1, pp. S1–S44, 1998. ·

131. R. H. Gargett, "Grave shortcomings: the evidence for Neanderthal burial," Current Anthropology, vol. 30, pp. 157–190, 1989.

132. R. H. Gargett, "Middle Palaeolithic burial is not a dead issue: the view from Qafzeh, Saint-Césaire, Kebara, Amud, and Dederiyeh," Journal of Human Evolution, vol. 37, no. 1, pp. 27–90, 1999. ·

133. P. Mellars, "Symbolism, language, and the Neanderthal mind," in Modelling the Early Human Mind, P. Mellars and K. Gibson, Eds., pp. 15–32, McDonald Institute for Archeological Research, Cambridge, UK, 1996.

134. J. Maroto, El pas del paleolític mitjà al paleolític superior a Catalunya i la seva interpretació dins del context geogràfic franco-ibèric, doctoral dissertation, Universitat de Girona, 1994.

135. M. Camps, The Mid-Upper Palaeolithic Transition in Iberia: Turning Data into Information, BAR International Series, S1517, Archaeopress, Oxford, UK, 2006.

136. M. Camps, "Where there›s a will there›s a way? 30 years of debate on the Mid-Upper Paleolithic transition in Western Europe," in The Mediterranean from 50,000 to 25,000 BP: Turning Points and New Directions, M. Camps and C. Szmidt, Eds., pp. 1–10, Oxbow, Oxford,

UK, 2009.

137. C. Renfrew, "Towards a cognitive archaeology," in The Ancient Mind. Elements of Cognitive Archaeology, C. Renfrew and E. B. W. Zubrow, Eds., pp. 3–12, Cambridge University Press, Cambridge, UK, 1994.

138. U. Eco, Trattato di Semiotica Generale, Bompiani, Milano, Italy, 1975.

139. L. Wittgenstein, Philosophische Untersuchungen, Bilingual edition, Crítica, Barcelona, Spain, 1988.

140. G. Ryle, The Concept of Mind, Hutchinson, London, UK, 1949.

141. J. L. Bintliff, "Archaeology and the philosophy of Wittgenstein," in Philosophy and Archaeology Practice: Perspectives for the 21st Century, C. Holtorf and H. Karlson, Eds., pp. 153–172, Bricoleur, Göteborg, Sweden, 2000.

142. J. A. Fodor, The Elm and the Expert, MIT Press, Cambridge, Mass, USA, 1994.

143. J. A. Fodor, Concepts. Where Cognitive Science Went Wrong, Oxford University Press, Oxford, UK, 1998.

144. J. A. Fodor, LOT2. The Language of Thought Revisited, Oxford University Press, Oxford, UK, 2008.

145. L. Wittgenstein, The Blue and Brown Books, Basil Blackwell, Oxford, UK, 1958.

146. N. Chomsky, "Some empirical assumptions in modern philosophy of mind," in Philosophy, Science, and Method. Essays in Honor of Ernest Nagel, S. Morgenbesser, P. Suppes, and M. White, Eds., pp. 260–285, St. Martin's Press, New York, NY, USA, 1969.

147. J. A. Fodor, Psychological Explanation, Random House, New York, NY, USA, 1968.

148. S. Savage-Rumbaugh, S. G. Shanker, and T. J. Taylor, Apes, Language, and the Human Mind, Oxford University Press, Oxford, UK, 1998.

149. M. D. Hauser, "A primate dictionary? Decoding the function and meaning of another species› vocalizations," Cognitive Science, vol. 24, no. 3, pp. 445–475, 2000.

150. N. Hornstein, A Theory of Syntax. Minimal Operations and Universal Grammar, Cambridge University Press, Cambridge, UK, 2009.

151. H. Lasnik and J. Uriagereka, A Course in GB Syntax: Lectures on Binding and Empty Categories, MIT Press, Cambridge, Mass, USA, 1988.

152. N. A. Khabbaz, "A geometric hierarchy of languages," Journal of Computer and System Sciences, vol. 8, no. 2, pp. 142–157, 1974.

153. O. Bar-Yosef, "Can Paleolithic stone artifacts serve as evidence for prehistoric language?" in Hot Pursuit of Language in Prehistory. Essays in the Four Fields of Anthropology in Honor of Harold Crane Fleming, J. Bengtson, Ed., pp. 373–379, John Benjamins, Amsterdam, The Netherlands, 2008.

154. N. Chomsky, The Architecture of Language, Oxford University Press, New Delhi, India, 2000.

155. R. Botha, "Theoretical underpinnings of inferences about language evolution: the syntax used at Blombos Cave," in The Cradle of Language, R. Botha and C. Knight, Eds., pp. 93–111, Oxford University Press, New York, NY, USA, 2009.

156. M. Camps and J. Uriagereka, "The Gordian Knot of linguistic fossils," in The Biolinguistic Turn. Issues on Language and Biology, J. Rosselló and J. Martín, Eds., pp. 34–65, Universitat de Barcelona, Barcelona, Spain, 2006.

157. M. Piattelli-Palmarini and J. Uriagereka, "The evolution of the narrow faculty of language: the skeptical view and a reasonable conjecture," Lingue e Linguaggio, vol. 4, pp. 27–79, 2005.

158. C. S. Adams, The Knot Book, American Mathematical Society, Providence, RI, USA, 2nd edition, 2004.

159. J. Hass, J. C. Lagarias, and N. Pippenger, "The computational complexity of knot and link problems,"Journal of the ACM, vol. 46, no. 2, pp. 185–211, 1999. ·

160. S. Balari and G. Lorenzo, "Para qué sirve un ballestrinque? Reflexiones sobre el funcionamiento de arfectactos y organismos en un mundo sin funciones," Teorema, vol. 29, pp. 57–76, 2010.

161. S. Balari and G. Lorenzo, "Computational phenotypes. Where the theory of computation meets evo devo," Biolinguistics, vol. 3, pp. 2–61, 2009.

162. G. F. Michel and D. A. Harkins, "Concordance of handedness between teacher and student facilitates learning manual skills," Journal of Human Evolution, vol. 14, no. 6, pp. 597–601, 1985. ·

163. J. Tracy, A. Flanders, S. Madi et al., "Regional brain activation associated with different performance patterns during learning of a complex motor skill," Cerebral Cortex, vol. 13, no. 9, pp. 904–910, 2003. · ·

164. T. Q. Gentner, K. M. Fenn, D. Margoliash, and H. C. Nusbaum, "Recursive syntactic pattern learning by songbirds," Nature, vol. 440, no. 7088, pp. 1204–1207, 2006. · ·

165. P. Perruchet and A. Rey, "Does the mastery of center-embedded linguistic

structures distinguish humans from nonhuman primates?" Psychonomic Bulletin and Review, vol. 12, no. 2, pp. 307–313, 2005. ·

166. V. M. Longa, G. Lorenzo, and J. Uriagereka, "Minimizing language evolution: the Minimalist program and the evolutionary shaping of language," in The Oxford Handbook of Linguistic Minimalism, C. Boeckx, Ed., pp. 595–616, Oxford University Press, Oxford, UK, 2011.

167. O. Soffer, J. M. Adovasio, and D. C. Hyland, "The 'Venus' figurines. Textiles, basketry, gender, and status in the Upper Palaeolithic," Current Anthropology, vol. 41, pp. 511–525, 2000.

168. F. d›Errico, C. Henshilwood, M. Vanhaeren, and K. van Niekerk, "Nassarius kraussianus shell beads from Blombos Cave: evidence for symbolic behaviour in the Middle Stone Age," Journal of Human Evolution, vol. 48, no. 1, pp. 3–24, 2005.

169. C. S. Henshilwood, F. d›Errico, R. Yates et al., "Emergence of modern human behavior: middle stone age engravings from South Africa," Science, vol. 295, no. 5558, pp. 1278–1280, 2002. ·

170. C. S. Henshilwood and B. Dubreuil, "Reading the artifacts: gleaning language skills from the Middle Stone Age in southern Africa," in The Cradle of Language, R. Botha and C. Knight, Eds., pp. 41–61, Oxford University Press, New York, NY, USA, 2009.

171. M. Vanhaeren, F. d'Errico, C. Stringer, et al., "Middle Paleolithic shell beads in Israel and Algeria,"Science, vol. 312, pp. 1785–1788, 2006.

172. N. J. Conard, M. Malina, and S. C. Münzel, "New flutes document the earliest musical tradition in southwestern Germany," Nature, vol. 460, no. 7256, pp. 737–740, 2009.

173. P. Mellars, "Symbolism, language, and the Neanderthal mind," in Modelling the Early Human Mind, P. Mellars and K. Gibson, Eds., pp. 15–32, McDonald Institute for Archaeological Research, Cambridge, UK, 1996.

174. P. Mellars, "Neanderthals, modern humans and the archaeological evidence for language," in The Origin and Diversification of Language, N. Jablonski and L. C. Aiello, Eds., pp. 89–115, Academy of Sciences, San Francisco, Calif, USA, 1998.

175. S. Mithen, The Prehistory of the Mind. A Search for the Origins of Art, Religion, and Science, Thames and Hudson, London, UK, 1996.

176. I. Tattersall, Becoming Human: Evolution and Human Uniqueness, Harcourt Brace, New York, NY, USA, 1998.

177. S. Balari, A. Benítez Burraco, M. Camps, et al., "Homo loquens

neanderthalensis? En torno a las capacidades simbólicas y lingüísticas del neandertal," Munibe (Antropologia-Arkeologia), vol. 59, pp. 3–24, 2008.

178. W. T. Fitch, "Three meanings of 'recursion': key distinctions for biolinguistics," in The Evolution of Human Language. Biolinguistics Perspectives, R. K. Larson, V. Déprez, and H. Yamakido, Eds., pp. 73–90, Cambridge University Press, Cambridge, UK, 2010.

179. N. Chomsky, Cartesian Linguistics. A Chapter in the History of Rationalist Thought, Harper and Row, New York, NY, USA, 1996.

180. C. Finlayson, The Humans Who Went Extinct. Why Neanderthals Died Out and We Survived, Oxford University Press, New York, NY, USA, 2009.

181. P. Mellars, The Neanderthal Legacy: An Archaeological Perspective from Western Europe, Princeton University Press, Princeton, NJ, USA, 1996.

182. C. Stringer and C. Gamble, Search of the Neandertals. Solving the Puzzle of Human Origins, Thames and Hudson, London, UK, 1993.

183. E. Trinkaus and P. Shipman, The Neandertals. Changing the Image of Mankind, Jonathan Cape, London, UK, 1993.

184. N. E. Collias and E. C. Collias, "An experimental study of the mechanisms of nest building in a weaverbird," The Auk, vol. 79, pp. 568–595, 1962.

185. M. H. Hansell, Bird Nests and Construction Behaviour, Cambridge University Press, Cambridge, UK, 2000.

186. C. Herzfeld and D. Lestel, "Knot tying in great apes: etho-ethnology of an unusual tool behavior," Social Science Information, vol. 44, no. 4, pp. 621–653, 2005.

187. F. L. Coolidge and T. Wynn, "A cognitive and neuropsychological perspective on the Châtelperronian,"Journal of Anthropological Research, vol. 60, no. 1, pp. 55–73, 2004.

Chapter 12

CITATION IN APPLIED LINGUISTICS: ANALYSIS OF INTRODUCTION SECTIONS OF IRANIAN MASTER'S THESES

Alireza Jalilifar (Ahvaz) and Razieh Dabbi (Mahshahr, Iran)

Shahid Chamran University of Ahvaz, Iran

Islamic Azad University in Mahshahr, Iran

INTRODUCTION

Appropriate reference to other sources is an important feature of academic writing. In writing scholarly papers, researcher writers do not want only to show their own credibility in research. But they also need to refer to other works, their findings, and their results. They make references to the works of others in order to frame and support their own work and also to establish a niche for themselves within their special discourse community. An important aspect is to learn how to cite other works in an appropriate style. To understand the importance of citation in the academic setting it would be enough to say that citation, if used properly, would be against literacy piracy.

Academic writers not only need to make the results of their research public and persuasive, they should also show that their success in gaining acceptance for their work is at least partly dependent on the strategic manipulation of various rhetorical and interactive features (White 2004: 341). White also regards citation as a complex communicative purpose with syntactic, semantic, and pragmatic variables (cf. White 2004: 112) which is of interest not only to EAP scholars (e. g., Charles 2006; Hyland 1999; Petric 2007; Swales 1986, 1990; Thompson 2001, 2005) but also information scientists (White 2004). In discourse analysis, citations have often been examined in terms of reporting verbs (Hyland 1999; Thompson/Ye 1991) which enable the writer to position their work in relation to the works of other research. Despite the differences in approaches and methods, researchers agree that the role of citation in scientific discourse is not only to acknowledge the works of others but also to promote the writer's own knowledge claims.

Hyland (1999) believes that one of the most important realizations of the research writer's concern for audience is that of attributing propositional content to the existing literature and demonstrating accommodation to the community knowledge. As a core tool in the research discipline, citations are crucial in any research to situate the work and to build on the works of others (Wohlin 2008). Because citation involves creating intertextual relationships between the citing and the cited texts, it is especially prone to occlusion. Indeed, occlusion is implicit in the existence of conventions for citation. The conventional signals for source reporting are, therefore, needed to allow the writer to reveal as much of the relationship as she or he thinks the reader needs to know (cf. Pecorari 2006: 6).

Thompson (2005) investigated the nature of genre and citation practices in eight Ph.D. theses within Agricultural Botany at a British university. He identified citation types and observed their relation to content, writer, and rhetorical purposes. In studying social science – Politics – and natural science – Materials – theses, Charles (2006a, b) found that reporting clauses were considerably more frequent in social sciences than in natural sciences. Other differences aside, both social and natural sciences made use of research sources roughly equally. This confirmed that reporting clauses were often associated with citation and they often occur as integral citations. In sum, the data revealed disciplinary differences in the frequency and the stance function of the clauses. Comparison of the two corpora showed that human subjects occurred more often in Politics while non-human and **it** subjects were more frequent in Materials. Thus, the writers created a stance that was appropriate to their discipline and purpose.

Petric (2007) aimed to identify the relationship between the types of citation and high- and low-rated master›s theses. The corpus used in that study consisted of 16 master›s theses (eight A-graded theses and eight lower-graded theses), written by second language writers from 12 countries in Central and Eastern Europe. She used Thompson›s (2001) classification of citation types (attribution or source, origin, reference, and example) with some modifications to classify both integral and non-integral citations. A total of 1981 citations were identified in 310›624 words, of which 1253 were in the high-rated theses (182›896 words) and 729 in the low-rated ones (127›728 words), alluding to greater citation density in high-rated theses with more syntactic and rhetorical complexities.

By taking the importance of citation role into account, the present study investigates intertextuality in terms of citations utilized in MA theses. Writers are seeking to position themselves in relation to members of the research community, as they perceive them, and this is most evident in the introduction section. How they position themselves varies from writer to writer. In the context of Iran, the investigation of the way that Iranian thesis writers cite in their introduction sections and position themselves within the discourse community has been overlooked although there have been a few works identifying citation in different sections of articles (Jalilifar 2010; Shooshtari/ Jalilifar 2010).

Thesis writing is a difficult process for native speaker students and often doubly so for non-native speaker students (Paltridge 2002: 137). Some researchers consider MA theses as one of the key genres used by scientific communities to disseminate knowledge (Koutsantoni 2006: 20); others consider MA theses as a high stakes genre at the summit of a student›s academic accomplishment (Hyland 2004a: 134). Samraj and Monk (2008: 194) acknowledge the abundance of works on published academic texts such as research articles, but they regret that in terms on graduate students› writing, to which MA theses belong, little work has been done. The ability to cite appropriately is of key importance in academic writing (Charles 2006b: 311), but it produces considerable difficulties for the novice writer. The investigation of citation patterns has particular value, since it can reveal the way that different writers express themselves, which can be linked to genre and/or disciplinary purposes. Paying attention to citation in academic writing courses would encourage students to examine the different types of citations, and also it will help them to become aware of the functions of citation within the text.

Introduction is considered as a specific and crucial «part-genre» (Dudley-Evans 1997: 5) to set out their research questions, in both research articles and MA theses (Hyland 2002: 542). Citation features of MA thesis introductions (MAIs) have even been a less charted territory area of consideration than research article introductions. According to Paltridge (2002: 126), one reason can be the accessibility of the text, that is «Theses and dissertations are often difficult to obtain in university libraries, and even more difficult to obtain from outside the university». In Iran, as a foreign language learning context, all English-major students are required to write their MA theses in English; such students (non-native), according to Samuelowicz (1987, as cited in Paltridge: 2002: 127) often have difficulty in meeting the demands of the kind of writing required of them at this particular level. Therefore, writing an MA thesis is perhaps the most significant piece of writing that any student will ever do (Hyland 2004a: 134). In MA theses, the supervisor and the reader may ignore citations because they know that in the defense session, apart from some general assumptions about citation and plagiarism, judgments may not depend so much on the ways students cite and the types of citations MA students use in their writing. This is a lethargic performance which may make students less attentive to this important textual feature of academic writing. Hence, MA students rarely are criticized for their citation behavior. By focusing on the nature of citation patterns in one of the «citation-dense chapters» (Pecorari 2003: 322), we can help students to write more successful MA theses.

Accordingly, the question that is posed in this study is: In what way are citations exploited in the introductions of Iranian MA English theses in applied linguistics?

THE DATA

Sixty five MAIs were selected on an available basis from the Iranian universities – Tehran University (UT), Shahid Chamran University of Ahvaz (SCU), and Science and Research Branch-Ahvaz (SRA). The corpus was assumed to comprise and represent samples of high-rated MA theses associated with these universities. Since generic structures and rhetorical structures are subject to variation across time, we selected those which were published between 2005 and 2009. In carrying out the study, one vexed problem was accessing MA theses from universities, which led to the unequal selection of MA theses from each university. The trend in Iran is that the Research Department of the faculties does not usually allow students to copy theses or borrow from the Research library. They are only allowed to use them on site. This constraint took us an extensive amount of time to sit and take notes. The theses were codified for ease of reference and anonymity of thesis writers (e. g., UTI 1 referred to an introduction from Tehran University).

Table 1: Number of Theses from each University

SCU	SRA	UT
16	28	21

Instrument

In this study, Thompson and Tribble's (2001) framework for integral and non-integral citations was used as the instrument to analyze and compare the materials. The main categories which Thompson and Tribbles (2001) set are as follows: a) integral citation consisting of three sub classes; b) non-integral citation consisting of four sub-categories. Thompson and Tribble's (2001) classification assumed to be comprehensive and it takes accounts of all the citations types. According to Thompson and Tribbles (2001: 95), non-integral citations are divided into four categories:

- Source or attribution: Source indicates where the idea or information is taken from, as in this example:
- Learning style is the biologically and developmentally imposed set of

characteristics that make the same teaching wonderful for some and terrible for others (Brown 2000). (UT)

b)   Identification: This citation type identifies an agent within the sentence it refers to. An example of this type is:

•   In fact, a great deal of work has been done in the area of learner autonomy... (Haughton/Dickinson 1988; Cotterall 1995; Murray 1999; Chan 2001, 2003; Spratt Humphreys/Chan 2002; Clegg 2004; White 2006). (UT)

c)   Reference: This is usually signaled by the inclusion of the directive "see", as in: acquisition is insufficient for L2 learners... (See Cobb/Meara 1998: 2). (SCU)

d)   Origin: This indicates the originator of a concept, technique or product, as shown in the following example: discourse markers, which are also known by a variety of names, such as pragmatic markers (Schiffrin 1987), discourse particles or discourse operators (Schourup 1999), and discourse connectives (Blackmore 2002). (SRA)

Thompson and Tribble (2001: 95f.) classify integral citation can be as follows:

a.   Verb controlling: The citation acts as the agent that controls a verb, in active or passive voice, as in:

1. Brown and Yule (1983: 183) point out that theme is not only the starting point of the message, but it also has a role in connecting what has already been said. (SRA)

b.   Naming: In this kind of citation, the citation is a noun phrase or part of a noun phrase. An example of this type is:

2.   According to Oxford (1994), a second language is a language studied in a setting where... (UT)

c.   Non-citation: There is a reference to another writer but the name is given without a year reference. It is most commonly used when the reference has been supplied earlier in the text and the writer does not want to repeat it, as in:

3.   Hyland states that citation represents choices that carry ....(SRA)

To identify stance in the verb controlling type of integral citation, Thompson and Ye's (1991) framework was used. According to this classification, one of the most important ways of evaluation in reporting verbs is identified through writer's stance. Based on this taxonomy, reporting verbs which writers use can be categorized into three sub-categories as follows: a) factive in which the writer portrays the author as presenting true information or a correct opinion, for example, *acknowledge, bring out, demonstrate, identify, improve, notice, prove, recognize, substantiate, throw light on*; b) counter-factive in which the writer portrays the author as presenting false information or an incorrect opinion, for example, *betray (ignorance), confuse, disregard, ignore, misuse*; and c) non-factive in which the writer gives no clear signal as to her attitude towards the author's information or opinion, for example, *advance, believe, claim, examine, generalize, propose, retain, urge, utilize* (Thompson/Ye, 1991:. 372). This framework has been extensively applied by researchers on different sections in different disciplines (e. g., Hyland 1999). See Appendix A for the verbs identified in verb controlling citations.

PROCEDURE

Once the corpora were compiled, citations were identified following Hyland's (2000) criteria. Each occurrence of another author's name was counted as one citation, regardless of whether it was followed by the year of publication or not. The analysis did not include textual elements outside of the main text, such as epigraphs and explanatory footnotes. After the selection of the text corpus, word count was run on in order to determine the length of the corpus. Then the data were stored according to Thompson and Tribble (2001) to identify and classify each type of citation. Finally, the frequency of integral and non-integral citations was calculated to detect the possible differences in the citation classes and judge whether the differences are significant.

The framework used in the study is functional, allowing us to look at the contextual nature of citations. Thus, our study provides analyses at both quantitative and qualitative levels.

RESULTS

The first step taken in the analysis of citation types in the introduction sections of MA theses was to run word count to determine the length of the corpus. A total of 1'134 citations were identified in 79'886 words, in the MA theses.

Table 2: Citations in M.A Theses

Av. per work Per 1000 words Total citations
MA theses 17.44 14.19 1134

Table 2 indicates the importance of citations in academic writing, with an average of almost 17.44 in thesis introductions, depicting the characterization that MA theses tend to employ citations.

Surface Forms of Citations in MA Theses

Different citation types are used to substantiate claims in thesis introductions. Table 3 demonstrates the variation in the ways Iranian MA students refer to sources, with a distinct preference for integral citation. As the results showed, the use of integral citations was more than one and a half that of non-integral citations.

Table 3: Citation Types in Thesis Introductions

	Integral	Non-integral	X^2	Df	Sig
Theses	699	435	61.46	1	.00
P < 0.05					Critical value = 3.84

To find out whether the existing differences between integral and non-integral citations were significant,*chi*-square test was applied. The value of *chi*-square (61.46) was higher than the critical value (3.84) at the significant level of P < 0.05. This showed a significant difference in the frequency of citation types in thesis introductions. Accordingly, the use of integral citations was considered more than one and a half that of non-integral citations. That is to say, writers tended to use integral citations far more than non-integral.

Integral Citations in MA Theses

Within integral citations (Table 4), greater emphasis was given to *Verb controlling* by Iranian MA students.

Table 4: Types of Integral Citation in Thesis Introductions

		Theses	
		F	(%)
	Verb controlling	453	(64.80)
Integral	Naming	189	(27.04)
	Non-citation	57	(8.16)
	Total	699	

As shown in Table 4, *Verb controlling* was the most frequent citation within integral citations of theses. Following Thompson and Ye›s (1991) classification of reporting verbs, the verbs were classified based on the fact that *writers* (the writer of the actual text) may represent the reported text of an *author* (the one who is cited by the writer) as a) true using factive verbs; b) false using counter-factive verbs; and c) non-factively, given no clear signal. Findings showed that MA theses tend to use factive verbs to represent the cited text as true in the *Verb controlling* citation frequently, as in:

1.   Swain and Lapkin (1995: 372) *point out* to the result of a ... (SRA)

Several sentences in theses were found in which the writer draws on factive verbs in order to represent the cited text as true (e. g. *acknowledge, point out, establish*, etc). Non-factive verbs received the highest frequency in theses by which writers represent neutral stance toward the cited text and withhold judgment, as in:

2.   Celce-Murcia (2001: 3) *believes* that one reason... (SCU)

Counter-factive categories in which the cited text was represented as false were found only three times in MA theses, as in:

3.   Knight (1994), however, *has rejected* this view... (SCU)

In the above sentence, the writer shows the author›s disagreement using the verb «rejected». Further examples of counter-factive verbs are *fail, overlook, exaggerate, ignore*, etc, which were not found in this study. (see Appendixes B for stance in integral citations).

In the present study as shown in Table 4, the *Naming* type occurs second in rank of the most frequent citations used in MA introduction sections. Close inspection of the different kinds of *Naming* citation in the theses revealed interesting findings in the discourse of this genre. Bear in mind that citation in *Naming* is within the sentence but it does not control the verb. In order to find out why this might be the case, concordance lines of the *Naming* citation were drawn. It was observed that certain patterns were regularly used, as those depicted in Table 5.

Table 5: Naming Citation Patterns in Theses

Naming citation patterns	Theses	
	f (%)	
according to X (2005)...	97	51.32
X' (2005) study/theory	24	12.69
...that/work of X (2005)	17	8.9
...in X (2005) /	7	3.70
...to X (2005) x is...	5	2.64
...for X (2005) x is...	5	2.64

...by X (2005)	10	5.29
based on X (2005)	9	4.76
following X (2005)...	5	2.64
in accordance/line with X(2005)	2	1.05
taken /adapted from X (2005)	8	4.23
Total	189	

The pattern "according to X" is clearly the preferred choice in the MA theses. In this pattern, the writer focuses on author who does not receive the agent position. The pattern which received the second highest frequency in the MA theses was the "X's study". MA students tend to use those noun phrases which function as modifier. Notice the following example:

4.   Oxford's (1998) study of students...

The use of "in X" pattern in MA theses was (f = 7), which is contradicts Thompson's (2001) study in which he found "in X" pattern the most common Naming citation pattern used in Agricultural Botany theses. This type of citation refers to the "work" of an especial author, but the word "work" is not mentioned explicitly. Here is an example of this pattern:

5.   It is not mentioned in Jordan (1997), even though this standard ...(SCU)

Other examples of preposition + Naming citation were found to be "by X (2005)" pattern, which was not frequent in MA theses, as in:

6.   the large scale cross-sectional study by MacIntyre et al. (2002) which...
      (SRA)

In this pattern, the overall focus is on the work of a particular researcher. Other patterns of *Naming*citation were rare in the data, and examples of Non-citation were still far less than Verb controlling and Naming in MA theses and (f = 57).

Non-integral Citation in MA Theses

Table 6 shows that non-integral citation was mostly realized by writers in the form of **Source** in thesis introductions, as a strategy to attribute information to an author.

Table 6: Distribution of non-integral citations

	Theses		
Non-integral	F	(%)	
Source	369	(84.82)	

Identification	42	(9.65)
Reference	8	(1.83)
Origin	16	(3.67)
Total	435	

Reference, used to persuade readers to see other texts, was found to appear less than other non-integral citation in MA theses (F = 8), as exemplified below:

1. acquisition is insufficient for L2 learners…(See Cobb/Meara 1998: 2). (SCU)

Origin, which can function as an indication of the origin of a theory, technique or product, was also found inconspicuous in MA theses, as in:

2. discourse markers, which are also known by a variety of names, such as pragmatic markers (Schiffrin, 1987), discourse particles or discourse operators (Schourup, 1999), and discourse connectives (Blackmore, 2002). (SRA)

In this example, the writer attributed the "known names for discourse markers", to several originators. Here, the difference between Origin and Source seems to be tricky but, according to Thompson and Tribble›s (2001: 95) definition, «where Source attributes a proposition to a source, Origin indicates the originator of a concept or a product". Iranian MA students exploited the latter type of non-integral citations infrequently (about 3.67% of non-integral citations). Instead, they prefer to denote the cited concept and proposition to an author (Source) rather than to introduce the creator of that concept (Origin). In Thompson›s (2005) study of theses, where he identified citations in different rhetorical sections, writers were more concerned with Origin citation in the method sections; however, in introduction sections of theses, no Origin was identified; accordingly, he considered it as «typical features of method sections» (Thompson 2005: 316), since in the method section the materials and methods are described for the analyses.

DISCUSSION

In view of the question which asks for the distribution of citations employed by MA students in the introduction sections of their applied linguistics theses, analysis showed significant differences in the citation practices. Integral citations tended to give greater prominence to the cited sources in MA theses. Results showed a pronounced tendency to use integral citations in which the name of the researcher appears as a sentence element with an explicit grammatical role.

Charles (2006b) believes that the choice of integral/ non-integral citation is a complex product of a number of factors including citation convention, genre, discipline and individual study type (cf. Charles 2006b: 317). In this study, however, the preference for integral citation does not seem to be only related to the citation conventions, but to the functions of citations in theses, in which writers prefer to emphasize the author especially in subject position (by using verb controlling citation). This complies with the communicative purposes pursued by MA students, since they tend to establish a strong support for their claims within the text by placing the citation within the sentence and emphasizing the researcher rather than the information.

Citation practices reflect students› social and epistemological conventions, their audiences, and citation conventions. MA students are not likely to show a high share of knowledge in applying different citation types according to the standards established by their target discourse community. They do not set a discursive framework of integral and non-integral citations in order to establish a space for their research and for their possible publication. In order to publish their work, a paper should meet certain characteristics, and these characteristics should be acceptable to the editors of the journals. It seems that MA students do not stick to those principles set by journals gatekeepers, which may arise from their unawareness of conventions of citation practices; as such their work may get little space for publication if they wish to publish it in condensed form.

In academic writing, especially in MA theses, students tend to choose appropriate information supporting their study, without offering any subjective interpretation by means of verbs (e. g. factive and counter-factive verbs). In fact, they do not evaluate the reported text, but they only tend to report it, often using appropriate grammatical patterns, that is, whether to place the author in the subject position in integral citation, or to enclose it parenthetically while they may ignore the rhetorical and discourse level of citation. Thompson and Ye (1991) argue that to concentrate only on the given information would in many cases be to miss or misinterpret the purpose. They add that «evaluation in text is the signaling of this purpose» (Thompson/Ye 1991: 367).

MA students tend to report previous research (hence more integral citations) rather than evaluate it, and they point it out for the purpose of creating a research space for their study in the introduction, simply by summarizing it and integrating it into their study. Taylor and Chen (1991, as cited in Fakhri 2004) also reported that the absence of evaluation of previous research can be attributed to the unacceptability of argumentative styles and self-promotion in the cultures considered. The descriptive rather than argumentative nature of MA thesis introductions may stem from the lack of competitive publishing environment and avoidance of self-promotion in the Iranian culture. The authors of the local studies are familiar with the academic practices in their respective culture and the socio-cultural stigmatization of direct confrontation and self-promotion. So lack of critical evaluation may be related to cross-cultural variation. Fakhri (2004) reports that communicative styles in different cultures vary in terms of directness, that is, the degree to which speakers and writers reveal their intentions. Western cultures prefer direct, explicit communication styles whereas the Japanese, Iranian, and Arab cultures value indirectness (cf. Fakhri 2004: 1131).

Moreover, Iranian students are likely to have fewer resources at their disposal when they come to cite the works of others because they are less skilled writers of academic discourse. Verb controlling citations are in some ways the easiest and most obvious ways of incorporating citations into text. However, professionals, especially if they are native-speakers, possess a wider range of linguistic options to draw which could fit in with the findings of the present study that the Iranian writers used more integral citation.

Of the citation types sporadically utilized in this study, one was reference used by writers as a «shorthand device» (Thompson 2001: 105) to direct the reader to another text in which exact details can be found. Writers should decide whether it is necessary to provide details or to use the word *see* and make the reader responsible for reading and understanding more details about the subject. For Hyland (2002), these devices (e. g. *see*) belong to "directives" which show somewhat the writer's ability for gathering information from sources as well as his ability to direct the reader. Reference, if used properly, can be one of the «conventional signals» which, as Pecorari (2006) claims, are needed for source reporting to allow the writer to reveal as much of the relationship as she or he thinks the reader needs to know.

The way that citations are manifested in MA theses may reflect the context in which citations are used by these writers. One determining element of this context is audience. MA students write mostly for Iranian readers with different attitudes and expectations. They may receive no critical feedback from their readers. Thus, they may not be aware of the rhetorical effect of citations as international writers do. MA students› preference for only two types of integral citation may be indicative of their less proficient knowledge citation.

Another reason is the size of the community they address. Iranian MA students address a small discourse community in comparison to international writers who address a much greater discourse community with quite different expectations and language knowledge. Looking at the results of the present study, one may claim that MA students make use of a distinct pattern of the citation types (namely integral citation) and they seem to have little knowledge. MA students are not at the appropriate stage of linguistic or intellectual development, and so they apply limited citation practices (Charles 2006b; Hyland 1999; Petric 2007; Thompson/Tribble 2001). This works against the inclination of expert writers for non-integral citations in published articles (Jogthong 2001; Okamura 2008), and/or their equal tendency toward these two types of citation. MA students focus on the explicit grammatical roles of citations and do not give an equal weight to the reported author and the message. The existing rhetorical patterns in the citation practices in the MA thesis introductions mark the underlying social structures accepted by novice writers in applied linguistics. As argued by Martin (2000: 9), "the stage a culture has reached in its evolution provides the social context for the linguistic development..." and this linguistic development "provides resources for the instantiation of unfolding texts". Therefore, citation as an important feature in academic writing brings to surface those social structure differences that exist and determine the way writers' intentions are shaped. This becomes more revealing to us in relation to MA theses that are not shaped by experienced academic writers.

CONCLUSIONS AND IMPLICATIONS

The findings of the present study have pointed to the existence of various citations across this academic writing type. The study revealed significant differences between MA students' tendencies to use integral and non-integral types of citation with the greater tendency to use the former. Findings also give a broad view of MA students' tendencies in the use of citation subtypes and that MA students define citation in different ways and consider that their readers cannot be assumed to possess the same interpretive knowledge. The breadth of citation reflects the complexity of citation practices, and this in turn makes it difficult for novice writers in learning to cite appropriately. In general, the findings therefore suggest that citation use should receive more attention in EAP courses. The study identified both the common rhetorical and linguistic features reflected in theses, which in turn, reflect the social and cultural contexts, as well as writers' aim of writing. The preference for a special type of citation within MA theses (i. e. integral) shows their familiarity with formal features of citation, for instance to use an author in a subject position and give explicit grammatical role to the author but their ignorance of the functional features of citation. We should bear in mind that citation practice is like a two sided coin, with formal and grammatical features constituting only one side. This might stem in unfamiliarity of Iranian MA students with the functional aspects of citation that each simple citation conveys because, in fact, they do not usually receive explicit instructions on citation practices.

In addition, Iranian students' less use of non-integral citation shows that they usually emphasize the authors in their writing rather than the information, leading us to conclude that supervisors may not criticize MA students' for their citation patterns or they may not pay due attention to the way their students cite in theses; instead, they focus upon linguistic and grammatical features of theses and ignore functional characteristics.

The way that we have looked at citation in the context of MA thesis writing has got its own newness. Moreover, the problems encountered by Iranian MA thesis writers might not necessarily be experienced by MA students representing other nationalities. This requires further studies before one can make generalizations about citations in this genre.

Investigating usual citation patterns used in theses, textbooks or articles will enhance students' understanding of what lies behind the citation choices. Accurate use of citation can be considered as one important way to prevent plagiarism, so, EAP teachers can provide a wide range of citation functions and different forms to teach novice writers. A particularly interesting direction for future research would be a cross-disciplinary comparison of citation patterns used by Iranian students and other researchers. This will allows us to see the disciplinary differences in citing authors in academic writing.

At the time of publication of this paper, Alireza Jalilifar is affiliated with the Shahid Chamran University of Ahvaz, Iran, and Razieh Dabbi is affiliated with the Islamic Azad University in Mahshahr, Iran.

REFERENCES

1.　Charles, Maggie (2006a): "The construction of stance in reporting clauses: A cross disciplinary study of theses". *Applied Linguistics* 27/3: 492–518.

2.　Charles, Maggie (2006b): «Phraseological patterns in reporting clauses used in citation: A corpus-based study of theses in two disciplines». *English for Specific Purposes* 25: 310–331.

3.　Dudley-Evans, Tony (1997): «Genre models for the teaching of academic writing to second language speakers: Advantages and disadvantages».In: Miller, Tom E. (1997): *Functional approaches to written text: classroom applications*. Washington, DC, USA: 150–159.

4.　Fakhri, Ahmed (2004): "Rhetorical properties of Arabic research article introductions". *Journal of Pragmatics* 36: 1119–1138.

5.   Hyland, Ken (1999). «Academic attribution: Citation and the construction of disciplinary knowledge».*Applied Linguistics* 20/3: 341–367.

6.   Hyland, Ken (2000): *Disciplinary discourses*: *Social interactions in academic writing*. Harlow: Longman.

7.   Hyland, Ken (2001): «Bringing in the reader: Addressee features in academic writing». *Written Communication* 18/4: 549–574.

8.   Hyland, Ken (2002): «Directives: Argument and engagement in academic writing». *Applied linguistics*23/2: 215–239.

9.   Hyland, Ken (2004a): "Disciplinary interactions: Metadiscourse in L2 postgraduate writing". *Journal of Second Language Writing* 13: 133–151.

10.   Hyland, Ken (2004b): «Patterns of engagement: Dialogic features and L2 understanding writing». In: Ravellie, Louise/ Ellis, Rod. (eds.) (2004): *Analyzing academic writing*. England, Continuum: 6–23.

11.   Jalilifar, Alireza (2010): "Research article introductions: Subdisciplinary variations in applied linguistics".*Journal of Teaching Language Skills* 2/2: 29–55.

12.   Jogthong, Chalermsri (2001): *Research article introductions in Thai: Genre analysis of academic writing*. Unpublished doctoral thesis, Morgantown, West Virginia, Department of Educational Theory and Practice.

13.   Koutsantoni, Dimitra (2006): "Rhetorical strategies in engineering research articles and research theses: Advanced academic literacy and relations of power". *English for Academic Purposes* 5: 19–36.

14.   Martin, James R (2000). «Analysing genre: Functional parameters». In: Christie, Frances/Martin, James R. (eds.) (2000): *Genre and institution: Social progress in the workplace and school*. London, Continuum: 3–39.

15.   Okamura, Akiko (2008): "Use of citation forms in academic texts by writers in L1 & L2 context". *The Economic Journal of Takasaki City University of Economics* 51/1: 29–44.

16.   Paltridge, Brian (2002): «Thesis and dissertation writing: An examination of published advice and actual practice». *English for Specific Purposes* 21: 125–143.

17.   Pecorari, Diane (2003): «Good and original: plagiarism and patchwriting in academic second-language writing». *Journal of Second Language Writing* 12: 317–345.

18.   Pecorari, Diane (2006): "Visible and occluded citation features in postgraduate second language writing".*English for Specific Purposes* 25: 4–29.

19. Petric, Bojana (2007): «Rhetorical functions of citations in high- and low-rated master›s theses». *English for Academic Purposes* 6: 238–253.

20. Samraj, Betty/Monk, Lenore (2008): «The statement of purpose in graduate program applications: Genre structure and disciplinary variation». *English for Specific Purposes* 27: 193–211.

21. Shooshtari, Zohreh G./Jalilifar, Alireza (2010): «Citation and the construction of disciplinary knowledge».*Journal of Teaching Language Skills* 2/1: 45–66.

22. Swales, John (1986): «Citation analysis and discourse analysis». *Applied Linguistics* 7/1: 39–56.

23. Thompson, Geoff/Ye, Yiyun (1991): «Evaluation in the reporting verbs used in academic papers». *Applied Linguistics* 12/4: 365–382.

24. Thompson, Paul (2001): *A pedagogically-motivated corpus-based examination of PhD theses: Macrostructure, citation practices, and uses of modal verbs* . Unpublished PhD Thesis, University of Reading.

25. Thompson, Paul (2005): «Points of focus and position: Intertextual reference in PhD Theses». *English for Academic Purposes* 4: 307–323.

26. Thompson, Paul/Tribble, Chris (2001): «Looking at citations: Using corpora in English for academic purposes». *Language Learning and Technology* 5/3: 91–105.

27. White, Howard D. (2004): «Citation analysis and discourse analysis revisited». *Applied Linguistics* 25/1: 89–116.

28. Wohlin, Claes (2008): «An analysis of the most cited articles in software engineering journals».*Information and Software Technology* 50/1: 3–9.

Chapter 13

INNOVATIONS IN STRUCTURING ARTICLE INTRODUCTIONS: THE CASE OF APPLIED LINGUISTICS

Ling Lin

Hong Kong Polytechnic University (China)

ABSTRACT

This study explores the rhetorical structure of introductions that are followed by an independent Literature Review (L) section. It is motivated by an increasing use or even the prevalent use of both the introduction and L sections in the opening phase of empirical research articles in many disciplines and the lack of systematic genre-based investigation of introductions with a following L section. Based on a detailed examination of 30 introductions with a subsequent L section in Applied Linguistics, this study found that they generally can be classified into two categories according to their communicative functions and structures. They are the traditional CARS type that largely follows the classic "Create a Research Space" (CARS) model and the innovative Two-move Orientation type. Some featured elements used in the introductions with a subsequent L are identified and the "Two-move Orientation" approach is formulated for the rhetorical structure of this new type of introductions. The interesting links between introduction and L are also suggested. The study contributes to our understanding of the structure and function of this important part-genre in a new generic context (that is, introductions being followed by an independent L section) and illuminates the current genre-based teaching of introduction writing.

INTRODUCTION

Increasing awareness and concern about the growing use of English as an academic lingua franca (Ferguson, 2007) and the long-term dominance of Anglo-American discursive norms in the publication world has given rise to a substantial body of research on various aspects of the genre of English research articles (RAs), e.g., its macro-structure, the rhetorical organization of its major sections, to name just a few. Regarding the macro-structure of the RA, the classic Introduction-Method-Results-Discussion (IMRD) model determines that there are four major sections in a "conventional" empirical article (namely, the Introduction, Method, Results and Discussion sections) with the Introduction as the only single section in its opening phase. Given the important position and pivotal role of the Introduction section, its rhetorical structure has in the past three decades attracted considerable scholarly attention, whose major focuses concern its variations across disciplines (Samraj, 2002), sub-disciplines (Ozturk, 2007) and cultures (Lee, 2001; Hirano, 2009; Sheldon, 2011). A number of studies have also explored the interrelationship between the Introduction and other parts of the RA such as abstracts in Samraj (2005). These studies mostly used Swales's (1990) influential "Create-a-Research-Space" (CARS) model and its revised version (Swales, 2004) as the basis of their analyses and generally validated the effectiveness of the models in accounting for the rhetorical structure of the introductions.

However, the existing studies either only studied introductions in the traditional IMRD context (nwogu, 1997; Kanoksilapatham, 2005; Loi, 2010) or did not define clearly the generic context of the introductions they analyzed (Anthony, 1999; Samraj, 2002; Hirano, 2009) – that is to say, whether the introductions selected appeared as the only section in the opening phase of the RAs or they were used in combination with other sections before Method, such as the Literature Review (L) section (Lin & Evans, 2012; Pérez-Llantada, 2013). As such, they have not yet systematically studied the rhetorical structure of the introductions that are followed by an independent L section. This would seem to be an important omission, because the use of both introduction and L before Method has become a common practice in contemporary research writing in many disciplines (Yang & Allison, 2004; Kwan, Chan & Lam, 2012; Lin & Evans, 2012; PérezLlantada, 2013) and to what extent, if any, the introductions used before the L section differ structurally from the traditional ones, especially those studied in the IMRD context, remains unknown.

The importance of L and the prevalent use of the "new" type of introduction (that is, the introductions with a subsequent L) have been demonstrated by a recent comprehensive survey of the macro-organization of empirical RAs based on a large corpus of 780 RAs selected from the 2007 volume of prestigious journals from 39 disciplines in the fields of applied sciences, engineering, social sciences and humanities (Lin & Evans, 2012). This study shows that over half (51.7%) of the empirical RAs investigated employ both introduction and L sections in the opening phase. In many disciplines (such as electronic and information engineering, management and marketing, industrial and systems engineering), over 80% of the empirical RAs have used the L section between Introduction and Method. Analogous findings are yielded from Kwan, Chan and Lam (2012), who studied evaluations of prior scholarship in the L section of RAs in the two sub-fields of information systems. By defining the L section as the section(s) between the introduction and the methodology sections where previous literature is reviewed, they found that in the two source journals following a strong behavioral science research, 100% and 93.02% of the RAs published in them respectively have used an L while in the other two respective journals that show a strong design science research paradigm, 82.86% and 92.43% of the RAs published in the specified period came with an L. Therefore, the L section is almost an obligatory part-genre of the RAs in this field. The use of the L section as an expanded RA constituent on the theme of the traditional IMRD is frequently found not only in traditional journal articles without the new online elements (research highlights, graphical abstracts, interactive graphs, embedded videos, hyperlinks) as support or enhancements, but also in the "article of the future" prototypes in disciplines such as business and palaeogeography, as reported in Pérez-Llantada (2013).

In view of the possible influences from the neighboring section on the structural movements and configurations of the introductions and the increasing use of the L section after the introductions documented in recent studies (Kwan, Chan & Lam, 2012; Lin & Evans, 2012; Pérez-Llantada, 2013), the rhetorical structure of the introduction section that is followed by a usually elaborate L section is an unexplored issue that merits systematic genre-based investigation. Perhaps due to this research gap and a lack of research-informed accounts on how to structure this kind of introductory phase consisting of both introduction and L in the current writing manuals and reference books, our student writers often feel baffled in this regard and pose questions like the following:

- Is there any difference between the introduction with a subsequent L and the stand-alone I without a following L in terms of their structures and functions? If yes, what is it?

- If the usually lengthy L section is used for reviewing previous literature, do we still need to review previous studies in introduction (as suggested by the classic CARS model)?

- Given that there is an additional section – L – used in the introductory phase, is there any connection between the introduction and L?

To bridge the research gap and facilitate our research writing teaching and training, these questions will be addressed by the present study. Another interesting question this study explores is whether the traditional CARS model (Swales, 1990 & 2004) is still applicable to account for the rhetorical organization of the introductions in a "new" generic context – that is, being followed by the L section.

To answer these questions, the current study conducted a genre-based structural analysis of 30 article introductions with a subsequent L in Applied Linguistics. The reason for choosing this discipline is that it is one of the many disciplines where research writers favor using both the introduction and L in the opening phase of the empirical RAs (see Lin & Evans, 2012). Through this analysis, significant findings have been obtained on the schematic structure and communicative function of the particular group of introductions with a following L section, including the identification of the two-move structure for the innovative Orientation-type introduction.

THE STUDY

Data Collection

To accomplish the research aims, 30 RA introductions followed by an L in applied linguistics were collected. These introductions were all drawn from empirical RAs published in the 2011 volume of the following five highimpact journals: English for Specific Purposes (ESP), Language Learning (LL), Applied Linguistics (AL), TESOL Quarterly (TQ), and Studies in Second Language Acquisition (SSLA). Excluding the special issue where all published works were written on the same theme, which may possibly influence the rhetorical structure of the RAs, the present author searched for all the introductions that fulfil the selection criterion – being followed by a clearly distinguishable L section – from the remaining issues until the required number (namely, six) of the introductions were selected from each journal. Among the 30 selected introductions, 14 are headed "Introduction" whereas as many as 16 are non-labeled. This is because most source journals such as TQ, LL and SSLA require their submitted manuscripts to follow the specifications of the APA Publication Manual (2010), which maintains that the introduction does not need to have a heading that labels it as introduction due to its clearly identifiable position in the article. All these introductions feature a clearly distinguishable L section employed after them. In this study, the L section refers to the section(s) placed between the Introduction and Method sections that provide varieties of "background" to the study such as the contextual, theoretical and methodological background (Lin & Evans, 2012). After these 30 introductions were collected, each of them was assigned a number, AL1 through AL30 for ease of reference. The next sub-section specifies the two stages of analysis.

Data Analysis

Categorizing Introductions

Before identifying the move structure of the genre, it is essential to understand the overall rhetorical purpose of the texts in the genre (Biber, Connor & upton, 2007). With the help of an expert genre analyst who is an associate professor having conducted a wide range of Applied Linguistics research for many years, the researcher, after multiple careful readings of the introductions, discovered that a considerable number of them indeed do not function to create a research space for the study when they are followed by an L (see Table 1). They also exhibit very different schematic structures from those of the traditional introductions as suggested by the conventional CARS model. Therefore, based on their major communicative purposes, the 30 introductions were firstly classified into two groups: the traditional CARS group and the unconventional group consisting of introductions that are not CARS-like.

Table 1: Two major categories of introductions: Their frequencies, average lengths and proportions in the full RAs

Categories of introductions	Traditional CARS	Orientation
No. of introductions	18 (60%)	11 (36.7%)
Ave. length per text (no. of words)	700.7	343
Proportion of the entire RA (%)	7.9	4.1

As shown in Table 1, 18 out of the 30 introductions fall into the traditional CARS group, indicating that they are conventional introductions displaying a close affinity to the CARS model. Among the 12 unconventional introductions, there is one special case termed "Building on the Writer's Own Previous Research" while the other 11 consistently reflect a distinct two-move structure with their purposes of identifying an issue to be addressed and informing the readers of the about-to-be-presented research. For this distinct group of introductions, an innovative two-move structural model – the Two-move Orientation approach – was proposed to account for their rhetorical organization (see Appendix 1). This Two-move Orientation type and the traditional CARS type are the two dominant categories of introductions with a following L section identified in the present data. Thus, their systematic structural analysis was undertaken using the frameworks detailed in sections 2.2.2 and 3.2 respectively

As for the only single introduction (AL 14) that is styled and structured very differently from the two major types, it is not suited for genre analysis. This unique case seems a "relaxed, story-telling" type that starts with introducing the present study and then recounts the author's whole research experience and process. In accounting for his research story, the author firstly stated what he had done on the topic previously, then pointed out the link of his previous study to the initial design of the present one, and finally described how he further reshaped his research design by integrating his observations and thoughts during the research process. The entire introduction as a selfnarrative account is unlike the traditional argumentative CARS type, which usually emphasizes niche establishment and occupation. While this introduction shows that the study it reports builds on the writer's own previous research, in its subsequent L section, the writer did review numerous previous studies by others and point out the gaps to be filled by his study.

Corresponding to its special structure, this "Building on the Writer's Own Previous Research" introduction is stylistically featured by a strong authorial voice and the frequent use of the first person pronoun "I" (eleven times) and its accusative case "me". This special kind of introduction seems more likely constructed by disciplinary experts with adequate authority and substantial research experience on particular topics, which enable them to confidently show the readers that their studies are an accumulation of experience along particular research lines. Although there is only one introduction of this type identified in the present data and we do not know how frequently expert writers favor this type in other disciplines, it is still worth being described. The description of this introduction not only gives readers a sense of structural variability of the introductions with a following L in Applied Linguistics, but provides useful reference for the future similar research of a larger scale in other disciplines.

As displayed in Table 1, Orientation introductions are nearly half of the traditional CARS introductions both in terms of their length and their proportions in the whole articles. This could largely be explained by the different content elements and structural components in them, which is further discussed in Section 3.2.

Analyzing the Structure of The Two Major Types Of Introductions

A two-level rhetorical analysis (moves and sub-moves) was undertaken of the two dominant categories of introductions: the traditional CARS type and the innovative Orientation type. In this study, moves are considered for "characterize[ing] a genre as prototypical rather than obligatory" (Lewin, Fine & Young, 2001: 36). Regarding move constituents, the reason for preferring "sub-moves" to the contrasting pair of concepts "steps" and "strategies"

(Bhatia, 2001; Kwan, 2006) is that "sub-moves" is a more inclusive term that is more applicable to the present analysis, whereas "steps" predicts the obligatory nature of the move constituents that occur in a fixed sequence and "strategies" indicates the opposite. However, in referring to relevant previous studies, the original terms the authors used (like "steps" or "strategies") are retained. Two other important principles were also adhered to: first, imperatives rather than gerunds and present principles were used to label the moves and submoves for foregrounding writers' actions, as practised in Stoller and Robinson (2013). Further, in the coding analysis, for a few sentences reflecting more than one rhetorical function, only the most salient one was considered (Ozturk, 2007; Del Saz-Rubio, 2011; Sheldon, 2011).

Swales's (1990 & 2004) CARS model was taken as a starting point for analyzing the 18 conventional CARS introductions. The move-level analysis is comparatively straightforward as the three moves of the model (namely, Move 1 "Establish a Territory"; Move 2 "Establish a niche"; and Move 3 "Present the Present Work") were found prototypical in the present data (see section 3.1). However, the coding and analysis of the sub-moves is more taxing, as there are a variety of sub-moves identified, including the majority set out in Swales's two versions of the CARS model, two elements newly devised in this study (that is, Sub-move 3.3 "State Theoretical Frameworks/Positions" and Sub-move 3.6 "Indicate the Literature Review Content" presented in Appendix 2) and several others proposed in recent introduction studies (for example, Del Saz-Rubio, 2011). As such, the three major moves with all these identified move elements constitute an integrated CARS model (see Appendix 2) that served as the coding framework for analyzing the traditional CARS introductions.

As shown in Appendix 2, for the moves and sub-moves conceptually shared in Swales's two versions of the CARS model yet with different labels, their terms in the revised version were followed if they were present in the data. Therefore, for instance, Move 3 in the integrated CARS model is "Present the Present Work" rather than the metaphorical term "Occupy the niche" used in the 1990 model.

With respect to the sub-moves, in his revised model Swales compressed all options in Move 1 into an exclusive broad category "Topic Generalization of Increasing Specificity", which is all-encompassing yet apparently overgeneralized and not helpful for identifying interesting strategies employed by the authors (Del Saz-Rubio, 2011; Sheldon, 2011). To overcome this limitation, this study followed Del Saz-Rubio (2011) in maintaining the separation of the three sub-moves "Claim Centrality" (S1.1), "Make Topic Generalizations of Increasing Specificity" (S1.2) and "Survey Items of Previous Research" (S1.3) while further classifying Sub-move 1.1 "Claim Centrality" into "Claim Importance in Research World" (S1.1a) and "Claim Importance in Real World" (S1.1b) (Samraj, 2002 & 2005).

Although some genre scholars such as Samraj (2002) and Kwan (2006) have noted the confusions about differentiating "Making Topic Generalizations" and "Reviewing Items of Previous Research", the two original steps within Move 1 in Swales's 1990 model, this analytical difficulty generally does not exist in this study. The instances of "Topic generalizations" in this study were mostly nonresearch phenomenon or practice description – see example (1) – and the summarized research state or established knowledge claims – see example (2) – with few cases being introductions of theoretical constructs/concepts – see example (3) – which could be attributed to the applied nature of the discipline (namely, Applied Linguistics) as well as the author's postponing of substantial reviews of research activities to the subsequent L.

1.   Advanced English for Academic Purposes (EAP) language learners encounter many challenges as they move through their education and begin producing academic written texts within their chosen discipline. (AL 19)

2.   Research has shown that the acquisition of second-language (SL) grammar and pragmatics differs for foreign language (FL) and SL contexts (Bardovi-Harlig & Dornyei, 1998; Kasper & Rose, 2002; Kasper & Schmidt, 1996...). (AL 1)

3.   ... the typological generalization called the noun phrase accessibility hierarchy (NPAH; Keenan & Comrie, 1977), the systematic way in which languages differ with respect to the types of RCs they allow. (AL 2)

Concerning the sub-moves associated with niche establishments, in addition to the "negative" and "positive" warrants, "Suggest Implicitly Inconsistencies Precluding Gap Signaling" newly devised in Del Saz-Rubio (2011) and having been alluded to as early as in Samraj (2002) was found in the present corpus, thus being incorporated into the integrated CARS model. The only instance of this sub-move is provided below:

1.   ... some recent studies that have investigated the issue of pragmatic and grammatical acquisition have found evidence in support of the hypothesis that SL environments foster awareness of pragmatic appropriateness, whereas FL environments focus on grammatical accuracy (e.g., Bardovi-Harlig & Dornyei (...) However, evidence has also been reported that English FL (EFL) speakers showed a higher sensitivity to pragmatic errors than their English SL (ESL) counterparts

(niezgoda & Rover, 2001). These somewhat controversial findings in the existing research ... (AL1)

Within Move 3, Sub-moves 3.2, 3.4, 3.5 and 3.7 in the integrated CARS model were drawn from Swales's (1990 & 2004) CARS model. Sub-move 3.1 ("Announce Research Purposes, Focuses, Research Questions, or Hypotheses") is a combination of Step 1 ("Announcing Present Research Descriptively and/or Purposively") and Step 2 ("Presenting RQs or Hypotheses") of Move 3 in the revised CARS model. This combination practice performed by Kwan (2006) in her genre analysis of the Literature Review chapters of doctoral dissertations was found applicable to the present data analysis and was thus adopted. Two new special elements perhaps characterizing the discipline and the CARS introductions with a following L are "State Theoretical Frameworks/Positions" (S3.3) and "Inform the Literature Review Content" (S3.6), as illustrated in examples (5) and (6), respectively:

1. ... it is argued throughout the present article that not only are multiword expressions much more common than popularly assumed, but they are also difficult for readers to both accurately identify and decode – even when they only contain very common words. (AL18)

2. Two areas of current literature will be reviewed. First, the effect of practice on the acquisition of cognitive skills ... Second, the effects of time distribution ... (AL 26)

As for the innovative Orientation-type introduction, a Two-move Orientation approach (2.2.1) was postulated for their discourse structure based on the general procedures for conducting a corpus-based move analysis expounded in Biber, Connor and upton (2007), with the help of the expert genre analyst who has provided advice for the classification of introductions. As this new type of introductions is the focus of the present study, more explications and clarifications of its functions and structural components will be presented in Section 3.2.

After developing the integrated CARS model and the Two-move Orientation approach as coding protocols of the two major types of introductions through repeated pilot-coding exercises and substantial discussions with the expert genre analyst, the researcher used WinMax's QDA program (MaxQDA, 2012) to code all texts. A trained coder who is an Applied Linguistics PhD candidate coded independently six texts (around 33.3%) from the traditional CARS group and five texts (around 45.5%) from the innovative Two-move Orientation group for our inter-coder reliability check. Our agreement percentages all exceeded 86%, generally indicating the validity of and consistency in our coding and analysis. Any remaining few discrepancies were resolved through discussion, criteria checking and further clarification.

RESULTS AND DISCUSSION

The traditional CARS introductions

Previous studies have mostly confirmed the strong explanatory power of Swales's CARS model in that it is generally stable at the move level with modifications mainly suggested at the sub-move level by other genre scholars (for instance, Anthony, 1999; Samraj, 2002). In line with this, the three moves of the CARS model are found prototypical in the conventional CARS introductions in the present study, though only Move 1 is obligatory (see Table 2). This suggests that a noticeable number of introductions still bear a structural resemblance to the CARS model even when they are followed by a usually lengthy L section that could possibly take over some communicative roles originally performed by them.

Table 2: Frequency counts of the three moves

Moves	Individual counts	No. of introductions with the move (%)
Move 1 Establish a territory	36	18 (100%)
Move 2 Establish a niche	30	16 (88.9%)
Move 3 Present the present study	22	17 (94.4%)

Only two out of the 18 CARS introductions (AL2, 30) have Move 2 missing while the only introduction without a Move 3 is AL 22, which is characterized with four consecutive alternations between Move 1 and Move 2 (see Table 3). Although a few introductions omit either Move 2 or Move 3, the repeated use of the three moves are common, as can be seen from their individual counts.

Table 3: Examples of the move configurations

Observed patterns	No. of articles (%)	Examples
Introductions following Swales's CARS model		
1-2-3	4 (22.2)	AL1, 16, 17, 19
1-2-1-3	2 (11.1)	AL4, 25
1-2-1-2-3	2 (11.1)	AL18, 23
1-2-3-2-3	1 (5.6)	AL3
1-2-3-1-2-3	1 (5.6)	AL21
1-2-1-2-3-2-3	1 (5.6)	AL10
1-2-1-2-1-2-1-3	1 (5.6)	AL20
1-2-1-2-1-2-1-2	1 (5.6)	AL22
1-2-1-2-1-2-1-2-3	1 (5.6)	AL5
Introductions deviating from the strict Swales's CARS model		
1-3	2 (11.1)	AL2, 30
1-3-1-2-3	1 (5.6)	AL6
1-3-1-2-1-3	1 (5.6)	AL26
Total no. of RAs	18 (100)	

Table 3 summarizes the move structure of this group of introductions. Generally congruent with the findings reported in most previous introduction studies on a similar discipline or sub-discipline (like Ozturk (2007) on second language acquisition and second language writing; Hirano (2009) on English for specific purposes; and Lee (2001) on English education), this study found that a significant proportion (66.7%) of the CARS introductions involve cyclicity, mostly with the repetition of two – for example, 1-2-1-2-3 (AL 18, 23) – or three moves – for example, 1-2-1-2-3-2- 3 (AL 10). However, the archetypal 1-2-3 structure is still the most common pattern and another three structures gaining prominence are 1-2-1-3, 1-2-1- 2-3 and 1-3. As stated before, only two introductions do not contain a Move 2, suggesting the central role played by this core component in the conventional CARS introductions. Despite four introductions showing salient deviations from Swales's CARS model and the existence of varied move structures, all introductions commence with Move 1 and close with Move 3, except AL 22 comprising four alternations between Move 1 and Move 2, as aforementioned.

Figure 1 displays the frequency of sub-moves within each major move. Within Move 1, the generalization element (S1.2) is the only obligatory submove, suggesting the importance of providing general background knowledge and contextualizing the research study in general sense in the introductions used before L. As for reviewing specific research activities, this element is frequently moved to L and only used in just over half (55.6%) of the introductions. This contrasts with the obligatory nature of this element maintained in Swales (1990) and recorded in many follow-up structural analyses of the introductions without a subsequent L such as the introduction in the IMRD context studied in Kanoksilapatham (2005). Therefore, much less use of reviewing individual research items to establish the territory is a prominent feature of the introductions with a following L, even though they mainly reflect the communicative function and move structure of the CARS model.

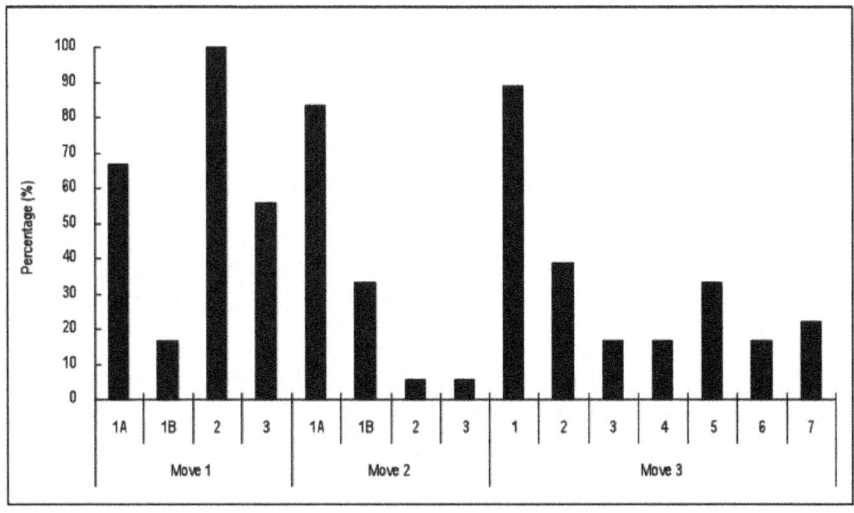

Figure 1: Sub-move frequency within moves in the traditional CARS introductions

The following text excerpts illustrate typically how the author just referred to the previous studies by listing them in a non-integral citation (shown in italics) when summarizing the research state of the field in introduction – see example (7) – while reviewing at length and critically the cited studies by using a number of integral citations (see the italicized part) in the subsequent L section – see example (8):

- The few studies that have addressed unattended this (Moskovit, 1983; Steinberg, Kaufer, & Geisler, 1984; Geisler et al., 1985) have focused on prescriptive uses and reader interpretations, with little empirical focus on the linguistic environment surrounding such structures. (AL 19)

- Few studies have focused specifically on the use of demonstratives in anaphoric reference and in relation to text cohesion. The studies that do exist primarily focus on the pronominal use, which may be a consequence of the prescriptive rules that exist. For example, Moskovit (1983) seeks to determine when pronominal this constitutes 'broad reference' (...)

Moskovit attempts to determine when broad reference is unclear by examining 28 examples (...) Steinberg et al. (1984) and Geisler et al. (1985) question Moskovit's interpretations (...) Although these early studies offer a starting point, they focus on establishing prescriptivism, a practice which has in some circles fallen out of fashion. In addition, the research methodologies are problematic (...) Furthermore, these studies focus primarily on the use of pronominal this, and little (if any) attention is paid to demonstrative determiners ... (AL 19)

In the L section, the detailed review of the studies referred to in the preceding introduction establishes the link between the two sections and recreates the research space for the study. The linking of this sort is frequently found in the introductions with a following L, including the traditional CARS type and the Orientation type. Regarding the two varieties of centrality claims, "Claim Importance in Research Word" (66.7%) is much more frequently employed than "Claim Importance in Real World" (16.7%). Although a similar tendency occurred in writers' choices of two gap-indication sub-moves (that is, research gap indication is far more favored), Sub-move 2.1b (33.3%) is still a prominent element, reflecting the great concerns of this discipline with real-world language-related problems. This could also be perceived from the frequentlycited definition of Applied Linguistics by Chris Brumfit (1995: 27):

[Applied Linguistics is] the theoretical and empirical investigation of realworld problems in which language is a central issue.

Both the "positive" warrant and Sub-move 2.3 are used in only one traditional CARS introduction. The only instance of the latter has been presented in Section 2.2.2. Of the seven variations realizing Move 3, Sub move 3.1 is most frequently employed (88.9%), followed by the method statement (38.9%) and the statement on announcing research significance (33.3%). As for the two new elements identified in the present study, Submove 3.3 and Sub-move 3.6 are respectively used in 16.7% of the introductions. Their degrees of importance need to be further examined by using a larger data set in this discipline. Table 4 demonstrates the frequently-used sub-move configurations within each move. The fact that the number of the sub-moves integrating these patterns is either one or two and the most frequently used patterns for the three moves are all a single sub-move structure indicates that the traditional CARS introductions used before L are not densely structured. However, there are a wide range of choices in the combined use of different submoves within each move. Besides the patterns listed in Table 4, there are many more different patterns (for example, S2.1b+S2.1a for Move 2, S3.1+S3.5 for Move 3), suggesting that these introductions are flexibly structured at the sub-move level.

Table 4: Frequently-used sub-move configurations in the three moves (No. of occurrences !3)

Move	Sub-move configuration	Count no.	% of intro
M1	S1.2 (Make topic generalizations of increasing specificity)	13	50
	S1.1a+S1.2 (Claim importance in research world+ Make topic generalizations of increasing specificity)	4	22.2
	S1.3 (Survey items of previous research)	3	16.7
	S1.2+S1.1a (Make topic generalizations of increasing specificity+ Claim importance in research world)	3	16.7
M2	S2.1a (Indicate a research gap)	22	72.2
	S2.1b (Indicate a problem or need in real world)	4	11.1
M3	S3.1 (Announce research purposes, focuses, research questions or hypotheses)	6	33.3

Two-move Orientation Introductions

Besides the classic CARS introductions, previous studies have identified other types of introductions with different structures, like the specificgeneral introductions in the Humanities and the problem-focused introductions in Law (Feak & Swales, 2011). In this study, an innovative type (namely, the Two-move Orientation introduction) is identified among the introductions with a following L. As aforementioned, unlike the CARS introductions, Two-move Orientation introductions do not function to create a research space for the study but mainly to identify the issue to be addressed and inform the readers of the research to be undertaken. They are essentially the brief, prologue-style introduction described in Lin & Evans (2012: 156). An example text of an Orientation-type introduction (AL9) is provided in Appendix 3.

The Two-move Orientation approach (Appendix 1) is formulated for the rhetorical structure of Orientation introductions. It contains two prototypical moves: Move 1 "Identify the Issue" and Move 2 "Present the Study". Move 2 is obligatory as it is used in all 11 Orientation introductions while Move 1 is present in ten of them as AL 15 is a single-move (namely, Move 2) introduction. Therefore, the two moves are essential in realizing the communicative functions of this type of introduction. In terms of move configurations, after AL 15 containing only a Move 2 excluded, eight out of the other ten Orientation introductions follow strictly the canonical pattern "M1-M2". As for the other two introductions, AL7 (M1-M2-M1-M2) and AL 13 (M2-M1-M2) display the cyclical structure. In all, most of the new types of introductions displaying the two-move structure are regularly and simply structured at the move level. The next two sub-sections detail the elements within the two moves. The same as in explicating the integrated CARS model, for the sub-moves that generally correspond to those in the CARS model, their definitions are not repeated due to space limitation.

Move 1 "Identify the issue"

In the Two-move Orientation approach, Move 1 is divided into three submoves. Sub-move 1.1 ("Survey non-research Phenomena/Practices or General Knowledge Claims of the Field") shares mostly the propositional content and semantic attributes of Sub-move 1.2 "Make Topic Generalizations" in the traditional CARS model. The instances of this submove are commonly general statements on the research state of the field, explanations of the key theoretical constructs/ concepts, accounts of the general beliefs on the theme, or descriptions of the non-research phenomena or activities. In AL 9 (see Appendix 3 for detail), two segments illustrate this sub-move.

Generally, the element of the specific review of individual studies does not exist in this type of introductions and thus there is no difficulty in distinguishing Sub-move 1.1 and the specific literature review element. It is not surprising since this group of brief, prologue-style introductions simply identifies the topic, purpose and structure of the paper and does not engage in a focused, gap-creating review of the literature, which has become a major task of the subsequent L (Lin & Evans, 2012). In this regard, AL 9 again provides a good example. It does not contain any review of previous studies on the theme (namely, the usefulness of imagery in the form of pictorial illustrations and etymological notes in idiom dictionaries), which is however included in the subsequent L. One extract from L illustrates this:

1. Extensive research has been conducted by Boers and his colleagues into the effects of mental imagery evoked by etymological elaboration (...) Gallese and Lakoff (2005: 4) propose that in order to understand a concept such as grasp (...) A positive influence of etymological elaboration on form and meaning retention has been reported in Boers (2001) (...)The question whether the strategy of etymological elaboration is equally effective (...) is addressed by Boers et al. (2004a) (...) In Boers et al. (2008), students' position on the verbalizer/imager continuum was correlated with their scores on the idiom comprehension ... (AL 9)

Owing to the absence of the detailed review of previous studies and the substantial niche-establishment move as well as much fewer complex recursive move patterns in these Orientation introductions, their length and proportions in the whole article are around a half of the conventional CARS introductions (see section 2.2.1). Sub-move 1.2 ("Establish Importance of the Field") resembles the centrality-claim element in the CARS model. However, among the ten instances of this sub-move, only one establishes importance in the research world and the other nine do so in the real world, which contrasts with what is revealed in the traditional CARS introductions (3.1). Sub-move 1.3 ("Suggest value of the Issue") is the special element in this type of introductions. Although Orientation introductions do not have a substantial niche-establishment move for justifying the study, they often use one or two sentences concisely indicating the potential value of a research issue which is worth studying. Though this sub-move is absent in AL9 (see Appendix 3), an example is provided here to illustrate it:

1.   ... the way in which raters assess lexis in writing is an area which should be of interest to a broad range of English language educators. (AL 13)

After suggesting the value of a research issue, for most of the cases the author immediately declares what he or she is going to do, hence this submove often being followed by Sub-move 2.1.

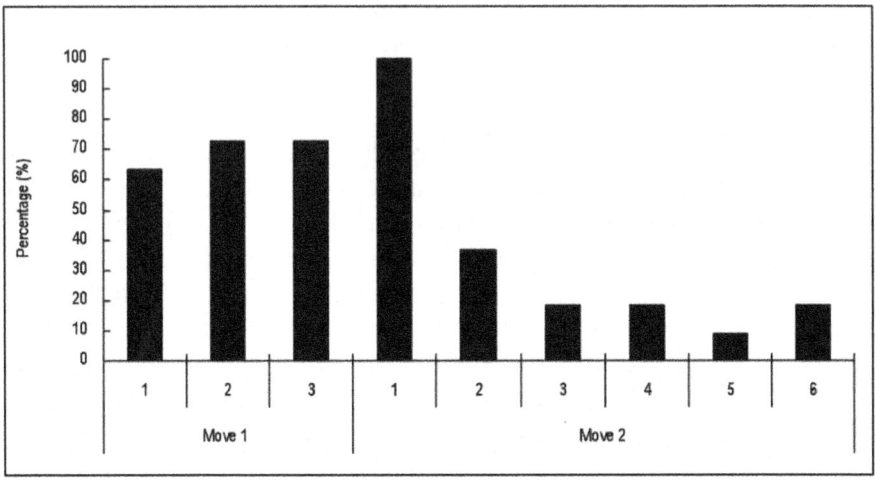

Figure 2: Sub-move frequency within moves in Two-move Orientation introductions.

The three sub-moves are prototypical constituents of Move 1 since they have been used in most of Orientation introductions (63.6%, 72.7% and 72.7% respectively) (see Figure 2). However, they co-occur in varied patterns and only AL 28 uses them in the canonical linear pattern of "1-2-3" (see Table 5); in nine out of the 11 Move 1 instances, the number of sub-moves integrating Move 1 is no more than three and only four Move 1 instances involve cyclicity. All these suggest that Move 1 structure of Orientation introductions is very flexible and irregular but not heavily informationloaded.

Table 5: Different sub-move combinations within Move 1

Observed sub-move patterns	Examples
Single sub-move	
Sub-move 3 only	AL7
Two sub-move configurations	
1-3	AL8, 27
1-2-1	AL9
1-2-1-2-1	AL7
2-1	AL29
2-3	AL11, 12
3-2-3	AL13
Three sub-move configurations	
1-2-3	AL28
1-2-1-2-3	AL24

Move 2 "Present the study"

Move 2 comprises six sub-moves. Among them, four (S2.2, S2.3, S2.4 and S2.6) are the same as those in Swales's two versions of the CARS model. Sub-move 2.1 is formed by integrating Step 1 and Step 2 of Move 3 in the revised CARS model, following Kwan (2006). This is also the first sub-move for Move 3 in the traditional CARS introductions. The reason has been stated in section 3.1 and also applies here. Sub-move 2.5 ("Indicate the Literature Review Content") is a unique element found in the introductions with a following L. It is different from the element "Outlining the Paper", which indicates the content of each major part of the RA. Instead, it only suggests what will be presented in the forthcoming L section, as illustrated below:

- The sections below review key theoretical concepts and various studies which have investigated creativity and language play for language learning. (AL 8)

The sub-moves for Move 2 in Orientation introductions is basically the same as those for Move 3 in the traditional CARS introductions except that the element "State Theoretical Frameworks/Positions" is absent in these much shorter Orientation-style introductions. The tendency in using sub-moves for presenting the study in Two-move Orientation introductions is also similar to that in the traditional CARS introductions: Sub-move 1 as an obligatory element is most frequently used, followed by the method statement (36.4%). All the other sub-moves are only used in a few introductions. Sub-move combinations within Move 2 vary greatly (see Table 6). However, "Sub-move 1 only" is the most frequently used configuration and the number of sub-moves integrating this move in most of its instances is only one or two. These confirm again that the rhetorical structure of this type of introductions is generally flexible yet straightforward. In all 11 Orientation introductions, Sub-move 1 is invariably present despite the different submove combination patterns used within Move 2, which indicates the importance and prominence of this element. These frequently used patterns identified for the two moves further our understanding of this innovative type of introductions used before L and have high reference value for the teaching of introduction writing in EAP classrooms.

Table 6: Different sub-move combinations within Move 2

Observed sub-move patterns	Examples
Single sub-move	
Sub-move 1 only	AL7, 13, 24, 27, 28
Two sub-move configurations	
1-2	AL13, 29
1-4	AL12, 15
1-6	AL7, 9
Three sub-move configurations	
1-2-3	AL11
Four sub-move configurations	
1-3-2-5	AL8

CONCLUSION

Compared to other genre-based introduction research, the present study is unique in its focus on the rhetorical organization of introductions that are followed by an independent L section in view of the increasing use or even the prevalent use of both introduction and L sections in the opening phase of empirical RAs in many disciplines (Kwan, Chan & Lam, 2012; Lin & Evans, 2012; Pérez-Llantada, 2013). The results reveal a discernible influence from the use of a subsequent L on the introductions both in the structural and functional terms. These introductions exhibit a mixture of rhetorical organizations in that 60% of them identified as the traditional CARS type display a close affinity to the CARS model while another significant proportion of them (around 37%), termed the Orientation type, consistently exhibit a two-move structure suggested in the Orientation approach simply to identify a research issue of potential value and to inform the readers of the research to be undertaken. Although the traditional CARS group of introductions generally follow the CARS model at the move level, they manifest some special features characterizing their generic context (that is, being followed by an L) and the nature of the chosen discipline, like the use of the newly devised sub-moves "Indicate the Literature Review Content" and "State Theoretical Frameworks/ Positions", and much less use of the element for reviewing specific research studies, which is often shifted to the subsequent L section. In Two-move Orientation introductions, the element for reviewing individual research items is even absent. They do not have the substantial "niche-establishment" move either as they do not intend to create a research space for the study based on a focused, gap-creating literature review.

Instead, they employ the featured elements "Suggest value of the issue" and "Indicate the Literature Review content".

The two major types of the introductions identified differ in terms of their lengths, functions and structures. In addition to the differences indicated above, at the move level, the traditional CARS introductions are much more complexly structured for involving much cyclicity while most Two-move Orientation introductions are regularly and straightforwardly structured. At the sub-move level, they are both flexibly yet simply structured with no dense use of elements. Because of their different structural components, communicative functions and content elements involved, Two-move Orientation introductions are generally much shorter than the traditional CARS introductions. All these revealing findings and the interesting links between introduction and L suggested in this paper are illuminating and valuable to the genrebased teaching of article introduction writing given that there is currently a lack of published advice on how to construct the introductions used before L and the possible similarities and differences between this kind of introduction and the traditional introductions without a following L, like those in the IMRD context. Our student writers, especially those coming from the disciplines where the use of both introduction and L in the opening phase of the RAs is favoured, need to be made aware of the structural variability of the introductions, the special features the introductions with a subsequent L exhibit, and the possible logical links between introduction and L.

This study only focuses on a single discipline (that is, Applied Linguistics); therefore, future research could extend the present study by studying introductions with a subsequent L in many other disciplines to assess the newly proposed Two-move Orientation approach and to examine the possible cross-disciplinary variations in structuring this particular group of introductions.

More insights are needed into disciplinary practices in arranging propositional contents and functional elements respectively in the two adjoining sections – namely, the introduction and L sections.

ACKNOWLEDGEMENTS

I am grateful to Editor Prof. Ana Bocanegra for her editorial advice and the reviewers for their helpful comments and support in the publication of this paper.

REFERENCES

1. Anthony, L. (1999). "Writing research article introductions in software engineering: How accurate is a standard model?" IEEE Transactions on Professional Communication 42: 38-46.

2. APA Publication Manual (2010). Publication Manual of the American Psychological Association, 6th ed. Washington, DC: American Psychological Association.

3. Bhatia, V.K. (2001). "Analyzing genre: Some conceptual issues" in M. Hewing (ed.), Academic Writing in Context: Implications and Applications: Papers in Honour of Tony DudleyEvans, 79-92. Birmingham: University of Birmingham Press.

4. Biber, D., U. Connor & T.A. Upton (2007). Discourse on the Move: Using Corpus Analysis to Describe Discourse Structure. Amsterdam: John Benjamins.

5. Brumfit, C. (1995). "Teacher professionalism and research" in G. Cook & B. Seidlhofer (eds.), Principle & Practice in Applied Linguistics: Studies in Honour of H.G. Widdowson, 27-41. Oxford: Oxford University Press.

6. Del Saz-Rubio, M.M. (2011). "A pragmatic approach to the macro-structure and metadiscoursal features of research article introductions in the field of agricultural sciences". English for Specific Purposes 30: 258-271.

7. Feak, C.B. & J.M. Swales (2011). Creating Contexts: Writing Introductions across Genres. Ann Arbor: University of Michigan Press.

8. Ferguson, G. (2007). "The global spread of English, scientific communication and ESP: Questions of equity, access and domain loss". Ibérica 13: 7-38.

9. Hirano, E. (2009). "Research article introductions in English for specific purposes: A comparison between Brazilian Portuguese and English". English for Specific Purposes 28: 240-250.

10. Kanoksilapatham, B. (2005). "Rhetorical structure of biochemistry research articles". English for Specific Purposes 24: 269-292.

11. Kwan, B.S.C. (2006). "The schematic structure of literature reviews in doctoral theses of applied linguistics". English for Specific Purposes 25: 30- 55.

12. Kwan, B.S.C., H. Chan & C. Lam (2012). "Evaluating prior scholarship in literature reviews of research articles: A comparative study of practices in two research paradigms". English for Specific Purposes 31: 188-201.

13. Lee, S. (2001). A Contrastive Rhetoric Study of Korean and English Research Paper Introductions. Unpublished doctoral dissertation, University of Hawaii.

14. Lewin, B.A., J. Fine & L. Young (2001). Expository Discourse: A Genre-based Approach to Social Science Research Texts. London: Continuum.

15. Lin, L. & S. Evans (2012). "Structural patterns in empirical research articles: A cross-disciplinary study". English for Specific Purposes 31: 150-160.

16. Loi, C.K. (2010). "Research article introductions in Chinese and English: A comparative genre-based study". Journal of English for Academic Purposes 9: 267-279.

17. MAXQDA (2012). VERBI Software. Consult, Sozialforchung, GmbH, Berlin, Germany.

18. Nwogu, K.N. (1997). "The medical research paper: Structure and functions". English for Specific Purposes 16: 119-138.

19. Ozturk, I. (2007). "The textual organization of research article introductions in applied linguistics: Variability within a single discipline". English for Specific Purposes 26: 25-38.

20. Pérez-Llantada, C. (2013). "The article of the future: Strategies for genre stability and change". English for Specific Purposes 32: 221-235.

21. Samraj, B. (2002). "Introductions in research articles: Variations across disciplines". English for Specific Purposes 21: 1-17.

22. Samraj, B. (2005). "An exploration of a genre set: Research article abstracts and introductions in two disciplines". English for Specific Purposes 24: 141-156.

23. Sheldon, E. (2011). "Rhetorical differences in RA introductions written by English L1 and L2 and Castilian Spanish L1 writers". Journal of English for Academic Purposes 10: 238-251.

24. Stoller, F.L. & M.S. Robinson (2013). "Chemistry journal articles: An interdisciplinary approach to move analysis with pedagogical aims". English for Specific Purposes 32: 45-57.

25. Swales, J.M. (1990). Genre Analysis: English in Academic and Research Settings. Cambridge: Cambridge University Press.

26. Swales, J.M. (2004). Research Genres: Explorations and Applications. Cambridge: Cambridge University Press.

27. Yang, R.Y. & D. Allison (2004). "Research articles in applied linguistics: Structures from a functional perspective". English for Specific Purposes 23: 264-279.

CITATION

CHAPTER 1

Yang, L. (2013) Evaluative Functions of Reporting Evidentials in English Research Articles of Applied Linguistics. Open Journal of Modern Linguistics, 3, 119-126. doi: 10.4236/ojml.2013.32016.

CHAPTER 2

J. (2014) Towards a Character Language: A Probability in Language Use. Open Journal of Modern Linguistics, 4, 333-349. doi: 10.4236/ojml.2014.42027.

CHAPTER 3

Liu, S. & Liu, H. (2014). A Review of Models in Experimental Studies of Implicit Language Learning. Open Journal of Modern Linguistics, 4, 54-64. doi: 10.4236/ojml.2014.41006.

CHAPTER 4

John Robert Schmitz, Some Polemical Issues in Applied Linguistics, http://www.scielo.br/pdf/rbla/v10n1/03.pdf

CHAPTER 5

Kanavillil Rajagopalan, Language politics and the linguist, http://www.scielo.br/pdf/rbla/v5n1/05.pdf.

CHAPTER 6

Gerard Steen, Metaphor in applied linguistics: four cognitive approaches, http://dx.doi.org/10.1590/S0102-44502006000300004.

CHAPTER 7

Wang Y, Liu Z, Sun M (2015) Incorporating Linguistic Knowledge for Learning Distributed Word Representations. PLoS ONE 10(4): e0118437. doi:10.1371/journal.pone.0118437.

CHAPTER 8

A. Effendi Kadarisman, Language Problems In Applied Linguistics: Limiting The Scope, http://journal.teflin.org/index.php/journal/article/viewFile/185/162.

CHAPTER 9

Yang, L. (2012). A Comparative Study of Evidentiality in RAs in Applied Linguistics Written by NS and Chinese Writers. Open Journal of Modern Linguistics, 2, 140-146. doi: 10.4236/ojml.2012.24018.

CHAPTER 10

Wang, J. and Xu, C. (2015) Cue Competition between Animacy and Word Order: Acquisition of Chinese Notional Passives by L2 Learners. Open Journal of Modern Linguistics, 5, 213-224. doi: 10.4236/ojml.2015.52017.

CHAPTER 11

Sergio Balari, Antonio Benítez-Burraco, Marta Camps, Víctor M. Longa, Guillermo Lorenzo, and Juan Uriagereka, "The Archaeological Record Speaks: Bridging Anthropology and Linguistics," International Journal of Evolutionary Biology, vol. 2011, Article ID 382679, 17 pages, 2011. doi:10.4061/2011/382679.

CHAPTER 12

Alireza Jalilifar (Ahvaz) and Razieh Dabbi (Mahshahr, Iran), Citation in Applied Linguistics: Analysis of Introduction Sections of Iranian Master›s Theses.ISSN 1615-3014

CHAPTER 13

Ling Lin, Innovations in structuring article introductions: The case of Applied Linguistics, ISSN: 1139-7241

INDEX

A

Academic disciplines 87, 88
Anatomic macrostructures 207
Applied linguistics (AL) 143
Applied Linguistics (AL) 262
Artificial grammar 49
artificial grammar learning (AGL) 47, 49

B

Biological activity 208

C

Character language 19, 21, 22, 27, 28, 38, 39, 40, 41
Chinese native speakers 181, 187, 193, 195
Chomsky Hierarchy of grammars 204
Cognitive processing 95, 99, 106, 110
Cognitive systems 203, 222
communicative language teaching (CLT) 158
Comprehensive understanding 57
Continuous Bag-of-Words Model (CBOW) 116, 136
Controversial issues 63

D

Distant language 21, 25, 27, 32
Distinctions introduced 97
Distributional semantic models (DSM) 116
Distribution pattern 6

E

Embedded videos 261
Empirical article 260
English for Specific Purposes (ESP) 262
English Language Teaching(ELT) 20
English native speakers (EN) 187
Epistemic modality 169
Extraordinary appeal 87

F

foreign language teaching (FLT) 149
Form-function mappings 184

G

General nature 100
Genre-based investigation 259, 261
Grammatical evidential systems 167, 168

Grammaticalised evidential systems 167, 168
Grammaticality judgment task (GJT) 188

I

Imaginable communicative act 203
Implicit learning 45, 46, 47, 48, 49, 50, 51, 52, 53, 54, 55, 56, 57
Indonesian language 20, 21, 28, 30, 32, 33, 34, 35, 36
Indonesia University of Education (UPI) 152
Information processing system 202
information source 2, 3, 4, 5, 6, 7, 14, 15
International Association of Applied Linguistics (AILA) 67
Interpersonal functions 165, 171, 172, 175, 176
Introduction-Method-Results-Discussion (IMRD) 260
Isolating language 182

K

Knowledge Regularized Word Representation (KRWR) 119

L

Language Learning (LL) 262
Language politics 81, 91
Learning distributed 115, 116, 123, 138
Linguistics Applied (LA) 144

M

Margin Regularizer (MR) 124
Microsoft Office Excel 172

N

Natural computational system 203, 204, 205, 219
Neural language 115, 116

neural language models (NLM) 116
neural-network language model (NNLM) 119
Neurological dysfunctions 205
Notional passives 181, 182, 183, 184, 185, 186, 187, 188, 189, 190, 191, 192, 194, 195, 196, 197, 198
Numerous models 46

O

Obligatory grammatical category 167

P

Pervasive linguistic phenomenon 165, 173
Philosophical nature 101
Positive definition 95
Pragmatic linguistics 23
Preference-based 118, 122, 134

R

Reaction time (RT) 46
Reporting evidentials 1, 4
Rhetorical complexities 244

S

Science and Research Branch-Ahvaz (SRA). 246
Second language acquisition (SLA) 75
Second Language Acquisition (SLA) 76
Second-language (SL) 266
Sequence learning (SL) 47, 49
Shahid Chamran University of Ahvaz (SCU) 246
Speaker meanings 146, 159
Systemic Functional Linguistics (SFL) 170

T

Television weather-forecasters 82
TESOL Quarterly (TQ) 262
Theoretical issue 48

U

Universal Grammar (UG) 159
University of Malang (UM) 151, 153

V

Various disciplines 95

vector space models (VSM) 115
Verbal forms 6, 8
Vocal-Auditory interface 209, 211

W

Word Association Network (WAN) 117